Golan and Globus celebrated their acquisition of Cannon with this full-page ad in *Variety* on May 9, 1979.

The Cannon Film Guide
Volume I (1980–1984)

Austin Trunick

BearManor Media

Orlando, Florida

The Cannon Film Guide: Volume I, 1980–1984
Copyright © 2020 Austin Trunick. All Rights Reserved.

No part of this book may be reproduced in any form or by any means, electronic, mechanical, digital, photocopying or recording, except for the inclusion in a review, without permission in writing from the publisher.

This book is an independent work of research and commentary and is not sponsored, authorized or endorsed by, or otherwise affiliated with, any motion picture studio or production company affiliated with the films discussed herein. All uses of the name, image, and likeness of any individuals, and all copyrights and trademarks referenced in this book, are for editorial purposes and are pursuant of the Fair Use Doctrine.

The views and opinions of individuals quoted in this book do not necessarily reflect those of the author.

The promotional photographs and publicity materials reproduced herein are in the author's private collection (unless noted otherwise). These images date from the original release of the films and were released to media outlets for publicity purposes.

Published in the USA by
BearManor Media
1317 Edgewater Dr. #110
Orlando, FL 32804
www.BearManorMedia.com

Softcover Edition
ISBN: 978-1-62933-580-3

Printed in the United States of America

Dedication

For my father, a man who enjoyed these sort of movies as much as I do.

Table of Contents

A Preservation of an Era: Foreword by Sam Firstenberg	ix
Preface	xii
Introduction	xvii
Chapter 1: *The Happy Hooker Goes Hollywood*	3
Interview with Actress Lisa London	
Chapter 2: *Schizoid*	15
Chapter 3: *Teen Mothers*, a.k.a. *Seed of Innocence*	23
Chapter 4: *Dr. Heckyl and Mr. Hype*	31
Chapter 5: *The Apple*	41
Interview with Actress Catherine Mary Stewart	
Chapter 6: *New Year's Evil*	61
Chapter 7: *Hospital Massacre*, a.k.a. *X-Ray*	67
Chapter 8: *Enter the Ninja*	73
Chapter 9: *Body and Soul*	89
Chapter 10: *Death Wish II*, *Death Wish 3*, and *Death Wish 4: The Crackdown*	97
Chapter 11: *Lady Chatterley's Lover*	121
Chapter 12: *The Last American Virgin*	131
Interview with Actress Diane Franklin	
Interview with Actor Joe Rubbo	
Chapter 13: *That Championship Season*	151
Chapter 14: *Treasure of the Four Crowns*	161
Chapter 15: *Nana*, a.k.a. *Nana, the True Key of Pleasure*	171
Chapter 16: *10 to Midnight*	179
Interview with Actor Andrew Stevens	
Chapter 17: *House of the Long Shadows*	197
Chapter 18: *Young Warriors*, a.k.a. *The Graduates of Malibu High*	207
Chapter 19: *Hercules* and *Hercules II: The Adventures of Hercules*	213
Interview with Director Luigi Cozzi	
Interview with Actress Mirella D'Angelo	

Chapter 20: *Revenge of the Ninja*   247
   Interview with Director Sam Firstenberg
   Interview with Actor Kane Kosugi

Chapter 21: *The Wicked Lady*   285

Chapter 22: *The Secret of Yolanda*   299

Chapter 23: *Over the Brooklyn Bridge*   303

Chapter 24: *Sahara*   311

Chapter 25: *Breakin'* and *Breakin' 2: Electric Boogaloo*   325
   Interview with Actor Michael "Boogaloo Shrimp" Chambers
   Interview with Screenwriters Jan Freya and Julie Reichert

Chapter 26: *Making the Grade*   357
   Interview with Actress Jonna Lee

Chapter 27: *The Naked Face*   369

Chapter 28: *The Seven Magnificent Gladiators*   377

Chapter 29: *Sword of the Valiant: The Legend of Sir Gawain and the Green Knight*   385

Chapter 30: *Love Streams*   395

Chapter 31: *Bolero*   409

Chapter 32: *Exterminator 2*   427
   Interview with Director William Sachs

Chapter 33: *Ninja III: The Domination*   447
   Interview with Stunt Coordinator Steven Lambert
   Interview with Actor Jordan Bennett

Chapter 34: *Missing in Action, Missing in Action 2: The Beginning,* and *Braddock: Missing in Action III*   469
   Interview with Screenwriter James Bruner

Epilogue   505

Acknowledgments   507

Index   511

A Preservation of an Era: Foreword by Sam Firstenberg

When I was a teenager attending high school in Israel during the 1960s, Menahem Golan was a household name all over the country. He directed some very popular Israeli movies in that period and always made sure that his name appeared above the title in big, bold letters in their advertisements—they were always "A Menahem Golan Film." I never met him in person until a chance meeting, far away from our mutual homeland, at a party in 1973 in Hollywood, California. I was attending film school at the time and he was preparing to produce and direct his first film in Hollywood. Golan impressed me right away as a very decisive man who made abrupt decisions with no hesitation. Looking for a break into the industry I asked him to join his production and he hired me to work on his production on the spot, without even blinking. Right away he impressed me as a very colorful man with a very loud and commanding personality. I worked for Menahem Golan in many different roles through the 1970s, from courier to production assistant to assistant director, and then as a feature film director beginning in the 1980s, after he and Yoram Globus acquired Cannon.

The creative atmosphere and the cinematic culture of Cannon were like no other film production organization of their time. There was a sense of openness and adventure amongst the rank and file of the employees, all emanating from the man at the top: Menahem Golan. Golan was the de facto, one-man creative department of the company and, in general terms, he was open and receptive to any "crazy" idea presented to him. It's not that every initiative taken ended up being a movie, but many did, and many were given the green light instantly, on the spot. Most of the other companies—majors and independent—were rigid and hesitant in approving projects, making decisions via endless committees and group meetings and, as a result, were not willing to take unproven chances. At Cannon, the creative decisions were based on Golan's gut feelings, and that's how they launched projects with Chuck Norris, Charles Bronson, John Cassavetes, and the likes of *Runaway Train*, *Otello*, *American Ninja*, *Breakin'*, and on and on and on. Some of these projects were financially risky, but nevertheless they were made. That's why so many moviemakers were attracted to work for Cannon.

In the 1960s, traditional, independent, low-budget exploitation and genre b-movies gave way to an emerging new wave of independent, expressive, and personal cinema and a different breed of American movies, the likes of *Easy Rider*, *Midnight Cowboy*, and so on. The major studios followed suit and started to produce more artistic, expressive, personal films, and Hollywood abandoned their "bread and butter" movies. Cannon Films seized on the opportunity and penetrated the vacuum that was created and, together with others, occupied this abandoned field. Certain types of audiences all over the world had felt betrayed and yearned for more of the old-fashioned genre flicks: action, horror, sci-fi, and the like. The 1980s also saw the emergence of the home video phenomenon, the videocassette tape rental economy and the rise to power of no major independent production and distribution companies to supply the product that was missing from the marketplace. Cannon became the largest of them all, producing more than 530 movies. At some point it was called a mini major.

In the 1990s, the major studios took notice of what was happening and started to produce the same type of movies that Cannon was making with the likes of Stallone, Schwarzenegger, Van Damme, and so on, but with much bigger budgets. Those new genre movies were much more elaborate, expensive, and better-looking, and consequently the majors reclaimed the market for themselves. By doing so, the majors pushed the independent companies back to the corners they came out of in the first place. Nowadays people talk about "the Cannon look," and there is a renewed interest in the company and its movies. Moviegoers who grew up with those films in theaters or at home are nostalgic about the movies created by Cannon under the vision of Menahem Golan.

There is one thing for sure: Menahem Golan and Yoram Globus left a stamp on the popular culture of America and the world over. In studying the history of filmmaking in Hollywood, there was a capsule of about 15 years, through the 1980s and the first half of the 1990s, which can be characterized or branded as the period in which Cannon revolutionized the role of independent genre filmmaking in Hollywood. This is definitely one undeniable chapter in the ever-evolving history of cinema and it's important to make sure it will not be forgotten. This book is an important block in this preservation endeavor.

Sam Firstenberg
Los Angeles, 2019

Sam Firstenberg is the director of numerous Cannon classics, including Revenge of the Ninja, Breakin' 2: Electric Boogaloo, *and* American Ninja.

Preface

Like many of you, I grew up in the era when your whole weekend's entertainment was decided during a Friday night trip to the video rental store. It was in those places where Cannon reigned supreme, and their recognizable logo could be found somewhere on almost every shelf in the store. Thanks to my local mom-n-pop shop's lenient policies toward renting violent, R-rated movies to minors, I was exposed at a young age to film classics such as *Invasion U.S.A.*, *New Year's Evil*, and *American Ninja*. I learned early on that a movie didn't need to be "traditionally good" to be *great*. For the rest of my film-loving life, the sight of the Cannon logo at the front of a movie would stir up happy, fluttery feelings within my heart. If you're reading this now, my guess is you might feel the same way.

I started *The Cannon Film Guide* as a way to revisit the movies I loved, write about them, and talk to people whose work I'd so long admired. I set out to create the first comprehensive book on the legendary b-movie studio's entire filmography. Eventually it turned out that such a project would actually call for three volumes.

Listening to the stories told by the films' creators, I found places where many of the tall tales surrounding Cannon and their productions long overshadowed what had really happened back in those days. (Menahem Golan's knack for mythmaking was as often responsible for this as anything else.) On the same hand, there were just as many moments where I discovered the truth was crazier than I could have ever imagined.

The release dates listed in this book correspond to the earliest U.S. theatrical release I could find for each title, or my closest approximation as to when it first hit video store shelves. It wasn't unusual for Cannon to stagger a release, opening a film on one coast or in select cities before packing up and shipping the prints along to their next destinations.

When it comes to franchises, I've chosen to write about direct sequels in the same chapters as the film that launched a series. Because these films obviously share so many elements, I found that this was a good way to cut down on redundancies. In this volume you'll find writings on all of the Cannon entries in the *Death Wish* and *Missing in Action* franchises, even the ones that were released in 1985 or later, because Cannon's first installment came out in the years covered here. While they're commonly viewed as a trilogy, I've written about each of the Sho Kosugi ninja films individually as they don't share any plot continuity.

While I strove to include as much of Cannon's catalog as possible, this is not a 100% complete survey of the company's output. Many movies appeared in video shops with the Cannon logo on the spine but were only secondhand pickups or distribution releases by the company. As a guideline I decided to include only the films that Menahem Golan and/or Yoram Globus produced themselves, or were significantly involved in their creation in some other way.

In addition, there are a number of Cannon films which received little to no domestic release, primarily because they were intended only for specific, international markets. If a movie was deemed not to merit a token VHS release in the United States when it was new, it's unlikely it will suddenly be made available here on Blu-ray more than 30 years later. Because of their unavailability, I've opted to write of these films only with passing mentions. That said, many relative obscurities from the Cannon library *are* included here with full-chapter studies—films that, as of this writing, are still only available

Preface

on decades-old videocassettes or, when lucky, as murky YouTube rips. I wish my readers the best of luck in tracking these down; as my writings on those movies will indicate, they're usually worth the effort.

Austin Trunick
Connecticut, 2019

Introduction

In 1979, a pair of Israeli cousins—Menahem Golan and Yoram Globus—snapped up controlling shares of the failing American company The Cannon Group, a minor independent film studio known for churning out drive-in caliber schlock. Golan was the pair's creative mind, a filmmaker responsible for several hits in his native Israel and with an Academy Award nomination for Best Foreign Feature under his belt. His much younger cousin, Globus, was an immensely savvy businessman with an unmatched talent for international film sales. The pair lived and breathed cinema, having grown up on American movies of the '30s, '40s, and '50s. These two eccentric outsiders were determined to transform Cannon into Hollywood's "seventh major studio." It was a lofty and totally unprecedented goal, but through an impressive stretch of the 1980s, it was one they very nearly succeeded in achieving.

Their first year of Hollywood production saw a trickle of the same sort of budget horror films and comedies that Cannon had been known for prior to the cousins' takeover. They topped off their inaugural year with *The Apple* (1980), a bombastic, sci-fi disco musical inspired by Old Testament stories and directed by Golan himself. The movie proved stunningly uncommercial, but offered a first glimpse at the sort of wild ambition that the Golan and Globus-led Cannon would come to be known for.

And then came their first hit: the martial arts film *Enter the Ninja* (1981), which kicked off a ninja craze that swept video shelves, Saturday morning cartoons, and toy stores throughout the entirety of the 1980s. They had two more unpredicted hits in rapid succession with *Death Wish II* (1982), a sequel to the violent, decade-old vigilante film that had made Charles Bronson famous, and the endearing teen sex comedy *The Last American Virgin* (1982), an English-language remake of a film Golan and Globus had produced in Israel several years earlier.

Nobody—not even Cannon—expected *Breakin'* (1984), a movie about Los Angeles hip hop street dancers, to debut at #1 at the U.S. box office and remain a top gainer for most of that summer. That same year Cannon signed a multi-picture deal with a middle-aged karate instructor-turned-actor named Chuck Norris. They funneled his niche talents into a string of hits which included *Missing in Action* (1984), *Invasion U.S.A.* (1985), and *The Delta Force* (1986). A few years later, a struggling Belgian martial artist named Jean-Claude Van Damme made an impression on Menahem Golan when he roundhouse-kicked over the movie mogul's head. Golan cast him in *Bloodsport* (1988), and a star was born.

Hits like these helped Cannon offset the many, many more films that failed to recoup their budgets in American movie theaters. The company managed to stay afloat in large part thanks to Yoram Globus' ingenious approach to film financing. As Cannon pre-sold their films to foreign, cable, and video distributors (sometimes with little more than a title or a mocked-up poster), they were able to churn out dozens of films per year without overly concerning themselves whether or not those films actually made any money when they hit U.S. theaters.

While Cannon are most beloved today for their many action movies which starred the ultimate pistol-packing badass, Charles Bronson, or high-kicking heroes like Chuck Norris, Jean-Claude Van Damme, and Michael Dudikoff, they also produced films by prestigious auteurs like John Cassavetes, Barbet Schroeder, Franco Zeffirelli, Jean-Luc Godard, and Robert Altman. In a few rare cases, a Cannon film was nominated for an Academy

Introduction

Award. More often, their movies brought home Razzies. While it's rare to find a critically acclaimed film bearing the company's famous arrow logo, it's even more difficult to find a Cannon movie that isn't thoroughly entertaining from its title screen to its final credit roll.

From 1980 through its eventual closure in 1994, The Cannon Group in its various forms left behind a legacy of more than 200 films spanning every imaginable genre found at your local video rental shop in the 1980s. These included musicals, science fiction, erotic thrillers and teen sex comedies, fantasy epics, action and adventure flicks, horror films, dance movies, children's fairy tales, and many that were simply impossible to categorize. Today, more than three decades removed from their heyday, Cannon is held in the highest regard by connoisseurs of cinematic cheese. They are the most beloved cult studio of what was arguably cinema's greatest decade: the 1980s.

Over three volumes, *The Cannon Film Guide* will celebrate and explore the output of the legendary b-movie studio in chronological order. Volume One—this book—covers the years 1980 through 1984, largely chronicling the studio's rise under its dual mavericks, Menahem Golan and Yoram Globus. Volume Two will track 1985 through 1987, Cannon's most prolific years, and include many of their most ambitious productions. Volume Three will span the widest range of years, 1988 through 1994, which entailed a bitter fallout between the cousins and a maelstrom of other misfortunes which amounted to the company's inevitable fall. (However, the period also included late-era classics like *Bloodsport* and *Cyborg* [1989], and numerous direct-to-video masterpieces.) Join me then, won't you, as we take a journey into all things Cannon: the good, the bad, the ugly, the awesome, the overblown, the badass, the sexy, the hilarious, the mind-boggling, the unbelievable, and *The Apple*.

Before we dive in, let's talk briefly about how we got here. To fully understand Cannon in the 1980s, one must familiarize themselves with the origin stories of Hollywood's most unlikely moguls: Menahem Golan and Yoram Globus.

Cannon's valiant leaders as they presented themselves on the front page of their 1983 sales catalog, along with an excellent summation of the company's ambitions.

Menahem Golan was born Menahem Globus on May 31, 1929, to Polish immigrants in Tiberias, a coastal city in what is now Israel. At the time the city was occupied by British troops in the wake of WWI, and a movie theater had been built there to entertain them. The theater screened an ever-changing rotation of imported Western hits, and the young Menahem became enchanted with the cinema at an early age. Seeing the latest Chaplin films and Hollywood musicals were more than a pastime for this particular youth, but an obsession. Regularly unable to afford his ticket, the intrepid boy eventually struck up a deal with the theater's projectionist: he'd offer his free labor by turning the crank which controlled the movies' Hebrew subtitles in exchange for seeing movies as they passed through town. As time went by, the young Menahem's aspirations shifted from simply seeing films to making them. Cutting photos from magazines and fixing them to the rotating dryer rack in the basement of his family's apartment building, he directed his first "motion pictures." He recalled that when he asked a penny for admission no one would show up, and so he resorted to paying his school pals a penny each for their attendance.

Menahem enlisted in the Israeli Air Force during the nation's War for Independence in 1948 and, in an act of patriotism, took on a Hebrew surname. Inspired by the hilly Golan Heights region visible across the water from his hometown, Menahem Globus would from then on be known as Menahem Golan. After leaving the armed forces, Golan traveled to study theatrical production abroad, first at London's Old Vic and then at the city's Academy of Music and Dramatic Art. Upon returning to his homeland Golan found considerable success as a stage director, sometimes tackling Hebrew-language versions of popular Broadway musicals.

The siren's song of cinema still surged strong through Golan, however, and in 1960 the 30-year-old film fanatic uprooted his family and moved to New York, where he took filmmaking classes and attempted to find financing for an Israeli spy thriller he'd written for the screen. It was tough going. Growing despondent after a year of non-starts in the United States, Golan eventually wrote a letter to Roger Corman, the prolific and influential b-movie filmmaker, asking him for work and tutelage. Famous for taking chances on aspiring movie-makers, Corman answered Golan's letter in just a matter of days. Corman explained that he would soon start shooting a new film, *The Young Racers* (1963), in Monte Carlo: if Golan could meet him at his hotel at the start of production, bring a car with him, and pay for all of his own travel and lodging expenses, he'd hire him on as his personal driver. So, Golan and his wife flew to Paris and rented an automobile, and Corman kept his word.

Golan not only worked as his driver, but in typical Corman fashion was asked to wear additional hats as a production assistant while his wife, Rachel, was hired on as a makeup artist.

The Young Racers isn't nearly as notable for its content as it is for the famous names who cut their teeth working on it. Menahem Golan served on that film crew alongside two other young, aspiring filmmakers: Francis Ford Coppola and an emerging screenwriter by the name of Robert Towne. The two would go on to be known for films such as *The Godfather* (1972) and *Apocalypse Now* (1979), and *Chinatown* (1974), respectively, and independently win six Oscars between the two of them. Another young, hungry maverick working on that set was frequent Corman collaborator Charles B. Griffith, best known for penning b-movie classics like *The Little Shop of Horrors* (1960) and *Death Race 2000* (1975).

There's a story that was regularly recounted by Golan which involved him pitching Corman the idea for a Hebrew gangster film, and the producer agreeing to give him the $20,000 left over from *The Young Racers*' production budget to make it. As Golan told the story, Coppola got wind of Corman's offer and told their mentor that he would be out of his mind dumping that kind of money into a black-and-white, Hebrew-language b-movie; if Corman instead gave Coppola that funding, he'd deliver a film that would sell to American audiences. Coppola rushed back to his room and banged out a story treatment overnight, which impressed Corman enough that he handed those funds to the American over the Israeli. While Golan showed a lifelong flair for exaggeration that was occasionally peppered with outright fabrication, at least part of this story can be confirmed. Using leftover budget from *The Young Racers* and many members of the same cast and crew, Coppola's resulting production would become his now-legendary breakthrough feature, the low-budget cult horror flick *Dementia 13* (1963).

Golan never held a grudge against Corman for rescinding his funds, and even cited the producer as one of his greatest teachers. Besides, that didn't stop him from making his movie. Golan returned to Israel and found another financier, which resulted in the Hebrew noir *El Dorado* (1963), Golan's directorial debut and one of the earliest screen appearances of Israeli superstar Chaim Topol. It fared very well with movie-goers in his homeland. Finally, Golan had his foot in the door of the film industry. Scraping together money however he could, he'd direct more movies over the next few years—including the Audie Murphy-led spy film *Trunk to Cairo* (1965), paid for by Samuel Z. Arkoff's hallowed American Independent Pictures—but there were always difficulties getting projects off the ground. That would change once Golan paired himself up with a brilliant producer and financial mind in the form of his younger cousin, Yoram Globus.

Yoram Globus was born in Tiberias on September 7, 1941, twelve years after his cousin Menahem. As a boy his family moved 50 kilometers west to the city of Kiryat Motzkin, where his father opened his first movie theater. At the age of five Yoram was helping out in the lobby, promoting new movies, swapping out posters and working the ticket counter. By the time he was 10 years old he was serving as a projectionist. As a teen, his parents moved to the much larger city of Tel Aviv and opened another theater. Coming of age and showing little interest in life beyond the family cinema, his father pleaded with Yoram's cousin, Menahem—who at this point was a well-known stage director—to help encourage his son. The cousins obviously shared similar passions. As Menahem told the story, he promised the younger Yoram that if he made it through business school the two of them would one day make movies together. Yoram took him up on the offer, and went to business school. A few years later, every b-movie fan's favorite opening credits line was born: "A Golan-Globus Production."

With his business degree in hand, Yoram reunited with Menahem in the early 1960s after the elder cousin returned from his time in New York and working under Roger Corman. The duo founded Noah Films, a production company named after Golan's father. Golan was widely viewed as the duo's creative mind, and Globus the shrewd businessman. Although the black-and-white, Hebrew-language movies they produced in their early years were primarily tailored toward the Israeli market, Globus quickly showed an uncanny ability to sell these seemingly-niche movies abroad to foreign theater chains and distributors. It was Globus' savviness as a salesman which kept the various Golan-Globus ventures afloat over their first 15 years, and laid the groundwork for Cannon's period of sustained success in the 1980s.

From the very outset of their collaboration, Golan and Globus formed a seemingly unstoppable team, producing film after film, with Golan occasionally writing the odd title or sliding into the director's chair. One of their first movies produced together, the broad Hebrew satire *Sallah* (1965), set Israeli box office records for a film produced from within the country—records that Golan and Globus themselves would best time and again throughout the 1970s—and would become Israel's first cinematic release to be nominated for the Best Foreign Language Film Academy Award. They'd receive the same Oscar nod for *I Love You Rosa* (1972), and again for *The House on Chelouche Street* (1973) the following year. The fourth time it was for *Operation Thunderbolt* (1977), this one directed by Golan himself and starring Klaus Kinski. Ironically enough, they lost that year to the French-language film *Madame Rosa* (1977), by Israeli filmmaker Moshe Mizrahi: the director of the second and third Oscar-nominated films that Gold and Globus had produced. Always the bridesmaids but never the bride, the absence of an Academy Award trophy would consistently drive Golan throughout the rest of his career. (More on that later.)

Lovingly dubbed "The Go-Go Boys" by the media because of their fast working pace and prowess at making deals, Golan and Globus delivered hit after hit for the Israeli market. One of the most notable among these was the ethnic musical *Kazablan* (1974), an adaptation of an older stage production that was given the bombastic flair of the old Hollywood musicals which captivated its co-writer and director, Menahem Golan, when he was a youth. More than just a box office smash, *Kazablan* was an outright pop culture phenomenon in its home country. Songs from its soundtrack topped the music charts and the film is still beloved there to this day, the Israeli equivalent of a *West Side Story* (1961) or *The Sound of Music* (1965).

Although Golan and Globus' efforts are regularly credited with pushing the Israeli film industry to new heights, few of their films from this period made much of a splash outside their homeland, receiving small releases targeting niche audiences. The exception to this was the raunchy teen comedy *Lemon Popsicle* (1978), directed by future Cannon regular Boaz Davidson. Revolving around the misadventures of sex-starved teen boys in the 1950s and featuring a soundtrack of American rock-and-roll classics, *Lemon Popsicle* went on to be one of the local film industry's all-time biggest hits. In Israel alone it took in more than quadruple its budget, one third of which had gone to licensing songs from Elvis Presley and Jerry Lee Lewis. With its universal theme of teen boys being horny, the movie found sound success abroad—especially in Japan, West Germany, and a few other parts of Europe. To date, the franchise includes seven sequels, one spin-off movie and a reboot film. Davidson himself returned to direct the surprisingly faithful American remake: the beloved Cannon coming-of-age comedy, *The Last American Virgin* (1982).

In Israel the Go-Go Boys were prolific and well-respected, arguably the most successful movie producers to come out of the country. What had eluded them thus far, however, was profit and prosperity in America. A passion for Hollywood films is what inspired Golan and Globus to pursue filmmaking, and producing Hollywood-style movies was what they continuously strove for. It wasn't enough for them to have revitalized their local industry and put Israeli filmmaking on the international map: they dreamed of being bigshot, studio moguls in the mold of Louis B. Mayer, Jack Warner, or Adolph Zukor. It didn't seem to matter to them that the old-fashioned studio system had all but died out in Hollywood by the late 1970s. It wouldn't stop them from trying to re-implement it—and, for a brief time, succeeding at doing so.

There was a level of inherent glamour and professionalism imbued within the Hollywood exports, and even the biggest, locally-grown Israeli hits only yielded a drop in the box office bucket compared to an American blockbuster. Golan and Globus found it hard to compete at home, where resources were limited along with the access to big-name, international movie stars. This led to their formation of a sister company under the awkwardly-spelled name AmeriEuro Pictures Corporation, which Golan and Globus used to launch joint American and European productions aimed at Western markets before switching to the more straight forward name, Golan-Globus Productions. First came the gangster picture *Lepke* (1975), which starred Tony Curtis and was shot in Hollywood, quickly followed by the heist flick *Diamonds* (1975), starring Robert Shaw, Richard Roundtree, Shelley Winters, and Barbara Hershey. The routine spy thriller *The Uranium Conspiracy* (1978) was shot across many picturesque locations but failed to make much a ripple. Most primed for success was the lavish romantic epic *The Magician of Lublin* (1979), adapted from an acclaimed novel by Isaac Bashevis Singer. It starred Alan Arkin, Louise Fletcher, and Shelley Winters (again), and featured a score by three-time Oscar winner Maurice Jarre and a theme song sung by Kate Bush. All of these were directed by Menahem Golan, and all were met with mixed reviews and middling box office returns. Undoubtedly more frustrating for the pair, America had entirely failed to take much notice of them.

By the late 1970s, Golan and Globus had come up with a new plan. In Hollywood, the late '70s were a time when many studios were regrouping to re-assess the way they did business. Distribution models were changing. Young auteurs would emerge from the independent film movement and establish a new upper echelon of studio filmmakers. This was the dawn of the blockbuster era, when hits such as *Jaws* (1975) and *Star Wars* (1977) would set hitherto unimaginable box office benchmarks and completely reinvent the way that movies were marketed. Meanwhile, many smaller and independent American production companies were facing financial difficulties. Golan and Globus spotted an opportunity to force their way in.

Founded in 1966 by film students Dennis Friedland and Chris Dewey, The Cannon Group was just such a struggling company, but that hadn't always been the case. They had success early on with an English-language re-release of the softcore Swedish porn film *Inga* (1968), and their biggest-ever hit with 1970's controversial *Joe*, starring Peter Boyle and helmed by John G. Avildsen. They kept their focus primarily on the low-cost exploitation markets, importing cheap monster movies, sex comedies, kung fu and gangster

Introduction

flicks from abroad for a quick buck, or funding homegrown, low budget productions such as *The Happy Hooker* (1975), another hit.

By the end of the '70s, however, a run of flops had left this first incarnation of Cannon on shaky financial footing. Enter Golan and Globus, who had come up with the idea that acquiring an American company with its own distribution arm would make it easier for them to disseminate their product stateside. That Cannon already had a catalog of around 80 films made the company particularly appealing to the duo. The cousins approached the flagging indie studio with an unusual proposal: they would use their considerable international sales skills to sell the company's product to untapped overseas markets, taking a commission on each sale. Those commissions were used to purchase controlling shares from its founders. By May of 1979, The Cannon Group officially belonged to Golan and Globus. Their first production under new management would be *The Happy Hooker Goes Hollywood* (1980), a direct sequel to a pair of movies that had made good money for the prior regime.

The rest, as they say, is history . . . and the subject of the very book you hold in your hands. Welcome to *The Cannon Film Guide, Volume One*.

The Cannon Film Guide
Volume I (1980–1984)

The Happy Hooker Goes Hollywood on Betamax.

The Happy Hooker Goes Hollywood

Release Date: May 10, 1980
Directed by: Alan Roberts
Written by: Devin Goldenberg & Alan Roberts
Starring: Martine Beswick, Chris Lemmon, Adam West, Richard Deacon
Trailer Voiceover: "How do you make movies? You make movies with money. Money comes easy to the girls of Xaviera Hollander!"

For Golan and Globus' first American production under their newly-acquired Cannon banner to have set a more suitable tone for their future filmography, it would have needed to star Chuck Norris fighting breakdancing ninjas. Not only was *The Happy Hooker Goes Hollywood* tiptoeing along a line that separated mainstream comedy from softcore pornography, but it was a loose-linked sequel to a franchise they had no hand in originating. (See: *Death Wish II–IV* and *Exterminator 2*.)

Jumping into the sauna with another *Happy Hooker* sequel made sense, at least, because the series' rights came along with Golan and Globus' purchase of Cannon, since the prior management had distributed its first two, moderately successful entries. By the time we got to this G&G-produced *Happy Hooker* threequel, the series had transformed into an unexpectedly meta affair. This was a sequel with a plotline surrounding the fictionalized making of the first movie in the series.

When *Goes Hollywood* begins, celebrity prostitute Xaviera Hollander is happy running a bustling brothel with a long, long wait list among New York City's most wealthy and influential patrons. (It's not the gritty, sad sort of place you typically imagine a whorehouse to be: this one's more of a bright, cheerful Disneyland of Screwing.) Her book, *The Happy Hooker*, stills reigns over bestseller lists, which is what brings her to the attention of Hollywood.

Warkoff Brothers Studios—their logo resembles the famed Warner Bros. shield almost exactly—is led by William B. Warkoff, an old school mogul, and he's hell bent on inking a deal with New York's most famous madam and turning her life story into his company's next big, hit blockbuster. In true screwball fashion, he promises that he'll name whichever of his three producers to be his successor as the head of the studio if they're able to successfully get her signature on a contract. Thus, a madcap competition begins.

Xaviera is flown out to Hollywood where she's wined, dined, and wooed by a variety of showbiz big shots. Joseph Rottman, Mr. Warkoff's son-in-law, is a buffoon, and his bid for the WBS empire is shot down just as quickly as his highly-falsified pitch session to Xaviera. Producer Lionel Lamely, a handsome lothario, gets closer by seducing the famous lady of the evening, but blows it when his girlfriend, a young starlet, clandestinely records the two of them getting busy and throws a fit. It's Mr. Warkoff's young, bashful grandson Robby, of course, who is able to win the prominent prostitute's good favor with his insistence that she can make the movie herself, outside the Hollywood system. (Robby is played by Chris Lemmon, son of Jack. He'd later co-star opposite Hulk Hogan in the short-lived '90s TV series *Thunder in Paradise* [1994].)

And so Xaviera, Robby, and their crack team of working girls embark on an independent filmmaking adventure. (It's less *Easy Riders, Raging Bulls* and more zany, hooker hijinks.) They quickly discover that making a movie costs lots of money, and the girls aren't exactly flush with liquid assets. They finance the film the best way they know how: by exchanging sexual favors. Need film stock? Screw the lab technician in the dark room. Need a mansion to use as a shooting location? Have two of your topless flunkies bang the real estate agent. Can't afford catering? Force yourself on the poor deli delivery guy. That sex can buy you anything you want or need is the crux of this movie's humor.

The jilted producers at Warkoff Brothers Studios are embarrassed by all of the press that Xaviera's production receives in the Hollywood trades, and tip off the police to her illegal activities. After the assistant director unknowingly offers sex to an undercover cop posing as a camera rental clerk, the production is raided. This sets back the shoot, and legal fees sap what little (non-sexual) budget they had. Xaviera decides to take her revenge by playing a long, elaborate prank on the slimeballs at Warkoff Brothers. To make a long story short, through a series of far-fetched deceptions, Rottman and Lamely wind up wandering through a fancy-pants industry shindig while in full drag, being solicited by a drunk Shriner, and then accidentally cold-cocking a cop.

With this public relations catastrophe being the final straw, Mr. Warkoff himself steps in and attempts to broker a peace treaty. He offers Xaviera $5 million dollars to finish her film, on the condition that she delivers it in time to play at the premiere of his brand new, Los Angeles movie theater. It's a bet, of sorts: if she fails to deliver the finished film, she receives no payment and the rights to the movie revert to Warkoff Brothers. After the obligatory movie-making montage, we cut to the big day, when Robby and a couple of hoes are retrieving their finished film from the processing lab just under the wire, hours before the show. Unfortunately it's been hijacked by a pair of Jewish gangsters! (One is played by Yehuda Efroni, a character actor who would hold the record for most appearances in Cannon movies: sixteen total, not including many more of Golan and Globus' pre- and post-Cannon ventures.) A wacky car chase ensues, but the print is finally secured just as the pre-movie previews wrap up. Xaviera's indie movie is a wild success and the world-famous madam becomes the toast of Hollywood. Presumably she lives happily ever after, since this wound up being the final movie in the *Happy Hooker* trilogy.

In case you weren't alive in the 1970s and were wondering: there *was* a real-life Happy Hooker. Xaviera Hollander was a former secretary at the Dutch consulate in New York who quit her job in 1968 to become a high-end sex worker. She eventually opened her own brothel and became NYC's best-known madam—until her arrest, and subsequent deportation, for prostitution in 1971. Her memoir, *The Happy Hooker: My Own Story*, was published that same year, and became a *New York Times* Bestseller, infamous for its sexual candidness in that era.

Of course, a film version of *The Happy Hooker* followed in 1975. (It was, in fact, the second "adaptation" of the book to appear that year, following *The Life and Times of Xaviera Hollander* [1976], a full-on pornographic film.) This movie starred Academy Award nominee Lynn Redgrave and was a comedy loosely based on the book. It received a few warm reviews and fared well at the box office, and so a sequel followed—this time, starring Joey Heatherton in the titular role. *The Happy Hooker Goes to Washington* (1977) saw Xaviera being summoned to testify in defense of sexual freedom in front of Congress, and featured a supporting rogues' gallery which included Rip Taylor, Billy Barty, and Harold Sakata, the actor who played Oddjob in *Goldfinger* (1964). This one flopped.

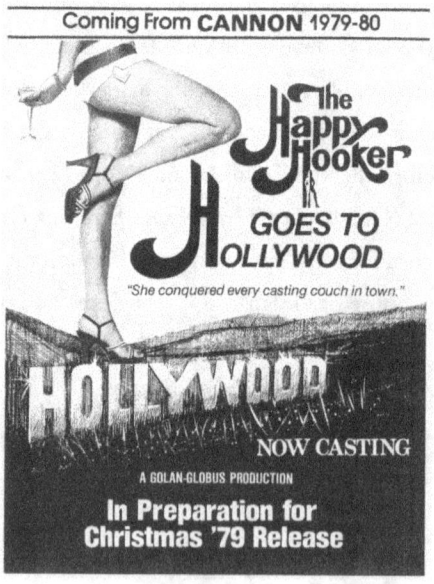

A full-page announcement for *Happy Hooker Goes Hollywood* in the May 9, 1979 issue of *Variety*.

When Golan and Globus took over Cannon and decided it was worth going ahead with a third *Happy Hooker* movie, Martine Beswick was brought in as the third actress to play the character in a trilogy which, by this point, bore little resemblance to the real-world Hollander's life. Beswick has the rare distinction of twice appearing as a Bond girl: in *From Russia With Love* (1963) and in *Thunderball* (1965). Beyond 007, her most famous role was in *One Million Years B.C.* (1966), in which she famously had a catfight with Raquel Welch and was terrorized by Ray Harryhausen dinosaurs. Not surprising for a James Bond movie veteran, Beswick brought some class back to the Happy Hooker role. It sounds as if she attempted to do the same with the entire production: the actress claimed to have stormed off the set when she arrived to shoot a swimming pool scene and found background extras engaging in *real* sexual intercourse.

The biggest surprise in the cast is Batman himself, Adam West, playing playboy movie producer Lionel Lamely. West spent the '70s and '80s trying to break out from under the shadow of the Caped Crusader, but mostly appeared in low-budget and direct-to-video flicks—including this, his first for Cannon. He'd later play an extraterrestrial in Cannon's *Doin' Time on Planet Earth* (1988). His performance in *The Happy Hooker Goes Hollywood* feels half-heartedly dialed in, but then it's not the most glamorous of roles, either, as a bumbling lady-killer who isn't exactly the suave Bruce Wayne you've come to know and love. When he's caught in a lie, Xaviera smashes a halved grapefruit into his crotch, complete with the sound effect of muted brass accompaniment. (*Wah wah wah wahhhhh*—there are a lot of those in this movie.) When he performs his big drag scene, he barely even attempts to inflect a feminine voice. He does briefly appear nude, however, so if you've ever had a burning desire to see Batman's butt, well, here you go.

West wasn't the only fading TV star hired on to *Happy Hooker III*; it appears to have been a running theme in the film's casting department. Phil Silvers, an old legend who originated the Sgt. Bilko character on his own *The Phil Silvers Show* in the 1950s, plays the wheelchair-bound William B. Warkoff. He's perpetually flanked by leggy, twin blondes played by Candi and Randi Brough, who'd appear again in Cannon's *Dr. Heckyl and Mr. Hype* (1980) this same year. As identical twin bombshells, Candi and Randi were popular pinup models in the early '80s, and probably most famous, acting-wise, as *BJ and the Bear* cast members in its final season. (When they moved to Hollywood, they leased their first apartment—a designated single—by fooling their landlord into thinking they were one person who just came and went more often than most.) Warkoff's son-in-law and West's drag partner, Joseph Rottman, is played by Richard Deacon, formerly of *The Dick Van Dyke Show* (1961–1966) and *Leave it to Beaver* (1957–1963). Fifties television personality Edie Adams has an appearance as a prickly talk show host; she'd hosted her own TV talk show in the mid-1960s. Until her husband's death in 1962, Adams and comedian Ernie Kovacs were one of TV's true power couples, a tier under Lucy and Desi. She may have been most famous as the long-term spokesperson for Muriel Cigars, where her famous catchphrase was the breathy, Marilyn Monroe-esque suggestion "Why don't you pick one up and smoke it sometime?"

The Happy Hooker Goes Hollywood also functions as a *H.O.T.S.* (1979) reunion, with Xaviera's brothel featuring actresses Lisa London, Susan Kiger, and Lindsay Bloom, who previously appeared together in the cult campus comedy. Lyman Ward, best known as the dad from *Ferris Bueller's Day Off* (1986), plays a real estate agent who's dragged onto a pool table by two topless ladies in lieu of rental fees. Speaking of '80s comedy dads, Paul Keith—the father in Cannon's hit *The Last American Virgin* (1982)—has a blink-and-you'll-miss-it role as a desk worker. Famed *Variety* columnist Army Archerd plays himself, covering Xaviera's big red carpet movie premiere.

The movie's associate producer, Ronnie Hadar, was part of Cannon's international sales division at the time Golan and Globus took over. He'd eventually have a huge hit to his name with (of all things) the numerous Mighty Morphin' Power Rangers children's TV shows.

However, director Alan Roberts' post-*Hooker* story is far and away the most intriguing—and mysterious. Prior to *Happy Hooker*, he'd mostly helmed '70s softcore porno movies like *The Zodiac Couples* (1970), *The Sexpert* (1972), and most famously *Young Lady Chatterley* (1977). He directed a few more films afterward, including a 1991 flick called *Karate Cop*, before settling into a career as a freelance film editor and occasional producer. This is where things get strange. In 2011, Roberts' name surfaced as the alleged director on documents pertaining to a low-budget movie titled *Desert Warrior*, described as a "historical Arabian Desert adventure film." It's unclear just how far Roberts' involvement with the film went: he never made a public statement about the movie, and other crew members refused to name the movie's director. Documents linked to the film and reported on by *Vice* contained the name Alan Roberts. ("Alan Roberts" being derived from his given name, Robert Alan Brownell.) In addition, *The New York Times* named Roberts as the movie's director. *Desert Warrior* was shot on a tiny budget around Los Angeles.

When a 14-minute portion of the film was uploaded to YouTube in 2012, it had been re-dubbed by other actors into an inflammatory, anti-Islam video under several titles, most notoriously *Innocence of Muslims*. The main character, whose name during shooting had been "Master George," was now being addressed as "Muhammad" and was portrayed as a philanderer and pedophile. This clip set off a chain of international coverage which incited protests, riots, and retaliatory attacks around the world. (News outlets estimated that the violent protests resulted in 50 deaths worldwide.) The entire 80-person cast and crew came out with a denouncement of the film, claiming that they were duped all along into thinking they were making an entirely different sort of movie. Eventually, the film's mastermind was revealed to be Nakoula Basseley Nakoula, a U.S. citizen of Egyptian birth, who wrote and produced the movie under a series of pseudonyms—and had previously been arrested in possession of meth-making supplies in the 1990s. It's no wonder that Roberts himself, the *Happy Hooker Goes Hollywood* director, kept a low profile in the wake of *Innocence of Muslims*, until his passing in 2016. Needless to say, it was a long, long way from the softcore pornos (and this Adam West sex comedy) on which he'd built his career.

An Italian theatrical poster for *Happy Hooker Goes Hollywood*. Note that even the title itself is wearing lingerie.

Interview: Actress Lisa London

The Happy Hooker Goes Hollywood was only Lisa London's second film, having made her screen debut in the cult campus comedy *H.O.T.S.* (1979). The actress and model would return to Cannon six years later in their women-in-prison film, *The Naked Cage* (1986). Other notable roles over the next decade included appearances in the Dirty Harry sequel *Sudden Impact* (1983) and a pair of movies from Andy Sidaris' notorious Bullets, Bombs, and Babes series:

Savage Beach (1989) and *Guns* (1990).

In addition to her acting, London was a member of the '80s girl group The Pinups. (She lends her own vocals to the soundtrack of *The Naked Cage*.) She continues acting to this day and has more than 50 credits to her name.

The Cannon Film Guide: Your very first movie was *H.O.T.S.*. As a way of launching your career, it's hard to go wrong with a cult classic like that one.

Lisa London: I know! It was so high profile. It's funny. As time has gone on and the industry has changed, it was technically a low-budget film but it was made for millions of dollars, and now people are making films for like $10,000 and getting them out there. It's kind of amazing the level I started on, because I think I only had one other audition before I got that, too.

Can you tell me how you arrived to that point? I know you moved to Los Angeles with nothing more than a dream—that it's one of those stores.

Yes, of course. Don't we all? [*Laughs*] My background was in journalism and broadcasting. I'd sang on stage a few times, but I had never acted on stage or in front of a camera. I had done a lot of modeling growing up in Palm Springs. Even though I was in college on a full scholarship for journalism, all I had ever wanted to do was act since I was born.

I was actually dating someone very famous who was transitioning from the sports world into acting. His agent was basically trying to get rid of me because I was a distraction, and so he sent me on this humongous audition. They were looking for girls to do a female version of *Animal House* (1978). It was a really big deal. Every starlet in town was up for one of the main characters. I thought I did so horribly at the audition that I didn't think there was any way I was going to get it. I'd never seen a movie script before! They handed me the script and told me they wanted me to read for O'Hara, but I saw both characters on the page and I thought "Oh, they must want me to change my voice and act out both parts." [*Laughs*] So I launched into it that way, literally stepping on the reader's toes.

There was this gorgeous woman in the room who was one of the writers. Her name was Cheri Caffaro. She stopped me and said, "Gentlemen, let me take Lisa outside." While we were outside for just a moment she tells me,

"This is great, but why don't we concentrate on *just* O'Hara? Let them read the other things." She coached me through it, and I ended up getting the part. It was a starring role right off the bat. Talk about beginner's luck, right?

Your next film after that one was *Happy Hooker Goes Hollywood*.

That was absolutely fantastic—it was a dream come true audition. Very rarely do you feel you did your best and know afterwards, "Oh my god, I know this character is mine. I got this." It's rare you get instant gratification from everyone in the room who is auditioning you. I felt that immediately. I felt like I was being offered the role while I was in the room, because the vibe was so strong. I actually became good friends with the director, Alan Roberts, who you know, then, later was the controversial director who shot that [*Innocence of Muslims*] video. That felt so bizarre, because you couldn't be around a cooler, nicer guy, and to think that he was embroiled in that—life is just so crazy! I will never forget when they revealed who the director of that video was and I was like, "Oh my god!"

Happy Hooker was a dream come true. I got to work with some iconic actors on that: Adam West, Richard Deacon, and Martine Beswick. Chris Lemmon and I became best friends on it. Phil Silvers told me I was great at comedy and that's when I knew I had arrived.

***Happy Hooker* was sort of a pseudo-*H.O.T.S.* reunion, with Lindsay Bloom and Susan Kiger also appearing in the film with you.**

Yeah, there were quite a few *H.O.T.S.* girls in that one. K.C. Winkler was in it, too. That was pretty wonderful. It was hilarious—you know, we're on location at places like LAX and the Ambassador Hotel. Getting to watch all of these people do their thing, that was really great. And the costumes! Hair and makeup, everything was so first class. Being so beautiful and glamorous was rather fun.

This was Cannon's first U.S. production after Golan and Globus took over. What were your impressions of the new studio?

The name "Cannon Films" seemed to have this power behind it, like it was a big name brand. It was an amazing journey to watch this new brand of filmmaking. They did this thing where they sold movies at Cannes that weren't even made yet, and that was kind of an unheard of thing to do. They were brazen. They were kind of gangsters, they were kind of cowboys. They didn't do things in traditional ways. I know there are stories where people were upset by the way they did things, but I have to say my experiences working for them were just fabulous. I can't complain at all. What a way to learn, that's what I'll say.

It sounds like a really fun set.

Are you kidding me? It was! And at the premiere I got to meet Jack Lemmon. Chris was like, "Lisa, this is my dad." [*Laughs*] You can't beat that.

You did several movies between *Happy Hooker* and your next Cannon film, the women-in-prison movie *The Naked Cage*. In the middle, though, you had a bit of a career as a pop star.

I did. I was the lead singer of a band called The Pinups, which was ahead of its time. We were the first girls to wear lingerie on national TV. We did it before Madonna, before anybody.

The director [of *Naked Cage*], Paul Nicholas, fought for me [to have a song in the film]. The powers that be at Cannon didn't want to pay for the song that I sang, and they finally agreed to do it because he insisted that it was perfect for the film. It was a trip to watch yourself doing a love scene to your own music, you know? [*Laughs*]

Quentin Tarantino does this retrospective movie night at The Beverly Cinema, and he featured *The Naked Cage*. It was amazing—it was completely sold out. It really stood out on screen. It's a beautiful film, and beautifully shot. It was really ahead of its time, and it shows so many things from racial tension to the issue of overcrowding in prisons and what goes on in them. It's really a great film with some great acting. It was really special, and I was surprised by how great it was. I didn't think it was going to hit me the way it did. It's a really well-done film. And it's a hysterical story, how I got that role.

Oh yeah?

You can't write this stuff.

Please share!

Sometimes in auditions they'll interview you, rather than have you read from the script. In those situations the most important thing is for them to talk to you and get a vibe from you. Then they'll cast you and just let everything unfold as it does. So, I think I had about four auditions with Paul Nicholas and Chris Nebe, the producer of *The Naked Cage*, before I'd really read anything.

I remember sitting in the big, gorgeous offices at Cannon Films—I think this was probably my third meeting with them. They said, "So, tell us a little about yourself. Is there any particular type of film that you're not into, or that you don't like?" And so I said, "You know, really, the only movies that I feel are kind of silly, to me, are women's prison movies." [*Laughs*] Of course I hadn't seen the script. They just looked at each other and didn't say anything. Around four days later I had a call back and was given the script, and I literally almost fainted. I called my agent and said, "Oh my gosh! They're never going to hire me!" But we actually became very good friends, and I did a couple other projects for them.

I actually met one of my best friends to this day on that set: Leslie Huntly. That was pretty amazing. I ended up introducing her to her now-husband of 25 years, and they have two kids. And so, *The Naked Cage* produced a lot of life. [*Laughs*]

Do you have any other memories you'd like to share from that set?

Oh, yes! We actually shot at [the Sybil Brand Institute], which was really intense. You can only imagine what it was like to be in an actual, functioning women's prison. I think they had shut it down at that point for some maintenance. There's a scene where I'm petrified about something and everyone thought my acting was so great, but that's because a gigantic rat had just run right over my bare feet. [*Laughs*]

But like I said, getting to have a song in the film was just crazy. Getting to work with Angel Tompkins, a veteran actress who is just gorgeous to this day . . . she was also at the [Beverly Cinema] screening. And it having this new life again, 30 years later—it's an amazing, full circle journey through the film acting world.

Schizoid

Release Date: September 12, 1980
Directed by: David Paulsen
Written by: David Paulsen
Starring: Klaus Kinski, Marianna Hill, Donna Wilkes, Craig Wasson, Christopher Lloyd
Trailer Voiceover: "Sick with revenge! Twisted with hate!"

Klaus Kinski is the scariest thing about *Schizoid*, and I'm not even talking about the character he plays in it. Always an imposing presence on screen, his notoriously erratic behavior off screen is the stuff of legend.

Klaus Kinski was born in the Free City of Danzig, now part of Poland, in 1926. Kinski was drafted into Nazi Germany's air force as a teenager, where he was injured and captured during his first combat. It was in a British POW camp where he started acting, appearing in shows to entertain his fellow prisoners. Kinski sought work in theater after the war. His rare acting talent was clear to many directors, but his frequent, often violent outbursts made it impossible for him to keep jobs for any significant length of time. In 1950, Kinski was confined to a state insane asylum for stalking and attempting to strangle an older woman he'd become romantically obsessed with. Records released after his death showed that doctors' initial diagnosis for Kinski was schizophrenia, but that their final medical conclusion was psychopathy. Although medically classified as "a danger to the public," he was released after three days.

Schizoid on VHS.

Kinski eventually made his way into film, landing frequent roles in European exploitation movies, spaghetti westerns, and horror films. His reputation grew, not only for being a great actor, but as an unpredictable egomaniac and womanizer. Kinski was married four times and had three children: Pola Kinski, Nastassja Kinski, and Nikolai Kinski. All three became actors themselves, with middle daughter Nastassja going on to the most fame as an international sex icon and a talented actress in her own right, famous for roles in Roman Polanski's *Tess* (1979), Wim Wenders' *Paris, Texas* (1984), and the 1982 remake of *Cat People*. She was also the star of Cannon's erotic post-War drama, *Maria's Lovers* (1985).

In a period of poverty, Klaus Kinski shared a boarding house with a 13-year-old young man who'd grow up to be the actor's greatest collaborator. In 1972, Klaus Kinski appeared in his first film for the German filmmaker Werner Herzog—the unforgettable *Aguirre: The Wrath of God*—and one of cinema's most beguiling actor-director relationships was born. They made four more films together: 1978's *Woyzceck*, 1979's *Nosferatu the Vampyre*, 1982's *Fitzcarraldo*, and 1987's *Cobra Verde*. In Kinski, Herzog found his greatest muse; in Herzog's films, Kinski found the perfect conduit for his wild, untamable energy. One possible explanation for their incredible creative chemistry is that, by any standard measure, Kinski and Herzog were both batshit crazy.

The behind-the-scenes stories from Kinski and Herzog's films together are unbelievable. Knock-down, drag-out fistfights, hours-long screaming matches, pointed guns and mutual death threats were all commonplace on their sets. Herzog has admitted to attempting to burn Kinski alive in his bed after one bad fight; during another, the director threatened to shoot them both when Kinski tried to walk off set. However, like any couple who seem to fight all of the time but deep down love each other very much, that anger and resentment channeled itself into mind-blowing makeup sex—and by makeup sex, I mean an infinitely fascinating, shared filmography. The duo's five movies together number among each of their best works, and are must-see cinema. After Kinski's death, Herzog assembled a documentary in tribute to his long time partner titled *My Best Fiend* (1999), which contains a lot of incredible, archival footage pertaining to their volatile friendship.

Schizoid was Kinski's first and only film for Cannon, yet he'd previously worked for Menahem Golan when he starred in his Best Foreign Film-nominated Israeli feature, *Operation Thunderbolt* (1977). *Schizoid* was written and directed by David Paulsen, who'd previously penned Golan's James Bond knock-off *The Uranium Conspiracy* (1978), and had helmed the slasher flick *Savage Weekend* (1979), a Cannon distro title. Preliminary marketing materials for the film sold it under the name *Murder By Mail*, though it was ultimately put out in the U.S. with a more sensational, if insensitive, title: *Schizoid*.

The film's working title, *Murder By Mail*, came from a series of threatening letters—cut-and-pasted from magazines, classic creepazoid-style—received by the film's heroine, a love advice columnist named Julie, played by Marianna Hill. (She's best remembered as Fredo's wife in *The Godfather: Part II* [1974] and her starring role opposite Clint Eastwood in 1973's *High Plains Drifter*.)

Julie largely ignores the threatening letters, dismissing them as the handiwork of a harmless nut job, until people in her therapy group start turning up violently murdered. The police are initially reluctant to help her pursue a connection between the letters and the murders, and the death toll escalates as Julie grows closer, romantically, with her German-accented therapist, Dr. Pieter Fales (played by Kinski.)

From the moment he appears on screen, Pieter seems suspicious. His wife died under mysterious circumstances. He has sexual affairs with more than one of his patients at any given time. He lives in a big, empty, Silverlake mansion. In one of his first scenes, he leers creepily through a doorframe as his teenage daughter undresses before a shower. Perhaps most disturbing of all: he's played by Klaus freakin' Kinski!

We watch members of Julie's therapy group get picked off one at a time, murdered by an unseen assailant in a stylish hat and trench coat. His (or her) weapon of choice is a pair of long, sharp scissors.

Schizoid moves slowly and isn't the most thrilling of slashers, but it does a good job of throwing suspicion on its cast, leaving viewers guessing as to the killer's identity until the very end. Even in spite of Kinski's inherent menace, there are multiple other characters who are believable suspects. *Is* it Pieter, the psychotherapist? Or could it be Julie's jealous ex-husband, Doug, whom she works with at a Los Angeles daily paper? Or is it someone from her therapy group, such as the spooky, old handyman? Or maybe it's Pieter's daughter, who seems to be just about as unhinged as her father? You'll have to watch *Schizoid* to find out.

A full-page ad promoting the film under its working title, *Murder by Mail*, from the May 7, 1980 issue of *Variety*.

You'll find many recognizable faces within *Schizoid*'s supporting cast. Julie's ex is played by Craig Wasson, who'd go on to star in De Palma's *Body Double* (1984) and then *A Nightmare on Elm Street 3: The Dream Warriors* (1987). The actress playing Pieter's daughter is Donna Wilkes, known to mainstream audiences from *Jaws 2* (1978) and to cult movie fans for starring as the title character in the 1984 sexploitation flick, *Angel*, in which she played a 15-year-old schoolgirl who moonlights as a prostitute and helps take down a serial killer.

These days, the most famous secondary actor in the film would obviously be Christopher Lloyd, appearing here as one of the more suspicious members of Julie's therapy circle. After wrapping five seasons on the sitcom *Taxi* (1978–1983), Lloyd had grown tired of film and television, despite memorable roles in *Star Trek III* (1984) and *The Adventures of Buckaroo Banzai* (1984). For a while he'd made up his mind to quit movies and return exclusively to the stage, but his agent talked him into taking one last film audition. He'd wind up landing that role: Dr. Emmett Brown, in 1985's *Back to the Future*—and the rest is history.

As it goes, *Schizoid* may not be one of the better slashers from an era that produced many, many, many of them, but it has a very strong cast, and they play a big part in its watch-ability. Seriously, half the fun is watching Kinski trying really hard to appear *not* creepy. Christopher Lloyd—even in a smallish role like this on—also has a way of elevating the quality of any project he's involved in.

In true "ripped from the headlines" tradition, the plotline for *Schizoid* was loosely inspired by a real series of events which happened less than a year before the movie's release. In 1979, *Chicago Tribune* syndicated columnist Bob Greene was the recipient of a string of bizarre, threatening letters from an anonymous person, signed "Moulded to Murder." In them, the individual threatened to commit a series of murders in Los Angeles county beginning after the New Year. In early January of 1980, police detectives set up an anonymous phone line for Greene, which he published in his column with an invitation for the person writing the letters to call so that they could talk it through. When the aspiring killer reached out to the writer, the LAPD was able to trace the call to a phone booth where they apprehended him before he could commit his planned murder spree.

The whole, thrilling ordeal was recounted for readers in Greene's nationally-syndicated weekly column, and by the articles and TV news programs which covered the story as it played out. Of course the first time Greene ever heard about Cannon's film inspired by his experience was when the studio sent out a press release boasting of how *Schizoid* was based on the "Moulded to Murder" story—much to Greene's horror. The journalist had turned down all offers to sell the film rights out of respect for the psychologically ill individual it centered on, worried that Hollywood would sensationalize his sad story. Lack of film rights didn't stop Cannon, obviously, who turned it into a lurid slasher flick named *Schizoid.*

Teen Mothers on videocassette.

Teen Mothers, a.k.a. *Seed of Innocence*

Release date: October 1980
Directed by: Boaz Davidson
Written by: Boaz Davidson and Stu Krieger
Starring: Timothy Wead, Mary Cannon
Tagline: "She was 14. He was 15. They had a baby. Their only shelter was the streets of New York."

Unplanned pregnancy! Homelessness! Incarceration! Prostitution! Being chased by a lecherous dwarf, and being shot at by the police! All these and more are (apparently) the dangers of... *teenage copulation*!

As you can probably tell from the way my tongue is pushing at my cheek, *Teen Mothers*—or *Seed of Innocence*, as it was titled originally—wasn't one of those informational sex education films intended to warn teenagers about the perils or premarital intercourse, but something far more sensationalized. It wasn't necessarily a new idea: grindhouse movies had been parading under the guise of informational films since 1936's *Reefer Madness*. Decades earlier, Jerry Gross' *Teenage Mother* (1967) made beaucoup bucks on the drive-in circuit while passing itself off as an educational feature by including real-life birth footage amongst its scenes of drag racing and juvenile delinquency.

Given the subject matter, a teen pregnancy film was a great cover for an exploitation movie, given that you pretty much *had* to show how the bun was placed in the metaphorical oven. Whether Cannon had these same intentions or not with *Teen Mothers* is unclear, but the final product is one that's wildly far-fetched, a tad sleazy, and much more fun than any stuffy educational film would ever have been. The movie stars Timothy Wead and the perfectly-named Mary Cannon—neither were first-time actors, nor were they ever particularly well-known—as the movie's accidental parents. They're supposed to be fifteen- and fourteen-years-old in this movie, but in real life were nearly a decade older than their characters. There are more familiar faces in *Teen Mothers*' supporting cast, but we'll get to them later.

We're introduced to our adolescent lovers, Danny and Alice, as they're—for lack of better terminology—screwing in a barn. The movie wastes zero time getting to its premise, as over the next two scenes we watch young Alice faint during marching band practice and then have a doctor confirm she's pregnant. While Alice's parents are occupied with slut-shaming their daughter, Danny's getting the snot beat out of him by Alice's older brother and practically being disowned by his own father. Alice's folks decide to do what's best for their little girl when she needs them the most, and lock her up in a convent until after the baby is born.

Judging by how steamily the opening sex scene is shot, it's clear from the outset that *Teen Mothers* isn't a cautionary tale like the promotional art seems to suggest. Soft focus, lighting that flatters, nude bodies gently thrusting atop a pile of hay—if their intent was to make sex look *un*-appealing to minors, well, this was the most wrong possible way they could have gone about it. Just compare this scene to a similar one in *Lady Chatterley's Lover* (1982), another Cannon film which featured characters humping in ecstasy on a perceptibly unsanitary barn floor. That scene isn't half as erotically-charged as this one—and that film starred Sylvia Kristel, one of the most famous erotic film stars of all time!

Once the film's plotline moves to the nunnery, though, things start to go fully bonkers. The maternity home in *Teen Mothers* is a palpably sinister place, run by a cruel Mother Superior who's a cross between *One Flew Over the Cuckoo Nest*'s Nurse Ratched and *Annie*'s Miss Hannigan. None of the knocked-up young ladies seem to be there voluntarily, and we learn that the nuns abscond with their babies shortly after birth to put them in Christian homes, regardless of whether or not the mothers want to keep them. During one harrowing scene, Alice's friend mouths off to the head nun and she slaps her face so hard that the poor girl suffers an instant, late-term miscarriage. This is obviously no place for our heroine mother-to-be, who's finally rescued by her boyfriend—he bull rushes his way into the convent as alarm sirens wail—while the other girls cheer them on.

Since Danny can now add kidnapping on top of the statutory rape charges Alice's parents threatened him with, it's pretty clear that he and Alice can't go back home to their small, conservative, Midwestern town. They impulsively make up their minds to run away to New York, the concrete jungle where dreams are made of, and find a new life for themselves. Unfortunately for these starry-eyed kids, this is New York City at the beginning of the 1980s, where crime was rampant, the streets were littered with trash, and Times Square was little more than a stretch of porno theaters. The New York City of *Teen Mothers* is more in line with the gritty, urban wasteland seen in *The Warriors* (1979) or *Death Wish* (1974) than the squeaky-clean, Disney-fied one it is today.

The rest of the film chronicles the young couple's many misadventures in the Big Apple. Within hours of their arrival they're hustled out of their automobile by a smooth-talking car thief who goes by the name of Captain, who eventually has a change of heart and offers them a place to stay. Two years later the actor who plays Captain, T.K. Carter, would take on his most famous role as the roller skating cook, Nauls, in 1982's *The Thing*. From 1984 to 1986 he'd play Punky Brewster's favorite teacher, Mr. Fulton, on the NBC series of the same name, and also appear in Cannon's *Runaway Train* in 1985.

Danny and Alice move into their new home which is, of course, a crumbling Bronx slum overflowing with criminals, nut jobs, and assorted misfits. Their roommate—Captain's sister, Denise—is a hooker, and played by *Playboy*

Playmate Azizi Johari. She'd play another hooker—one quite bluntly named "Pussy"—in Cannon's *Body and Soul* (1981).

Our teenage lovebirds' next-door neighbor is an escaped mental patient named Leo, played by the unmistakable Vincent Schiavelli. Standing six-and-a-half feet tall with distinctive features characteristic of the genetic disorder Marfan syndrome, Schiavelli found a steady career in character work for nearly four decades. That included roles in both classics and cult films, such as *One Flew Over the Cuckoo's Nest* (1975), *Fast Times at Ridgemont High* (1982), *The Adventures of Buckaroo Banzai Across the Eighth Dimension* (1984), *Batman Returns* (1989) and *Ghost* (1990), among many others.

On their very first night in the new digs, pregnant Alice is propositioned by one of Denise's visiting johns and flees terrified into the streets, where she's chased through a thunderstorm by two leering, grotesque hobos waving torches over their heads. (One of them is a dwarf because, why not, I guess?) Our heroes' situation seems pretty dire at this point in the film, but for two runaway teens with a baby on the way, it could be worse.

Danny gets a job as a busboy at a diner run by Shirley Stoler (of *The Honeymoon Killers* [1970], *The Deer Hunter* [1978], and *Pee-wee's Playhouse* [1986–1990]), where he's held up at knifepoint by a young William Sanderson. Astute television viewers will recognize Sanderson's warbling voice from HBO's *Deadwood* (2004–2006) and *True Blood* (2008–2014), or from his long tenure as the eccentric Larry on *Newhart* (1982–1990). He also had memorable roles in the science fiction classic *Blade Runner* (1982) and the pre-Cannon Chuck Norris action vehicle *Lone Wolf McQuade* (1983).

After thwarting the robbery Danny goes to a strip club to celebrate, then arrives home drunk just as Alice goes into labor. They welcome their new bundle of joy—a bouncing baby girl, whom they name Laura—and swiftly learn, as you'd expect, that caring for a newborn is no walk in the park. Eventually Danny throws a temper tantrum at work, quitting his job and tossing their happy little family's financial stability out the window. During an argument, he angrily suggests that Alice get off her lazy, baby-raising butt and go get a job, and so she storms out of their apartment and does the first thing any sensible young woman would do: goes straight to her prostitute friend, Denise, and inquires for work. (Why she never even briefly considers any other profession we'll never know.) Naturally, she has second thoughts the first time she's alone in a motel room with a sleazy businessman and runs home to Danny, whose first reaction is to smack her in the teeth as soon as he finds out where she's been. All of this drama is eventually resolved when *he* finally forgives *her*.

In this alternate advertisement, Danny and Alice hardly let their baby come between them and their canoodling.

Are you still with us? Are you starting to think that baby Laura perhaps might have perhaps been better off being taken away by the sinister nuns? Well, Danny and Alice realize they're overmatched by the big city and decide to head back home with the hope that their families will welcome them with open arms. You would that would be as simple as packing up their stuff and climbing onto the next Greyhound bound for farm country, but nooooo, no no no. Not for Danny and Alice. As the young father ducks into a supermarket to pick up a pack of diapers, Captain shoplifts a rubber duck as a going-away present for little baby Laura. A security guard catches him and things escalate at record speed: within seconds, Danny has stolen the guard's gun, the boys have fled the store, and Captain has been gunned down by the New York Police Department. (It's an incredibly action-packed sixty seconds of screen time!) Danny is hauled off to jail, but the movie promptly ends with him being acquitted of any wrongdoings in front of a courtroom overflowing with their family and friends. One of the final images we get is baby Laura erupting from the back of the courtroom, screaming "daddy!" and stumbling towards Danny's open embrace in slow motion. It's as glorious an ending as it sounds.

It's all pretty silly, sure, but it's also fun in a campy, melodramatic way. A lot of entertainment value was mined from presenting the ludicrously precipitous fallout of Danny and Alice's underage hanky-panky. Cannon screened the film under its somewhat pretentious-sounding original title, *Seed of Innocence*, at Cannes in 1980, but opted to release it under the more enticing name *Teen Mothers* when it hit video in the United States. (The plural in "mothers" is a little misleading, as the movie is only really about the one teen mother.)

Stars Timothy Wead and Mary Cannon both left Hollywood entirely by the late 1980s. Wead dedicated himself to religion and formed Performance Ministries, where he travels around the country acting out sections of the New Testament as a one-man show for church congregations.

The script was co-written by Stu Krieger, who'd become better known for writing the screenplay for the classic Don Bluth animated film, *The Land Before Time* (1988), a movie with significantly fewer prostitutes and unplanned pregnancies.

Writer-director Boaz Davidson was able to make *Teen Mothers* something of a family affair, with his wife, Bruria, working as an editor on the film, and casting their daughter as baby Laura. While *Teen Mothers* may not have been the best indication of things to come, Boaz Davidson's name is one you'll be reading many times across these pages as one of Cannon's most prolific movie-makers and, later, most successful alums. As the filmmaker behind their hit, Israeli comedy *Lemon Popsicle* (1978) and other successful films in Golan and Globus' native country, the producers were already very familiar with Davidson and his work when they made their way to the United States and set up shop in 1979.

Davidson was born in Tel Aviv and had trained in filmmaking at the London Film School before returning home to make his mark on Israeli cinema with numerous, well-received movies—in particular the aforementioned *Lemon Popsicle*, which went on to be one of the country's highest-grossing films of all time. By pure coincidence, Davidson had already relocated to Los Angeles just before Golan and Globus acquired Cannon, and the cousins wasted no time in reuniting with their golden goose director. *Teen Mothers* would be the first movie he made for the duo after their move stateside, followed by *Hospital Massacre* (1982). Over the next decade and change Davidson was one of the studio's primary collaborators, helming further Cannon features such as 1982's *The Last American Virgin* (an Americanized remake of *Lemon Popsicle*), *Going Bananas* (1987), *Salsa* (1988), and *American Cyborg: Steel Warrior* (1993). He also had a hand in the screenplays for both *Hot Resort* (1985) and *Delta Force 3: The Killing Game* (1991).

After Cannon's demise in the early 1990s, Davidson would pivot into a producer's role. He'd become a major player with Nu Image, founded by fellow Cannon alum Avi Lerner, whom he'd later follow to the newly-formed Millennium Films and there head up development. Launched in 1996, Millennium has reigned for more than two decades as Hollywood's most successful independent studio. Specializing in action movies with global appeal, Millennium can be viewed in many ways as something of a spiritual successor to Cannon. Starting in 2010, Davidson would once again employ several of Cannon's biggest stars in his most successful movie franchise, *The Expendables*, including Sylvester Stallone, Dolph Lundgren, Chuck Norris, and Jean-

Claude Van Damme; the series would gross over $270 million globally across its first three entries. While few would few would have imagined it, the cheap, silly *Teen Mothers* wound up being the first foray into Hollywood for a man who would eventually become one of the Industry's major power players. Indeed, everyone has to start *somewhere* . . . .

Dr. Heckyl and Mr. Hype

Release Date: October 1980
Directed by: Charles B. Griffith
Written by: Charles B. Griffith
Starring: Oliver Reed, Sunny Johnson
Trailer Voiceover: "Horribly hilarious... You'll love the brute and you'll hate the brute!"

Robert Louis Stevenson's classic 1886 novella, *The Strange Case of Dr. Jekyll and Mr. Hyde*, is one of literature's most-adapted works, and has made its way into motion picture dozens of times since the first, silent movie version of it was released in 1908. Innumerable filmmakers over the years have taken the tale's ageless themes of dual identity and transformation and put their own twist on it. In these re-imagined versions, the hero doesn't necessarily drink a potion and turn into a violent murderer, but something else entirely. Across various takes on the story, nerds have turned into ladies' men (1963's *The Nutty Professor*), White men into Black men (1976's *Dr. Black, Mr. Hyde*), and men into women (1995's *Dr. Jekyll and Ms. Hyde*). I guarantee, none of these versions are as strange a case as Cannon's singular *Dr. Heckyl and Mr. Hype*.

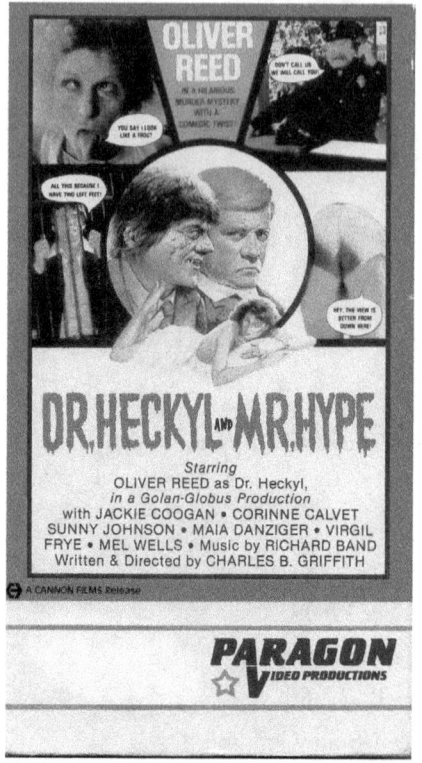

The VHS slipcover for *Dr. Heckyl and Mr. Hype*, complete with talking buttocks. This copy was rented by Video Hits in Kalamazoo, Michigan.

The film was written and directed by Charles B. Griffith, one of the more prolific talents to emerge from Roger Corman's filmmaking family tree. Griffith wrote dozens of screenplays for Corman from the 1950s through the 1970s, including b-movie classics such as *The Little Shop of Horrors* (1960), *It Conquered the World* (1956), *The Wild Angels* (1966), and *Death Race 2000* (1975). He also acted in, produced, or worked as second unit director on many of those features. Few scribes are as highly revered as Griffith among enthusiasts of that era's schlock cinema; even Quentin Tarantino has cited Griffith as one of his all-time favorite screenwriters.

Griffith knew Cannon's co-chief, Menahem Golan, with whom he'd worked on the crew of Corman's *The Young Racers* (1963), and the two were old friends. (The same film crew had included future bigshots Francis Ford Coppola and Robert Towne.) Just after Golan took over Cannon in 1979 he had tried to hire Griffith to write *The Happy Hooker Goes Hollywood*, but details weren't agreed upon in time and Cannon moved on. That same year Griffith put together a list of joke movie titles and premises to pitch to Francis Ford Coppola at his annual Christmas party, including one called "Dr. Feelgood and Mr. Hype," about a hippie who turns into an advertising executive. Coppola got a good chuckle out of the list and nothing more than that, but when Golan read it he saw an opportunity. Griffith was given the greenlight to make a comedic take on *Jekyll and Hyde*—but only four weeks to write the script before shooting had to begin!

This *Variety* ad for the movie's Cannes debut emphasizes their famously handsome star's presence by showing him, for once, *not* covered in grotesque makeup.

In prototypical Cannon fashion, Griffith pounded out a 200-page screenplay which Golan cut down simply by tearing whole pages out. The budget was set at a lean $750,000. That may not sound like a lot, and it wasn't; even by 1980, an average studio film already cost millions to make. However, if you look at the budgets for a few other, successful, "small" movies that came out the same year—*Mad Max* (roughly $250k USD), *Maniac* ($350k), and *Friday the 13th* ($550k)—it's easy to see that budgets can be stretched with a little creativity. Griffith was given a four-week shooting schedule, and then two weeks to edit the film together. Things went . . . well, read on.

The movie's first major issue stems from its central miscasting. Griffith had written the film with Dick Van Dyke in mind to play the dual, lead roles of Heckyl and Hyde. Once it was discovered that Van Dyke wouldn't be available during the movie's tight filming window, Golan went out and hired Oliver Reed instead, who was certainly a fine actor but a *much* different one than Van Dyke.

For a period of time Reed had been one of Great Britain's most bankable leading men, starring in hits like *Oliver!* (1968) and *Tommy* (1975). By this point in his career, however, the former A-lister was probably less famous for his acting than he was for being an outspoken misogynist and a very, very heavy drinker. He once publicly boasted of drinking more than *one hundred* pints of beer over a single bender. Reed passed away at 61 years old while filming 2000's *Gladiator*, from a heart attack brought on by one of his famous, boozy binges. *Dr. Heckyl and Mr. Hype* was the second adaptation of this particular tale Reed had appeared in, having made an uncredited appearance in the Hammer production *The Two Faces of Dr. Jekyll* (1960).

In *Dr. Heckyl and Mr. Hype*, Oliver Reed plays the homely Dr. Henry Heckyl, a man with the misfortune to look like one of the zombies from *Dawn of the Dead* (1978) who had come down with a terrible case of scoliosis. He has blue-grey skin cratered with ugly wrinkles, a potato-like nose, mismatched eye colors and a hunched back. Regardless of his monstrous appearance, he's earned a reputation as a highly skilled podiatrist, seeing a steady string of patients in a medical office he shares with doctors of other curious specialties.

We learn early on that Heckyl pines for a pretty blonde named Coral, played by Sunny Johnson. While the radiant, young Johnson was only cast a matter of mere hours before shooting began, she is one of this film's bright spots. Her only other, truly notable role was playing Jeanie, the figure skater, in *Flashdance* (1983). Tragically Johnson died of a brain aneurysm shortly after appearing in that film, at the young age of 30.

More promotion for the movie's screenings at Cannes. Now that's a face only a mother could love.

In the movie, Heckyl is far too shy and self-deprecating to work up the nerve to talk to Coral, and is content to watch her board her bus each morning from afar. After moping around for the first chunk of the movie—both in willowy voiceover, and in his dialogue with others—he decides that he'll end it all, and take his own life. "Goodbye, you old, ugly piece of shit," he says to himself in the mirror as he prepares to cut his own head off with an oversized pair of scissors. He's interrupted at the last possible second by another doctor, who has invented a miraculous weight loss drug: one sip turns a fat, plain woman into a skinny, beautiful model in a matter of minutes. Better yet, the only side effect to this miracle drug they've discovered so far is "a little diarrhea."

Let's talk a little about the tone of the film, which never quite jives in a way that feels right. The script and premise seem to be going for a madcap, Mel Brooks-style comedy along the lines of *Young Frankenstein* (1974). The gags are lowbrow, and the movie's side players give uber-broad performances. The soundtrack is packed to the gills with silly, cartoonish sound effects—we're talking slide whistles and springy "boi-oi-oi-oi-oing" noises—and the cornball character names seem to support the theory that everything about the movie was meant in jest. There are characters named Clutch Cooger, Mack Druck, Dr. Lew Hoo, Herringbone Flynn, and the best of them all: Miss Finebum. (Her name sounds like would happen if an eight-year-old was asked to come up with his own Bond girl.)

On the other hand, Reed's performance completely clashes with the all-out wackiness that surrounds it. Reed plays the meek, deformed Heckyl like a tragic outcast, as if he were playing, say, the Phantom of the Opera or the Hunchback of Notre Dame. Meanwhile his malicious alter-ego, Mr. Hype, is a frightening, egotistical psychopath. Neither character is remotely as goofy as their surroundings, even while Reed is uttering comedic lines in a ridiculous makeup job.

As you expected, Heckyl eventually guzzles the magic potion and is transformed into the handsome Mr. Hype; the transformations themselves appear particularly low-budget, involving a lot of wide-eyed, puckered-lip faces, zany sound effects, and psychedelic strobe lights. His first priority after this life-altering transformation is, of course, to go out and lose his virginity. The problem, though, is that Mr. Hype has a bad habit of murdering the unfortunate women he takes to bed before he can consummate the deed. ("She's dead ... and I'm still a virgin!" he laments after sticking one hussy's big toe into a lamp socket and electrocuting her to death.) Mr. Hype then proceeds to stalk Heckyl's dream girl, Coral, who it turns out isn't attracted to the good-looking maniac but (surprise!) has fallen for the kind-hearted fuggo of himself, Dr. Heckyl.

This ad, which appeared in Cannon's sales catalogs, somewhat oddly decided to focus on the movie's foot stuff.

Of course the potion magic proves to be unstable and Heckyl/Hype has a hard time keeping his urges in check as he flip-flops between the two personas at random intervals. Lots of mistaken identity hijinks and sped-up, Benny Hill-style chases ensue. If you've seen one screwball take on *Jekyll and Hyde*, you've seen them all. This one looks even cheaper than its reported budget would lead you to believe.

Still, *Dr. Heckyl and Mr. Hype* should be of interest to Roger Corman fans, as it features a handful of cameos from his regular stable of actors. Mel Welles plays the portly, *very* Jewish doctor who invents the magical shape-shifting serum. (He was Mr. Mushnik in the original *Little Shop of Horrors* [1960], and would appear in two, future Cannon movies, *Body and Soul* and *The Last American Virgin*.) Dick Miller, a prolific and versatile character actor who appeared in at least twelve Corman-produced ventures, appears a garbage man; he'd go on to have a career renaissance in the 1980s, appearing in classics such as *The Terminator* (1984) and *Gremlins* (1985). Additionally you'll find an appearance from silver screen icon Jackie Coogan as a police commander. Coogan's starring turn in Charlie Chaplin's classic *The Kid* (1921) made him one of Hollywood's first child stars, but he grew even more famous four decades later when he became Uncle Fester on TV's *The Addams Family* (1964–1966).

Numerous other supporting players would return for bigger roles in other Cannon features. *Revenge of the Ninja*'s Virgil Frye plays a detective in this one, while Charles Howerton, later of *Asssassination* (1987), takes on the glamourous role of a gangster with ugly feet. This was also the film debut for Tony Cox, who would work on Cannon's *Invaders from Mars* in 1986 (as a puppeteer) and *Rockula* in 1990. He's most famous today for playing the elf, Marcus, to Billy Bob Thornton's surly Santa Claus in the anti-Holiday classic *Bad Santa* (2003). In *Heckyl*, he plays a dwarf who drinks Heckyl's magic solution and grows to an average height. The movie also features an early, jazzy score by Richard Band, a composer who'd go on to become synonymous with another famous '80s b-movie studio, Empire Pictures.

You'd think that Griffith would have done more films for Cannon, but while a number were discussed over the years, none ever panned out. (He had, at some point, worked on *Oy Vey, My Son Is Gay*, a longtime pet project of Golan's which wasn't made until 2009, but Griffith was never a credited writer.) Griffith next wrote and directed *Smokey Bites the Dust* (1981) and the direct-to-video sword and sorcery film *Wizards of the Lost Kingdom II* (1989), but largely left Hollywood behind to focus on travel writing until he passed away in 2007.

"The Power of Rock…in 1994." The slipcover for *The Apple*'s rare VHS release.

The Apple

Release Date: November 21, 1980
Directed by: Menahem Golan
Written by: Menahem Golan (script),
Stars: Catherine Mary Stewart, George Gilmour, Vladek Sheybal
Trailer Voiceover: "The Apple is success. The Apple brings you everything. The Apple is the temptation. The Apple is the experience. The Apple is the forbidden fruit. The Apple takes your soul!"

The music business is (literally) hell in the far-off future year of 1994. Welcome to *The Apple*!

Movie musicals had fallen into a dark period by the end of the 1970s. The cheery, golden days of song-and-dance legends like Gene Kelly, Judy Garland, and Fred Astaire were long passed. The early part of the decade saw the arrival of interesting, maturely themed musicals such as *Cabaret* (1972), The Who's fascinating-if-not-necessarily-good *Tommy* (1975), another exceptional remake of *A Star is Born* (1976) starring Barbra Streisand and Kris Kristofferson, and the grand poohbah of midnight movies, *The Rocky Horror Picture Show* (1975). Then *Saturday Night Fever* (1977) came along with a disco soundtrack that sold 16 million copies and ruined musicals for everyone. The Rodgers, Hammersteins, and Sondheims of the traditional musical world had gone out of style; the format was largely hijacked by record labels and studio executives for the cynical purpose of selling soundtrack albums.

The fallout years of *Saturday Night Fever* brought us such garish productions as 1978's *The Wiz*, an R&B retelling of *The Wizard of Oz* which starred Diana Ross, Michael Jackson, and Richard Pryor. Then came *Sgt. Pepper's Lonely Hearts Club Band* (1978), in which the Bee Gees, Peter Frampton, Aerosmith, and other '70s-centric celebrities butchered beloved classics from the Beatles catalog. (Its soundtrack famously went Platinum, then lost its Platinum status when four million copies of the steaming, vinyl turd were returned, unsold, to distributors and eventually had to be destroyed by the label.) The situation was bleak, and it was about to get worse.

Golan and Globus announced *The Apple* with this ... *interesting* ... full-page *Variety* ad from May 1979. "The BIG Science Fiction Romantic Rock Opera of The 80's" had yet to be cast.

The decline of the Hollywood musical in the late 1970s coincided with the rise of disco music, which led to an inevitable, mutant crop of disco musicals. The most famous of these famous flops is *Xanadu* (1980), a ridiculous Olivia Newton John musical about a Greek goddess who returns to Earth as a human roller skating enthusiast, falls in love with a dweeb, and helps him open a nightclub. *Can't Stop the Music* (1980) was a fictionalized account of how the Village People formed, in which the singing group played themselves opposite Steve Guttenberg and Bruce Jenner. There was also *Thank God It's Friday* (1978), a musical set in a Los Angeles disco club which stars a young Jeff Goldblum and Debra Winger; and *Roller Boogie* (1979), which centers on a post-*Exorcist* Linda Blair as a competitive roller dancer, and *Skatetown, U.S.A.* (1979), starring baby-faced Patrick Swayze and Scott Baio, about rival roller skaters. (It's incredible how closely the disco and late '70s skating fads coincided.) Even rare, non-disco musicals such as *Grease* (1978) and *Fame* (1980) felt compelled to tack on disco theme songs to help move soundtrack units.

Finding a good movie musical from this period is like playing Russian roulette with five bullets in the cylinder. They do exist, but for every interesting or creatively daring musical like *All That Jazz* (1979) there are ten steamers along the lines of Robert Altman's horrifying *Popeye* (1980) live-action film, or the bankrupt Neil Diamond remake of *The Jazz Singer* (1980).

One of Menahem Golan's talents was spotting trends and getting out slightly ahead of them, and the Cannon co-honcho wasted little time jumping on the disco bandwagon. *The Apple* had its origins as a Hebrew-language stage musical written by Coby and Iris Recht, married songwriters who'd had some previous success as pop singers in Israel. When their original vision for the play proved too expensive to stage, the Israeli duo brought their idea to Golan, who proposed that they adapt their manuscript into an English-language screenplay. After they did so Golan took his own pass at their revised script, removing scenes and adding new characters. The resulting product was *The Apple*. In a niche genre of movie musicals known for being loud, weird, and uncommonly garish spectacles, *The Apple* may be the craziest of the bunch.

The movie opens at the Worldvision Song Festival, a fictionalized take on the real-world Eurovision Song Contest: an annual, televised music competition that's aired in European countries since the 1950s. (Contemporary American audiences seeing *The Apple* likely wouldn't have gotten the reference.) A sequin-plastered disco act called BIM entertains a youthful, enthusiastic crowd with their highly repetitive hit theme song "BIM," an addictive earworm of a track that effectively functions as the bad guys' theme music. Behind the scenes, we see Satan—errrr, "Mr. Boogalow"—closely monitoring and manipulating his pop act's audience ratings.

In this incredible, illustrated French poster, the movie's main villains can be spotted lurking overhead.

The Apple doesn't beat around the bush here: the movie makes it unmistakably clear, right up front, that Boogalow is a bad guy. (That's pronounced "Boogaloo," as in *Breakin' 2: Electric Boogaloo*.) First off, Boogalow has a goatee. Second, he wears a burgundy tuxedo and a single, humongous diamond, dangle earring, which is an outfit only Lucifer or maybe Prince's evil, secret twin could pull off. He's played by Polish character actor Vladek Sheybal, with such villainous gusto that he may as well be twirling his moustache while smoking a cigarette from the far end of a long, skinny stick. (Sheybal's best remembered for his role as the sinister chess player, Kronsteen, in the 1963 James Bond entry *From Russia With Love*.)

When his assistant, Mr. Shake, announces that Bim are in the lead—a lead measured, inexplicably, in "heartbeats"—Boogalow vows that he'll turn BIM into the biggest stars of the decade. (Actor Ray Shell instills Mr. Shake with a level of flamboyant camp that makes Chris Tucker's *Fifth Element* [1997] character look subdued.)

BIM's elaborately gaudy stage show soon ends, and the master of ceremonies introduces the next act: a clean-cut, Canadian folk duo who perform under their first names, Alphie and Bibi. At first they're nearly booed off stage, but once the rowdy kids stop heckling them long enough to hear their song, they begin to be swayed by its romantic lyrics. (Although only the two singers and an acoustic guitar can be seen on stage, an invisible drummer and a lush string section accompany them through their song.) Backstage, Boogalow begins to panic as the audience is wooed by the Canadians' music—these nobodies are registering more heartbeats than his beloved BIM! He orders his minions to use the P.A. system play some sort of mind control cassette, which makes the audience once again turn against these two, comely Canucks. Amid a sea of jeers, Bibi flees the stage in tears.

Just as clearly as *The Apple* marked its villains, it's obvious that this wholesome pair will be our heroes. Bibi is played by the ever-charming Catherine Mary Stewart in her film debut. Stewart would go on to be a fixture of '80s cult cinema, starring in classics like *The Last Starfighter* (1984), *Night of the Comet* (1984), *Dudes* (1987), *World Gone Wild* (1987), and *Weekend at Bernie's*

(1989). This was actor George Gilmour's first and only film appearance, however, playing Alphie. There's little to no record of what he did after *The Apple* and it's a shame he never turned up in another film, as he's hardly the movie's worst actor.

Back at the Worldvision Song Festival, Boogalow is rushed by reporters on his way out and answers their questions about his hip, new disco group in multiple languages. We also learn that BIM's song was selected by the American government for their "national fitness program." One brazen reporter—a cameo by frequent Cannon composer George S. Clinton, not to be confused with the Parliament Funkadelic mastermind of the same name—asks Boogalow to comment on allegations that the festival is rigged, which Boogalow responds to by informing the journalist that he'll soon be out of a job. It's clear the reach of Boogalow's evil stretches far beyond the music industry.

A subdued ad from a Cannon sales catalog. The movie is described as "A futuristic, musical fantasy about the over-sexed, over-drugged, glamorized decadence of the music world in 1994."

While *The Apple* was shot in Cold War-era West Berlin, the city's grey and blocky, post-war architecture is meant to stand in for a futuristic American megalopolis, likely New York City, in 1994. Why exactly Golan singled out that specific year as the setting of his futuristic dystopia is unclear, other than perhaps it was exactly fifteen years from when the movie went into production.

Alphie and Bibi arrive at a Worldvision afterparty being thrown by Mr. Boogalow, where the evil mogul is showing off his new lineup of BIM-related merchandise. The most notable object here is the "BIM Mark": a glittering, triangular sticker which everyone immediately slaps on their foreheads without question. Boogalow greets the young couple at the door, introduces them as his guests of honor, and immediately pairs them off with Dandi (Allan Love) and Pandi (Grace Kennedy), the two members of BIM, who dress like forgotten members of a 1980s X-Men lineup.

Bibi buys right into the party culture—immediately accepting drinks from Boogalow, and drugs from Dandi—while Alphie remains suspicious and guarded. Bibi and Dandi head upstairs together to the rooftop garden for an impromptu make-out session, while the remaining guests downstairs break into an impromptu dance number. Dandi serenades Bibi with a fairly heavy-handed seduction tune titled "Made For Me." Alphie then catches her kissing the disco space prince and drags her out of the place, because obviously it's no fun to find your girlfriend making out with some other guy she just met at a party.

The next morning they head to a meeting at Boogalow International Music headquarters, which from the outside looks like a drab office building surrounded by guards who wear all-black and carry riot shields shaped like the BIM Mark. On the inside, however, it's clearly an airport terminal ... an airport terminal filled with clowns, wizards, showgirls, jugglers, opera singers, and medieval minstrels! Bibi and Alphie are asked to wait in the lobby, where they learn that strange-looking folks are all members of a pop group called Ballet 2000. Cue the musical number "Showbizness," and holy shitballs, this is the moment when the movie goes from simply insane to insanely amazing.

Literally everyone we see starts dancing. Boogalow and Mr. Shake show up and start to rap about how sinful showbiz is in 1994. There are tap dancers, mime acts, fire breathers, a top-hatted dwarf, and feather boas being twirled left and right. A chorus line shakes their assets in sequined bikinis, BIM receptionists make synchronized phone calls wearing see-through plastic raincoats and bondage gear, and we get multiple winks from Boogalow directly into the camera. It's a spectacle that's both mind-blowingly flamboyant and mind-blowingly nonsensical.

Our heroes are finally brought to Boogalow's office, which is covered in a prismatic wallpaper that makes it look like an early '90s Trapper Keeper. Bibi and Alphie are asked to sign recording contracts. Bibi, of course, doesn't ask any questions. Meanwhile, the more sensible Alphie wants to have a lawyer to read it over, which is probably the smart thing to do when a guy who is clearly Beelzebub-made-flesh asks you to sign your name to a contract.

If *The Apple*'s thinly-veiled metaphors haven't made it entirely clear that Bibi and Alphie's eternal souls are on the line here, then Alphie's sudden, positively demonic hallucination will chase away all doubts. The first thing he envisions is an earthquake; second, a lightning storm; finally, a full-blown musical number that takes place in Hell itself. This is where *The Apple* throws metaphor out the window and starts using a sledge hammer to get its Biblical pseudo-message across. (I say pseudo-message because it's never obvious what exactly *The Apple* is trying to get across to viewers. Doesn't a message usually need to *say* something?)

We're teleported into a cavern bathed in dim, red lights, where Alphie and Bibi are now almost nude, except for leaves covering their naughty bits. Boogalow is there—now dressed like Dracula—as are Dandi, Shake, skeletons, werewolves, and Napoleon, for some reason or another. The Devil—er, Boogalow, sorry—orders up his "special hors d'oeuvre:" an oversized apple, which he encourages the gullible Bibi to bite into. This triggers yet more dance choreography. Dandi sings the movie's title track, which features the lyrics "It's a natural, natural, natural desire / Meet an actual, actual, actual vampire!" The scene makes the wacky airport, circus dance-off from a few scenes back look sensible in contrast. Convinced by His Satanic Majesty's garish pageantry, Bibi takes a big ol' bite of the proverbial apple. Alphie storms away in a huff.

Bibi (Catherine Mary Stewart) prepares to take a bite from the symbolic apple in this Spanish lobby card.

Cue another song, "How To Be A Master," which features yet more rapping on the part of Boogalow, this time over a reggae beat. The song takes place during a montage where Bibi receives rock star training, complete with aerobics classes and a glam makeover. Bibi takes off on a solo tour, and we see her perform her new hit song "Speed"—which is either about doing drugs in America, or America itself doing drugs, depending on your interpretation of the lyrics—alongside a bunch of boogying bikers.

We cut back to lovelorn Alphie, who's wallowing in his sorrows in a cheap apartment. An indeterminate amount of time has passed during the two previous musical numbers, wherein America has become a police state ruled outright by Boogalow and BIM. We watch a kind, Jewish stereotype get ticketed by a police officer for not wearing a BIM Mark on her face. It turns out she's Alphie's landlady, played by Miriam Margolyes (or Professor Sprout, to all of you *Harry Potter* fans.) Poor Alphie's behind on his rent and is barely scraping by as a solo songwriter. He plays for his landlord a depressing new song which no music publisher wants to purchase because it's depressing, and also not a very good song.

Soon afterward, *The Apple* has its third "Holy shit, am I really seeing this?" moment when government loudspeakers announce that it's time for everyone to take part in the mandatory fitness program, or "BIM Hour." This involves everyone dropping whatever it is they're doing for a synchronized, hour-long dance routine set to "BIM," the song we heard BIM perform at the beginning of the movie. In a series of surreal images, a group of firefighters stop putting out a raging fire to dance; doctors drop their scalpels mid-surgery to flail their arms to the music; a gaggle of nuns high-kick to the song. *Everybody* is dancing, from construction workers and police officers to senior citizens and even more leather-clad bikers. There is no reason for this nightmarish musical interlude other than to make the audience question whether the first 50 minutes of *The Apple* pushed them over the brink of their sanity.

Alphie tries to talk to Bibi after one of her sold-out concerts, but only gets a beating from Boogalow's goons for his troubles. Seeing this makes Bibi suddenly feel bad for treating her ex-boyfriend so poorly, so they unwittingly sing a duet about how much they miss each other as Bibi gets weepy-eyed in her silver tower and Alphie crawls back to his crappy apartment to get wasted.

It's heavily implied in the next scene that Alphie tried to kill himself off-screen, but that's never stated explicitly in spite of it seeming like a pretty significant plot point. His landlady advises that he stops moping around the house and go out to find Bibi, which turns out to be a terrible idea because she's currently attending a crazy sex party at BIM Headquarters. Moments after his arrival, Pandi slips Alphie a roofie, and Alphie starts tripping balls. He demands that Boogalow release Bibi from her contract. (Boogalow now has a single, devilish horn growing out of the side of his head, in case anyone missed the first 100 clues that identified him as a living incarnation of the devil.) The Boog suggests to Alphie that he himself ask Bibi whether or not she wants to be released from her contract. Alphie runs around the party looking for her, and then *The Apple* serves up its fourth "My God, my eyes! I can't believe my eyes!" moment.

The song is titled "I'm Coming," and it's meant in the filthiest way that can possibly be read. There's no subtlety in the song, no innuendo: just pure, unadulterated dirty talk. As soon as Pandi sings Alphie lines such as, "Let me feel every inch of your love," "Fill me up with your fire," and "I'll drain every drop of your love," it's clear that *The Apple* is *going* there. (And if it somehow isn't, then Pandi's pantomimed blowjob and orgasmic moans should hammer the point home.) During the song, Pandi guides the drugged Alphie through the orgy and seduces him. There are cutaways to scantily-clad couples "dancing" on mattresses, although what they're doing looks more like a synchronized demonstration of positions from the Kama Sutra. At the height of his ecstasy, Alphie screams out Bibi's name and storms away to find her, only to catch his ex-girlfriend in bed with Dandi, the evil moon prince.

"She became a star ... thanks to the devil!" Another wonderful French poster for the film.

Alphie wakes up from this psychedelic sex nightmare in an open field, where an old, bearded man who looks like the flower power version of Hagrid from *Harry Potter* informs him that he was screaming in his sleep. (He's played by the prolific British actor Joss Ackland, perhaps best known for playing the bad guys in both *Lethal Weapon 2* [1989] and *Bill and Ted's Bogus Journey* [1991].) This man takes Alphie to his hippie commune, to live among a bunch of long-hairs wearing headbands and bellbottoms. Weirdly, the hippies seem to live inside a cave. If the sudden appearance of hundreds of hippies feels out-of-place, it's because that particular stereotype had all but died out by this time, considering that Woodstock had happened more than a decade before this movie's release. *The Apple*'s suggestion that hippies would still be a thriving subculture in a dystopian 1994 seems like a stretch—even by this movie's elastic standards.

Meanwhile, at BIM headquarters: Bibi is hungover from her drug-fueled orgy, and Pandi starts to show some remorse for boinking her ex-boyfriend the night before. Pandi tells Bibi she should go to Alphie, and then they let her go. (It turns out that all Bibi had to do was ask!) Bibi and Alphie have a happy reunion inside the hippie cave, which appears like it may be the same set they used for the Hell scene, but without the red lighting.

The movie jarringly jumps ahead an undisclosed amount of time: it's said that Bibi's only been at the compound for just over a year, but she and Alphie suddenly have a child that's at least two years old. (Someone's math was off.) The happy family lives among the hippies, who sing a groovy anthem called "Child of Love." They're soon rounded up by an army of BIM riot police, and Boogalow shows up to demand Bibi repay the $10 million dollars she owes them for bailing on her contract. She doesn't have the dough, of course, so the police force them all on what we presume has to be a death march. Alphie's a totally chill bro about the whole situation, and he reassures Bibi that a never-before-mentioned "Mr. Topps" will come to save them. Bibi has no idea who or what Alphie is talking about, and that's okay because neither does the audience. This is where *The Apple* breaks out its final, most insane scene of all.

The hippies stop marching and look to the sky. We hear a bunch of far out, science fiction-y sound effects and suddenly a glowing, golden car flies out of the clouds. A man in a white suit descends from the heavens. This must be Mr. Topps, whom we've never met before and was only mentioned for the first time 15 seconds earlier! Nevertheless, he's here to save the day. It turns out Mr. Topps is actually God himself and he's tired of Boogalow's hijinks. (Topps is played by Ackland again, the same actor as the hippies' leader.) Mr. Topps invites the hippies to follow him up an invisible stairway to Heaven, and then informs the disappointed Boogalow that he's going to take them all to live on a new planet. The end.

"The power of rock ... the magic of space." The movie's English poster didn't care that the movie has nothing to do with outer space.

If you need a little time to soak that in, I understand. Go take a walk. Maybe a bath. Pour yourself a glass of wine and change into something comfy. It's not easy to process *The Apple*'s last few scenes. This may be one of the most WTF endings in movie history. At the very least, it's the most literal deus ex machina ever committed to film, considering that God himself actually descends from the heavens in a flying car to rapture the hippies out of Boogalow's police state.

When the movie had its first screening at The Montreal Film Festival, the audience was given promotional copies of the movie's soundtrack on vinyl. Many of these were used as projectiles when the booing crowd started tossing them like Frisbees at the screen midway through the movie. Menahem Golan was so distraught by their reaction that he fled the theater and said that he considered throwing himself off a hotel balcony before his cousin, Yoram, talked him down. (Thank goodness he didn't, or else cinema would have been robbed of the so many wonderful film he'd continue to produce.)

The Apple was recut after the disastrous Montreal screening and received limited distribution in theaters around the world, but fared poorly with both critics and audiences. It ultimately failed to recoup its budget. For the next 20 years *The Apple* languished in obscurity, before its DVD release brought it back to the attention of kitschy movie fans.

The thing is, despite everything it has going against it—the terrible fashion, silly song lyrics, over-obvious allegory, and nonsensical plot jumps—*The Apple* has oodles of charm. There are so many insane musical numbers that need to be seen to be believed, and the songs have a habit or burrowing their way into viewers' brains and staying there for days afterward. *The Apple* is certainly never, ever boring. Once you get past your initial disbelief, it's one of the rare bad movies that gets better each time you watch it. After your third or fourth trip down the *Apple* rabbit hole, you'll swear it's a masterpiece. The movie's cult following should only grow as more weird cinema fans are given the chance to see it.

Bibi (Catherine Mary Stewart) belts out a thinly-veiled drug reference during the musical number for "Speed."

Interview: Actress Catherine Mary Stewart
Throughout the 1980s, few actresses made appearances in more cult classics than Catherine Mary Stewart. Born in Canada, Stewart had only ever intended to make her career as a dancer—but was discovered, personally, by Menahem Golan during a cattle call audition for *The Apple* in London. With little to no acting experience, she was cast in the musical's starring role. Having been bit by the proverbial acting bug during the filming of *The Apple*, she moved to Hollywood afterwards to pursue a career on screen.

One of the most recognizable faces from so many '80s classics, her many roles include appearances in *Nighthawks* (1981), *The Last Starfighter* (1984), *Night of the Comet* (1984), *Mischief* (1985), *Dudes* (1987), *World Gone Wild* (1988), and *Weekend at Bernie's* (1989). There was hardly a shelf in the video rental shop where you wouldn't have found one of Stewart's movies.

The Cannon Film Guide: **I've had the pleasure of speaking to many people who could talk about Menahem Golan, the producer. Not as many, though, can talk about Menahem Golan, the director. Can you describe what he was like to work with?**

Catherine Mary Stewart: Menahem was a large man with a large personality. He loved filmmaking and *The Apple* was a passion project for him. This was going to be the movie that broke him into the American film market. So as you can imagine, he was passionate about every aspect of making this movie to the point where he didn't trust anyone else to direct it. His passion was tangible on the set every day, from being thrilled with what was going on to being very frustrated when things weren't going the way he wanted. He held everyone to the very high standard that he demanded of himself and there was never a question about how he felt from moment to moment.

For me specifically, I had a direct run in with Menahem when I misread a call sheet and thought I had a day off, so I was out all night long enjoying the city of West Berlin. When I didn't show up for my pickup to take me to the set all chaos broke loose. I think I was still out somewhere. When I finally got back to the hotel the mistake I had made was clear. I ended up being very late to the set which throws the entire schedule off, and is very costly. Menahem was not happy, as you can imagine, and as I was getting my make-up done for the scene that I was very late for, he told me in no uncertain terms that I would never work in this business again. He was quite understandably angry and was not one to hold back. In an odd way it didn't bother me as much as you might expect it to. At that point, frankly, I hadn't really considered the idea of working in the business again. I was still so new and inexperienced. I probably thought I would just go back to dance. I think that was really the only time he lashed out at me and ultimately he was a big supporter and cheerleader for me when I decided to pursue acting professionally.

I know you went into your audition almost entirely in the dark as to what the film was that you were trying out for. What were your first impressions of the script, or the story?

I was completely in the dark during the audition process. I went in by chance and completely unprepared, tagging along with some friends in London who I happened to bump into on their way to the audition. I was asked to read a scene and sing a song. It was a cold reading and an even colder singing audition. I guess I must have been given the script after that, because I was asked to come back the next day. I don't really remember my reaction to the script. This was all totally new to me. I'd never really ever read a movie script before. I don't remember finding it risqué or weird. I do remember reading it over and over again after they offered me the job. By the time we shot the movie I pretty much knew everyone's lines in the entire script.

Stewart pulls triple duty on a Spanish advertisement for the movie. Rough translation: "It was acid rock in the Sixties. Disco rock in the Seventies. Punk Rock in the Eighties. And now, in the Nineties, it's the rhythm of Bim. The music, love, and power in 1994."

As someone newly initiated into showbiz and movie-making, did you see a bit of yourself in your character, Bibi?

I never thought about it at the time. In retrospect I absolutely see my younger self in the character, and Menahem definitely saw a lot of Bibi in me. I embraced the innocent, naiveté of the character as an actor, but it wasn't much of a stretch.

You've mentioned how you were too naïve when shooting *The Apple* to pick up on the innuendo in songs like "I'm Coming" and "Speed," which sounds adorably innocent. Do you recall the moment or your reaction when you finally caught on to the themes the music was not-all-too-subtly hinting at?

Yep, it took me way too long to figure it all out. I wasn't being asked to do anything I felt uncomfortable with and I was always treated professionally and with the greatest respect. To me, it was much later that I really grasped how suggestive these songs were. They are suggestive but there is nothing outright graphic. It all still puts a smile on my face.

What was it like shooting in West Berlin at that time? When I think of Berlin at the end of the 1970s, I think of David Bowie, Iggy Pop, and Brian Eno doing some of their best work there. It sounds like a very interesting, artistic scene was going on there at the time.

The places we shot were just normal locations. I didn't have a lot of time to really absorb West Berlin from the perspective of someone like David Bowie, but I certainly learned a lot about the recent history of the city. I was only somewhat aware of the significance of West Berlin versus East Berlin, the Wall, and Checkpoint Charlie.

Joss Ackland and I spent a day in East Berlin. We were allowed to go in, but no one from there was allowed to come out. That right there pretty much illustrates the insanity of walls, whether it's to keep people out or keep people in. West Berlin had a crazy, colorful, circus-like atmosphere. East Berlin had a sort of grey, quiet, sad feel. I learned so much about the geo-politics of that area at that time and its history.

Who were your best friends on set?

I hung out with lots of different people, from my fellow actors to many of the dancers. There was not a lot of down time for me, but I had fun.

You were coming to the film as a professional dancer. What did you think of the movie's choreography?

I loved it! Most of the dance numbers were huge production pieces with wild costumes. I thought it was terrific. The whole experience was kind of like a fantasy that I just dove into and committed to. It felt like a big, happy family.

Some actors, such as Vladek Sheybal, had some creative input into their character's costuming. Do you remember ever weighing in on your makeup or wardrobe?

Oh my god, absolutely not! Vladek was a seasoned actor. He knew exactly what he was doing and how he wanted to come across. I knew nothing and I didn't pretend to know anything. I was in heaven being fitted for the costumes and having the make-up applied by these incredibly talented and creative people.

There aren't many scenes without dozens of dancers or extras, wild set decoration, and fabulous costumes—it's an incredible amount to absorb when you're watching it, and there's always something new to find on repeat viewings. Was it as dizzying to be there, on set?

The bigger, more complicated scenes are the ones that take the longest to set up and shoot, so dizzying would not describe the feeling on set. I was fascinated by all aspects of shooting a movie at that point so I was never bored, but as they say, there was a lot of hurry up and wait. The effect you describe is created in the editing.

Looking back at it all these years later, is there one day of shooting you can pick out as your favorite? A scene you remember most fondly?

I loved the scene where I'm looking for Alphie. That whole sequence is memorable for me. The very first day of the shoot, we shot the scene where I'm on the monorail after Pandi has helped me escape. Movies are rarely shot in sequence, so the rest of that scene was shot on different days, but I loved the romantic nature of looking for Alphie, finding his apartment, being told he's hanging out with some hippies under a bridge, crossing paths with Joss' character, finding Alphie in a cave and embracing him as the camera spins around us. All the while, the music swells. *Loved* it!

You briefly worked in Cannon's public relations department while you were first getting acclimated to life in Los Angeles. Can you tell me more about how that came about? Can you recall what movies you helped out on, and what you did?

I was encouraged to move to Los Angeles, and Menahem was very kind in introducing me to people and agents, and helping with a job. I basically helped to organize and log films and publicity, and prepare material for different festivals. I don't remember specific movies. *The Apple* may have been one of them. I know they did a lot of sequels with big stars.

Given that this was your first film, was there a lesson you learned on *The Apple* that you carried with you through the rest of your career?

Check your call sheet very, very carefully, be prepared, and be on time!

New Year's Evil

Release Date: December 26, 1980
Directed by: Emmett Alston
Written by: Leonard Neubauer & Emmett Alston
Starring: Roz Kelly, Kip Niven, Grant Cramer
Trailer Voiceover: "One terrifying night of unspeakable evil!"

Holidays! They're a reason to celebrate and gather with friends or family, overeat, overdrink, and maybe even get out of the office for a day or two. Who *doesn't* love a holiday?

Nubile co-eds in slasher movies, that's who!

Allowing bloodthirsty maniacs to run loose around holidays has been a tradition which filmmakers have kept alive throughout the entirety of the modern horror era. It does really make a lot of sense when you think about it, though: people tend to gather during the holiday season, so it's a convenient time to slaughter them—speaking purely from a maniac's point of view, of course.

Many holidays are considered a sacred time, or at the very least a safe one, associated with warm, fuzzy feelings, rather than the feeling that someone is about to stab you. By subverting our expectations and making those carefree days a time of terror, filmmakers are able to dial up the horror by several degrees. (It's a trick they use in action movies, too—see *Die Hard* [1988] and

Invasion U.S.A. [1985] for examples of Christmas-timed bloodshed.) And then, of course, there is a lot of familiar iconography that can be played with and turned on its head. Imagine: red-rimmed eyes glaring at you over the fake white beard of a Santa Claus costume, the glow of Christmas tree lights reflected in his knife . . . .

Christmas is naturally one of the big ones for murderous cinematic psychopaths, with films like *Black Christmas* (1974), *Christmas Evil* (1980), *Silent Night, Deadly Night* (1984) and the similarly-titled *Silent Night, Bloody Night* (1972) among the more notable movies of this Yuletide subgenre. Fourth of July has *Uncle Sam* (1996). For a long time, Easter was only represented by *Critters 2* (1988), but recent years have given us the absurd likes of *Easter Casket* (2013) and *Easter Bunny Kill! Kill!* (2006). The slasher *Blood Rage* (1987) took place at Thanksgiving, and was following by the rampaging turkey flick *ThanksKilling* (2008). Even holidays you wouldn't get off work have their own dedicated horror movies: Valentine's Day comes with *My Bloody Valentine* (1981) and Cannon's own *Hospital Massacre*, St. Patrick's Day has the *Leprechaun* franchise, and April Fool's Day has, well, *April Fool's Day* (1986). Let's not forget about Mother's Day (*Mother's Day* [1980]) and Father's Day (*Creepshow*'s opening segment, "Father's Day" [1982]). While they may not be proper holidays, per se, we *have* to count prom night (*Prom Night* [1980]) and Friday the 13th (the *Friday the 13th* franchise, at a dozen films and counting.) You can rest assured Birthdays aren't safe, either, thanks to *Happy Birthday to Me* (1981) and *Bloody Birthday* (1981).

To what do we owe such a rampant number of holiday-themed horror movies? That would, of course, be John Carpenter's classic *Halloween* (1978), the godfather of all slasher flicks. While *Black Christmas* may have technically done it first, Carpenter's groundbreaking slasher was certainly the one that made it a trend. (Being the spookiest day of the year, more horror films are set at Halloween—or Samhain, All Hallow's Eve, the Devil's Night, and what have you—than any other holiday. It's kind of a no-brainer for the genre.) After the $300,000-budget *Halloween* raked in $47 million in U.S. ticket sales alone, suddenly *every* tagalong slasher flick seemed to be set on or around one of our country's holidays. These special dates made marketing the films especially easy, as there was always an obvious spot on the calendar to schedule the release near.

If there was a prevailing trend in movies—and more importantly, one that appeared to be reflective in robust box office receipts—you can bet that Cannon would try to get in on it. Golan and Globus recruited Emmett Alston, a USC film school graduate who'd worked as a motion pictures officer in the Air Force during Vietnam. Alston made a total of seven movies during the 1980s, including Sho Kosugi's wild *Nine Deaths of the Ninja* (1985). He was originally set to direct 1981's *Enter the Ninja*, but was bumped to second unit director when Golan himself took the helm.

Alston was given a budget in the ballpark of half a million dollars, but only three weeks of pre-production time—and only three weeks to shoot the film! To make matters slightly more complicated, this took place during a three-month-long SAG-AFTRA strike in the late summer and fall of 1980, meaning special contracts had to be signed with all union laborers involved in the film. This didn't seem to hinder or slow down filming of *New Year's Evil* at all. In fact, Cannon pulled the plug on the shoot with five days left on the schedule, informing the cast and crew they had already had enough footage for a movie to be cut together. The movie was prepped, shot, and edited in just a few months and then let loose in theaters on the very last weekend of 1980, just in time for New Year's Eve. Although the movie holds together really well all things considered, there are moments where you can tell where quality control was sacrificed for speed—such as how the credits misspell their producer's name as "Yorum" Globus.

Unlike some other holiday-centered horror flicks, *New Year's Evil*'s setting isn't arbitrary. It fully embraces the New Year's Eve theme, making that special date an integral part of the film's plot. The movie is set in Los Angeles and centers on an evening-long telecast hosted by Diane "Blaze" Sullivan, played by Roz Kelly. (Kelly is best remembered for playing "Pinky" Tuscadero, the Fonz's girlfriend on *Happy Days* from 1976–1977.) We learn that Blaze is a celebrity and second-tier rock-and-roll icon in the Dick Clark vein, if Dick

Clark had been a hip, New Wave rocker chick. While Blaze and a roster of pop metal acts welcome the New Year as it dawns in successive time zones, she takes live calls from viewers at home. Unfortunately, one of her first callers happens to be a murderous psychopath who promises he'll kill each time the clock strikes midnight in a new city.

New Year's Evil makes a really clever move around ten minutes into the film: it shows us the killer's face. Unlike the majority of slasher movies which spend most of their runtime making the audience guess at their killers' identities, we meet *New Year's Evil*'s boogeyman, sans mask, as he makes his first call from a pay phone. He introduces himself as "Evil" (pronounced "*Eeeeeeee-ville!*"), speaking through an electrolarynx—one of those electronic boxes used by throat cancer survivors—to distort his voice.

The tones produced by the actual electrolarynx proved too monotone to act through, so we're listening to actor Kip Niven do that creepy voice on his own, without electronic assistance. Niven passed away in 2019 with nearly 100 credits to his name, the most prominent of which was the antagonist "Red" Astrachan in *Magnum Force* (1973), the second Dirty Harry movie.

Although we know for sure what he looks like, we have no idea who the heck Evil is. Evil makes good on his promise to go on a killing spree, preying mostly on women and using the fact that he's a handsome, smooth-talking guy to his devious advantage. (He's a disguise wiz, too, donning a fake moustache, nurse's outfit, priest vestments, and even a cop's uniform at various points in the film.) While he's off running around, slicing and dicing his victims—or suffocating one victim with a giant bag of marijuana—Blaze cooperates with the LAPD by keeping Evil on the line for as long as possible each time he phones in to give her his hourly murder update. Meanwhile, the bands play on for the rock 'n' roll fans celebrating at home . . . and Blaze's creepy son lurks around the venue's backstage area with a pair of his mother's pantyhose pulled down over his head.

It's worth noting now that her teenage son, Derek—Grant Cramer, star of *Hardbodies* (1984) and *Killer Klowns from Outer Space* (1988)—is an aspiring actor with a few *very* visible psychological issues. While his mom's hosting the biggest party of the night, he's off moping in her room, playing with a knife while stretching pantyhose over his face and popping suspicious-looking pills. In any other slasher movie we'd be pointing a finger at this clearly-unhinged boy: there's no way he *wouldn't* be the killer, right? But we know he isn't, because we've *seen* the killer doing his dirty work and know he's definitely not *this* particular weirdo.

Evil eventually makes his way to the venue, intent on making Blaze's murder the grand finale of his all-night kill-a-thon. The concert sequences of the film were shot at Hollywood's Steve Allen Playhouse, not only the location where Steve Allen broadcast the first incarnation of *The Tonight Show*, but where Groucho Marx filmed *You Bet Your Life*. (It burned down in 1990.)

There comes a twist when the killer reveals his identity and it's actually surprising, so I won't give it away here. Without spoiling anything, Evil traps and torments Blaze as the police close in on him. They chase him onto the roof of the hotel—in actuality, this scene was shot on the roof of Cannon's Los Angeles offices—where he stands on the edge of the building, reciting a passage from *Hamlet* and wearing a cheap, creepy Stan Laurel mask. (Out of the many killers' masks in '80s slasher movies, I somehow find this one of the most unnerving.) He jumps to his death below, but the movie ends on one final, sly wink which suggests that Evil's reign of terror might not be over. However, it definitely was over: there was never a *New Year's Evil 2*.

New Year's Evil may not be as tense or frightening as the decade's finest slashers but it's certainly fun, and one of the better mid-tier masked murderer movies. Everyone involved appears to have been aware that what they were making was a little bit goofy, and seem to ham it up a little extra for the camera because of that. (I mean, just listen to Evil's *voice!*) When our masked murderer evades a gang of vengeful bikers, he does so in a drive-in movie theater showing the trailer for Herschell Gordon Lewis' 1963 film *Blood Feast:* a knowing nod to the style of sensational, bloody, only half-serious schlock they were making here. The rest of the cast includes many faces who'd turn up in Cannon features in coming years, including Chris Wallace (*Body and Soul*), Taaffe O'Connell (*Hot Chili*), Louisa Moritz (*Hot Chili* again, and *The Last*

American Virgin), and John Greene (*Schizoid*).

The film fared poorly with critics, but it's hard to fault them when they'd been deluged with these sort of holiday horror movies. It holds up a lot better today. Cannon's pre-sale arrangements assured that the film was a financial success for them, even when the ticket-buying public didn't necessarily show up in droves. Like the many other studios which jumped on the same bandwagon, Cannon learned the hard lesson that simply setting a horror movie on a holiday wouldn't immediately translate to flashing dollar signs, and the trend eventually faded (although it never fully burned out.)

New Year's Evil on VHS. This copy was rented by Video Update in Youngstown, Ohio.

Hospital Massacre, a.k.a. *X-Ray*

Release Date: April 1982
Directed by: Boaz Davidson
Written by: Marc Behm & Boaz Davidson
Starring: Barbi Benton
Tagline: "The checkup that became a nightmare!"

Like *Schizoid* and *New Year's Evil* before it, *Hospital Massacre* rode a wave of low-budget slasher movies that flooded the American horror scene in the immediate wake of the mega-hits *Halloween* (1978) and *Friday the 13th* (1980). While it was initially marketed under the endearingly goofy working title *Be My Valentine . . . or Else!* and sold overseas as *X-Ray*, it hit U.S. video shelves under the utterly more descriptive title *Hospital Massacre*. (Cannon changed the title after Paramount's *My Bloody Valentine* [1981] and their own *New Year's Evil* [1981] flopped, concluding that holiday-themed horror no longer sold at the box office.)

The movie's lone star with any name recognition is Barbi Benton, a former Playboy Playmate most famous for being Hugh Hefner's girlfriend through much of the 1970s. The diminutive model—born Barbara Klein—appeared on the famed nudie mag's cover four times, and was briefly the co-host (with Hefner) of *Playboy After Dark* (1969–1970). Her acting career included appearances on *Hee Haw* (1969–1971), *The Love Boat* (1977–1987), and *Fantasy Island* (1977–1984). Following *Hospital Massacre*, Benton co-starred in the first film of the *Deathstalker* (1983) franchise and put out a string of pop country records before retiring from show business.

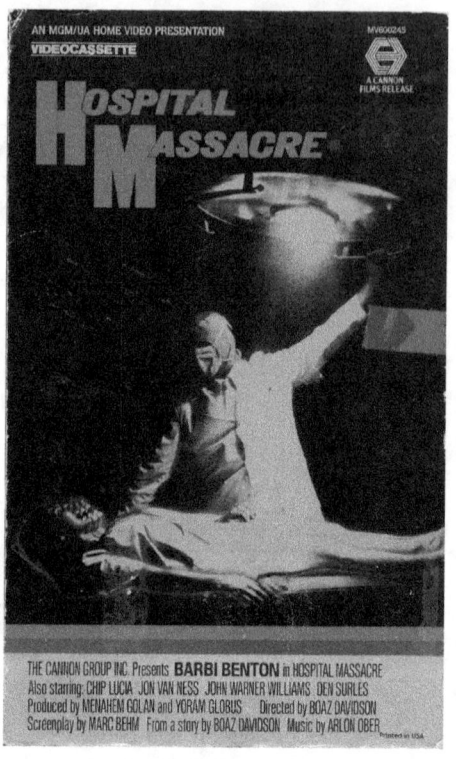

Hospital Massacre on VHS. This was the first of Cannon's movies to be distributed on MGM/UA Home Video.

Hospital Massacre didn't give Benton much room show off her acting range beyond screaming, running, complaining about the hospital's wait times, and lounging about in the nude, but her presence alone was enough in 1982 for Cannon to print her name in an extra-large font across the movie's advertisements. (The film was first announced with a former Bond girl, Jill St. John, playing the lead.)

Originally an Austrian financier had been slated to direct the film. When this mysterious Aussie failed to front his share of the budget by the time shooting was slated to begin, Golan and Globus fired him and brought in their frequent collaborator Boaz Davidson to direct. Davidson had most recently made *Teen Mothers* (1980) for the studio, and had directed the producers' biggest international hit, *Lemon Popsicle*, in 1978.

The movie begins with a brief prelude which takes place nineteen years before the meat of the movie. (The "massacre," if you will.) Two youngsters—a boy and a girl—play with a toy train at "Susan's House, 1961," as the title card reads. Another boy, named Harold, leaves a handmade Valentine for the little girl, Susan. He watches, peeping tom-like through a window, as the two mean-spirited children laugh at the card, crumple it up, and toss it away. Jilted little Harold then breaks into the home, murders the rival little boy and then leaves his corpse swinging from a hat rack for his young crush to discover. Will this disturbing little intro scene come into play again by the time the movie's over? You bet it will! (But only at the *very* end.)

We pick up again in the 1980s, and Susan (Benton) is now a 30-something divorcee with a tween daughter and a brand new boyfriend. Her new guy gives her a ride to the hospital to pick up some unspecified test results—the same hospital "where they had all the trouble last year," he ominously mentions as she's stepping out of the car. We learn that a patient "broke loose and ran amok," which makes the place sound more like an old mental asylum than the general care hospital it appears to be from the outside, but that's beyond the point. (Susan laughs off his concerns, anyway.) The heavily-decorated lobby informs us it's Valentine's Day, which you'd think would be slightly disconcerting given Susan's holiday-themed childhood trauma, but she barely acknowledges it. Meanwhile, many doctors spend a lot of screen time pursing their lips while squinting at x-rays of Susan's lungs and intestines. They whisper to each other about how seriously ill she is, but no one ever lets the audience in on whatever they believe is wrong with her.

The biggest thing most viewers notice in *Hospital Massacre* is that everyone—and I mean *everyone*—stares at Susan in creepy ways through the entire length of the movie. A few of these stares are your garden variety, perverted leering, but the majority of characters Susan encounters shoot her some serious, out-of-nowhere "I'm going to kill you" eyes. This makes every minor character in the film seem potentially evil. Her ex-husband, her doctors, their patients, the nurses, the janitor, the *fumigators*, and even a trio of little old ladies—they all give Susan long, disturbing looks when she passes. This leads viewers to spend a lot of their time guessing just which of the many creepazoids Susan meets actually intend to do her harm. When we do eventually see the killer, he's wearing full surgical garb. We can guess that he's likely a male based on his size and frame, as well as the hunch that it's *probably* that preteen psychopath who terrorized her in the film's opening scene, but that's all we have to go on.

As Susan wanders about the hospital looking for someone who can sign over her test results, a killer sneaks around a spooky, mostly-unused storage floor, picking off Susan's real doctor and tampering with her paperwork to prolong her wait time. Most of us would agree that hospitals are generally bustling with people and activity, but this one appears to be almost empty—which makes for an extra eerie setting, if not a particularly realistic one. (*Hospital Massacre* was shot on several abandoned floors of a Los Angeles medical center; the production was restricted to shooting nights so that they'd not disturb any of the hospital's real patients or staff.) Benton, of course, receives her obligatory nude scene when a doctor performs the world's most perverted physical examination on her.

Two thirds of the film pass before Susan ever crosses paths with the murderer, as he flits about in dimly-lit hallways and manages to violently slaughter a bunch of random employees without the rest of the staff ever catching on. The kill methods, of course, are doctor-themed: knives, a syringe, acid, and even a bone saw are used to butcher his victims. (Many of these kills were trimmed from the British release for it to receive an 'X' certificate; the U.S. version runs roughly nine minutes longer than the one released in the U.K.)

For the better part of the film's final half hour, Susan is chased and toyed with by the murderous psycho who, in the last few minutes, reveals his identity to her and—surprise!—it's Harold, the little boy who never forgave her for throwing away his Valentine's Day card nineteen years earlier. We were supposed to have seen that coming all along, right?

The movie's big reveal can be read one of either two ways, both of which are equally silly. In one scenario, Harold's over-complicated revenge scheme required that he obtained a medical degree and landed a position at the hospital where Susan would eventually have tests done two decades after she rejected him. Or, we're supposed to believe that Harold was the same loony patient who ran amok the prior year, was never caught, and then spent twelve months hiding within the hospital's abandoned wing and lying patiently in wait for Susan to come in for a routine visit—which finally happened, *entirely coincidentally*, on Valentine's Day.

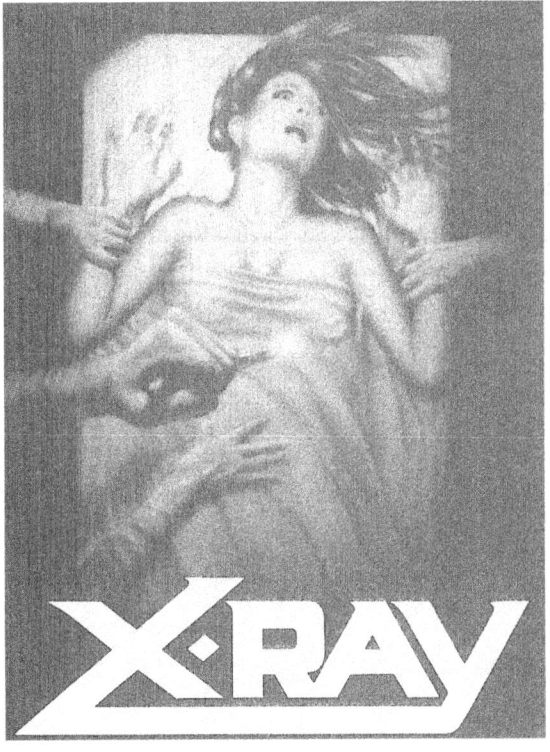

A lurid ad for the movie from Cannon's sales catalog.

You'd normally suspect that casting a Playboy Playmate in a lead role would limit a film, but Benton does a fair job in her one-dimensional role and is hardly the movie's biggest issue. That dubious honor would go to the script, which drags its feet all the way to a conclusion that everyone could see coming from the outset. Screenwriter Marc Behm had previously penned the stories for two 1960s classics—the Grant/Hepburn romantic adventure *Charade* (1963) and The Beatles' madcap *Help!* (1965)—as well as Menahem Golan's English-language directorial debut, *Trunk to Cairo* (1965). Cannon would also hire him to handle two of their early, erotic literary adaptations: *Lady Chatterley's Lover* (1982) and *Nana: The True Key of Pleasure* (1983).

It's not a classic slasher, by any means, but it's far from the worst. Horror fans may even get a kick out of how far-fetched it all becomes, even by the standards of the subgenre. How is Susan the *only* person in the entire hospital who notices there's a spree killer on the prowl? And why does she not bother to, you know, attempt to leave the hospital until we've passed the midway point of the movie? And then, of course, the method in which literally *everybody* is made to look like they could be the killer is so over-the-top that it makes *Hospital Massacre* a lot of unexpected fun.

Director Boaz Davidson has mentioned that people have approached him over the years who mistook the film for a comedy. He's said that comedy wasn't his intention—but I'd vouch that it's the best way to approach this one if you want to get the most enjoyment out of it.

Enter the Ninja

Release Date: October 2, 1981
Directed by: Menahem Golan
Written by: Dick Desmond & Mike Stone
Stars: Franco Nero, Susan George, Sho Kosugi, Christopher George
Trailer Voiceover: "Hired assassins. Trained killers. Masters of the most deadly art known to man. If you take on a ninja, no matter how many you are, be prepared for the consequences!"

Before the Teenage Mutant Ninja Turtles. Before *3 Ninjas*. Before *Ninja Gaiden*. Before *Surf Ninjas*. Before *Beverly Hills Ninja* and *Ninjas vs. Zombies*. Before *American Ninja*. Before *American Ninja II, III,* or *IV*. Before *American Ninja V,* even!

Before all of those, there was *Enter the Ninja*.

From a distance, it may look like Menahem Golan's *Enter the Ninja* was nothing more than an attempt to cash in on the martial arts movie craze that blew up in the wake of Bruce Lee's untimely death. (I mean, just look at that title!) It wound up being so much more. In true Cannon Fashion, they stumbled into an international box office hit which helped kick start the ninja mania of the 1980s and early '90s. It was a cultural obsession that spread throughout movies, cartoons, comic books, and video games of the era.

Enter the Ninja on videocassette. By the time the movie reached VHS, Sho Kosugi had become a major star. This is the reason why he's featured on the tape's cover over the movie's actual leading man, Franco Nero.

The post-*Enter the Ninja* video shop landscape saw hundreds of poorly-dubbed martial arts movies with the word "ninja" in the title flood store shelves. Often the branding was totally arbitrary, where the word "ninja" was haphazardly slapped on the box of a kung fu movie which didn't even feature a character who wore the traditional shozoku (ninja pajamas). Many knock-off filmmakers, however, quickly saw the hidden value in the shozoku; in particular, the way it covered most of an actor's or stunt person's face.

Thanks to these masks, directors could get away with casting no-name martial artists as their anonymous heroes or villains when they were making a ninja film. (A crafty producer could raid a local karate dojo and come away with a film's entire ensemble.) One particularly prolific Hong Kong filmmaker named Godfrey Ho directed a whopping 49 movies with the word "ninja" in their English titles between 1982 and 1993—these included such memorably-named features as *Full Metal Ninja, Ninja Terminator, Ninja Kill* and *Ninja Demon's Massacre*.

Cannon, of course, stayed on the front line of that sweet ninja action, and followed up *Enter the Ninja* with two only loosely-linked sequels—*Revenge of the Ninja* and *Ninja III: The Domination*—before launching into their five-part *American Ninja* series.

Cartoons and comic books enthusiastically jumped on the ninja bandwagon as well. The most famous of these animated ass-kickers of Eastern origin, of course, were the Teenage Mutant Ninja Turtles. Their adolescent, reptilian presences have graced TV shows, feature films, video games, and comics for more than three decades. Before they led impressionable children towards a diet of only pizza, cartoonists Kevin Eastman and Peter Laird created the Turtles as a parody of legendary comic book creator Frank Miller's wildly popular run on Marvel's *Daredevil* comic book series. Miller had popularly introduced Daredevil's villain-turned-ladybaby, Elektra: a female ninja who wore a red bikini instead of the traditional, black shozoku. Batman, Spider-Man, Ghost Rider, the X-Men, and G.I. Joe were all given allies and/or foes who wore masks, scaled walls, and tossed shurikens. Ninjas, of course, were already a fixture of their mother country's popular fiction—especially in anime and manga—but even the Japanese saw a rise in ninjutsu practitioners infiltrating their entertainment in the 1980s. These stealthy assassins also leant themselves well to the burgeoning video game arena. By the time the fighting game boom took off in the '90s, some games went so far as to give players a plentitude of colorful ninjas to choose from.

Historians typically trace the ninja's real-world roots back to the fifteenth century, where references were made to groups of "shinobi"—a term interchangeable with "ninja" that sees more prevalent use in Japan—who were described as skilled mercenaries. In feudal Japan, the samurai were bound by a code of honor that required them to settle their disputes in face-to-face duels. This necessitated a need for hired fighters whenever there was dirty work needing to be done. The shinobi, who were believed to have been from lower classes in contrast to the customarily upper-class samurai, could work as assassins, spies, thieves, or in any other clandestine role where stealth and anonymity were of the utmost importance.

And with that info dump—congratulations! You now know more about ninjas than many of the people who worked on *Enter the Ninja*.

As the story goes, Golan and Globus got their hands on a martial arts script about what was at the time a little-known, masked Japanese warrior known as the ninja. The story was conceived by karate World Champion Mike Stone, who for a period was slated to star as the movie's lead White Ninja. At the start of production Golan decided he wanted someone with more experience and star power, and re-cast the lead role. (Stone remained on board as a fight choreographer, stunt man, and body double; he'd also work behind-the-scenes in various capacities on many of their *American Ninja* films, and play a villainous on-screen role in the franchise's second installment.)

This two-page *Variety* ad for the film's Cannes premiere placed Nero front and center. The ninja whose eyes can be seen looming in the background is Mike Stone, who had been originally cast as the movie's lead.

Now finding himself without a ninja, Golan trawled the Manila Film Festival for a leading man he could sign as a last-minute replacement. It was at a café where he spotted Spaghetti Western legend Franco Nero—the rugged, blue-eyed Italian star best known for playing Django in Sergio Corbucci's 1966 cult film of the same name—who was game to star in Cannon's new action movie, which was due to start shooting right away in the Philippines. It wasn't a big deal to Golan that Nero, with his thick, Italian accent, might not sound believable playing an American. It also didn't matter to him that Nero, having no formal martial arts training of any kind, might not make a very convincing ninja, either.

Golan's choice to cast 40-year-old Western star as his film's (literal) "white ninja" may seem suspect, but this odd piece of casting is just where the delightful nuttiness of *Enter the Ninja* begins. To understand how this movie made ninjas look so damn cool you only have to watch the film's opening credits.

Wearing a black shozoku against a black background, martial artist turned actor Sho Kosugi demonstrates the weapons of the ninja arsenal, one-by-one, as the credits roll. He twirls his sais, dramatically cuts through air with a katana, loads a dart into his blowgun, swings caltrops about, and for good measure demonstrates a handful of cool weapons that a real ninja likely never would have used, such as nunchaku, or nunchucks. Golan demanded that nunchucks be included because Bruce Lee had used them; it didn't matter that real-life ninjas never would have used them. (Historically, nunchucks would have been highly ineffective against the swords, spears, and bows that were the popular weapons of the ninja's day.) They definitely looked cool, though, and stayed part of the pop culture ninja's arsenal from that point on. If Michelangelo was your favorite Turtle, you have *Enter the Ninja* to thank for his historically-inaccurate weapon selection.

Let's stop for a moment here and appreciate the infinite badassery of cinema's Ninja of Ninjas, Mr. Sho Kosugi. We'll be talking about him a lot throughout the pages of this book, so a little background information is necessary. (And oh, what an incredible backstory he has.) Born just outside of

Tokyo in 1948, Kosugi began studying martial arts at the tender age of five. As a young child he befriended an elderly hermit who lived near his town. Defying his parents' advice, Kosugi visited the old man several times a week, where he would be taught the techniques of Ninjutsu—the martial art practiced by ninjas. After years of teaching, Kosugi found his mysterious master had strangely vanished without warning. Nevertheless, the student continued his studies of more mainstream martial arts, attaining black belts in three different styles by the time he was eighteen and becoming an All-Japan karate champion.

Entering adulthood, Kosugi decided he'd attend college in the United States. On his first day in Los Angeles he was the target of an attempted mugging—two of his assailants fled after Kosugi left the third bleeding on the sidewalk with a single kick. (Generously, Kosugi waited with the man until an ambulance arrived.) Stateside, Kosugi continued his martial arts studies while working as a karate instructor, and eventually opened his own dojo. Thanks to his being local to the Los Angeles area, Kosugi was recruited regularly throughout the 1970s for small roles in movies when casting directors needed someone to perform martial arts moves, but not necessarily speak. By 1980 Kosugi had befriended fellow karate star Mike Stone, who had just sold a script entitled "Dance of Death" to a newly-restructured studio known as The Cannon Group. Stone tapped his friend to appear in the movie—now re-titled *Enter the Ninja*—as the movie's villainous ninja and the rest, as they say, is history.

Kosugi would not only co-star in *Enter the Ninja*, but double for many of the masked bad guys and act as the film's uncredited ninja consultant thanks to his lifelong dedication to Ninjutsu. Although the movie's producer-director had little interest in portraying realistic ninjas on the screen, Kosugi brought to the film a degree of authenticity that had yet to be seen on screen in the West. Quite a few of the film's weapons were either designed by Kosugi, or came from his personal collection.

With *Enter the Ninja*'s widespread popularity, Kosugi became the face of the Hollywood ninja. As their popularity boomed, comic book and VHS cover artists would base their characters' poses on Kosugi's press photos. The stars of knock-off films, having never practiced this obscure martial art, would copy techniques from Kosugi's filmography. As for the martial artist-turned-actor himself, he suddenly found his services in high demand.

Cannon were wise to snap up Kosugi for two unrelated sequels: *Revenge of the Ninja*, and *Ninja III: The Domination*. (He played the hero in the former, and a villain again in the latter.) After Cannon trimmed out a lengthy martial arts sequence from the third movie and left his character with minimal screen time, Kosugi parted ways with Cannon and took on work with other studios. The first one was the short-lived TV series *The Master* opposite Lee Van Cleef, which only ran for one season in 1984. He followed that with the feature film *9 Deaths of the Ninja* (1985), helmed by *New Year's Evil* director Emmett Alston, and the movies *Pray for Death* (1985) and *Rage of Honor* (1987) by Gordon Hessler. His last, major starring role in an American movie came with 1988's *Black Eagle*, which was more notable for featuring a pre-fame Jean-Claude Van Damme playing its generic, '80s Russian villain. By the end of the 1980s, the ninja action subgenre had gravitated towards kiddie fare featuring gymnasts in rubber suits (1990's *Teenage Mutant Ninja Turtles*). Martial arts movies in general had moved on to new stars, such as the aforementioned Van Damme and Steven Seagal. With the changing of the guard, Kosugi's time in the spotlight was over.

And now, back to *Enter the Ninja*.

Sho Kosugi's awesome weapon demonstration continues for several minutes while the credits roll. Suddenly, in slow motion—and completely out of nowhere—a white ninja jumps in from out-of-frame and flying-kicks Kosugi to the face. How could you *not* want to continue watching this movie after that? The best news is that things only continue to get cooler from here.

We're introduced to middle-aged badass Cole (Nero) in the midst of what appears to be a covert, somewhat sloppily-edited assassination mission. (Cole seems to teleport between locations, and the weapons his assailant ninjas wield occasionally change from cut to cut. Or, is that just another one of the ninja's mystical powers?) Dressed in an all-white shozoku, Cole is pursued by the black ninja and his posse of red ninjas, whose bright-colored uniforms offer little camouflage in the forest where the battle takes place. He quickly dispatches the red-garbed enemies, slashing one's throat, running another through with his katana and killing a third by lodging a shuriken right into the poor guy's forehead. There's a final showdown between Cole and the black ninja, who we know is evil by the way his eyebrows persistently angle downward, but it's a bit of a letdown: Cole escapes with a slow-motion dive over the side of a waterfall.

We re-join the White Ninja—played by Nero in close-ups, and by Mike Stone whenever he's doing actual ninja-y stuff—as he's approaching what can only be described as a quaint, ninja village. He dukes it out with a few more red ninjas before taking on the black ninja for yet another showdown. Just as Cole is about to deliver the killing blow, he allows his opponent to surrender, unexpectedly sparing his life. He proceeds onto the building's patio, where an elderly, sage-looking Asian man stands calmly surveying the action. The White Ninja bows to him, draws his katana and—as slow motion kicks in once again—lops off the old man's head. (Don't worry, it's only a dummy.)

The White Ninja proceeds into the building and—surprise! This action-packed opening sequence wasn't a deadly, high-stakes battle at all, but Cole's final exam at Ninja school. His classmates remove their masks to reveal that they're all okay, and the Master Ninja enters carrying his own, wax dummy head. Given how gruesome the kills we just witnessed were, are we supposed to believe the student ninjas go through the trouble of rigging themselves up with tubing to squirt fake blood every time a classmate undergoes one of these tests? And how the heck did one dude take a ninja star directly to the brain and come out relatively unscathed? Never mind. Let's continue.

Once the initiation ceremony is over, Cole is declared a master of ninjutsu. This sparks serious beef with his classmate Hasegawa, the black ninja (Kosugi). Hasegawa feels very strongly that this non-Japanese fella has no business being a ninja, which seems kind of racist. This becomes important later on.

Cole packs up his ninja gear and heads to the Philippines, where he's been summoned mysteriously by an old war buddy named Frank Landers (Alex Courtney). Choosing to climb over their front gate rather than ring the doorbell, he's understandably greeted at the end of a shotgun by Frank's new wife, Mary Ann. She's played by Susan George, a wonderful English actress best known for playing Dustin Hoffman's wife in the controversial *Straw Dogs* (1971), and for memorable roles in the cult movies *Mandingo* (1975) and *Dirty Mary Crazy Larry* (1974).

Mary Ann disarms Cole with her beauty; Cole disarms Mary Ann with a well-placed karate chop. Frank welcomes his buddy in. Over dinner, it becomes obvious that everything isn't peachy-keen in Frank and Mary Ann's marriage. It turns out that Frank's been hitting the bottle really hard ever since an evil corporation started trying to force them off their land. Frank and Mary Ann run what appears to be a coconut farm with loose rules about employing child labor, and where the local Filipino farmhands regularly drop whatever they're doing at a moment's notice to hold impromptu cock fights.

Cole heads into town, where he witnesses a pudgy thug known as The Hook roughing up a shop owner. The Hook is played by Israeli actor Zachi Noy, who co-starred in the goofy fat kid role in Golan and Globus' hit *Lemon Popsicle* series—he'd appear again in Cannon's *The Ambassador* (1985) and their Movie Tales version of *The Emperor's New Clothes* (1987). A friendly American peddler named Dollars informs Cole that The Hook—so named for the hook that's replaced his left hand—has been extorting money from all of the local businesses. Dollars is played by Will Hare, best remembered as the old farmer who nearly puts a shotgun hole through Marty McFly when he mistakes him for an alien in *Back to the Future* (1985).

Returning to the farm, Cole and Mary Ann find a group of thugs beating up their head farmer, Pee Wee. (*Great* name.) Cole naturally kicks the living daylights out of these bad guys and save the day, but that doesn't stop the local farmers from handing Mary Ann their resignation notices, leaving the couple's coconut farm without any workers. The next morning they head back to town to recruit laborers at a local bar, where The Hook shows up again to intimidate the local work force. It's here where we finally hear The Hook's over-the-top, Dr. Strangelove-esque German accent. (His voice is dubbed only slightly better than Franco Nero's faux-Texan accent: little effort was made to find a voice actor who sounded anything like the well-known Italian star.) Cole's Ninjutsu training comes in handy yet again as he dispatches the goons with a variety of kicks and haymakers.

A theatrical poster from Germany, where the movie was released with a title which quite awesomely translated to "Ninja: The Killer Machine."

Licking his wounds, The Hook retreats to a fancy skyscraper where we learn that he works for an evil businessman named Venarius, who is delightfully played with utmost, moustache-twirling cheese by the former star of TV's *The Rat Patrol* (1966–1968), Christopher George. Venarius has closely studied every page of the Bond villain handbook: he lives in a fancy tower, wears ornate smocks, has a swimming pool filled with bathing beauties *in his office*, and buys matching white suits for his private army of henchmen. (Let's not forget that his head enforcer has a hook in place of his hand, either.) Venarius wants Frank's farmland for its rich oil reserves, and he sends his thugs back to the Landers' farm to again terrorize the impoverished, cockfight-loving villagers who live on it. Luckily Cole still happens to be hanging around to once more kick the shit out of these guys, but not before poor Pee Wee is tied up and drug behind the bad guys' jeep. Cole sends a strong message by ripping off the Hook's hook with his bare hands, leaving the whimpering goon with a bloody stump. ("Hey, you forgot something!" Cole calls, and tosses the severed limb to the fleeing thug. The soundtrack follows that with a sad trombone noise. Yep, *Enter the Ninja* goes there.)

Later, Frank receives an invitation to meet with Venarius' men to discuss a monetary offer for his land. Cole rides along to an old, creepy, abandoned fort which is a very suspicious place to hold a business meeting. Frank meets with Venarius' dapper, British henchmen, who make him a seven-figure offer on his farm that he must accept immediately. Meanwhile, Cole's been creeping around the perimeter and silently knocking out the armed guards. (They also have matching white suits. It's cute.) When the bad guys in charge summon their hired goons to intimidate Frank, they're surprised to find only a few remain. Cole bursts in and dumps a large pile of assault rifles at their feet. Everyone else drops their weapons, and they have a big ol' kick-fight which Cole wins, obviously. Afterwards they head to a bar where Frank ties on a few too many and starts saying things he'll regret later. When Cole asks whether Mary Ann wants kids, Frank drops one little nugget of too much information: "Don't get me wrong, she's a sexy lady. She *wants it* all the time, but I can't get it up for her lately." The camera slowly zooms in on Cole here, and it's clear that he's thinking *long* and *hard* about what his best friend just said. *Long* and *hard*.

You can guess where this is going, right? In the *very next scene* we watch as Mary Ann enters Cole's bedroom wearing a diaphanous nightgown and climbs into his bed, and then as Cole switches off the lights. By now, Cole is starting to seem like a bit of a dick. It doesn't matter how big a lush your best friend is, or how many thugs you've kicked to death while defending his coconut farm: you don't sleep with his wife.

By the midway point we'd forgive any viewers who might have forgotten this movie was called *Enter the Ninja*. Since the movie's opening there hasn't been a single reference to ninjas. While Cole does show off a few sweet, ass-kicking moves, there's nothing about this middle-aged, Italian hunk with an overdubbed American accent that really screams "ninja." But that's about to change. Remember when I asked you not to forget Cole's grudge-holding classmate, Hasegawa, the black ninja? One of Venarius' brighter goons makes a wild leap of logic and figures out that Cole might be a secret ninja, and they come to obvious conclusion that the only way to kill a ninja is with *another* ninja. ("Only a ninja can stop a ninja" is the most common motif across all of Cannon's ninja films, and was even one of the taglines for *Enter*'s follow-up, *Revenge of the Ninja*.)

Conveniently, Cole's most bitter rival is available for hire at the very same ninja school he just graduated from. Venarius' goon travels to Japan, where Cole's beloved mentor basically has Hasegawa put on a karate-themed dance routine for his prospective employer before putting him on a plane to go kill his former classmate.

Back in Manila, Cole breaks in to Venarius' office hoping to get to the bottom of his beef with Frank. He has Dollars distract the security guards with some pornographic photos before he knocks them out and steals their uniforms. While there, they find a reel of film that shows Hasegawa slicing off a gangster's arm: we're supposed to believe that it's candid footage of the black ninja in action, even though it's shot from multiple angles and slickly edited. This tips Cole off that trouble is coming his way.

Meanwhile, the black-garbed Hasegawa sneaks into the Landers' farmstead. He makes short work of their personal guards, killing one by slamming a pair of ninja climbing claws through his face. This weapon is known as the tekagi-shuko, or "hand tiger." They're usually pretty badass-looking, but the one in this movie kind of looks like a hairbrush taped to Sho Kosugi's hand.

Not only does Hasegawa hate white ninjas, but he might be totally insane. The biggest clue is the villainous laugh he makes while he murders people, which is actually more of a nefarious chuckle. (To approximate that ridiculous noise, read this line out loud through clenched teeth: "Hee hee hee hee hee!") Frank grabs a baseball bat and tries valiantly to protect his wife, but baseball bats are no match for ninja steel. Hasegawa kills Frank, then sets fire to the homes of all the Filipino farm workers because Hasegawa is damn crazy.

When Cole returns home to find his best friend dead and Mary Ann kidnapped, it triggers Full Ninja Mode. We watch him gear up and don his snow-white shozoku, then head straight to Venarius' office building where he shows no mercy killing every single guard who gets in his way, as well as the building's unarmed receptionist. (Being killed by a shuriken just because you answer phones for a guy who pissed off a ninja? Talk about a shitty way to go.) Cole keeps on killing Venarius' employees until one of the top goons invites him to meet with his boss. "You didn't have to kill half of our guards," he points out, and we agree!

They head to the local cockfighting arena, where Venarius and more than a dozen of his best men are holding Mary Ann captive. The evil CEO insists he only wants to talk, but white ninja don't play that way. Cole kills pretty much everybody present using all of the nifty weapons we saw in the movie's opening credits. Christopher George gives an amazingly campy performance in this scene: he whines and screams orders at his soldiers as he powerlessly watches Cole pick them off one by one, and wonders out loud where his hired ninja might be. He screeches one of the film's most quotable lines like a stereotypical. spoiled rich kid: "I want my black ninja, and I want him *now*!"

Once all of his employees have been killed, Venarius tries to bargain his way out of death by offering Cole a job working for him. Cole politely declines by nailing him with a ninja star, cuing arguably one of cinema's most hilarious death scenes. As Venarius falls backward in slow motion, he shrugs and mugs a face that absolutely can be read as "What the heck, ninja?"

But, we're not done yet! Cole spins around to find that Hasegawa has arrived late and taken Mary Ann hostage in the center of the arena's cockfighting ring. Cole enters the ring and Hasegawa releases Mary Ann, but she doesn't flee the area, because if two ninjas are about to duel to the death you bet your ass you'd be sticking around to watch, too. Cole and Hasegawa have it out—white ninja versus black ninja—and their showdown doesn't disappoint, even if it does feel a little underwhelming after Cole's lengthy bad guy murder spree. When Cole wins, Hasegawa pleads that he allow him to die with honor. Cole agrees, and then lops the head off a dummy wearing Hasegawa's black shozoku.

Perhaps one of the best final frames ever committed to celluloid.

The movie's dénouement is appropriately goofy. Cole coldly leaves the smoldering Mary Ann behind in Manila and heads off to the airport to go home. At the terminal Dollars casually asks Cole, "So, who you gonna kill next, Mr. Ninja?" Cole corrects him, clarifying that a true ninja only kills in self-defense. (Which, based on the movie's last 40 minutes, is complete bullshit.) A moment later the recently-unemployed Hook rolls up with a luggage cart and asks Cole whether he could use a porter. When he realizes who he's talking to, he flees in terror. Cole turns to Dollars and adds that sometimes a ninja will make an exception to their self-defense rule, then turns to the camera, smiles, and winks. Freeze frame. Movie over.

Enter the Ninja is a great deal of fun, even in the few moments where the movie stops making any logical sense. Franco Nero oozes so much charisma from behind his bushy moustache that it's easy to forget how implausible he seems as this particular story's hero. Christopher George plays the pinnacle b-movie bad guy: equal parts spoiled brat and remorseless killer. The plot is thin and predictable, but it wastes little time connecting the dots between the nearly non-stop fight scenes. Where *Enter the Ninja* truly succeeds is in making ninjas look unbelievably awesome, from its violent opening scene to its even more violent closing scene. There's a reason why ninjas were everywhere from this point on. *Enter the Ninja* started that craze, and that alone is enough to place it among the many high points of the Cannon canon.

This sun-faded, VHS copy of *Body and Soul* was rented by Video Dreams of Coral Gables, Florida.

Body and Soul

Release Date: October 23, 1981
Written By: Leon Isaac Kennedy
Directed By: George Bowers
Starring: Leon Isaac Kennedy, Jayne Kennedy, Muhammad Ali
Trailer Voiceover: "He was one man. He gave his body—they wanted his soul!"

In the late '70s and early '80s, Jayne and Leon Isaac Kennedy were one of Hollywood's true power couples, glamourous and good-looking, with everything they touched seeming to turn to gold. Appearing on television shows and on the covers of magazines, they were super-famous for a period of time. Even before they got into the movie business, the husband-and-wife duo were trailblazers: Leon for his pioneering work in Black entertainment, and Jayne for breaking several racial barriers in her role as a public figure.

Leon Isaac Kennedy was a Cleveland kid, born and raised, who had attended the same Shaker Heights high school from which actor Paul Newman had graduated a few decades earlier. That inspired in Leon a longing for the spotlight, and by the age of sixteen he'd landed a job as a radio disc jockey: the youngest-ever in a major national market. Adopting a persona known as "Leon the Lover," his popularity skyrocketed, and his show was syndicated across the country. He channeled this radio success into gigs on a pair of television variety shows: *Teenarama* out of Washington, D.C., which he hosted at the age of eighteen, and *Outta Sight*, which he wrote, produced, and co-hosted while still a teenager. The latter had the distinction of becoming the first African American television series to receive national syndication, just narrowly beating *Soul Train* to the punch.

Jayne Kennedy was born Jayne Harrison, and was also from Cleveland. In 1970 she was the first African American to be crowned Miss Ohio. Following her win, she made an appearance on *Outta Sight* where she met (and soon, married) the show's young producer, Leon Kennedy. Not long after tying the knot—singer Smokey Robinson was the best man at their nuptials—the handsome couple relocated to Los Angeles to break into acting. Jayne quickly scored a job on *Laugh-In* (1968–1973) alongside a handful of small TV roles. Her biggest break came in 1978 when she won a heavily-publicized talent search to become the new host of CBS's *The NFL Today*, making her one of the first female sports announcers. At the height of her career, she appeared on numerous magazine covers and was a spokesmodel for popular brands such as Diet Coke and Tab cola. In July of 1981, she made pop culture history by becoming the first Black woman to appear on the cover of *Playboy*—nearly three decades after the magazine's launch.

Meanwhile, Leon spent the 1970s working in radio and television, and opening a chain of successful discos as he worked toward his big screen break. He wrote, produced, or starred in a string of low-budget Blaxploitation films, and then in 1979 came *Penitentiary*. Leon produced and starred in this brutal feature directed by Jamaa Fanaka, which cleverly combined elements of boxing movies with those of a prison film. In the film Leon played Martel "Two Sweet" Gordone, a man wrongly imprisoned and forced to fight another inmate in the boxing ring or else become his sex slave. (Rocky Balboa certainly never faced such high stakes.) It was lurid, but the boxing in particular was very well done. The independent film was a huge success, raking in $18 million on a budget of less than $500,000. (Kennedy reprised the role twice more for the same director, in *Penitentiary II* [1982] and *III* [1987].)

When Cannon locked in a deal to produce and distribute Leon Isaac Kennedy's next film, it had to have looked like a slam dunk for the rising studio. Not only was it another boxing film from the indie wunderkind fresh off the hugely successful *Penitentiary*, but it would co-star his arguably even more famous wife, Jayne, in their first on-screen role together. The fact that superstar boxing legend Muhammad Ali had signed on to play a supporting role was just the icing on the cake. How could *any* movie producer have not have been licking their lips at such a surefire opportunity?

Leon himself wrote the film's screenplay, loosely adapted from a 1947 movie of the same name starring John Garfield. This "remake" has a few things carried over from the original—chiefly, the story of a boxer being lured into temptation by unsavory promoters, despite the protests of his disapproving mother—but for the most part it's its own film.

Leon Kennedy plays Leon Johnson, a talented amateur boxer who declines going pro because he's "a lover, not a fighter." After watching him win a thrilling match in the ring, we soon get to better know our hero better inside a men's room bathroom stall, where he's balls deep in some lady of presumably low moral caliber. In one of his first lines of dialogue, Leon frantically announces that he's about to ... *finish*, let's say. "Not in here. Someone might come!" his comely consort pleads. "The only one about to come is *me*," he tells her, "and it doesn't matter where!" (Leon the lover, ladies and gentlemen.)

Meanwhile, a fancy party is happening outside the bathroom, where famous sports reporter Julie Winters—Jayne Kennedy, playing a role that you have to assume was inspired by her professional persona—makes an appearance to present Leon with an award. He zips up in time to take the stage, where he promptly makes crude, sexist jokes at Julie's expense. She surprisingly warms up to him, however, following around 30 seconds of disco-dancing.

After opening the film as an insufferably arrogant, chauvinist assclown, we're presented with a more humanizing side of Leon when we meet his little sister, Kelly. Leon just adores the little girl, who is hospitalized with sickle-cell anemia. The doctor gives her low odds of surviving for much longer, but those chances would be raised slightly if she were to receive the best medical treatment. Those treatments cost lots of money, and Leon only has one viable way of earning that sort of dough, which draws ire from his disapproving mother. ("You are keeping your Black behind in college and becoming a doctor!" she screeches at him, seeming to forget that her daughter needs treatment *right away*.) Leon ultimately goes against her wishes and, with his best friend Charles (Perry Lang, who'd appear again in Cannon's *Sahara*), decides that if he's going to go pro, he'll do it by training with the best.

When you think of boxing and "the best," Muhammad Ali is usually the first name who comes to mind. This is true both in the real world and the world of *Body and Soul*. As one of the greatest athletes of the century, a pop culture hero, and a civil rights icon, Ali hardly needs any introduction. He was one fight away from retiring at the time of *Body and Soul*, but he still would have been one of the most famous people on the entire planet when the movie was released. Ali was a personal friend of the Kennedys, and Leon specifically wrote him into the movie.

In the next scene, Leon walks into Muhammad Ali's gym and demands training from the greatest boxer of all time. Ali takes Leon under his wing after he manhandles his best fighter in the gym's sparring ring. (Leon's personal trainer is played by Mike Gazzo, best remembered as Frankie "Five Angels" Pentangeli in *The Godfather: Part II* [1974].) The movie picks up steam here thanks to numerous montages in which Leon trains, courts Julie, knocks out fighter after fighter, and endows his little sis with gift after lavish gift. He eventually adopts the over-the-top persona of "Leon the Lover," and skyrockets to fame and fortune. (You might remember that "Leon the Lover" was also Leon Kennedy's disc jockey name.) In the film, he plays up the part by handing out roses—and kisses—to women in the audiences of his boxing matches, and wearing his name with hearts embroidered across the backside of his athletic shorts.

For the rest of the way *Body and Soul* follows a pretty standard course. Leon falls in with a crooked promoter named Big Man, played by ex-Rat Packer Peter Lawford, and becomes caught up in a debaucherously fast world of money, drugs, and loose women. Not only does he lose his way, but he loses his girl. Julie walks in on him in bed with a high-end hooker subtly named Pussy, played by *Teen Mothers'* Azizi Johari. Leon follows Julie to her car, half-nude, and begs for her forgiveness. She rebuffed him with the fantastic line, "I just wish that you were double jointed so that you could turn around and kiss your own ass!"

Time goes on and Leon's career falters. Eventually Big Man offers him money to take a dive during his next big match, and Leon is convinced that it might be his only way out.

An illustrated sales ad for the movie.

The latter portion of the movie builds up to Leon's big championship fight with "Mad Man" Santiago, a character who's not only a mildly offensive Latin American stereotype—he rides down to the arena on the back of a bull, wearing a sombrero—but is made out to be pure, unadulterated evil. Mad Man is the kind of boxer who hits below the belt, spits racial slurs, and nearly kills his sparring partner. He even makes cheap cracks about Leon's sick kid sister, and then hurls a woman's baby at the ground when it pees on him during a television interview. Yeah, Mad Man is a pretty bad guy.

Julie reconciles with Leon, and helps him find his competitive spirit again. The old gang—Julie, Charles, Muhammad Ali, and Kid Sis—helps him get back into fighting shape, and the rest of the movie dedicates itself to a legitimately exciting, fifteen-round finale bout between Leon the Lover and Mad Man Santiago. (I'll let you guys guess who goes home with the championship belt.)

While *Body and Soul* is about as formulaic as they come, it succeeds in a lot of the places it needs to. The boxing scenes, importantly, are pretty damn good—both in the choreography and the editing—and when *isn't* it fun to see the great Muhammad Ali light up a screen, even in a small movie? As far as chemistry goes, Leon and Jayne Kennedy are a predictably good on-screen fit. Their performances in *Body and Soul*, however, were overshadowed by their off-screen lives before the movie ever made it to theaters.

The theatrical release of *Body and Soul* coincided with two big PR hullabaloos surrounding the Kennedys. Just a few months before the film landed in theaters, Jayne became the first Black woman to appear on the cover of *Playboy*, marking a significant racial milestone, if not necessarily a feminist one. Inside the issue were a number of steamy, much talked-about bedroom photos of Jayne with her husband, nude and engaging in some hot-and-heavy fake sex. (Leon explained that the images were outtakes from their movie, *Body and Soul*, after some controversy had swirled around them.) The real bombshell dropped a week before the film's release, when the news broke that the high-profile celebrity couple were getting divorced. The topic of their ending marriage, of course, consumed the promotion of the film they starred in together. The couple jointly cited diverging careers and busy schedules as the reason for their amicable split.

Despite the controversies—or, perhaps in part thanks to them—*Body and Soul* went on to modest box office success, and did very well relative to its trim budget. Cannon signed on to produce Leon Isaac Kennedy's prison boxing threequel, *Penitentiary III*, in 1987.

Leon and Jayne Kennedy have another claim to fame in the annals of pop culture history; unfortunately, it wasn't the sort of new ground they had any desire to break. Shortly after their divorce, a VHS tape was stolen from their home which featured the two engaging in private, sexual activities for the camera, making Jayne and Leon Kennedy the very first victims of a celebrity sex tape scandal. This was long before the internet would have made such a video viewable by thousands within seconds of its release; the Kennedys' tape was passed hand-to-hand between perverts in increasingly-deteriorating videocassette dubs. Still, the damage was enough to tarnish Jayne's wholesome image and derail her promising career in broadcasting.

Leon kept making movies throughout the '80s, including his two *Penitentiary* sequels, *Hollywood Vice Squad* (1986) alongside Carrie Fisher, and *Lone Wolf McQuade* (1983) with Chuck Norris. In an example of extreme image makeover, the action star ladies' man eventually left the film business entirely to reinvent himself as an Evangelist pastor. He now runs the Kennedy Healing Love Ministries, which are based out of Burbank.

Cannon's first installment of the franchise in its VHS reissue.

Death Wish II
Death Wish 3
Death Wish 4: The Crackdown

Release Date: February 19, 1982 (II), November 1, 1985 (III), November 6, 1987 (IV)
Directed by: Michael Winner (II and III), J. Lee Thompson (IV)
Written by: David Engelbach (II), Don Jakoby [as Michael Edmonds] (III), Gail Morgan Hickman (IV)
Starring: Charles Bronson
Trailer Voiceover: "It happened once before . . . it's about to happen again! When violence rules the city and the police can't stop it, one man will . . . *his* way!"

The original *Death Wish* was produced by famed Italian mogul Dino De Laurentiis and released in U.S. theaters by Paramount in the summer of 1974. Seemingly no one involved in its making expected it to be a hit, but the film grossed more than five times its budget (and even more abroad) and was one of the most-discussed releases of its year, thanks in no small part to its incendiary content. Whereas its gruff leading man, Charles Bronson, had been a box office draw in foreign countries thanks to his appearances in hit Westerns and war pics, he was hardly as well-known to audiences back home in the United States. *Death Wish*, however, transformed him into an American icon.

Bronson was born Charles Buchinsky, the 11th of 15 children, deep in the mining region of western Pennsylvania. His father died when Charles was only ten years old; during the Depression, the young boy went to work in the coal mines to help support his family. He enlisted in the United States Army Air Forces after WWII broke out, eventually serving as a B-29 aerial gunner on the Pacific front and earning a Purple Heart for a bullet wound sustained during one of his missions. After the war he studied art and acting on the G.I. Bill, moved to Hollywood, and landed numerous bit parts in films and TV shows. Worried that he'd lose out on roles with an un-American sounding name—this was during the height of the McCarthy era—he adopted the surname Bronson. He did quite well for himself, being regularly cast in leading roles on short-lived TV shows and in low-budget genre films, but his biggest break came when he played one of the seven titular gunfighters in 1960's *The Magnificent Seven*, which was an especially huge hit abroad. He followed it up with memorable turns in *The Great Escape* (1963) and *The Dirty Dozen* (1967). These three movies vaulted Bronson into superstardom in Europe, where the actor was offered work left and right. During this period he played the villain of Sergio Leone's 1968 classic *Once Upon a Time in the West*. (Leone had badly wanted him for the lead of his legendary Man With No Name trilogy; when Bronson declined, Leone had to settle for Clint Eastwood.) At this point pushing 50 years old, Bronson was a bankable A-lister in places like France, Italy, and Japan, but he was rarely viewed as anything more than a supporting actor with a memorable, weathered face in the United States. That would all change with *Death Wish*.

Rather loosely based on the novel of the same name by author Brian Garfield, Bronson plays a mild-mannered New Yorker whose wife and adult daughter are brutally assaulted by home invaders. Unable to cope with his anger in non-violent ways, he's compelled onto the city streets at night to exact revenge upon unwitting muggers with the aid of his .32 revolver. The film also follows the police as they hunt for the vigilante, who becomes a folk hero to a populace that has become fed up with their law enforcement's inability to control urban crime.

The original *Death Wish* was to be directed by the great Sidney Lumet and star Jack Lemmon in the lead role; after Lumet dropped out, directorial duties went to an on-the-rise British filmmaker named Michael Winner. In dire need of a new star, Winner eventually coaxed Charles Bronson into the role, having worked with the actor previously on 1972's *Chato's Land* and *The Mechanic*, as well as 1973's *Stone Killer*. (Many years before Winner had dated Bronson's longtime wife, Jill Ireland, when she was only a teenager, an unbelievable coincidence that helped bring about the actor and director's productive fifteen years of collaboration.)

The *Death Wish* script had to be retrofitted to suit Bronson's cool, stony machismo: the Paul Benjamin protagonist of the novel, a meek accountant, became Paul Kersey, a tough-minded architect. Winner himself made wholesale changes to the script, most notably changing the novel's off-screen assault of Kersey's wife and daughter into a drawn-out, unnecessarily brutal, and extremely hard-to-watch rape and attack scene that lasts for several minutes in the film. At the time, it was easily the most graphic of its sort to appear in any studio release: the scene had to be altered significantly for the movie to be released in other countries. Also new was the ending. By the end of the book, Paul had become a complete madman, killing unarmed kids and turning into something arguably worse than the muggers he'd been executing. The film ends with Kersey quietly run out of town by the police, who didn't want to turn him into a public martyr to a populace who had come to regard the nameless vigilante as a hero. The movie closes with Kersey getting off a train in Chicago and encountering a gang of rowdy, young ruffians. *Death Wish*'s famous closing shot is a close up of Kersey cocking a finger-gun towards the youths and smiling, suggesting that his vigilante days are far from over.

Upon its release, *Death Wish* was largely despised by critics who generally viewed it as morally repugnant. Even those who were able to look past the violence and see it as a decent revenge thriller warned readers against its questionable (if not outright irresponsible) messaging, which seemed to champion gunning down criminals without due process. The movie was a box office hit despite this, particularly in big cities where the crime rates were rising out of control. In New York City, where the movie was set, theater owners reported record attendances. The controversy surrounding the movie, if anything, only contributed to its ticket sales. Paul Kersey instantly became Bronson's most iconic role. *Death Wish*'s impact had a rippling effect felt throughout the industry, spawning an entire subgenre of formulaic revenge thrillers that can be found within the action genre to this day. (Every time Liam Neeson must use his "very particular set of skills" to rescue a kidnapped family member, you can thank *Death Wish*.)

Although *Death Wish* had been a big financial success, it wasn't necessarily a movie to which anyone was clamoring for a sequel. Watching it as a stand-alone feature, *Death Wish* is a film that feels like it said what it wanted to say. In spite of its famous closing shot which left the door open for follow-ups, it feels like a natural ending point for Paul Kersey's story. Bronson himself showed little interest in revisiting the character, and director Michael Winner commented that he'd thought the idea had already been played out in the first film. Meanwhile, novelist Brian Garfield so disliked the way they'd grossly altered his work that he was driven to write a sequel book—*Death Sentence*, published in 1975—in which the character hunts down and confronts a copycat vigilante in hopes of stopping him. The market was flooded with cheap *Death Wish* knock-offs throughout the rest of the 1970s, while Bronson enjoyed a variety of roles in his newfound position as a Hollywood star.

Of course the newly emerged, Golan and Globus-led Cannon would see things differently.

Early in G&G's tenure at the company's helm, Cannon released an advertisement boasting about their upcoming slate, one film of which would be sequel to *Death Wish*. The problem with this was that Cannon did not own the rights to make said sequel, and that their wishful advertisement was the first time many involved with the first movie had ever heard about it. (This wasn't an entirely uncommon occurrence for Cannon, who made a habit of taking out ads for movies with big-name stars who'd yet to sign any sort of contract.) Dino De Laurentiis, who'd produced the original and still held the rights, had his lawyers call up Cannon and basically strong-arm them into purchasing it for a handsome, six-figure sum. Their hand forced, Cannon had no choice but to make a *Death Wish II*. Their problem, then, was that Bronson had no interest in doing the film—that is, until they offered him a cool $1.5 million to reconsider. By that point they'd already sunk nearly $2 million into a movie and had little more than a title and a star to show for it.

Cannon recruited young screenwriter David Engelbach to draft a script that would give Kersey ample reason to clean up the streets for a second time. Engelbach had already written the competitive arm wrestling adventure *Over the Top*, a screenplay with which Golan was reputedly enamored but would not be able to turn into a film until 1987. Engelbach initially passed on drafting *Death Wish 2*, but finally struck a deal in which Cannon would finance his directorial debut in exchange for his writing services. (His film would become their 1986 post-apocalyptic parody, *America 3000*.) Engelbach set the screenplay in San Francisco, which was quickly swapped out for Los Angeles since it would be cheaper for Cannon to shoot there. In Engelbach's version, Kersey was heavily armed and outfitted with body armor by a group of sympathetic survivalists, turning him into more of the one-man army you'd see in later sequels. In the filmed version of *Death Wish II*, like in the original movie, Kersey does most of his killing with a pistol.

Golan envisioned himself directing what he foresaw to be the biggest, hit sequel of the 1980s. Bronson balked, however, at anyone other than Michael Winner handling the feature, and put his foot down. Golan eventually gave in and Winner, who had arrived at a slump in his once promising career, was hired onto the film. His first order of business was to heavily re-tool Engelbach's script to better fit his personal filmmaking style, most notably by adding gratuitously detailed rape scenes.

Bronson had one other stipulation and it was that his wife, actress Jill Ireland, be cast as his romantic counterpart. Bronson and Ireland had married in 1968 after meeting on the set of *The Great Escape*, in which Ireland's first husband, actor David McCallum, had appeared with Bronson. (McCallum is best known for playing Illya on *The Man from UNCLE* from 1964 to 1968, and Donald "Ducky" Mallard on *NCIS* starting in 2003.) The two were madly in love, and rarely did Bronson leave behind his wife and their six children—two their own, and four more from their prior marriages—despite his busy filming schedule. Ireland appeared in sixteen of her husband's films in total, including a pair of Cannon pictures: *Death Wish II* and 1987's *Assassination*. She was diagnosed with breast cancer just two years after *Death Wish II*'s release, and courageously took a public stand against the rising costs of treatments, serving as a spokesperson for the American Cancer Society until her death in 1990, at the age of 54. Until the end, Mrs. Bronson was every bit as tough off-screen as her husband was on it.

Death Wish II opens with Kersey now living in Los Angeles, having left Chicago to work as the in-house architect for one of the city's leading radio networks. He seems to be carrying on better than can be expected after the events of the first film, which occurred either two or five years earlier depending on which of the film's own contradicting timelines you choose to believe. He's in a healthy relationship with hard-hitting reporter Geri Nichols (Jill Ireland) and having regular visits with his still nearly-comatose daughter, Carol (Robin Sherwood.) After a brief run-in with a group of thugs, Kersey's home is broken into by the same gang, who rape and murder his housekeeper. When Kersey and his daughter walk in on the criminals in the middle of the act, Kersey is roughed up and Carol taken as a hostage.

A long, violent rape scene was the most controversial element of the original *Death Wish*, and for whatever perverse reason Winner seems to have felt a need to top it in his sequel. The housekeeper's rape goes on for several minutes and needed to be heavily edited in order for the movie to obtain an R rating. Winner spent six grueling days shooting the scene, finally disgusting the film's first cinematographer, Thomas Del Ruth—who would go on to film '80s classics like *The Breakfast Club* (1985) and *Stand By Me* (1986)—so much so that he quit the movie and had to be replaced mid-shoot by Richard Kline, a cinematographer most famous for his Oscar-nominated work on the 1976 *King Kong* remake. Even the gang of thugs, all staunch method actors who'd spent weeks living inside their roles and who rarely broke character, would stop to comfort actress Silvana Gallardo when shooting was over.

Each of *Death Wish II*'s featured rapists, who were given wacky names like Stomper, Jiver, and Cutter, was encouraged to come up with his own, individual look. Most recognizable among them is Laurence Fishburne, an actor best known these days for his role as Cowboy Curtis on *Pee-wee's Playhouse* from 1986 to 1990. (Oh, and for movies like *Apocalypse Now* [1979], *Boyz n the Hood* [1991], and *The Matrix* [1999].) He spends the movie wearing neon pink, wrap-around sunglasses. Kevyn Major Howard, later of *Full Metal Jacket* (1987) fame, used a razor to remove his eyebrows and push back his hairline halfway up his head. Thomas F. Duffy, who plays the movie's ultimate goon, Nirvana, wears a newsboy cap over his long, fluffy hair; he'd go on to be quite prolific, appearing in movies such as *Independence Day* (1996) and the *Jurassic Park: The Lost World* (1997). Actors Stuart Robinson and E. Lamont Johnson round out the gang. Unlike the first movie, it's important to remember their faces as Paul Kersey will be spending the rest of *Death Wish II*'s runtime hunting them down.

The print advertisements for *Death Wish II* were dark and grimy, much like the film's contents.

Michael Winner apparently wasn't finished sickening his audiences, however, as Kersey's poor, mute daughter Carol also winds up raped a few scenes later by the gang as they're hiding out in an abandoned warehouse. As if that weren't bad enough, Carol finally slips free of her attackers only to flee straight through a plate glass window and get impaled on a spiked fence two stories below. Like the prior scene, Carol's assault and death are heavily trimmed in the theatrically-released version of the movie. Her death was part of Engelbach's original script, but the sexual assault was naturally added by Winner himself. (The screenwriter was so incensed by these additions that he considered having his name removed from the credits.)

In a full watch-through of this famously violent series, these two scenes make the first 30 minutes of *Death Wish II* the hardest part of the marathon to get through. Not only because the back-to-back rape scenes and the unnecessary impaling of a woman rendered near-comatose by her prior sexual assault are utterly tasteless, but because the chances of this exact thing happening to the same guy in two different cities two years apart feels absolutely absurd. Imagine if Bruce Wayne, having become Batman to avenge his parents' death, cleaned up Gotham City and then moved to Metropolis to start his life anew, only to witness yet another family member killed in a random mugging. Really, what are the chances?

If Kersey's calm reaction and unwillingness to cooperate with the police following Carol's death seems odd, it's because the original script had the LAPD ruling Carol's death a suicide, thus making Kersey skeptical of cops. (This helpful context was trimmed out.) After taking minimal time to mourn, Kersey digs a Beretta out of his closet and sets off for vengeance. By day he put on a normal front, somehow maintaining his job and relationships as if nothing's out of the ordinary. By night, he rents out a room at a dive motel on the sleaziest strip of skid row, disguising himself as a homeless man and stalking his daughter's attackers.

The Paul Kersey we see in *Death Wish II* is far better-equipped for action than the one we met the first time around. *Death Wish*'s Paul Kersey is about as meek a character as Bronson could believably play, his mistakes and injuries giving us the sense that he's a relatively normal guy pushed to extreme measures. Whereas the original Kersey was a perfectly-suited anti-hero for the gritty realism of 1970s cinema, an '80s *Death Wish* called for an '80s style of action hero. The Paul Kersey of *Death Wish II* mixes powerful hand-to-hand combat in with his pistol play. He hunts criminals as efficiently as the Predator: every time he leaves the motel room he winds up exactly where his prey is, however improbable that seems in a city as big as Los Angeles. He's also been given an arsenal of smooth one-liners. In one of *Death Wish II*'s coolest scenes, Kersey notices a large crucifix hanging on a chain around one his attacker's neck:

Kersey: You believe in Jesus?

Stomper: Yes, I do.

Kersey: Well, you're going to meet him.

And then he *blows the dude away*.

Eventually the LA police draw a connection between their vigilante and the one that ran loose in New York two to five years earlier. They put in a call and the NYPD sends out Lieutenant Frank Ochoa, the cop who trailed Kersey on his first vengeance spree. (Ochoa's again played by the excellent Vincent Gardenia, who'd later play the florist Mr. Mushnik in 1986's *Little Shop of Horrors* musical remake, and then be nominated for his supporting performance as Cher's father in 1987's *Moonstruck*.) Initially out to stop Kersey, Ochoa is shot to death while protecting his former nemesis during a gunfight with a few heavily-armed criminals. His killer, Nirvana, the last surviving member of the gang that assaulted Kersey's daughter, escapes.

Fortunately for Nirvana, he's apprehended by the police before Kersey catches up with him. He avoids the electric chair thanks to a bum insanity plea and is committed to the exact rehabilitation facility where Kersey's girlfriend, Geri, happens to be researching a magazine article. Kersey spends the rest of the movie forging a fake ID so that he can sneak in as a doctor, get into a fistfight with Nirvana, and finally electrocute the murderer to death with the hospital's shock therapy machine. Geri figures out what her vengeance-seeking boyfriend has been up to this whole time and calls off their engagement, but Kersey doesn't seem fazed. The movie ends with a co-worker asking Kersey whether he's free to come to a party one night soon. Kersey shrugs, mugs for the camera, and utters the line: "What else would I be doing?" The final shot of the film is Kersey's shadow stalking in the night, implying that he's made cleaning up the streets a full-time hobby.

Cover art for the *Death Wish II* soundtrack album, with music by Jimmy Page.

While *Death Wish II* has a handful of great action scenes and a characteristically cool performance from Bronson, it's neither as gritty and exciting as the original, nor as goofily fun as the sequels to come. Still, like its predecessor, it does a great job of capturing the feel of the sleazier parts of the city in which it was filmed, as Winner shot only on location and grabbed real street people to fill his frames, rather than professional extras. Another one of its highlights is its hard rock soundtrack by former Led Zeppelin guitar god Jimmy Page. Cannon had initially desired that Isaac Hayes provide the movie's score, giving it a similar flavor to the ones he'd supplied for Blaxploitation films like *Shaft* (1971) and *Three Tough Guys* (1974). However, Page just so happened to be Winner's next door neighbor. When the director invited him over to see an early version of the film, the musician volunteered his services for the soundtrack. The resulting album was recorded in only a few weeks and was Page's first release after the breakup of his legendary rock band.

Death Wish II was released in February of 1982, a relatively quiet time for action films, to largely negative reviews. The public, on the other hand, had a surprisingly large appetite for a sequel to an eight-year-old movie starring a leading man who'd just celebrated his 60th birthday. The movie made more than $16 million in U.S. theaters and almost another $30 million abroad. Cannon, who had sold away the distribution rights to help finance the picture, didn't see much of that profit, yet it was still a big hit for them under their new leadership, and a major boost to their legitimacy as a studio.

Death Wish 3 arrived for rental in one of MGM's iconic, oversized, book-style boxes.

Cannon announced *Death Wish 3* at the Cannes Film Festival in 1984. Since the release of the second film in the series, Bronson had gone on to star as a fed-up cop in another Cannon feature, the superb slasher/thriller *10 to Midnight* (1983), and the very successful hitman picture *The Evil That Men Do* (1984). (The latter had initially been offered to Cannon, but Golan declined to pony up $200,000 for the screenplay rights.) While Bronson had been quietly reluctant to return to his Paul Kersey role the first time, he was far more vocal in his unhappiness about the direction the third movie took his character. If you can believe it, Bronson complained to the press about *Death Wish 3* being *too* violent.

This time around the screenplay was drafted by Don Jakoby, who would go on to write two of Cannon's three Tobe Hooper-directed features: *Lifeforce* (1985) and *Invaders from Mars* (1986), as well as their unproduced, science fiction retelling of *Pinocchio*, which was slated to star Lee Marvin as Gepetto and also be directed by Hooper. (Jakoby would go on to write the spider-centric 1990 horror flick *Arachnophobia*, the Jean-Claude Van Damme/Dennis Rodman joint vehicle *Double Team* [1997], and John Carpenter's *Vampires* [1998].) In a similar experience to Engelbach's on *Death Wish II*, Jakoby's script was heavily re-written once it got into director Michael Winner's hands. Unlike the prior writer, Jakoby succeed with having his real name removed from the film and replaced with the pseudonym "Michael Edmonds."

Death Wish 3 presented another major leap forward for Kersey, transforming him from simply a highly-skilled bad guy exterminator to a one-man, hoodlum-massacring army. The screenplay repositioned Kersey as a mash-up of *First Blood*'s John Rambo of *First Blood* (1982) and Kevin McCallister of *Home Alone* (1990), gunning down goons with machine guns and jury-rigging traps for would-be home invaders. It was no longer enough for him to hunt down and pick off the gang members who'd hurt his family; this time, Kersey would be deep-cleaning the streets of *all* criminals. Even Michael Winner himself, who'd returned to direct his third entry in the series, considered this sequel to have a more comedic tone than the films that preceded it. Watching the frequently hilarious final product, you can't help but question how much of that humor was intentional.

Fresh out of family members to be humiliated and killed, *Death Wish 3* had to get creative and seek out new relations of Kersey's to be murdered so to incite his latest quest for vengeance. Kersey returns to New York City via Brooklyn to visit an old war buddy only to find the elderly man freshly battered in his apartment by thugs. Kersey's pal dies in his arms just moments before the police burst through the door and arrest him on suspicion of murder. At the jail, an inspector by the name of Shirker (Ed Lauter) recognizes Kersey as the city's infamous vigilante of the 1970s. They strike an unorthodox deal: Kersey is given carte blanche to kill as many street thugs as he likes without repercussion, just so long as he works as an informant to the NYPD while doing so.

In Italy, the franchise was released with a title which translated to "The Night Executioner."

The newly-sanctioned vigilante heads back to Brooklyn and sets up shop in his dead buddy's apartment. There he befriends the deceased's pal, Bennett, also a fellow veteran. (Bennett's played by Martin Balsam, best known for his role as Detective Martin Aborgast in Alfred Hitchcock's 1960 masterpiece, *Psycho*; he'd also have a part in Cannon's *The Delta Force* in 1986.) Kersey is told that the area gang is led by a creep named Fraker, the same low-life whom Kersey had butted heads with during his brief time in lockup. Sporting a spectacular reverse Mohawk, Fraker is played with slimy gusto by Gavan O'Herlihy. (The same actor played Richie's older brother, Chuck Cunningham, on the first season of *Happy Days* (1974); when he asked to leave the show, his character was written out of the series and mysteriously never mentioned again.) Consistent with the prior film, Fraker's top henchmen go by silly nicknames like The Cuban and the Giggler, and are played by recognizable faces such as Ricco Ross (*Aliens*, 1986), Kirk Taylor (*Full Metal Jacket*, 1987), and a baby-faced Alex Winter, later the "Bill" of *Bill & Ted* fame. (Winter would also co-star in Cannon's gothic drama, *Haunted Summer*, in 1988.)

As the senior citizens tell it, this crime-ridden area of Brooklyn had once been a nice part of town, home to many upwardly mobile immigrant families. (Some exterior scenes were shot in the then-run down East New York region of Brooklyn, but the bulk of the movie—including its climactic gang war—was actually filmed in London.) True to his well-honed vigilante form, Kersey becomes the besieged neighborhood's de facto protector. When senior citizens are burgled, Kersey rigs up a trap that smashes out the front teeth of aspiring intruders. When two hoods attempt to steal a car, our vigilante shoots a couple holes through them. When a neighbor's wife is raped to death—because apparently it wouldn't be a Michael Winner film without gratuitous sexual assault—Kersey takes it as a cue to upgrade the weapons in his arsenal. (The assault woman in question is played by Marina Sirtis, last seen engaging in a topless whip fight with Faye Dunaway in another Winner/Cannon film, *The Wicked Lady* [1983]. She'd later co-star as Deanna Troi on *Star Trek: The Next Generation*, from 1987 to 1994.)

This time around Kersey's weapon of choice is a Wildey .475 magnum, a no-messing-around handgun that fires ammunition normally intended for use in big game hunting rifles. This explains why his enemies are blown ten feet through the air every time he blasts one. The actual firearm used on screen belonged to Bronson; its designer, Wildey Moore, served as a consultant on the movie.

Bronson's Wildey .475 featured prominently in many of the film's adverts, including this Italian poster with incredible, painted artwork by Sandro Symeoni.

There's a lot of comedy—accidental or not—which arises from the absolute joy the seemingly normal folks living in Kersey's neighborhood experience every time he blows the head off a local gang member. They hoot, whistle, holler, and cheer him on ("Right on, man!") like he's their favorite quarterback who just threw a perfect touchdown, rather than a heavily-armed 64-year-old who just gunned down a young, Hispanic purse-snatcher.

Another violent billboard advertisement by painter Sandro Symeoni, a legend of Italian film poster art.

When he's not casually dealing out death like it's hand after hand of blackjack, Kersey finds time to romance his attractive, much younger public defender, Kathryn (Deborah Raffin). If we've learned anything from a *Death Wish* movie, however, it's that you can't get close to Paul Kersey without being caught in the crossfire of his one-man war against crime. Poor Kathryn winds up getting blown up in a fiery car crash while Kersey's picking up his latest mail-order firearm from the post office.

Death Wish 3's action-packed finale may be the high point for the whole franchise. In a long, over-the-top firefight which spans several city blocks, Kersey wages war against a near-endless army of punks, bikers, and pushers. Buildings explode! A little old lady is set on fire! Several of Kersey's new-found senior citizen pals load up and join him in the wholesale exchange of bullets. It occupies almost a full quarter of the film's runtime and is nothing less than spectacular in its ridiculousness. The movie ends, appropriately, with Kersey blasting Fraker point-blank with a rocket launcher, blowing him clear through the wall of a building. (Coincidentally, this is almost the exact same way Chuck Norris K.O.'s his nemesis at the end of 1985's *Invasion U.S.A.*, which Cannon had released in theaters just a few weeks before *Death Wish 3*.)

For many fans, *Death Wish 3* is the pinnacle of the series. It's easily the most absurd entry, and you'd have a hard time arguing that it doesn't boast the best production value or highest body count. It's the best blend of the early films' violence and the later films' silliness. *Death Wish 3* is the series' biggest crowd-pleaser.

Critics once again were brutal in their reviews of the film, but time had proven twice before that reviews didn't matter when it came to a *Death Wish* movie. Cannon gambled that audiences still hadn't had enough of a pissed-off Charlie Bronson killing urban ne'er-do-wells, and it payed off. They shipped more than 1,400 prints across the United States, where it opened at #1 in the pre-holiday box office and raked in over $10 million dollars in its first ten days of release. The movie brought home over $16 million in domestic total, and the combination of its international box office, video sales, and a lucrative cable deal were a much-needed cash injection at a time when Cannon was significantly increasing the number and the size of the films they were producing each year.

Cannon was keenly aware of Bronson's enduring bankability as a star, especially in the sort of low-to-mid-budget action films they specialized in making, and were masters at selling these movies abroad. Cannon would make five more movies with Bronson (for a total of eight.) One of those, as you'd expect, was yet another *Death Wish* movie. Bronson made *Murphy's Law* (1986) and *Assassination* (1987) with the studio before once again assuming the role of Paul Kersey for *Death Wish 4: The Crackdown*. The subtitle is a deceptively clever play on words referencing both Kersey's lethal crackdown on the local mafia, as well as the crack cocaine they're peddling on the streets. This was 1988, in the midst of America's deadly crack epidemic.

An early sales ad for *Death Wish 4*, made before the movie was shot and making use of a photo from *Death Wish III*.

This third sequel was penned by Gail Morgan Hickman, who had been hired to write *Death Wish 3* but whose drafts were ultimately passed on in favor of the version written by Don Jakoby and then over-written by Michael Winner. Hickman's first credit as a screenwriter had been the Dirty Harry sequel, *The Enforcer* (1976). He also wrote *Murphy's Law* and the oft-delayed *Number One With A Bullet* (1987) for Cannon.

Filmmaker J. Lee Thompson was hired to direct this time, being a long-time favorite of both Cannon's and Bronson's. (Thompson made eight films with the studio, and nine with the star; you can read about his full, illustrious career in this volume's chapter on *10 to Midnight*.) Michael Winner, who'd directed every entry in the *Death Wish* series thus far, had his hands full making the Agatha Christie adaptation *Appointment with Death* (1988), which Cannon would release the following year.

This time around we find Paul Kersey back in Los Angeles and in a relationship with another journalist, Karen, played by Kay Lenz, an actress three decades his junior. (Lenz is well-known to horror fans for starring in 1985's *House*.) He's become something of a father figure to her teenage daughter, Erica, played by Dana Barron, who had previously played Chevy Chase's daughter, Audrey, on *National Lampoon's Vacation* (1983). Of course such a happy home life can't possibly last more than a few pages into a *Death Wish* script, and Erica soon dies from a crack overdose given to her by her boyfriend's dealer. Kersey, not one to stand by and let the law run its course, stalks the drug dealer to a local amusement park and shoots him to death in a cool sequence that's inter-cut with the chaos of a bumper cars ride.

Kersey soon receives a phone call from a mysterious millionaire named Nathan White, who is played with an unplaceable, Soviet-sounding accent by the ever-magnificent John P. Ryan. (Cannon fans may recognize the perpetually intense Ryan from his other villainous turns in 1985's *Runaway Train*, 1986's *Avenging Force*, and 1990's *Delta Force 2*. If they needed an over-the-top bad guy, there was no better actor for them to call.) In a stunning twist, White reveals that he knows about Kersey's vigilante past, and that he wants to hire Kersey to enact revenge upon the narcotics pushers who were responsible for his own daughter's death. Enticed by White's limitless finances to fund his arsenal and purchase criminal information, Kersey can't resist the opportunity to wipe out an entire drug ring.

White explains to him that the illegal narcotics trade in Los Angeles is controlled by two crime families. One is led by mobster Ed Zaccharias, played by Perry Lopez, best remembered as police Lieutenant Escobar in 1974's *Chinatown*. (Lopez appeared in another Cannon film, 1989's *Kinjite: Forbidden Subjects*, also opposite Bronson.) The other family is led by the Romero brothers, Tony (Dan Ferro) and Jack (Mike Moroff).

In a plot reminiscent of 1961's *Yojimbo*—Hickman's screenplay was inspired by the Kurosawa film as well as its Western remake, *A Fistful of Dollars* (1964)—Kersey pits the two gangs against each other by picking off a few of their most prominent members and making their deaths look like the work of a competitor in the drugs game. In *Death Wish 4* Kersey relies on cleverness as much as his revolver, sneaking into a crime lord's birthday party by posing as a caterer and later killing off a trio of enforcers—one played by a young Danny Trejo—with explosives hidden inside a bottle of fine wine. He goes on to snuff out a ruthless hitman, blow up a drugs processing plant, and take out a dealer posing as a video store manager in a scene that's literally wallpapered in posters for other Cannon movies.

The entire time Kersey is pursued by a pair of cops, Reiner (George Dickerson of *Blue Velvet* [1986]) and Nozaki, who was played by Soon Tek-Oh and last seen as Chuck Norris' torturer in the 1984 Cannon film *Missing in Action 2: The Beginning*. Nozaki is revealed to be crooked, and gets killed by Kersey in a failed attempt on his life. Kersey eventually lures the leaders of both cartels into a peace summit at an abandoned oil field, where he snipes Zaccharias from a concealed spot, spurring a violent shootout in which the remaining gang members essentially massacre one another. Soon afterwards Kersey learns that he was hoodwinked by his enigmatic benefactor: White, it turns out, wasn't the suspiciously wealthy and concerned citizen he was posing to be, but a competing drug lord with his sights on taking over the LA narcotics trade, and whose job Kersey just made a whole lot easier.

When White's attempts to have Kersey removed from the picture fail repeatedly, he kidnaps the beautiful, innocent Karen to lure the pissed-off vigilante out of the shadows. This leads to another lengthy, very cool shootout to close a *Death Wish* movie, which begins in a parking garage—filmed in the garage attached to Cannon's headquarters—and makes its way through a crowded roller rink, finally ending in a showdown between White and Kersey behind the building. White kills yet another one of Kersey's love interests in cold blood, and Kersey retaliates by blowing him up with Cannon's now-signature finishing move: a short-range blast from a rocket launcher.

The fourth movie's video release was a bigger success than its theatrical one.

The fourth *Death Wish* may not match its predecessor's insane levels of violence or the first movie's grit and tension, but it's my personal favorite of the series. Bronson's performance is comfortable and lively here. At least, he doesn't seem visibly embarrassed that he's appearing in the film (as he does in parts of *Death Wish 3*.) Hickman's screenplay, though far-fetched, isn't as preposterous as the last movie's script, and its stabs at dark comedy feel more intentional and land far better than *Death Wish 3*'s. Plus, J. Lee Thompson comes off as a far more proficient director than Winner, with several sequences—such as the roller rink chase and the bumper cars shootout—being among the most visually exciting of the entire franchise. (The director's son, Peter Lee-Thompson, edited *Death Wish 4* and five other Cannon movies, include *10 to Midnight* and 1985's *American Ninja*.)

By its fourth installment, theater-goers were finally losing interest in the increasingly hard-to-believe exploits of vigilante Paul Kersey. Cannon gave the film an early-November release date, similar to the one with which they'd had so much success for *Death Wish 3*. The movie failed to crack $7 million in domestic box office, nearly $10 million less than the prior entry. (Ironically, it was *Death Wish 4* which received the best reviews out of all of the sequels.) Some relatively fantastic video sales and successful international releases helped make up the difference for Cannon, but the fourth entry would be the final one the company would produce, at least officially.

The onset of the 1990s was a dark time for both Bronson and Cannon. Jill Ireland, Bronson's wife, succumbed to her long and public fight against breast cancer in the early summer of 1990. This happened only six months after the death of her adopted son, Jason McCallum, from a drug overdose. Grieving over the loss of his wife and the stepson he raised, Bronson is said to have lost much of his passion for making movies.

Meanwhile, years of questionable bookkeeping and financial overextension led to the near-death of Cannon as a film company. A buyout may have briefly saved the Cannon brand, but it couldn't save the relationship between its colorful heads, Golan and Globus. The cousins suffered a bitter falling out. Globus, the duo's money man, stayed behind with the Cannon survivors while Golan, the creative mind, left to become the head of another production company, the 21st Century Film Corporation. While his new company did not survive into the actual twenty-first century, it made a number of movies that were very much Cannon films in spirt, including a fifth (and final) *Death Wish* movie.

Released in the early weeks of 1994, *Death Wish V: The Face of Death*—a movie featuring so much death that they had to mention it twice in the title—

was Bronson's final leading role which showed in movie theaters. While he'd returned to acting by this point, it was mostly in easier TV movie roles. Golan had reportedly offered him $5 million to reprise his famous Kersey character one last time, and Bronson probably found that hard to refuse. His paycheck appears to have been higher than the rest of *Death Wish V*'s shoestring budget and much, much higher than the $1.7 million it made back in theaters. Golan, who was in rather dire financial straits at the time, had to repeatedly cut back the movie's budget, eventually removing original director Steve Carver (Cannon's *River of Death*, 1989) and replacing him with Canadian filmmaker Allan A. Goldstein, solely because our northern neighbors offered attractive tax breaks to studios who would film there with a majority Canadian cast and crew. While the plot of the movie takes place in New York City, it was rather unconvincingly filmed in Toronto.

Death Wish V ends the storied franchise not with a bang, but with a deflated whimper. Bronson, who was now in his 70s, was less keen on filming action scenes, and had expressed his desire to make the character more sympathetic. Here he's once again in a relationship with a much younger woman, and a father figure to her daughter. This time it's the mom's turn to die, and Kersey has to fight to keep the girl safe from her birth father—who implausibly happens to be a murderous crime boss played by another classic character actor, Michael Parks. The prolific Parks was a favorite of many cult directors, appearing in movies such as *From Dusk til Dawn* (1996) and *Kill Bill* (2003), and had a recurring role as the villainous Jean Renault on the seminal TV series *Twin Peaks* (1990–1991). His lone Cannon performance was as Chuck Norris' traitorous partner in their 1991 film, *The Hitman*.

Once again, here Kersey relies as much on his brain as bullets and brawn to dismantle the mob. In one of the movie's funniest highlights, Kersey kills a Mafioso by hiding a bomb inside a remote-controlled soccer ball.

After the disaster that was *Death Wish V*'s theatrical release played out, Bronson was done with Paul Kersey. Golan announced plans to make a *Death Wish VI* which would introduce a new vigilante following in Kersey's footsteps, but his company went bankrupt before the film could come to fruition.

Bronson's only remaining screen appearances were in a trilogy of made-for-TV thrillers, and he made his retirement permanent in 1999. In his remaining years, Bronson struggled through Alzheimer's. He passed away in 2003, at the age of 81.

For all of its notoriety, the *Death Wish* series proved bountiful to both its star and the studio that produced it. For Bronson, the Paul Kersey role is the one that finally earned his name top billing on a Hollywood film, and kept it there through the final decades of his career. To think that without *Death Wish*, most of us would probably only remember Bronson as a memorable supporting character in a few really good Sixties war movies and Spaghetti Westerns, rather than as one of cinema's all-time ultimate badasses. For Cannon, it provided a string of successes which provided not only financial benefits for the company, but a glimmer of legitimacy in an industry that had not previously taken them seriously. Even if they carried over all of the original movie's violence and none of its nuance, their *Death Wish* sequels—at least numbers *3* and *4*—are quintessential Cannon movies.

Lady Chatterley's Lover

Release date: May 7, 1982
Directed by: Just Jaeckin
Written by: Marc Behm, Just Jaeckin, Christopher Wicking
Starring: Sylvia Kristel, Shane Briant, Nicholas Clay
Trailer Voiceover: "She was beautiful, and sensual, and bold. She had everything money could buy, but she had a husband whose manhood was crippled by war. A man who could give her everything, except . . . *love.*"

What is erotica, really, but pornography with pretense? When it comes to cinema, at least, there's often very little that separates an "erotic film" from pornography; even today, there are plenty of movies playing in arthouse theaters that are more explicit than what you'd catch late at night on a pay cable channel. There is typically a stronger plot running through a piece of erotic cinema, and perhaps a more caring approach to aesthetics. Sometimes there are well-known talent in front of or behind the camera, and these directors or stars will choose to shoot only semi-explicit sex scenes just so that nobody can actually call what they're doing "porn." Other times it comes down to the overall quality of the picture. Most often, however, the only thing drawing a line between a movie being called an "erotic film" or falling under the label of that dreaded p-word is the film's *attitude*. Does the film feel like something cultured folks will discuss over fine wine and caviar, or something that will be watched on a grubby VHS dub by a teenager with a tissue in his hand?

Cannon makes their first foray into erotic literary adaptations: *Lady Chatterley's Lover* on VHS.

Erotic cinema boomed in the 1970s. In 1972 the U.S. saw the release of Bernardo Bertolucci's infamous *Last Tango in Paris*, which starred no more prestigious an actor than Marlon Brando. The movie released a floodgate of controversy over its graphic content, but in spite of its X-rating it was a triumphant, box office smash and opened the doors for many more dirty, artsy-fartsy movies to follow. The same year also saw the release of the porn-and-proud-of-it *Deep Throat* (1972), one of the first pornographic movies to be discussed by both mainstream film critics and television talk show hosts like Johnny Carson. It went on to be one of the highest-grossing films of the era and ushered in what historians later dubbed The Golden Age of Porn. It was a boom that was echoed through European cinema, as well.

Cannon would produce a good number of artsy, erotic films throughout their run, but their first was their most ballyhooed. It was a movie they took out a full-page ad for in *Variety* to proudly boast that "Cannon Presents Box Office Gold For 1981:" an adaption of D.H. Lawrence's landmark literary work *Lady Chatterley's Lover*, one of history's most famous, controversial, and highly-regarded pieces of smut. For their star, they would turn to none other than soft-porn royalty: Miss Sylvia Kristel.

Sylvia Kristel (left) with Nicholas Clay in a Spanish press still for the film.

Born in the Netherlands, Kristel had been a beauty queen and model before entering the film industry. She appeared in only a handful of small roles before she was cast in her most famous film, *Emmanuelle*, in which she played the young wife of a diplomat who passes her time by engaging in taboo sex acts with a rogue's gallery of extramarital lovers. Released in France in 1974, *Emmanuelle* became one of the country's most successful films of all time, playing in one Parisian theater for ten straight years. The movie made its way around the world, too, raking in loads of cash—especially in the U.S. and

Japan—and then again on home video. (*Emmanuelle*'s totals are estimated to be north of $100 million.) It was a touchstone for softcore pornography, spurring six official sequels—four of them featuring Kristel—and many, many exploitative knock-offs, such as the *Black Emmanuelle* series out of Italy and a ridiculous American series called *Emmanuelle in Space*.

The film's unprecedented popularity catapulted the young Kristel to international sex symbol status. (In a 2007 profile feature, the U.K. newspaper *The Independent* respectfully dubbed her "the world's most famous porn star.") Unfortunately, though, it also torpedoed any hopes she had of becoming a serious, mainstream actor. She was typecast into roles where clothes weren't simply optional, but were barely an option at all. As she put it herself, audiences preferred her with her clothes off—although, she admitted later in life that financial issues stemming from her troubles with drug and alcohol necessitated her taking roles she probably shouldn't have.

That reputation didn't stop her from giving a mainstream career a go, however, and a move to Hollywood led to appearances in films like *The Fifth Musketeer* (1979), *Get Smart* reboot *The Nude Bomb* (1980), an *Airport* sequel, and the taboo teen sex comedy *Private Lessons* (1981), in which she plays a foreign housemaid who seduces a teenage boy. Two of her highest-profile American films of this era, however, would come from The Cannon Group: *Lady Chatterley's Lover* and *Mata Hari* (1985).

It's easy to see why Golan and Globus considered scoring a contract with Kristel to be a major coup for their budding company. Here they had one of France's biggest box office stars: a tried-and-true sex icon with a built-in international audience. How could they possibly lose? To further ensure their first movie with her would be a can't-miss hit, Cannon reunited their new leading lady with her *Emmanuelle* director, French filmmaker Just Jaeckin.

Emmanuelle had been Just Jaeckin's first movie; his training to that point had been in photography. He'd followed up his rookie hit with the even racier, S&M-driven *The Story of O* in 1975. (This one's famous for its butt-branding scene, and because it was effectively banned in the U.K. for 25 years.) With these two films—both shot with far more of an eye for style than the average exploitation movie—Jaeckin firmly established himself as a premier erotic filmmaker. His movies weren't just filthy: they were a somewhat *classy* kind of filthy.

The copy accompanying this sales catalog entry described the film as being "based on the most erotic novel of our century."

Jaeckin adapted D.H. Lawrence's novel with screenwriter Christopher Wicking, who'd written a great many enjoyable Hammer horror films. (Marc Behm—co-writer of Cannon's *Hospital Massacre*—also had a hand in *Chatterley*'s screenplay.) Sylvia Kristel's contract with Cannon reputedly contained a number of special stipulations, including that she would have say over the casting of the male lead—with whom she'd be performing more than a few intimate love scenes—and that the film would be cut in a way that would leave enough to the imagination for it to receive the equivalent of a PG-rating. (If true, that stipulation had certainly gone out the window by the time the movie had arrived at the editing room.) Filming occurred mostly at Wrotham Park in Hertfordshire, England, a shooting location popular for its stately, eighteenth century elegance.

We're introduced to young Lady Constance Chatterley (Kristel) on the eve of the First World War. She's at a party held by her pompous, ass-hat of a husband, Clifford Chatterley (Shane Briant), presumably to show her off to his fellow members of the English aristocracy. Although he shows no outward signs of it in the film, we're to believe that Clifford possesses some attractive qualities beyond his title and enormous wealth, as Constance—or Connie, as he calls her—is hopelessly devoted to the man. Their stuffy celebration is deflated by the all-time, ultimate party killer as war breaks out during their champagne hour. Soon we see Clifford heroically charge into battle, rifle raised, under intense gunfire. He's wounded and falls, only to be rescued by allied medics.

Then, the war is over as quickly as it broke out. (Literally: the first few minutes of the film span the entirety of WWI.) Clifford has returned home, where he's doted upon by his adoring wife. He's also paralyzed from the waist down, thus totally unequipped to get down and dirty with his smoldering bride. Well aware that he can't satisfy all of her sexier, physical needs, he makes an indecent-yet-surprisingly-generous proposal: he permits her to take a lover, just so long as it's not some dirty, scrubby peasant boy.

So what does Connie do? She goes out and falls madly for the first lower-class fella she lays eyes upon. Oliver Mellors is a vulgar, earthy guy with a handsome body and even handsomer moustache. It's literally lust at first sight as Connie wanders in on him showering in the forest. Her brief glimpse of his well-lathered butt becomes the focal point of the soft-focus masturbation montage we're treated to soon afterward. An affair between the two quickly follows. Unfortunately for Mellors, he's one of those dirty poor people that Clifford despises so much; worse still, he's employed as the groundskeeper of her husband's estate, and lives in a shack in the woods just behind their house. It's far from the ideal setup for a covert love affair.

Actor Nicholas Clay, best remembered for playing Sir Lancelot in *Excalibur* (1981), was the filmmakers' third choice to take on the role of Mellors in *Lady Chatterley's Lover*. Their first choice had been actor Ian McShane, who had been romantically involved with Kristel for several years prior to shooting; he'd since remarried, and his new wife forced him to drop out as she was (understandably) uncomfortable with him shooting sex scenes with his ex-lover. Oliver Reed—who'd just filmed *Dr. Heckyl and Mr. Hype* for Cannon—was also offered the role, but he turned it down, and the part went to Clay.

Early on in the film, Clifford seems weirdly tickled by the thought of his wife getting her rocks off with another man. When the pompous paraplegic starts to figure out just who is laying it to his spouse, however, their happy little arrangement quickly sours. This is decidedly different from Lawrence's book, wherein Clifford is mostly unaware of his wife's affair with Groundskeeper Willie until the very end. The choice to stray here is actually a good one, as it adds a bit of drama and suspicion to break up all of the artfully-photographed humping. As Clifford's jealousy grows, he finds creative ways to demean Mellors in front of Connie, making his servant go so far as to carry around his limp-ass body and push his wheelchair through ankle-deep mud. To stress just how much Clifford hates the poor, he even refers to the lower class as no better than "human meat," which is something you're only allowed to say if you're a cannibal or a tyrannosaurus rex. War hero or not, this guy is pretty hate-able.

Really, though, it's all just padding for the film's myriad sex scenes, which are truly the cream filling of this literary and cinematic Twinkie. There are (expectedly) quite a few erotic scenes, although some—depending on your point of view—are more weird than arousing. There's one in which Constance and Mellors give in to their carnal passions on the floor of a chicken coop, surely contracting E. coli from all of the bird shit under their bucking asses. The strangest, though, comes straight from the book, where Mellors covers his nude lover's intimate bits in a layer of freshly-picked flowers. It's not his turning her into a human funeral bouquet that struck me as strange, but the way he follows it up by sticking flower petals in his own mouth, and then

French-kissing all of that vegetation into hers. I assume some people out there are into being force-fed fauna, but you can't imagine it tastes very good.

It all comes to a head, in a rather underwhelming manner, when Clifford catches his wife and her lover in the act, and then Connie decides to take a trip abroad to mull over whether or not she'll leave her husband. We don't get to see much in the way of fallout from her decision, which is disappointing. It all resolves super quickly, and feels very abrupt.

A German lobby card featuring Sylvia Kristel as a fleshy flower pot.

Cannon—Golan, in particular—had wanted to meddle with *Lady Chatterley's Lover* in the editing room. Jaeckin put his foot down by refusing to do any of the erotic scenes unless he had full creative control. You can guess who won.

In the end, *Lady Chatterley's Lover* wasn't the box office smash that Cannon was banking on, but that didn't stop them from trying again with another Sylvia Kristel starring vehicle in *Mata Hari* just three years later. We have to assume this particular movie's lack of success was disappointing to the actress, but it was clear she was quite proud of the feature when she told *The Sydney Morning Herald* that *Lady Chatterley* was "the first time [she'd] liked acting." Critics were lukewarm on her performance, but to be fair Kristel wasn't given much room to act—her dialogue had been dubbed over by another, anonymous actress in post-production, presumably to give her character an English accent rather than a Dutch one.

The movie fared better on video and in late-night cable showings. (For obvious reasons.)

Our heroes emerge from an unbuttoned fly in the U.S. artwork for *The Last American Virgin*.

The Last American Virgin

Release Date: July 30, 1982
Directed by: Boaz Davidson
Written by: Boaz Davidson
Starring: Lawrence Monoson, Steve Antin, Joe Rubbo, Diane Franklin
Trailer Voiceover: "*The Last American Virgin*: See it ... or be it!"

The 1980s were the Golden Age for teen comedies. Mixing the goopy sentimentality of John Hughes' films with the barefaced raunch of sex comedies like *Porky's*, 1982's *The Last American Virgin* is not only Cannon's most memorable foray into the genre, but among the highest-regarded films in all of the Cannon canon.

One of Golan and Globus' earliest plans for their newly-acquired Cannon Films was to do an Americanized remake of *Lemon Popsicle*, a low-budget teen movie they'd produced in Israel in 1978 and had gone on, quite unexpectedly, to be a global smash. The racy little comedy—written and directed by Boaz Davidson, and based on his own youth in Tel Aviv—sold more than a million tickets in its native country within its first year of release, turning it into one of Israel's highest-grossing films of all time. Hundreds of additional prints were made and sent abroad, and the movie proved quite popular across Europe and, perhaps most surprisingly, in Japan. It was nominated for a Golden Globe, was Israel's official submission to the Academy Awards, and spawned a long-running franchise of sequels, spin-offs, and reboots. This was the sort of wildfire success that a producer could hang their hat upon, and had played a major role in building up Golan and Globus' reputation within the international film community.

The United States was one market where the original *Lemon Popsicle* had failed to take off. The Cannon producers recruited the movie's original filmmaker, Boaz Davidson, to helm the remake. Davidson had since moved from Israel to the U.S. seeking his own fortune in Hollywood, just like Golan and Globus. What followed was a movie that, save for a few extra shots of boobies and butts and some changes to better localize the story to an early '80s SoCal setting, was remarkably faithful to the Israeli original.

Our heroes, from left to right: Gary (Lawrence Monoson), Rick (Steve Antin), and David (Joe Rubbo).

The Last American Virgin revolves around a trio of lads, seniors at a Los Angeles area high school. The film's de facto lead is Gary, a skinny kid with a pizza-delivery job, a greaser hairdo, and a romantic heart. He's played by Lawrence Monoson, who was just sixteen at the time and making his acting debut; he actually had to present the producers with a fake ID saying he was eighteen so that he could be hired on the film. Monoson would go on to have roles in the 1980s cult classics *MASK* (1985) and *Friday the 13th: The Final Chapter* (1984), and become a steady television actor.

Gary's best friends are the more popular and good-looking ladies' man, Rick, and the husky jokester, David. Rick is played by Steve Antin, who went on to play the bully, Troy, in *The Goonies* (1985) and the titular Jessie in the music video for Rick Springfield's "Jessie's Girl." David is played by Joe Rubbo, who'd have a very similar role in a subsequent Cannon teen comedy, *Hot Chili* (1985).

Rick's caught in the act with a girlfriend (Gerri Idol) in this press photo, which ran alongside many European reviews of the movie.

The Last American Virgin rolls out largely as a series of vignettes chronicling our boys' tireless attempts to get laid. The movie opens with one of its most memorable sequences, in which the trio picks up three teenybopper girls from a local fast food joint by inviting them to a big party at Gary's house. (The party is, of course, a lie.) When they get there not only is there no party—but the boys have to scramble to find a way to cover up the fact that they don't actually have any of the hip drugs that they had promised the girls. Making use of what little resources they have on hand, they cut white lines from Sweet'N Low packets, which are then passed around the living room and snorted. It turns out the girls, like the boys, are only pretending to have experience with this sort of stuff: not only do they believe them that the sugar substitute is cocaine, but they make comments about its high quality.

As their makeshift party starts to pick up, David disappears into a bedroom with the blond Brenda (Tessa Richarde) and Rick goes off with a redhead named Roxanne (Gerri Idol). This leaves Gary alone in the living room with the ostensibly prudish Millie (Winifred Freedman). Despite putting on that she's thoroughly disinterested in any hanky-panky, she allows Gary to remove her blouse just in time for his parents to arrive home, catching him on the couch with a partially-undressed young lady; his pal, Rick, with a topless harlot; and their son's buddy, David, undressed in their marital bed.

The movie, of course, has one of those obligatory, girls' locker room peephole scenes, which a lot of people will blame on *Porky's* (1981), but this movie actually predates that one. (*Virgin* was filmed in 1980, but it took two years before it saw theatrical release.) The peeping scene is followed by a ridiculous dick-measuring contest, complete with a parade of fake boners tenting out countless pairs of whitey-tighties.

Another memorable scene is when the three boys visit the home of an older woman (and evident nymphomaniac) named Carmela, played by Cannon regular Louisa Moritz. As the three boys sit half-dressed on her couch debating the order in which they'll take each of their turns in her bedroom, her sailor boyfriend unexpectedly returns home early—which sends the boys fleeing for their lives. It's a simple but very funny scene, and one that Cannon

THE CANNON FILM GUIDE, VOL.1 (1980–1984)

was so clearly pleased with that they repeated it again in 1985's *Hot Chili*, all the way down to having Moritz paired again with her *Virgin* co-star, Joe Rubbo.

The other guys eavesdrop as Rick undresses Carmela (Louisa Moritz).

Moritz was a Cuban-American character actress well-known for playing prostitutes and ditzy blondes. She made memorable appearances in *One Flew Over the Cuckoo's Nest* and Roger Corman's *Death Race 2000* (both 1975), *Up In Smoke* (1978), and *Chained Heat* (1983), as well as Cannon's *New Year's Evil* (1980). Contrary to the airheaded roles she typically played throughout her career, Moritz studied at Yale University and practiced law after she had largely moved on from entertainment. Near the end of her life she was suddenly again, but for an unfortunate reason: as one of the prominent victims in Bill Cosby's sexual assault scandal.

In *The Last American Virgin*, the glue that holds together of all these sequences of wacky, adolescent lechery is a stormy love triangle which develops between Gary, Rick, and a beautiful new girl in school named Karen, played by Diane Franklin. Franklin is probably most often recognized as the French foreign exchange student who wins John Cusack's heart in *Better Off Dead...* (1985). She was also very memorable as one of the time-traveling princesses in *Bill & Ted's Excellent Adventure* (1989), and as the star of the Empire Pictures b-horror classic *TerrorVision* (1986). This was the curly-haired actress' first movie role.

Gary falls hard for the comely transfer student at first sight, but she's only got eyes for his more handsome best friend, Rick. While Gary dreams of true, blue, everlasting love, Rick's number one priority is to get into Karen's pants as quickly as possible. Gary lacks his friend's good looks and confidence, and so rather than assert himself he passively steps aside and lets Rick have the girl. Karen winds up tossed aside, and worse: pregnant. Still head-over-heels for her, Gary pawns off most of his belongings and scrapes together the money needed to pay for Karen's abortion, believing foolishly that it might help her see him for the good guy that he is.

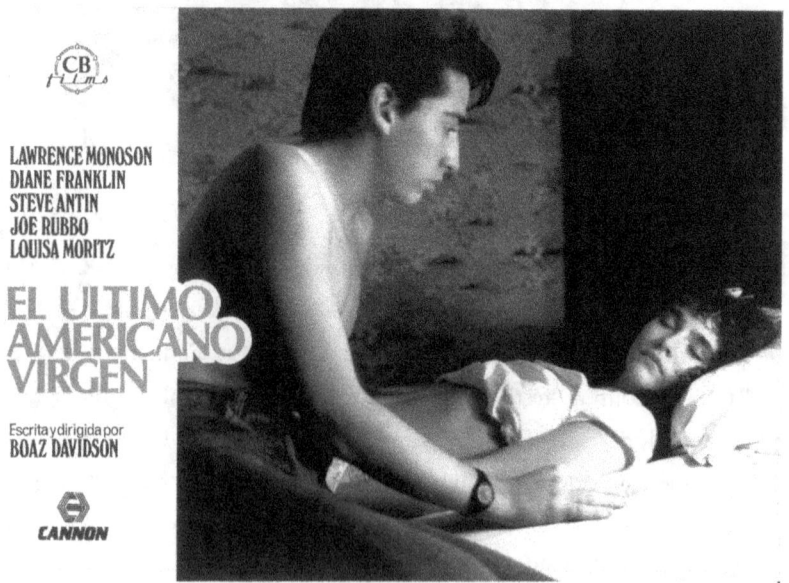

Gary pines hopelessly over the sleeping Karen (Diane Franklin).

The Last American Virgin's abortion scene is infamous. As U2's jarringly chipper "I Will Follow" plays on the soundtrack, Karen is stripped naked and strapped down to an operating table. (The song choice is even more disturbing when you learn that the lyrics are about a mother's unconditional love for her child.) The scene itself is filmed in a way that's more intimate (disturbingly) scintillating than the movie's sex scenes. Whether intentional or not, it leaves most viewers feeling sufficiently icky afterwards.

While the abortion sequence and its poppy soundtrack were controversial, it's the movie's abrupt, unhappy ending that is more divisive among viewers. After Gary pays for Karen's expensive procedure, he confesses his love for her. Believing for himself that, for once, the good guy has finally landed the girl, Gary attends Karen's birthday party only to find the girl of his dreams once again making out with slimy Rick, the guy who had tossed her aside after getting her into trouble in the first place. The movie ends with Gary driving away from the party in silence, tears streaming down his face.

It's a real damn heartbreaker, I'll tell you. There's not a single person in the audience who isn't rooting for Gary to land the girl, but most of us—adults, at least—are wise enough to know that life, especially when we're adolescents, doesn't always turn out the way we hope it will. We also understand teenagers can be pretty shitty people. At some point, most people have probably been on one side or the other of Gary's unrequited, youthful infatuation.

Some people walk away from the ending of *The Last American Virgin* absolutely hating the fact that the hero doesn't win. Others often admire the film for its frankness. Not everyone gets their happy ending, after all.

It really helps a lot that *The Last American Virgin*'s cast members look and talk like real-life teenagers. Of the four main characters, none had done a feature film before. Boaz Davidson has said that he preferred working with newcomers, as he felt that their performances would feel rawer than a seasoned screen actor's. His theory rings true here at least, as the performances across the board are more believable than any you'd get from the slick, polished teens you'd see in the bigger, studio films and sitcoms of the era. They're also much preferable to "teens" played by actors in their late 20s, as you'd see in most other, R-rated sex comedies.

This full-page ad ran in *Variety* before the cast was even finalized. At this point, Gary Dubin (Punky Lazaar on *The Partridge Family*) and future *Days of Our Lives* star Kristian Alfonso were slated to play the roles of Gary and Karen, respectively.

A few more notable fresh faces making their screen debuts include Kimmy Robertson, who'd play the spacy receptionist, Lucy Moran, on *Twin Peaks* (1990–1991). (If you've watched the, you can still conjure up her voice.) Playing the dowdy, cocaine-loving young lady who was paired off with Gary at the boy's "party" is character actress Winifred Freedman, who later co-starred on the *Happy Days* spinoff *Joanie Loves Chachi* (1982–1983) and also appeared in

The Naked Gun (1982) and one of Cannon's mid-era Chuck Norris vehicles, *Hero and the Terror* (1988). Brian Peck, best known as a punk rocker, Scuz, in *Return of the Living Dead* (1985), played the nerdy classmate with an enormous pecker.

The open fly motif was retained on this Turkish poster, which also advertises the soundtrack credits. The artist apparently either wasn't given a cast photo, or just didn't care that much about capturing anyone's likeness.

Let's talk about the movie's amazing soundtrack for a bit, shall we? Just as they'd done with *Lemon Popsicle*—which spent almost a third of its budget licensing songs from Bill Haley, Little Richard, Chuck Berry, and other 1950s pop idols—the music is woven throughout *The Last American Virgin* and cements it within its chosen time period. To update their American remake for the new decade, Davidson and Cannon moved away from oldies in favor of a modern, New Wave soundtrack by cutting edge artists like Blondie, Devo, The Police, The Cars, Journey, Tommy Tutone, and a pre-superstardom U2. Among the songs featured most prominently is Gleaming Spires' "Are You Ready For The Sex Girls?", utilized to quite humorous effect in *Virgin* and then later re-used in 1984's *Revenge of the Nerds*. (Those with a VHS copy of *The Last American Virgin* will also hear The Human League's "Love Action," which was used without the band's permission and then removed from subsequent releases of the movie.) The songs and bands picked for this soundtrack were legitimately hip, and Cannon splurged and went so far as to release the film in a stereo mix, which in those days was rare for a movie of this size and genre.

Alas, *The Last American Virgin* failed to live up to the high expectations that the studio held for it at the box office—after all, *Lemon Popsicle* had spawned a very profitable franchise in its native Israel. *The Last American Virgin* failed to gain much ground in its surprisingly small theatrical release in the late summer of 1982. The final box office tally was just under $6 million, in contrast to the cool, $105 million brought in by the similarly-themed *Porky's* (1981). This naturally put the kibosh on Cannon making any sequels, even though they'd signed the cast on to a multi-picture option from the start. A second movie was announced but never came to fruition, and would have placed the *Virgin* gang on a cruise ship opposite Cannon's favorite softporn starlet, Sylvia Kristel.

Perhaps the ending was too much of a bummer for American moviegoers, or maybe some of the subject matter too serious for audiences hoping for another brainless, T&A-fueled sex comedy. Fortunately, the videocassette release proved popular—sporting provocative cover art and heavily touting its trendy soundtrack—and frequent cable showings helped the movie find its way to impressionable youth, allowing it to achieve a well-deserved cult following over the decades since its release. *The Last American Virgin* may not have been among the highest-earning of the '80s teen sex comedies, but those who saw it were unlikely to forget it.

The curly-haired Karen (Diane Franklin) was brought to the forefront of the movie's Spanish print ads.

Interview: Actress Diane Franklin

One of the 1980s' iconic starlets, you might recognize Diane Franklin as the French exchange student who captures John Cusack's fancy in *Better Off Dead* ... (1985), a time-traveling princess in *Bill & Ted's Excellent Adventure* (1989), or from her scream queen roles in *Amityville II: The Possession* (1982) or *Ter-*

rorVision (1986). Of course, Cannon fans will know her from her big screen debut as Karen, the hero's unrequited love interest in their classic teen comedy *The Last American Virgin*. It was the role that launched her career, and a performance that few who have seen the movie are likely to forget.

Franklin stays very busy to this day, both as an actor and as a writer. Her autobiography, *Diane Franklin: The Excellent Adventures of the Last American, French-Exchange Babe of the 80s*, was released in 2012, and offers a candid, first-person account of being a young film actor in the 1980s. (The book is a treasure trove of wonderful anecdotes about the making of *The Last American Virgin*). In her second book, *Diane Franklin: The Excellent Curls of the Last American, French-Exchange Babe of the 80s*, she explores how she kick started the decade's curly hair movement in Hollywood.

A self-motivated young woman who had done a lot of modeling but had yet break into movies, Franklin decided at the last minute to leave during a college science exam so that she could audition for *The Last American Virgin*. We pick up her story there.

The Cannon Film Guide: You skipped out in the middle of a chemistry test to audition for *Last American Virgin*. What was going through your mind that day?

Diane Franklin: I knew that was a sad moment in my science career, and a low point in my scholastic education. Luckily I was able to drop the class. The moment I left, it wasn't like I knew I would never be a chemistry major, but I did know that particular test was a no-go.

When I got to the audition, they told me they wanted me to fly out the next week and that we would be shooting that weekend. That all took me by surprise! So I did the film, and then when I came back, I went back to school. I just thought, "Okay, so I missed that semester, I'll just go on to the next semester." But then when I started back at school, what happens? I got *Amityville II* (1982). Every time I went back at school, all of a sudden my career would start moving forward.

I guess I just didn't want to wait around for a career to happen. I just went, "I'm going to keep living life." I was going to keep auditioning as I was going to school, and whatever direction life took me, I'd follow.

You had to meet with Menahem Golan and Yoram Globus before shooting. What do you recall of your meeting with them?

The first time I was at the Cannon offices was in Los Angeles. Oh my gosh, it was so exciting. Thinking back now on the building, it was kind of old and wasn't that glamorous, but to me it was so exciting. It was in this tall office building on Hollywood Boulevard. I went in there and I remember meeting with Boaz Davidson and his wife, Bruria, who did the editing.

I auditioned with a few different guys: a couple different Gary's, but only one Rick. We just knew right away. Lawrence [Monoson] was so sweet. And Steve Antin, it's funny—he's so nice in person, but he was such a jerk when he was playing Rick in the movie. It was so amazing. I was very happy to be there. It was such a wonderful feeling to be around so many people you felt you could trust.

You were asked to stay over in Los Angeles, and shooting began right after that. How much time did you have to prepare yourself before cameras starting rolling?

Not much! [*Laughs*] By that point, though, I'd pretty much memorized the script. I usually tried to memorize a script before I went on the first audition. My attitude was that if you made the extra effort and knew the character so well, the director could tell you to go to any scene and you could do it. I was ready to do it because I'd already memorized it. That way, then, I could also just be free, and be the character.

Boaz did want me to see a scene from *Lemon Popsicle* because it clarified a moment in the film. I met Joe Rubbo—he and I were the only two flying in for the movie, so they put us up in a hotel. We were at the Holiday Inn in Hollywood. I don't think it even exists anymore, but it had a rotating restaurant at the top and we'd go up there for breakfast. A car would pick us up to take us to the locations. *Everything* in that movie was shot on location.

It all happened so quickly. Because they went through my agent and SAG, it felt to me like it was a real movie and that I could trust them. The paperwork was all signed, and the stipulations about nudity were written in the contracts. I knew what I was going to be doing in the movie; there was no last-minute, "Hey, why don't we try this?"

You mentioned that you watched part of the original movie, *Lemon Popsicle*, to help you understand the character. Did the whole cast watch it together?

When I watched it, it was just a scene and it was just me and Boaz. I will say that I knew *Lemon Popsicle* had sequels. When I went to do *Virgin*, in my contract they hadn't signed me on to do sequels. I knew that they'd signed the guys on, but not me. I was kind of like, "Aw, really? Why not me?" [*Laughs*] But I heard that the *Lemon Popsicle*s didn't have me in the sequels, either.

How would you describe Boaz Davidson as a director, and as a person?

Oh, he is very nice! Very nice! He was in his . . . late 30s? I don't know. Maybe he could have been younger. Anyway, to me he was very calming and direct. He was sensitive, more than anything. He's probably one of the most sensitive directors I've ever worked with. Obviously he knew I'd have to be doing the nudity, and he knew how to handle that. He'd done enough films with young women. I was over eighteen when I did *Virgin*, but he still knew he was dealing with someone very young. When you want to bring out these performances, you have to be mature enough to know how to work with young actors.

To this day I thank him so much for casting me in this film, because it meant so much to me—and I think it's because it meant so much to him. I think that's why all of us did so well in it. For most of us, it was our first big film. It was all because we trusted him, and because he loved the film so much.

Can you pick one scene or day on set that stuck most vividly in your mind, or that you hold closest to your heart?

It would have to be the last scene, for sure. We shot all the party scenes in the same house, so we shot that last scene the same day we shot all the party scenes. I had to bring that ending into the film on maybe the third or the fourth day of shooting.

I remember, I devoted that moment to my first love, my first boyfriend.

We had to break up and it was very heart-wrenching. When I did that scene, I thought of that moment, and talking to him. The relationship had meant so much that I wanted to pay homage to it.

Gary (Monoson) tries to comfort Karen (Franklin).

In the context of the film, most people probably saw it and thought I didn't care about Gary. Really, what it was is when you love someone, but you know that it's not the right time in your life. And so you break up with someone and it hurts, but you know it's the right thing to do. It's just not the right timing. In my character's case in that movie, I wasn't strong enough to leave Rick. It was like, "I want to be with you, but he's got me now." The way I played her, I wanted her to be someone who, if you were nice to her, she was nice to you. But if there's someone nicer, she's nice to that person. She doesn't have a core. But that's what that scene was all about to me.

That last scene is so amazing. Aside from it being unexpected, that moment is just my favorite.

It is wonderful, and I'm sure it's a scene that taught a lot of young viewers a hard lesson about love and life.

Originally I thought, "Who's going to see this film?" I thought maybe it would go on TV and it would never be in the theaters. Then it goes on not only to be a cult classic, but a respected cult classic. It goes to show that no matter what film you do, as long as your heart is in it and you put yourself out there, you never know.

Initially I was a little bit hesitant about doing the film, obviously, but because my storyline was so deep I wanted to do it. I loved my storyline. I felt I could bring some passion and some dignity into it.

You and your co-stars were all young and very early in your careers. Did that build a camaraderie on set? Were there friendships made?

Everybody on that film was friends with everybody. I think that happens on a first film, where everybody really bonds. It wasn't like it was just our first film, though . . . I guess, in a way, we were all virgins in that sense. We bonded. We were all different ages, but we appreciated having gotten the roles and we were all so nice to each other.

I think I hung out with Lawrence more after the film. When you're doing the part, you're kind of creating the character and the relationship, so you don't want to get to know the other actor *too* well during the shoot. But afterwards, it's okay.

We just all loved being together. We'd go out to restaurants, we'd go out for a night on the town. It was great.

Your big screen career really took off right after *The Last American Virgin*. How much of that do you feel was the right parts coming along at the right time, or did *Virgin* give you a leg up on what came next?

When I did *Last American Virgin*, I don't think I realized how much it kick started my career. But, it kick started everything. Even when I got *Better Off Dead* . . . , [the director] Savage Steve Holland had seen me in *Last American Virgin* and wanted me for that film.

In your mind, what has given *The Last American Virgin* its lasting power?

Virgin specifically did a lot of things all at once. It is a time capsule of '80s music and '80s style. It's a time capsule of '80s issues: abortion, cocaine, and the teen point of view. It's not a movie that makes a judgment on those issues. It's a movie that says, "This is what was going on at the time." When people see it today they probably think, "What? How come this movie isn't all about kids doing cocaine? Why isn't this an issue? They just gloss over it." It gives you the idea of, okay, that's just what life was.

And then there's the simplicity of the story, which everyone can identify with. It's timeless. Adults can watch it today and think, "I went through that." Teenagers can watch it and go, "Oh, I'm him" or "I'm her." It's very specific in its time period, yet it's got this very timeless message.

And then, the ending. You say to people, "I can't explain this movie to you. You just have to see it." That's why people keep watching it over and over again. You can't explain the movie to people, they just have to experience it, and then you go, oh, wow, I get it. That's what I think makes it so amazing.

David (Joe Rubbo) attempts to romance Rose (Kimmy Robertson).

Interview: Actor Joe Rubbo

A Bronx native, seventeen-year-old Joe Rubbo played David in Cannon's classic teen coming-of-age comedy *The Last American Virgin*. Cannon brought him back again for their similar follow-up, *Hot Chili*, in 1985. Other film and TV appearances included *The World According to Garp* (1982) and *Striptease* (1996), as well as recurring appearances in sketches on *Late Night with David Letterman* throughout the 1980s.

Rubbo is an executive producer and on-screen personality for *VIP Television* (2010), an entertainment and lifestyle program covering exclusive events across Miami and Southern Florida.

***The Cannon Film Guide*: You were fresh out of high school when you made *The Last American Virgin*. What inspired you to get into acting?**

Joe Rubbo: When I was in high school I was always the class clown. I played the drums in a band, and I liked to be in the limelight. I wasn't shy at all. When I graduated from high school, I just decided to give it a shot.

What do you remember about your audition?

I remember the first time I auditioned was in New York. I met the producers, but I hadn't met Boaz yet. They liked me a lot and called me back a second time. The second time, it was between me and another person and they hadn't made up their mind yet. When I was in the waiting room, the other person was there—it was [John Cassisi], who was on that show, *Fish* (1977–1978), and was in the Scott Baio movie [*Bugsy Malone*, 1976] where he played Fat Sam the Man. I went in that day and they told me they wanted me to go out to Los Angeles to meet the director. I flew out there, but I was only seventeen at the time and had to bring my mom with me, since I was a minor. They'd told me to pack my clothes, but bring extra, because I might have to stay if I got the part. I did the reading in L.A. and got the part.

Things moved fast—they started shooting very quickly.

Yes, it did. Things moved *really* fast.

I imagine you didn't have much downtime, but what was the shoot like when the cameras weren't rolling? Did you get out and see the town?

I was only seventeen, so I couldn't do much. [*Laughs*] I hung out with

Diane a lot. We were the only ones there from New York, so we spent Thanksgiving together: me, her, and my mom. She was a little older than me, so she could do more. But we became really good friends. I also became really good friends with Steve [Antin]. When I had to go back and do a voiceover, I stayed at his place. Back then when you had to do voiceovers, you had to do it in a studio. I do my own productions now, and these days you can do almost everything over the computer or over the phone, but back then I had to fly back and go in to the studio—MGM, I guess it was. When I was at the studio I got to meet Sylvester Stallone, Walter Matthau. I was there with Christopher Lloyd, but I didn't know who the hell he was. [*Laughs*] *Back to the Future* hasn't come out yet.

The cover of the film's Spanish press kit took an unexpectedly cartoonish angle, playing up the "American" aspect of the movie's title by crudely pasting Gary's head onto a doodle of the Statue of Liberty.

Looking back, when did you have the most fun on set?

At the beginning of the movie I was scared. They did the part with Carmela [Louisa Moritz] first, so I was shitting my pants. [*Laughs*] But Boaz is a very intelligent man, he got that right out of the way. He thought, "Let's get the bullshit out of the way first." All the nudity, you know. After that it was fine, like a party, like a big family. We all became really close. It was cool.

They made so many teen movies during the 1980s. In your opinion, what's made *Last American Virgin* stand out as one of the better-remembered ones?

I wish I knew! It freaks the shit out of me that people still recognize me, and know lines from the movie. I don't know—I guess because the movie's relatable, you know what I mean? There's no blowing up cars, special effects, nothing crazy like that. It's just three teen boys going out and trying to get laid, and having fun. Oh, and the music was incredible.

There made a bunch of *Lemon Popsicle* movies in Israel. Were there expectations that there would be a sequel?

Yes, there was. Believe it or not, I was going to be a star—we were all going to be stars. When I signed my contract, I actually signed on for three or more movies. There was a fallout between the director and the producers at Cannon films, and that's why we didn't do any more movies. But Boaz is doing very well—he's made a bunch of movies.

I did one more afterwards, it was called *Hot Chili* (1985). We did that one next. I wouldn't call it a sequel or a prequel, but it was the same storyline, basically, but with different characters. It wasn't as good as *The Last American Virgin*. I had fun on *Hot Chili*, but we were in Mexico in shitty surroundings. It was really hot. There were rumors that the place was haunted, and people were getting bit by scorpions. When we were there, we all wanted to get the hell out of there. We couldn't wait to get away from there. But again, I made a lot of good friends.

That Championship Season

Release Date: December 9, 1982
Directed by: Jason Miller
Written by: Jason Miller
Starring: Bruce Dern, Stacy Keach, Martin Sheen, Paul Sorvino, Robert Mitchum
Trailer Voiceover: "For one brief moment, they were the greatest."

My God . . . it's full of stars!

Before we get into *That Championship Season*—its merits, history, context, and trivia—let's spend a moment taking a good, long look at its cast. Holy moly, talk about a group of lauded thespians. This wasn't one of those cases where a filmmaker rolls the dice on a bunch of young, promising actors who go on to higher places in their careers, either: all five of *That Championship Season*'s lead actors were bona fide stars when the film was made.

You have Bruce Dern, who at this point had been nominated for an Academy Award for *Coming Home* (1978), and already had a 20-year career under his belt that included films like *Hang 'em High* (1968), *They Shoot Horses, Don't They?* (1969), *The King of Marvin Gardens* (1972), and *Black Sunday* (1977). Stacy Keach's filmography heretofore included the 1968 adaptation of *The Heart is a Lonely Hunter*, Robert Altman's *Brewster McCloud* (1970), and John

Huston's *Fat City* (1972). Martin Sheen, of course, was coming off a string of critically-acclaimed roles in little movies like *Badlands* (1973), *Apocalypse Now* (1979), and *Gandhi* (1982). Paul Sorvino had not yet made the splash he would later make with *Goodfellas* (1990) or *Law & Order* (1990–2010), but was already a well-respected Broadway actor who'd had memorable parts in films like *The Panic in Needle Park* (1971) and *Reds* (1981).

A handsome, pencil illustration of the film's star-studded cast adorns the cover of *That Championship Season*'s American VHS release.

Finally, we have one of Hollywood's true G.O.A.T.s in Robert Mitchum, a living, walking legend in the twilight of his career. He'd inhabited some of cinema's darkest, most iconic roles in classics such as *Night of the Hunter* (1955), *Out of the Past* (1947), *Cape Fear* (1962), and *The Friends of Eddie Coyle* (1973). This is a man who Roger Ebert, upon watching him work on the set of *That Championship Season*, described as "the last of the old lions." Sure, by this point in his life he was a notoriously temperamental alcoholic—a sickness that plagued him throughout his professional life, alongside chain smoking and a proclivity for starting brawls—who had resigned himself to making b-movies and cashing checks, but he was nevertheless an imposing screen presence and, by golly, when he wanted to, he could still act with the best of 'em. This was hardly ever more evident in his latter-day filmography than it was among the distinguished ensemble that surrounded him in *That Champion Season*.

The highly respectable cast, from left to right: Stacy Keach, Bruce Dern, Robert Mitchum, Paul Sorvino, and Martin Sheen.

That Championship Season, on the surface at least, is about four middle-aged men and their former coach reuniting to celebrate the 25th anniversary of their high school state basketball championship. What begins as an innocuous, social occasion explodes into an evening of bitter infighting, as secrets are spilled and the men are forced to confront their weaknesses and failures. Bruce Dern's character, George, is the ineffective, incumbent mayor of the decaying city of Scranton, Pennsylvania. He's a laughingstock among the locals, and is almost sure to lose the looming election to a younger, up-and-coming politician. Stacy Keach plays James, his campaign manager and the local middle school principal, who has ridden George's coat tails for his whole life in hopes it will one day lead to a prominent role of his own. Paul Sorvino, Phil, is one of the city's richest businessmen but also the most corrupt; his wealth has brought him a hollow happiness, and he compensates for that with drugs, fast cars, and loose women. Finally Sheen plays Tom, James' wayward brother, who is the only one to have left their hometown, stumbling from one place to another in an alcoholic stupor and constantly finding himself facing legal problems.

Normally all of their troubles are forgotten for a single night every year as these friends and former teammates gather to reflect on their one moment of glory: an unexpected, underdog victory in the Pennsylvania state basketball championship a quarter century ago. This annual tradition goes down at the home of their aging coach. Played in stately manner by Mitchum, the coach—he's only ever addressed as "Coach"—was forced to retire early, at a time when he felt he still had gas left in the tank. With no vocation to keep him occupied, the years are catching up with him rapidly. Normally, the five men can leave their problems behind as they hang out, drink, make jokes, shoot the shit, reminisce, and relive those thrilling, glorious final seconds of their championship season of 1957.

Until this year, that is, when failed ambitions suddenly give way to midlife crises, flared tempers, and long-buried tensions that bubble to the surface over the course of one emotionally supercharged evening. (Getting old sure isn't pretty at all in *That Championship Season*.) For one night, the lifelong friends find myriad reasons to hate one another. One is having an affair with another's wife. Another feels he is being taken for granted. Not one of them believes George has any credibility left in him as a politician, and Tom's boozing has gone on for so long that even his own brother is sick of bailing him out of his troubles. Alcohol certainly doesn't help matters for anyone on this particular night. The men all drink *too* much. Insults and ethnic slurs are hurled. Punches are thrown. A hunting rifle is pointed in threat. A man is physically assaulted with a basketball. The nervous and emotional breakdowns on display are exciting and, in the hands of such a capable group of performers, *That Champion Season* is absolutely captivating.

The cover of the movie's Spanish press kit.

The Championship Season's path to the big screen was long and rather circuitous. It began its life as a play by Jason Miller, a writer, director, and actor best known for playing Father Karras, the young priest, in *The Exorcist* (1973). After a ballyhooed premier run Off Broadway in 1972, *That Cham-*

pionship Season moved to Broadway, where it stayed for two years and 700 performances. (Paul Sorvino, who co-stars in this film, originated his role in the stage version.) The show received rave reviews and sold out many nights of its run. Greater prestige would follow: in 1973, it won the Tony Award for Best Play. While Miller was on the set of *The Exorcist*, he received a phone call informing him that it had won him the Pulitzer Prize for Drama.

Film producers were interested bringing *That Championship Season* to movie theaters before Miller himself was. Near the start of its acclaimed stage run, the play's film rights were jointly purchased by Playboy Productions and producer Max Raab, who had previously been instrumental in bringing *A Clockwork Orange* (1971) from novel to screen. This earliest incarnation of *That Championship Season* was to be distributed by Warner Bros. and executive produced by Hugh Hefner.

Miller himself first adapted his play for the screen in 1975. Studios were quite eager to bring the highly-lauded theatrical production to cinemas, but for years each planned version fell apart for one reason or another. Often it was due to Miller sticking to his guns, refusing to make changes that producers felt would make a movie adaptation more marketable to wider audiences. One studio wanted him to write the men's various women—their wives, girlfriends, mistresses—into the script, which went against Miller's vision of the play as being strictly about male bonding. In 1976, Columbia Pictures offered to produce the movie if Miller would relocate its setting from his hometown of Scranton, Pennsylvania to Pasadena, California. Once again, Miller refused to make the change; to him, Scranton itself was practically a character within the play. Not only did Miller desire that the story remain set there, but he wanted to actually shoot the movie in Scranton.

Other seemingly insurmountable issues arose, too, that were certainly no fault of Miller's. It looked as though the movie would finally happen by 1981: Miller's *Exorcist* director, William Friedkin, was slated to direct, and famed *Patton* (1970) and *Dr. Strangelove* (1964) actor George C. Scott attached to star in the film as the old Coach. Within the space of months, however, Scott dropped out because his salary demands could not be met, and Friedkin was forced to leave because of a prior commitment to direct a Broadway run of the play *Duet for One*. (Coincidentally, Cannon would also produce a film adaptation of *Duet for One*, starring Julie Andrews, in 1986.)

Miller, who was also an accomplished stage director in addition to his award-winning body of work as a playwright and actor, resolved to take over in the director's chair himself. George C. Scott was replaced with another Hollywood legend, William Holden, of *Stalag 17* (1953), *Sunset Boulevard* (1951), and *Network* (1974) fame. Just as rehearsals were set to begin, Holden drunkenly fell and gashed his head on the edge of a bedside table. Alone, he was unable to call for help before bleeding out, and died at the age of 63. The unexpected death of their star finally proved too much for the filmmaker and producers of *That Championship Season*, and production was once again postponed indefinitely. This is where Cannon stepped in during the spring of 1982.

Menahem Golan had caught a Hebrew-language stage version of *That Championship Season* in Tel Aviv and was a huge fan. He promptly got in contact with Miller. Cannon offered to let him make the movie with a greatly reduced budget, but the tradeoff would be that Miller could do the film the way he had always wanted it done: in Scranton, with himself as the director.

Cannon was still at this point a mostly-unknown commodity in Hollywood, and if *That Championship Season* became a hit it would be a prestigious boost to their young studio. By June, the movie was cast—with Robert Mitchum now in the Coach's role—and by July filming was already underway in Scranton. The high-ups at Cannon had requested a release date for December of that year, and so production moved quickly. The crew shot for grueling, twelve-hour days, six days a week, for a total of seven weeks. (Three weeks of exteriors in Scranton, and four more weeks of interiors shot on a sound stage in Los Angeles.) Miller was only granted ten weeks on top of that to edit the movie, which all added up to a svelte eighteen weeks from start of shooting to delivery of the final print. To polish it off, composer Bill Conti—fresh off Oscar nominations for *Rocky* (1976) and *For Your Eyes Only* (1981)—was brought aboard to provide the movie's effective score.

Ironically, much of the footage Miller had fought to shoot in Scranton didn't make the final cut of the film. Miller had "opened up" his screenplay a great deal from the stage version, bringing in additional locations and fleshing out back stories for several of the characters that were only alluded to in the play. These were removed when the filmmaker and producers reviewed an early cut and decided they would prefer the movie to be more like its acclaimed stage version.

Unfortunately, despite strong reviews which praised its performances and direction, it was Robert Mitchum's personal demons that managed to hijack the movie's publicity cycle. Cannon had booked out a section of the famed Waldorf Astoria hotel to hold a press day for the movie's big, New York City premiere. When he showed up at the hotel that morning for a long day of chatting up journalists, the old Hollywood bad boy—whose 40-year career was storied with temperamental outbursts, bar brawls, and arrests—was already stinking drunk. Following several hot, surly exchanges with interviewers, the 65-year-old Mitchum was sent back to his hotel early in hopes that he would sober up before the gala premiere that evening. Instead, he showed up to it even more intoxicated than before.

It was at this party, attended by many prominent figures of New York's upper crust, where things went truly south. Mitchum continued drinking, become steadily more belligerent, up until the director and principal cast were gathered together for a photo op. Miller and the four other actors were ushered around Mitchum, who was handed a basketball so that they would better resemble the old teammates they portrayed in the movie. It was during this posed shot that Mitchum—for reasons that are still unclear—became angry and hurled the basketball at the face of photographer Yvonne Hemsey, who was snapping photos at the event for *TIME* Magazine. Her camera was broken, her face was bloodied, and her two front teeth were knocked out. Witnesses, including Martin Sheen and Menahem Golan, rushed to her aid. Mitchum, meanwhile, was said to have appeared in a daze, perhaps in disbelief of the horrible thing he'd just done. The incident obviously made the papers, and Hemsey later filed a lawsuit against the screen legend for $30 million dollars.

A Spanish lobby card depicts the cast posing with a basketball, similar to what was attempted when Mitchum broke a photographer's teeth at the film's premiere party.

It's unclear whether it was this terrible piece of PR, or simply lackluster distribution and promotion, which derailed the movie at the box office. In either case, the movie performed very disappointingly. This had to have been upsetting to its set of esteemed actors, who'd agreed to reduce their shooting salaries in exchange for shares of its profits. For Mitchum, the drunken outburst with the basketball cost far more than his *That Championship Season* fee by the time he settled out-of-court with the assaulted photographer.

And thus, a film which Cannon had once viewed with Oscars in their eyes quietly disappeared in its winter release window. None of the big names whom had signed on for the film would ever work for Cannon again. All, that is, except for Robert Mitchum, who despite all of the trouble he caused them between his reported on-set drunkenness and the basketball face-smashing incident, would return to the Cannon fold to make *Maria's Lovers* (1985), *The Ambassador* (1985), and *Midnight Ride* (1990). This would wind up being the only movie Jason Miller ever directed, as he decided he'd return permanently to theater after his fraught experience bringing *That Championship Season* to screen.

Looking at it now, it's a damn shame that the movie never made the splash it should have. In the decades since its release, *That Championship Season* has aged very well. With incendiary performances from a top-notch cast and skillful direction which captured the intimacy, energy, and tension of the play while never feeling overtly stage-y, it's truly an overlooked and often forgotten gem. As for Cannon, this wouldn't be the only time they'd make a bid for prestige by packing their marquee to the brim with headline talent, but *That Championship Season* may have been the only instance where their gallery of stars approach paid off with a truly effective ensemble.

Treasure of the Four Crowns

Release Date: January 21, 1983
Directed by: Ferdinando Baldi
Written by: Tony Anthony & Lloyd Battista
Starring: Tony Anthony, Ana Obregon, Gene Quintano & Francisco Rabal
Trailer Voiceover: "You've seen *Raiders* . . . *Star Wars* . . . *Aliens* . . . and *Close Encounters* . . . But you are about to experience a totally new dimension in entertainment!"

Believe it or not, 3D movies have been around for almost as long as film itself. The first patents for stereoscopic motion picture processes date as far back as the 1890s; by the 1920s, rudimentary 3D films were already being screened for public audiences. The format didn't come into its own, however, until the early 1950s, with the release of groundbreaking, three-dimensional hits like *Bwana Devil* (1952) and *House of Wax* (1953). Many of these early features were genre films, which capitalized on the gimmick to produce cheap thrills, such as spears hurled directly at the camera, reanimated skeletons floating into the audience, or lions leaping out of the screen. *Creature from the Black Lagoon* (1954), perhaps the closest thing to a *Citizen Kane* of three dimensional movies, was released at this time.

By the tail end of this golden era, even the major studios were getting in on the game with big-budget, 3D musicals such as *Kiss Me, Kate* (1953) and Biblical epics like *The Robe* (1953). Even Alfred Hitchcock joined in on the fun by shooting *Dial M for Murder* (1954) with 3D projection in mind. The 3D technology of this era, however, was neither reliable nor cost-effective. Film prints broke down through the normal wear-and-tear of theatrical screenings, and any small drop-off in picture quality could render a 3D movie almost unwatchable. Over the years, 3D films gained a reputation for causing headaches and dizziness, and movie-goers seemed to tire of having objects continuously thrust at their faces. The fad eventually died off.

The rather misleading cover art for the VHS release of *Treasure of the Four Crowns*, which was sadly not in 3D.

Independent studios continued to release the occasional 3D film throughout the 1960s and 1970s, but these typically tended to be low-budget horror titles or softcore pornography films. In the early 1980s, 3D saw a sudden renaissance, spurred by the unexpected success of 3D movies like the spaghetti western *Comin' At Ya!* (1981) and the slasher sequel *Friday the 13th Part III* (1982). It was a short-lived craze which crested in the summer and autumn of 1983, a year which saw the release of movies like *Jaws 3-D*, *Amityville 3-D*, *Metalstorm: The Destruction of Jared-Syn*, and *Spacehunter: Adventures in the Forbidden Zone*—and, of course, Cannon's own expected foray into the third dimension, *Treasure of the Four Crowns*.

Treasure of the Four Crowns came from the same team responsible for the 3D mega-hit, *Comin' At Ya!*— writer/producer/star Tony Anthony, director Ferdinando Baldi, and producer/actor Gene Quintano—which had helped kick start the latest 3D movie craze in 1981. While *Comin' At Ya!* received mostly lukewarm to negative reviews upon release, it brought in a very cool $12 million at the domestic box office. This was an incredible sum for a Western in that particular era, not to mention one that had shot on a very modest budget. Its use of 3D was pretty inventive, too, with everything but the kitchen sink being hurled directly at the camera and into viewers' face, from bats to bubbles to a baby's bare ass. (Yes, really.)

A pair of the psychedelic 3D glasses that were handed out at screenings of *Treasure of the Four Crowns*. On the reverse side was a promo for *Hercules*.

Tony Anthony's path to movie-making is particularly interesting. Born as Roger Pettito in West Virginia, Anthony cut his teeth in the industry by writing and producing small, independent features before moving to Europe, where he continued his career. In Italy he starred in a successful series of Spaghetti Westerns playing a mysterious character known as The Stranger—a role similar to Clint Eastwood's in the wildly popular Man With No Name trilogy. Anthony also played the hero in 1971's *Blindman*, another Italian Western, this one directed by Ferdinando Baldi, with whom he'd collaborate on three more films, including *Treasure of the Four Crowns*. (*Blindman* is best remembered today for its bizarre casting of former Beatle Ringo Starr as one of its villains.)

In *Treasure of the Four Crowns*, Anthony plays an adventurer named J.T. Striker. The film opens with a lengthy, dialogue-free prologue; in fact, no dialogue is spoken until nearly 22 minutes into the movie. Dressed in brightly-colored leather outfit which makes him look more like a Formula 1 racer than a daring explorer, Striker retrieves a magical key from a haunted tomb deep under a Spanish castle. As he descends into the ancient chamber, he's attacked (mostly in slow motion) by an aviary's worth of large birds, from a vulture to a hawk to several owls and, most surprisingly, a living, breathing pterodactyl. After fleeing the fowl, slipping past a snake, and dodging several dogs—there is a *lot* of wildlife living in this abandoned palace—he stumbles into the castle's treasure-filled catacombs.

He immediately sets about pillaging the place, which not only triggers a zillion booby traps, but angers the spirits whose eternal peace he's so carelessly violated. The next ten minutes are all about survival, as the skeletons and suits of armor come to life around him, crossbows levitate and fire their arrows directly at the camera, dry ice fog pours out of pottery, and a whole variety of deadly weapons are magically thrown at our hero. It's a 3D smorgasbord! The filmmakers show off their special effects prowess by rapidly tossing as much as possible at the audience. Each time they find a particularly neat effect, they milk it for all its worth by repeating the same shot two, three, or four more times at different film speeds. As the chaos builds, Striker is eventually chased by rolling boulders. It's just like that famous scene from *Raiders of the Lost Ark* (1981), except there are *two* boulders, and they're *on fire*! (They're apparently not very heavy boulders, either, since Striker is able to stop one by tipping over a table in front of it, which the boulder bounces off without damaging.) After this goes on for quite a while, our hero manages to escape the castle, which explodes behind him—in slow motion, of course.

Striker (Tony Anthony) flees the burning catacombs as all kinds of crazy, 3D shit happens.

This is when the action switches to downtown Madrid, and where *Treasure* sheds its Indiana Jones-ish, adventure movie trappings to become your standard heist film. Striker hands off the key to his friend, Ed, an academic who specializes in mythical artifacts and works out of Spain's Royal Armory. Ed is played by co-producer Gene Quintano, who'd become a regular member of the Cannon family and earn writing credits on many films of theirs, including *Making the Grade* (1984), *King Solomon's Mines* (1985), and *Allan Quatermain and the Lost City of Gold* (1986). Away from Cannon he'd pen three different *Police Academy* sequels, *National Lampoon's Loaded Weapon* (1993), and the classic war film *Operation Dumbo Drop* (1995).

Ed recounts to Striker a legend about four magical crowns created by the Visigoths in the sixth century. One was accidentally broken by Arabs centuries ago, but another is in the possession of the professor. Locked inside the other two—which can only be opened with the fancy-ass key Striker pilfered in the opening scene—are magical stones which have untold powers of good and evil. The crowns' powers are never really explained any further than that, but we're given a chance to see their magic in action later on (and it's pretty balls-to-the-wall nutso.)

Unfortunately, the last two crowns are in the possession of the nefarious, Manson-like Brother Jonas (Emiliano Redondo), a former Brooklyn hoodlum who now leads a scary, mask-wearing cult from his mountaintop fortress. Though he's somehow still skeptical of the crowns' supernatural abilities despite being attacked by ghosts (and a dinosaur) just a few minutes earlier, Striker agrees to steal the crowns back from the heavily-armed cultists.

Before he can get in the heisting, however, Striker has to assemble his team—and boy, what a sad bunch of misfits they are. The first guy on Striker's list is Rick Martin (co-writer Jerry Lazarus), who was once the best mountain climber in the world but now spends his time drinking himself to death in a remote log cabin. At first Martin rebuffs Striker's offer of a cool $100,000 for a three-week job, as he's no longer interested in anything that doesn't come in a bottle. With impeccable timing, however, Striker's magical key comes to life and some serious poltergeist shit starts going down. As the key glows and flies about the room on a very visible string, making a grating, electronic noise like a short-circuited Theremin, flames shoot from Rick's pots and pans, his spice jars explode, blankets fly off his bed and the drawers shoot out of his dresser and spill his clothes all over the floor. This wildly gratuitous display of the movie's 3D effects is enough to change Martin's mind about joining the expedition.

In addition to co-writing this film, actor Jerry Lazarus became another Cannon regular. He'd play small roles in six more of their movies, including *Over the Brooklyn Bridge* and *Breakin' 2* (both 1984), *Hot Chili* (1985), *The Delta Force* and *Murphy's Law* (both 1986), and *Surrender* (1987).

Next up for recruitment is Socrates, played by Francisco "Paco" Rabal, a busy Italian actor who took on more than 200 roles over a film career that lasted sixty years. Notable among those parts were collaborations with Luis Bunuel (*Nazarin* [1959], *Viridiana* [1961], and *Belle de Jour* [1967]), Michelangelo Antonioni's *L'Eclisse* (1962), and William Friedkin's *Sorcerer* (1977). His daughter, Liz, is played by Ana Obregon, a Spanish actress who'd become more famous for her part in another Cannon movie: playing Bo Derek's globe-trotting bestie in the erotic catastrophe *Bolero* (1984).

Socrates is an aging strong man who now performs as a clown in a Spanish circus called Los Muchachos, where his daughter performs alongside him as an acrobat. (Or rather, Liz may possibly be Socrates' lover. The nature of their relationship is never explicitly spelled out, but we *hope* it's a father/daughter situation given their age difference, and because circus clowns presumably don't make great sugar daddies.) Socrates takes on the job because he knows the money will set Liz up for life even after he's gone—you see, Socrates has a bum ticker and was given only six months to live, a secret of his that will become a problem later on.

The gang assembles back at headquarters, where they've built an absurdly detailed model of the cult's compound. Ed, it's revealed, is also the token "gadget guy," and the team's fifth member. The fortress' many traps, guard towers, and other security measures are mapped out, setting the crew up for a seemingly impossible mission, which actually turns out to be far less exciting than we were led to believe once it's underway. Before the scene can end we're treated with yet another, sudden, psychedelic, 3D nightmare composed of crazy sounds, bright colors, abstract shapes, and a goat's head with glowing eyes. This is just the key once again proving that yes, it's definitely magical.

This finally brings us to Brother Jonas' temple, where the bearded and jingle bell-clad prophet is occupied with stereotypically weird, cult-y stuff, including various initiation rituals, healing rituals, and hair-cutting rituals. Striker and his gang have no trouble sneaking past his guards (who for some reason wear pig masks) and their machine guns to get inside the compound.

The bulk of their caper takes place in the cathedral where the crowns are stored, protected by an electrified gate and surrounded by a pressure-sensitized floor. (At the time of release, Cannon's press materials bragged that this was the biggest single set built in Spain in more than a decade.) From this point on, nearly *twenty minutes* of runtime are dedicated to the crew slowly rappelling across a ceiling beam, from one side of the room to the other. It seriously sucks the momentum out of the movie. Showing the robbery process in quiet, intense detail has long been an established trope of the heist movie genre, exemplified by films like *Rififi* (1956) and *Le Cercle Rouge* (1970), but there's nothing tense or exciting about watching the heroes of *Treasure of the Four Crowns* slowly and methodically crawl across a ceiling. Who in the editing room thought we *needed* to watch them carefully attach and secure each cable and harness before moving on to the next one?

A Spanish lobby card celebrating the movie's inexplicable, twenty-minute-long ceiling-crossing scene.

Once they're almost within reach of the crowns (finally), the whole plan is nearly compromised when Socrates inconveniently dies of a heart attack mid-caper. They still manage to make it to the altar, but shit hits the fan as soon as Striker lays hands upon the crowns. Spikes shoot from the walls and impale Rick; alarms sound; a statue comes to life and crushes Ed as venomous snakes fly from its mouth and bite him. None of this stops Striker. As he tries to remove the stones from the crowns, the room catches on fire, his head spins 360 degrees, and half of his face melts. You can't make this stuff up. The ending of *Four Crowns* makes next to no sense, but good golly does it present a spectacle of visual insanity.

As the cultists watch, understandably stunned into speechlessness, Striker turns around and fires flames from his hands. This makes the cultists spontaneously explode as lasers rip Brother Jonas' face apart in slow motion. This all happens while Ennio Morricone's lush score swells in volume. That's right—*Treasure of the Four Crowns* has a score by the great Morricone, the maestro of such unforgettable soundtracks *The Good, The Bad, and The Ugly* (1966), *The Untouchables* (1987), and *The Thing* (1982), among many others. His only other Cannon scores would be for *Nana, the True Key of Pleasure* (1983) and the Brooke Shields romantic adventure *Sahara* (1984).

A sales ad for the *Treasure* team's abandoned science fiction follow-up, which at this point was going to be about a man who escapes from his planet's "death mines" to lead a slave uprising against his former childhood friend. Think *Ben-Hur* (1959), but in outer space.

The carnage eventually subsides, and thankfully the crowns heal Striker's hideous facial scarring. Judging the stones' power to be too much for humanity to wield, he tosses them into the flaming remains of the dead Brother Jonas. The team's two surviving heroes—Striker and Liz—are soon rescued from the destroyed compound by helicopter. Before the credits roll, we're treated to a totally random scene where a monster emerges from a swamp and a creepy fish hurtles toward the camera. No, it doesn't make sense, but it does feel like the right way to cap off the movie's lovably batshit ending.

Treasure of the Four Crowns was released in either Super-Vision 3-D or Wonder-Vision 3-D, depending on which particular movie poster you looked at. Both were bullshit terms that Cannon invented to make *Four Crowns'* 3D process sound new and innovative, despite already having been used on *Friday the 13th Part III* just a few months earlier. For technical buffs, the film was shot using a Marks 3-Depix Converter, which stacked the movie's left and right images on top of one another using a single strip of film.

While the general, critical consensus was that the plot of *Treasure of the Four Crowns* was silly and mostly disposable, but the 3D effects were inventive and fun, which is a totally fair assessment. (Sadly, unless you saw the film in its original run you've probably never had the chance to see it in 3D, as home video releases have favored the 2D version.) The movie went out and made decent money at the box office.

Cannon announced a follow-up Wonder-Vision 3-D movie to be titled *Escape from Beyond*, but it never existed past a handful of trade advertisements. The science fiction story would have been set on another planet and follow either a space bounty hunter or intergalactic chariot racers, based on where it was in development at the time. By the end of the summer of '83, though, the bottom had dropped out of the 3D movie market following a flurry of disappointing, three-dimensional, sci-fi flops—including the high profile *Spacehunter: Adventures in the Forbidden Zone* and *Metalstorm: The Destruction of Jared-Syn*—which canceled out any hopes for *Escape from Beyond* ever being made.

It's a shame when you think about what might have been had *Escape from Beyond* made it to production; one can only imagine the fun that Tony Anthony and Ferdinando Baldi would have had in finding things to throw at their audiences in zero gravity. (And then again five or six more times, per object, at different film speeds.)

Nana, a.k.a. *Nana, The True Key of Pleasure*

Release Date: March 4, 1983
Directed by: Dan Wolman
Written by: Marc Behm
Starring: Katya Berger, Jean-Pierre Aumont
Tagline: "The erotic saga of forbidden love!"

Who ever said that literature can't be sexy? Certainly not Cannon! *Nana*'s formula was one the studio would attempt several times: take a classic novel that's famous for being dirty, cast a scandalous young starlet in the lead, crank the sexual element up to 11, then sit back and wait for big bucks to roll in from the box office. (Or for the movie to flop, as was the case each time Cannon attempted one of their literary softcore pornos.)

At least the filmmakers were pretty honest up front about the product they were delivering. The opening credits state that *Nana* is "loosely adapted from the novel by Émile Zola," and extra emphasis should be placed on the term "loosely." Zola's 1880 novel of the same name is a tale of a young actress who goes from rags to riches working as a high-end prostitute, only to meet her tragic end. Cannon's version of *Nana* is also a rags to riches tale, except here the crafty young prostitute flits from one lover to next accumulating wealth while sabotaging her lovers' lives, all on her way to a happy ending in which the Parisian elite gather to applaud her as she flies off on vacation in a hot air balloon. Along the way, there's lots and lots (and lots and lots) of screwing.

The movie is an odd-duck mélange of comedy, arthouse pretense, and occasionally graphic sex that ultimately boils down to 90 minutes of implausible, late-night cable fare. Shot by Cannon's Italian unit, Golan and Globus turned to Israeli filmmaker Dan Wolman for directorial duties. Screenwriter Marc Behm—who'd also worked on Cannon's *Hospital Massacre* (1981) and *Lady Chatterley's Lover* (1982)—handled the "adaptation."

Nana (Katya Berger) is embraced by the wealthy Count Muffat (Jean-Pierre Aumont) on the cover of *Nana*'s hard-to-find VHS release.

If compliments must be paid, it should be said that the film *looks* great: cinematographer Armando Nannuzzi had shot several classics of Italian cinema, including *I Knew Her Well* (1965) and Luchino Visconti's acclaimed 1969 film *The Damned*. He also shot Cannon's *Sahara* (1984). Nannuzzi famously lost his right eye when a remote controlled lawnmower went haywire on the set of 1986's *Maximum Overdrive*, running over a piece of wood and spraying shrapnel into the cameraman's face. Nannuzzi sued director Stephen King and others over unsafe work conditions in a case that was eventually settled out-of-court. The one-eyed cinematographer hardly slowed down after the accident, shooting almost twenty more films in his remaining years.

Nana features a score by the ever-mercenary Ennio Morricone, whose only other works for Cannon were the adventure film *Sahara* (1984) and the 3D adventure film *Treasure of the Four Crowns* (1983). His first name was somehow misspelled "Enio" in the opening credits, which might have gone unnoticed were he not, like, one of the most famous and respected film composers of all time.

A sales ad for the film, which was drawn from a still photo of Katya Berger that was taken on set.

The producers found their sexually-adventurous ingénue in nineteen-year-old actress Katya Berger, stepdaughter of prolific spaghetti western actor William Berger, who would soon show up for a deliciously hammy, villainous turn in Cannon's two *Hercules* movies. Katya Berger had a handful of credits to her name for playing salacious parts at very young ages, including leading roles in the Lolita-like *Little Lips* (1978)—remembered for its skeezy, underage nude scenes—and Joe D'Amato's infamous video nasty, *Absurd* (1981). She's an actress with limited range, but it's clear from the way the filmmakers strip her nude only five minutes into the film that she may not have been hired for her skills as a thespian.

Many of the story's developments unfurl in the sticky back rooms of a turn-of-the-century Parisian bordello known as The Minotaur. Here, the city's wealthy elite gather to socialize and/or get their rocks off with the club's many, multi-talented showgirls. Every crusty old fart in the joint falls in love with Nana the very moment she makes her debut on the stage. (Her name isn't pronounced "Nana" as in the synonym for a grandmother, but more like "Nah-nah," as in "Nana, nana, nana, nana—*Batman*!")

It's not long before Nana's manager is fielding generous monetary offers from her many admirers to take the young lady to bed. Once she realizes how much money her pimp is pocketing for her services, Nana takes business matters into her own hands and soon counts counts, barons, sheiks, and bankers among her aristocratic clientele.

Nana has zero trouble manipulating her many suitors to her fiscal advantage, milking them for beautiful clothes, a posh apartment, and even goading one into taking out a loan on his mansion to purchase her an African slave—errr, "professional fighter." Her actions rarely make a whole lot of sense, and she's never really given any clear motivation beyond the age-old desire for mo' money and mo' sex. It certainly doesn't help that all of the stuffy, rich guys in fancy suits who Nana takes to bed have a way of blending together. What little plot there is there exists solely to connect one nude scene to the next and, boy howdy, there are a lot of them.

We watch Nana as she bathes. We watch her perform in a pair of old-timey, silent porno flicks. We watch as old men spy on her through hidden peepholes into her dressing room. We see Nana naked in a scene she's not even in, when one old creep flips through nude photos of her. In case you're also wondering whether Katya Berger is the only person frolicking about in the buff: no, she's certainly not. Beyond every sexual partner the precocious young Nana lures into her bedchambers—or horse-drawn buggies, or stables—even the background extras frequently strip off their clothes to get in on the down and dirty action. Basically, if you see a character and they're not given a name, you're probably going to see their naughty bits within a few minutes' screen time.

Another sales catalog ad for the film.

With the sheer amount of nudity in this 90-minute movie, it was clear the filmmakers needed to be creative in order to squeeze every extra butt and boob in without it getting downright tiresome. In one weirdly-inspired scene, actors pantomime an erotic shadow play behind a backlit screen. Later, in the film's most gratuitous sequence, naked women are hunted by men on horseback (and their beagles) through a forest as a crowd of bourgeois spectators gleefully watch through binoculars. As each buxom, young woman is caught, the hunters doff their boots and red jackets to copulate with their eager prey, and the gathered rich folks cheer them on. Note that explicit nudity is reserved for the movie's female cast alone, as per Hollywood tradition: no willies, peckers, dongs, or what-have-you ever appear on screen in *Nana*.

At the hunting party Nana meets eyes with the socialite Satin, played by the lead actress's real-life stepsister, Debra Berger. This casting choice suddenly turns *very* weird when, just a few scenes later, Nana pays her a visit and the sisters spontaneously engage in a fully nude sex scene. No, they weren't related by blood, but you still have to imagine it was a bizarre experience. (How often do you think somebody brings it up at family reunions?) Debra Berger would go on to appear in several more Cannon films, including *Dangerously Close* (1986), *Invaders from Mars* (1986), and *52 Pick-Up* (1986). Their other sister, Carin Berger, was married to filmmaker Tobe Hooper in the 1980s, and worked in the costume department for many Cannon features, including *Nana*, *The Last American Virgin* (1982), *Lifeforce* (1985), and *The Texas Chainsaw Massacre 2* (1986), in addition to having a small role as the absurdly-named Nurse Lushtush in *Dr. Heckyl and Mr. Hype* (1980). Indeed, the Bergers were a Cannon family.

The movie rolls along as Nana chews up her men, relieves them of their fortunes, and then spits them out again. ("Every man I've ever met has adored me," she tells a smitten, young student whose father she has also seduced.) For some of these men, Nana proves to be their downfall. One poor count, Muffat, bears the brunt of her torture. Muffat is played by French leading man Jean-Pierre Aumont, best known for the award-winning *Lili* (1953).

Not long after Muffat becomes her newest sugar daddy, she begs him to buy her the aforementioned slave—ugh, here we go again, "professional fighter"—whom Nana promptly sneaks off to fellate behind a horse in her friend's stable. When he at first refuses to spend half a million francs on such an idiotic investment, Nana spitefully convinces one of her associates into entering an affair with Muffat's wife, Sabine, played by Mandy Rice-Davies.

Not nearly as famous for her acting, Rice-Davies was notorious in Great Britain for her role in the Cold War-era Profumo scandal. Her roommate, Christine Keeler, was discovered to be having secret affairs with both a British special agent and a Soviet secret agent simultaneously, an understandable compromise to national security. When called to the stand in 1963, Rice-Davies was told that another high-profile figure in the scandal, Lord Astor, had denied sleeping with her, to which the young woman gave her now famous, oft-quoted reply: "Well, he would say that, wouldn't he?"

Eventually Muffat caves in to Nana's demands and takes out a loan on his mansion in order to buy the slave . . . *fighter* . . . she asked for. While he's referred to as a "professional fighter" the movie and never as a slave, having the White characters buying and selling the movie's lone Black character of any consequence smells incredibly racist to me. There's also an uncomfortable cabaret "magic" trick where a White, naked lady is "transformed" into a Black, naked lady. Issues can also be taken with the movie's "sheik" character, who brings a goat with him into Nana's bedroom. It would be one thing if all of these occurrences were ripped from the pages of Émile Zola's 1880 novel, but most of them were fabricated by the filmmakers for this particular movie more than a Century later.

Nana enters her brand new slave into a dehumanizing "human cock fight," in which he's humiliatingly dressed as a chicken and forced to fight another man to the death. Nana's fighter is immediately and savagely killed, and Count Muffat loses his home. He then catches his wife porking another man, whom he has no choice but to kill in a duel. As if all of that wasn't bad enough, Nana shows up at Muffat's son's wedding, where she flashes her knockers at him, inspiring the boy to dump his bride at the altar and climb into Nana's carriage for some good, old-fashioned bumping of uglies. In our itemization of Muffat's myriad humiliations at the hands of the wicked crumpet, Nana, we've somehow failed to mention a scene where she makes the poor man pretend he's her pet dog during a bit of sex-play. Muffat works so hard to play along that he uses his teeth to fetch a stick when she throws it his way.

Nana's ending comes on rather abruptly. Rather than, say, showing how her character developed as a result of her actions, Nana just decides off-screen that she's had enough of her sex-and-extortion (sextortion?) lifestyle, and that she's going to leave Paris. Despite practically everyone in the city's upper-crust having one reason or another to despise her, they all show up to throw Nana a grand farewell as she flies away to India in a hot air balloon. As the balloon floats away, a man is revealed to be hiding in the bottom of the basket. He ducks under her dress and a sly smile forms on Nana's lips as (we have to assume) the stowaway gentleman performs cunnilingus on her. You wouldn't possibly have thought *Nana* was going to end on a classy note, did you?

Meanwhile, Émile Zola's original novel ended with dying horribly of smallpox, describing her as, I quote: "a heap of pus and blood, a shovelful of putrid flesh." Talk about a softened ending for movie audiences, won't you say?

As far as literary adaptations go, *Nana, the True Key of Pleasure* isn't going to help anyone ace their book report on the novel. As far as erotic comedies go, it's not nearly as fun or outlandish as some of the other films in Cannon's library. (For a similar mixture of comedy and melodrama peppered with gratuitous nudity, we'd recommend the more entertaining *The Wicked Lady* from 1983.) Director Dan Wolman went back to directing Israeli films, while *Nana* served as Katya Berger's final leading role before taking a two-decade hiatus from acting.

10 to Midnight

Release date: March 11, 1983
Directed by: J. Lee Thompson
Written by: William Roberts
Starring: Charles Bronson, Andrew Stevens, Gene Davis, Lisa Eilbacher
Trailer Voiceover: "When there is no justice, this man is the law!"

Not only is *10 to Midnight* among the most exciting films Cannon ever produced, but perhaps one of the most underrated thrillers of the 1980s. A unique and electrifying blend of police procedural, vigilante movie, and slasher film, *10 to Midnight* was also the film that brought J. Lee Thompson, one of Cannon's most relied-upon directors, into the company fold.

After 1982's *Death Wish II* turned out to be a roaring financial success for the Golan and Globus-led Cannon, it's natural that the rising studio would want to follow it up with the next Charles Bronson feature. Golan reached out to producer Pancho Kohner, Bronson's good friend and de facto manager, to feel out what the star had in mind for his next project. Kohner and Bronson made many films together throughout their careers, including six for Cannon (*10 to Midnight*, *Murphy's Law* [1986], *Assassination* [1987], *Death Wish 4: The Crackdown* [1987], *Messenger of Death* [1988], and *Kinjite: Forbidden Subjects* [1989].) Pancho was the son of Paul Kohner, a super-agent in Hollywood's

Golden Age, who had represented big names like Greta Garbo, Billy Wilder, and Marlene Dietrich.

Golan and Globus were on their way to the Cannes Film Festival in a couple of weeks, and hoped they could start selling their next Charles Bronson movie there. Kohner pitched them a script—for what would eventually become another Bronson classic, *The Evil that Men Do* (1984)—with a price tag to option it at $200,000. Cannon balked. Who needed to pay $200,000 for a screenplay? Was a screenplay even necessary at all to sell a film? In Cannon's case, the answer was no.

The VHS cover for *10 to Midnight*, the best non-*Death Wish* movie Bronson starred in for Cannon.

Cannon agreed to make a Charles Bronson feature, but not *The Evil that Men Do*. They'd figure out exactly what film that would be at a future date, but in the meantime they needed to come up with a placeholder name they could use to pre-sell the movie to foreign territories at Cannes. Golan gave the then-imaginary movie its title, *10 to Midnight*, for no other reason than he thought it sounded cool. Under that title they mocked up a crude drawing of Bronson firing an Uzi in front of a globe, called it an "international thriller," and loosely described a plot that involved an "ultimate vigilante" getting even with terrorists. This as-yet-nonexistent movie sold like hot cakes.

A Spanish advertisement featuring the slapped-together artwork that was used to sell the movie at Cannes.

Back in the States with a budget in hand, it was finally time for the producers to find a script for their project. Kohner reached out to Lance Hool, a fellow producer with whom he and Bronson had worked on a movie called *Cabo Blanco* (1980). Hool would later play an instrumental role in Cannon's

Missing in Action franchise, as series producer and the writer-director of the second film. (You'll read more about him in that chapter.) Hool had been developing a script under the working title *Blood Bath*, which Kohner knew was a potential fit for Bronson. Written by veteran screenwriter William Roberts, *Blood Bath* was loosely inspired by the case of real-life serial killer Richard Speck, who murdered eight Chicago nurses in one horrific night in 1966. Roberts had been famous for writing numerous "man's movies," including the classic Western *The Magnificent Seven* (1960), which also featured Bronson. More surprisingly, Roberts was also the creator of the long-running family sitcom, *The Donna Reed Show* (1958–1966). You read that correctly: the guy who wrote this ultra-violent, nudity-filled Bronson thriller also created one of the most wholesome sitcoms to ever grace television. (I guess he had a sensitive side?)

Another early, international ad. The roughly-sketched artwork here more closely resembles what was eventually used for the American videotape release, even if the tagline doesn't reflect the movie accurately.

The *Blood Bath* script was not an international thriller and had nothing to do with terrorism, both of which were things the original sales art had advertised. Even the title itself, *10 to Midnight*, was meaningless once pasted overtop the *Blood Bath* script. None of that mattered now that their money was already in hand.

A serious-looking Bronson appears in a Spanish lobby card for *10 to Midnight*.

To direct the film, Cannon hired the consummately professional veteran director J. Lee Thompson. The tiny-framed Thompson had served as a B-29 tail gunner during the Second World War. Afterward, a short stint as a West End playwright led to his entryway into the film industry. He came up in the waning years of the British studio system; his final film for his native country, *The Guns of Navarone* (1961), starring Gregory Peck, is one of Britain's best war films. He set sail for Hollywood immediately afterward, and the first film he made in his new home was *Cape Fear* (1962), a classic also starring Peck and featuring Robert Mitchum in one of his all-time greatest roles. From there, Thompson became something of a journeyman, taking on a wide variety of projects, notable among them films like *Mackenna's Gold* (1969), the fourth and fifth *Planet of the Apes* movies, and three movies with Charles Bronson: *St. Ives* (1976), *The White Buffalo* (1977), and the aforementioned *Cabo Blanco*.

Proven by his great working relationships with actors like Bronson, Mitchum, and Peck, Thompson had a way of hitting it off with actors whom other directors couldn't. Bronson especially liked Thompson and felt comfortable working with him, which no doubt factored in to Cannon's hiring him. It proved to be a fruitful relationship: Thompson would go on to direct seven more movies for the studio following *10 to Midnight*, including *The Ambassador* (1985), *King Solomon's Mines* (1985), *Firewalker* and *Murphy's Law* (both 1986), *Death Wish 4* (1987), *Messenger of Death* (1988), and *Kinjite: Forbidden Subjects* (1989). The latter four films were also Bronson vehicles.

In *10 to Midnight*, Bronson plays Leo Kessler, an honored and well-respected detective in the Los Angeles Police Department. Kessler has spent his decades-long career playing by the rules, but makes no effort to hide how fed up he's become with the justice system. He's sick of seeing depraved criminals protected by lawyers, and let off with only a slap on the wrist; he's the type of cop who loudly laments that he "remember[s] a time when *legal* meant *lawful* . . . now it means *loophole*." Kessler's been burned by the establishment too many times, and you sense that he's nearing a breaking point. Once you meet the sort of scum whose job it is his to bring down, you understand.

A pulpy, Italian poster by Enzo Sciotti and his longtime assistant, Renzo Cenci. Responsible for many iconic pieces of Italian horror film artwork, Sciotti has painted more than three thousand movie posters across his prolific career.

There's a serial killer loose in Los Angeles: a dangerously intelligent slasher preying on beautiful young women and leaving behind no evidence. Warren Stacey (Gene Davis) is a lowly office repairman, young and good-looking but clearly a "creep," as women familiar with his pervy advances never hesitate to describe him. The film opens with a detailed look into his deadly methods, as Warren surreptitiously watches a pretty, young lady climb into a van with a strapping suitor. Warren doesn't follow, but goes to the movie theater. After putting the sleaze on two teenyboppers—making sure they would recall meeting him there, and thus provide an ironclad alibi—he sneaks out through a bathroom window and stalks his comely victim to a secluded area of the nearby park, where the woman is making love to her boyfriend in the back of his van. He strips himself of all his clothes, and then yanks open the door. The woman screams, and briefly escapes while the knife-brandishing nudist makes short work of her boyfriend. Before long, though, he catches up with her; he makes no attempt to hide his identity from his victims, and she uses his name as she pleads with him to let her live. There's no changing his mind, and he delivers the killing blow. Within minutes, he's climbing back through the theater's bathroom window, flushing his rubber gloves down the toilet, and returned to his seat before the lights come up—no one around him having the slightest notion he was ever gone.

Only minutes after arriving at the murder scene, Kessler already knows he's seen the killer's handiwork before in a young woman whose body was discovered in the same park a few months ago. Not one to normally let emotions get in the way of his work, Kessler's knocked for a loop when he realizes the victim is an old friend of his grown daughter, Laurie's. With the help of his fresh-faced new partner, Detective Paul McAnn (Andrew Stevens), Kessler now has a personal motive for getting this psychopath off the streets.

Kessler pokers around the victims' apartment and questions her roommate, played by a future Real Housewife of Orange County, Jeana Keough. (She's also recognizable as the star of many, many Z.Z. Top music videos, and is credited here under her maiden name, Tomasina.) Every clue point seems to point Kessler toward the slimy little Warren Stacey, who it turns out had been the victim's co-worker. Not only does Stacey speak fluent Spanish—the victim was receiving frequent, dirty phone calls from an unknown "Mexican" male—but the dead girl's diary provides a clear motive, detailing the times she'd coldly rebuffed Stacey's flirtations. Kessler is truly convinced, however, the moment he combs Stacey's apartment and finds an electronic masturbation device under the bathroom sink. (Kessler demonstrates a keen eye for profiling murderous, sexual deviants, as he coolly theorizes during the autopsy of the first victim: "If anybody does something like this, his knife gotta be his penis.")

When another victim turns up dead—the roommate this time—they bring Stacey in for questioning, where it's revealed that he once did time in juvenile hall for animal cruelty and for slashing a little girl with a knife. Kessler *knows* this is their man: he grills Stacey about the last time he "made it" with a woman and completely loses his cool, and he whips out Stacey's plug-in fuck machine—which looks like a rubber vagina affixed to the end of an electric carving knife—and waves it in the suspect's face.

The super-creepy killer Warren Stacey (Gene Davis) stalks Karen (Jeana Keough) from inside her bedroom closet.

"Do you know what this is, Warren?" Bronson's detective screams. "It's for jacking off!"

Stacey's lawyer rescues him from the enraged Kessler's wrath. Having nothing to hold him on, the police have no choice but to release Stacey once the movie theater teenyboppers confirm his alibi. Without evidence, the district attorney can't bring charges against him. (The D.A. is played by Cannon regular Robert F. Lyons, who was also in *Death Wish II* and *Murphy's Law* with Bronson, and co-starred in *Platoon Leader* [1988] opposite Michael Dudikoff.)

It appears as if Stacey has won, at least this time. He might have gotten away with it scot-free, too, if not for his arrogance. He tries to get back at Kessler by crank-calling his daughter, Laurie, a nurse at the local hospital. This manages to rattle Kessler, yes, but it also pisses him off *real* bad.

Bronson's daughter is played by Lisa Eilbacher, a former child actor who went on to be something of an "it girl" in the 1980s, making notable appearances in *An Officer and a Gentleman* (1982) and *Beverly Hills Cop* (1984). Here's another bit of trivia: both she and co-star Andrew Stevens were up for the lead roles in *Star Wars* (1977), losing out to Carrie Fisher and Mark Hamill, respectively.

The detectives are able to match a voice print for Stacey to the latest batch of dirty phone calls, and convince the chief of police (Wilfred "Die-uh-beet-us" Brimley) to arrest Stacey. Brimley, known for his marvelous moustache and memorable roles in films like *The Thing* (1982), *The Natural* (1984), and *Cocoon* (1985), is among the most consistently fantastic character actors of the '80s. He's probably better known, though, as a spokesperson for Quaker Oats and Liberty Medical. His ads for the latter company—which featured his odd and oft-imitated pronunciation of the word "diabetes"—became an early viral video, and one of the first clips that Internet hucksters remixed into song form.

Although Stacey's about to be arrested and charged with harassment, that's not enough for Kessler. He wants to take this deranged maniac off the street, and he'll need to make sure he can pin him with the murders. So, Kessler sneaks into the forensics lab at night—the weed-smoking technician on guard is played by Bronson's stepson, Paul McCallum—and makes off with a syringe of blood from the case's evidence stash. He then breaks into Stacey's apartment and plants the blood on his clothes. When the police promptly find this "evidence," Stacey is charged with murder one.

For a while, it seems like Stacey's case is cut and dry. Kessler and McAnn are painted as heroes. Meanwhile, Stacey's shyster lawyer starts coaching his client, who insists the evidence is fake, for a potential insanity plea. Stacey's lawyer is played by Geoffrey Lewis, a hard-working character actor known for his recognizable scowl, who appeared in more than 200 films and television roles, including many of Clint Eastwood's movies. (He was the father of actress Juliette Lewis.)

Eventually the honest McAnn, who is due to testify during the trial, figures out that his partner indeed planted the blood and confronts Kessler about it. At first, Kessler encourages him to "forget what's legal and do what's right," but in the end, rather than ask his junior colleague to commit perjury, Kessler comes clean to the judge. Naturally this blows up in the LAPD's face. Kessler is fired, and Stacey is released.

Bronson's unmistakable eyes loom over the film's French poster.

Once again, Stacey's arrogance leads him to make a dumb mistake. Kessler receives a late-night ring from the freed killer, who's calling to taunt Kessler and let him know he'll have his revenge. Kessler has other ideas. Finding himself with lots of free time suddenly on his hands, Kessler dedicates himself to making the stabby slimeball's life a living hell. The ex-cop follows him around in his car, breaks into his apartment to mess with his head, and goes to his workplace to hang gruesome crime scene photos all over the bulletin board. (Never mind how Kessler got into the office without notice: tacking up photos of naked, dead girls in a public setting requires *major* cajones.)

If we thought Stacey was insane before, well, Kessler's antics drive him *really* crazy. Stacey snaps. With murder on his mine he heads straight to the hospital dormitories, where Kessler's daughter shares an apartment with three of her fellow nurses.

Do Laurie's besties look familiar? Ola Ray, who plays "Bunny," was Michael Jackson's shrieking girlfriend in the landmark "Thriller" music video. And Kelly Palzis, playing the blond Doreen, would eventually change her name to Kelly Preston and appear in movies such as *Twins* (1988), *Jerry Maguire* (1996), and the terrifying train wreck that was Mike Myers' live-action *The Cat in the Hat* (2003). Palzis/Preston also appeared in Cannon's *52 Pick-Up* (1986). She was briefly engaged to Charlie Sheen in the late '80s, but that was called off shortly after it was widely reported in the news that he had accidentally shot her in the arm. She eventually became Mrs. John Travolta in 1991.

Kessler learns that Stacey is on his way to the dorm but can't get there fast enough, and the fully nude Stacey murders her three roommates as Laurie stays hidden nearby. This entire sequence—easily the film's most tense and terrifying—is the one most closely inspired by the real-life Speck murders of 1966, in which one of the killer's intended victims survived by hiding under a bed while her eight friends were murdered within the apartment.

Laurie barely escapes from the apartment alive, only to be chased through the streets by the naked butcher. Just as Stacey is about to catch her, Laurie runs directly into her father's protective arms—while Stacey runs into the barrel of Kessler's revolver. Police cruisers arrive seconds later, their flashing lights bathing this final showdown between the sick-of-it-all ex-cop and the nude psycho in shades of red and blue. Stacey realizes he's trapped. His last line of defense kicks in, and all of his lawyer's coaching for a potential insanity plea comes flooding back to him.

Kessler clutches his daughter (Lisa Eilbacher) close during their final confrontation with the naked and bloody Stacey.

"Go ahead, take me in. You can't punish me! I'm sick!" the madman shouts, loudly enough for the converging officers of the law to hear. "All you can do is lock me up ... but not forever! One day I'll get out – that's the law! ... I'll be back, and you'll hear from me! You and the whole fucking world!"

Kessler growls through gritted teeth:

"No, we won't."

He pulls the trigger, putting a bullet-sized hole through Stacey's forehead. The credits roll.

It's the perfect ending for a fantastic thriller, even when you consider that Kessler—at this point of the film not even a rogue cop, but a lone wolf vigilante—would likely face prison time for killing a man as police were about to bring him into custody. Stacey is so awful, so despicably terrible a human being that Kessler's trigger-pull feels 100% justified. An original ending had Kessler wrestling down and stabbing the nude maniac, but this was supposedly altered because Bronson wasn't comfortable with the scene, and pages were cut from the script because they attempted to humanize Stacey in a way. In the case here, it feels as if every change made was a wise one. (You can read the cut-out scenes—and so many more fantastic details about this film—in Paul Talbot's exceedingly awesome book, *Bronson's Loose Again!*.)

A Spanish lobby card using a still photo from the alternate, underwear version of the movie's ending.

Actor Gene Davis, too, does his part in making Warren Stacey so inherently hate-able. Davis was best-known at this point in his career for playing a cross-dressing police informant in the Al Pacino flick, *Cruising* (1980); he'd play a killer again in the later Bronson/Thompson/Cannon vehicle, *Messenger of Death*. Warren Stacey was a difficult role, and one for which by all reports the script offered very little guidance. Davis plays his cards close to the chest; we're offered little insight into his reasons for killing, which makes his actions all the more disturbing. The sickening confidence that Davis instills in him (and is ultimately the villain's undoing) puts us entirely on Kessler's side when the gun goes off. Not only did he have to perform his murder and chase scenes wearing no clothes or shoes (this was shot during a cold, wet winter in 1982), but he had to do them all twice. Cannon was savvy enough to plan for two different versions of the movie: one for theaters and video, and one censored for cable television. Davis had to do each scene naked, and then all over again in small, black undies.

It's not surprising at all, but critics absolutely *hated* this extremely violent, nudity-filled thriller. None other than Roger Ebert opened his scathing, zero-star review by calling it a "scummy little sewer of a movie"—to be fair, he couldn't even get its name right, repeatedly referring to the film as "From Ten To Midnight" throughout his write-up. (Ebert was likely confusing it with Bronson's 1976 Western, *From Noon Till Three*.) Audiences, however, gave it a much better response, bringing home more than $7 million in domestic ticket sales and much more abroad; the cable broadcast rights and video rental deals were even more lucrative. For a movie that Cannon spent less than $5 million to make, it was a big success—the second in a row for the studio and their favorite, stone-faced star.

Paul McAnn (Andrew Stevens) jumps to action in *10 to Midnight*.

Interview: Actor Andrew Stevens

Andrew Stevens played Charles Bronson's partner, detective Paul McAnn, in Cannon's crime thriller *10 to Midnight*.

The multi-talented Stevens has worked—very successfully—in many different facets of the film industry since the 1970s. At the time of *10 to Midnight*, Stevens was best known for his acting work in films such as Sidney J. Furie's *The Boys in Company C* (1978) and *Death Hunt* (1981). Since that time he's also worked extensively as a director, screenwriter, and executive at several different independent studios. To date he's produced more than 175 films, most notably the cult classic *The Boondock Saints* (1999), *The Whole Nine Yards* (2000) starring Bruce Willis, and *3000 Miles to Graceland* (2001).

The Cannon Film Guide: **You appeared in *Death Hunt* just two years prior to co-starring with Bronson again in *10 to Midnight*. Did that factor at all into your casting in the latter film, or was it more of a coincidence?**

Andrew Stevens: They were completely unrelated. Different studios and different production companies. Different directors. The only common denominator was Bronson.

Do you recall what excited you most about the film, or the role?

After many years of playing the coming-of-age young man, or the "son of," in so many films and television shows, I liked that the role was an adult, with an autonomous point of view, in a position of authority. I think at the time I particularly liked that I was not playing the Gene Davis role.

Can you describe what J. Lee Thompson was like to work with, as your director?

J. Lee Thompson was a slight and impish ball of fire who was very compassionate and had a decisive point of view about things. He was very supportive of me. Subsequently, I worked with him on the pilot of the ABC TV series, *Code Red* (1981–1982), which was produced by Irwin Allen.

Your career as a producer took off after you'd spent nearly two decades working as a professional actor. What initially led you in that direction?

I fell out of love with acting and was looking for a way out and away to make my own films. After learning I had a bit of cachet in the independent film market, I strategically and premeditatedly bartered my services as an actor to get films made as a writer, producer, and director, and also to parlay that into ownership of my own films.

Yet another take on the Bronson pistol pose by the great Spanish movie poster artist Enrique Mataix.

In what ways did your experience in front of the camera prepare you for the many roles you've played behind it?

I spent many years working with a lot of people who were talented, and I assimilated other sides of the business by observing and retaining both information and the specific abilities which made something work. I also spent many years, particularly in routine television and independent films, working with subpar journeymen who either were punching the clock and phoning in pedestrian work, or had lucked into a position of being able to direct a film and had no clue how to work with actors, much less make a movie from a technical standpoint. I learned as much by the squandered opportunities of those I observed as I did from the top-notch talent I worked with over the years.

Menahem Golan and Yoram Globus were famous for their international sales, and for being among the first producers to recognize the full potential of the video market. You're also well-regarded for your ability to sell films abroad and for utilizing alternative markets like video and cable. Do you have a respect or admiration for what Cannon was able to pull off for much of the 1980s?

The "go-go boys" were certainly groundbreakers in the independent business and much like Avi Lerner, were able to attract a level of talent in independent films. My partner and I were able to do the same thing at Franchise Pictures, but we had an output deal with Warner Bros. for major distribution and Prints & Advertising, which deviates a bit from the Cannon model. I met them over the years and they were thought of by my colleagues with a kind smirk, as fossils who made a great impact on the independent film business and then the business passed them by.

House of the Long Shadows

Release Date: June 17, 1983 (U.K.)
Directed by: Pete Walker
Written by: Michael Armstrong
Starring: Vincent Price, Christopher Lee, Peter Cushing, John Carradine, Desi Arnaz Jr.
Trailer Voiceover: "What lives in this house? What stalks these halls? What hides in these shadows, and *who* is playing that piano? Welcome to the House of the Long Shadows!"

Four true legends of the macabre teamed up for the first (and only) time to film what was essentially a classic horror version of *The Expendables* (2010). The resulting *House of the Long Shadows* is an enjoyable mystery which managed to both parody and pay homage to these screen icons' prior filmographies. Introductions probably aren't necessary for these old-school titans of terror, so we'll be quick about it.

Vincent Price was one of the horror genre's most beloved actors, and who you could easily argue possessed its most recognizable voice. (Not to mention, many of horror's most fantastic moustaches.) Price possessed a unique style of gentlemanly creepiness, a sort of debonair charm that made him seem like the sort of new boyfriend your grandma might bring to holiday dinner but may actually be a 400-year-old vampire. Famous for appearing in many other classic chillers named after houses—including *House of Wax* (1953), *House on Haunted Hill* (1959), and *House of Usher* (1960)—Price was a staple in horror movies for decades. By the early 1980s, even youngsters who had never watched a black-and-white horror film likely still would have recognized Price's unmistakable vocal timbre from his spoken word guest appearance in Michael Jackson's record-breaking pop hit, "Thriller."

House of Long Shadows on VHS. They couldn't have assembled a better cast of living, horror legends than this.

Christopher Lee was most famous for playing the best of the batty bloodsuckers, Count Dracula himself, a whopping *ten separate times* throughout his career. For the hallowed British horror studio, Hammer Films, he also played Frankenstein's Monster, Rasputin the Mad Monk, and the Mummy, forever securing the maximum possible level of street cred as a horror icon. To top it off, he then starred in 1973's *The Wicker Man,* one of the greatest British horror films of all time. (Not to be confused with the 2006 remake starring Nicolas Cage, which is also incredible—but for all of the wrong reasons.) Christopher Lee's badassery essentially knew no bounds: he played Saruman in *The Lord of the Rings* movies, Count Dooku in the *Star Wars* prequels, and the man with the golden gun in the Bond flick *The Man With The Golden Gun* (1974). Prior to acting, he served in the Royal Air Force during World War II, then continued to work in the Central Registry of War Criminals and Security Suspects to hunt Nazis when the war was over. In the very last decade of his life he spent his free time recording heavy metal albums. Yeah, Lee may have been the most badass actor to have ever lived.

Meanwhile, Peter Cushing played the scientist, Victor Frankenstein, opposite Christopher Lee's monster in *The Curse of Frankenstein* (1957), as well as vampire-hunter Van Helsing opposite Lee's Dracula in *Horror of Dracula* (1958), both for Hammer Films. Cushing and Lee appeared in 24 films together over their storied careers—with *House of the Long Shadows* sadly being their final performance as a duo. He was a genre movie fixture throughout the rest of his career, from playing Sherlock Holmes in *Hound of the Baskervilles* (1959) to Grand Moff Tarkin in *Star Wars* (1977). He'd make one more Cannon movie appearance in their loopy, high fantasy film, *Sword of the Valiant* (1984).

John Carradine—patriarch of the prodigious Carradine Hollywood dynasty—was one of cinema's hardest-working actors. With more than 300 credits to his name stretching all the way back to filmmaking's golden age, Carradine had worked with everyone from John Ford to Martin Scorsese, Cecil B. DeMille to Woody Allen. While no other of his roles were ever as famous as his turn as Jim Casy in *The Grapes of Wrath* (1940), he was once considered a go-to actor for old Hollywood horror films thanks to appearances in spooky classics such as *Revenge of the Zombies* (1943), *The Mummy's Ghost* (1944), *House of Dracula* (1945) and *House of Frankenstein* (1944).

Long Shadows' cast posed for a series of now-iconic photos to promote the movie ahead of its release.

By 1982, filmmaker Pete Walker had effectively retired from the moviemaking business, having made a career of directing sleazy exploitation movies with lurid titles like *School for Sex* (1969), *The Flesh and Blood Show* (1972), and *Die Screaming, Marianne* (1971). He'd purchased a handful of English theaters and had been in the process of building his own, independent chain when he received a call from Golan and Globus, who were seeking films for the newly-formed Cannon.

Walker and screenwriter Michael Armstrong—who'd later do some uncredited script work on *Lifeforce* (1985)—agreed to a pitch meeting, in hopes they might be able to sell the burgeoning studio on a horror script they'd developed together called *Deliver Us Fârom Evil*. While Golan was not keen on that particular project—about, no joke: a murderous, aborted fetus that returns to take revenge on its killers—the producer made them a counter-offer. As a lifelong movie fanatic, Golan had dreamed of seeing the big-name stars of the spine-tingling flicks of yesteryear—Vincent Price, Christopher Lee, Peter Cushing, and John Carradine—share the silver screen together. Though attempts had been made at this sort of all-star horror picture by other filmmakers, none had been successful in casting that many of them in a single film. As these guys were all getting up there in age, Golan probably felt the clock ticking down on his chances at pulling off this feat. Carradine, Cushing, and Price were in their 70s by the time *Long Shadows* was released. Lee was the youngest at 61—hardly a spring chicken. (Walker claimed that Golan had also requested Boris Karloff and Bela Lugosi, not knowing that both were already deceased.)

While the sort of horror flick Golan was asking for was slightly outside of their wheelhouse, Walker and Armstrong didn't want to let a good opportunity pass them by. They agreed to return with a new proposal, and decided they'd approach it as a nostalgia piece. At first they'd hoped to remake a 1932 Boris Karloff venture titled *The Old Dark House*, but were unable to secure the rights from Universal. Instead, they opted to reimagine *Seven Keys to Baldpate*, a 1913 novel by Charlie Chan creator Earl Derr Biggers, which had been adapted for the screen at least half a dozen times already. The duo kept the original premise, setting, and twist ending, and tossed almost everything else out the window. Over two weeks, Armstrong pounded out a new script which played on the more clichéd elements of the classic, Gothic horror films that had made their dream cast so famous.

The ploy worked: Cannon seemed thrilled with the treatment, and all four stars signed on shortly after receiving the script. Production started and moved along relatively quickly: the film was shot briskly over five weeks and almost entirely at Rotherfield Park, a stately British manor house which was already dressed much like how it's seen in the movie.

House of the Long Shadows begins with Kenneth Magee (Desi Arnaz Jr.), a bestselling novelist, taking a meeting with his longtime editor, Sam (Richard Todd). They get into friendly, barbed debates over everything from the nature of love to the literary value of Emily Brontë. This leads to a high-stakes wager between friends, as Kenneth bets Sam $20,000 dollars that he can bang out a novel like *Wuthering Heights* in just 24 hours if given a peaceful and inspirational environment in which to work. Sam suggests Baldpate Manor, a mansion in Wales which has sat empty for years, and whose owner he already knows. They shake on it, and Kenneth sets off for Baldpate.

Desi Arnaz, Jr.—here credited (somewhat confusingly) without the suffix—is the son of television royalty, Lucille Ball and Desi Arnaz. He primarily worked in television, most notably on *Here's Lucy* from 1968–1972, opposite his real-life mother and sister, and as a lead character on the short-lived ABC science fiction series *Automan* from 1983–1984. (The latter roles was opposite Chuck Wagner, the future star of Cannon's post-apocalyptic comedy *America 3000*, released in 1986.) As of this writing, Arnaz has only appeared in one theatrical feature post-*Long Shadows*: 1993's *The Mambo Kings*, in which he played his own father. Meanwhile, actor Richard Todd starred in *Stage Fright* (1950) for Alfred Hitchcock and more than 50 other films. Coincidentally, he starred in a famous 1953 BBC production of *Wuthering Heights*—the same novel he challenges Arnaz's character to top in *House of the Long Shadows*.

Kenneth has a little trouble finding Baldpate Manor—that's character actor Norman Rossington, best remembered for playing the Beatles' road manager in *A Hard Day's Night*, playing a wary stationmaster—but he eventually makes it to the spooky, old house after an extended journey. He's surprised, though, to find that not only is he not alone there, but he's unwittingly part of some wacky flash mob when one oddball character after another arrives at the manor under mysterious circumstances.

First to arrive is a pretty, young blonde, Mary Norton (Julie Peasgood), with the preposterous claim she's being followed by a terrorist organization—and whom Kenneth believes to be a ruse sent by his editor to distract him from their bet. The pair next cross paths with an elderly couple claiming to be the house's caretakers, who are later unveiled to be Lord Elijah Grisbane (Carradine) and his daughter Victoria, both members of the aristocratic family who've long made Baldpate their home. (The Victoria character had originally been written for actress Elsa Lanchester—the original *Bride of Franken-*

stein [1935]—but actress Sheila Keith stepped in when the former was too ill to take on the role.) They're followed by the brothers Sebastian (Cushing) and Lionel (Price) Grisbane, who have been away from the family estate for four decades. Finally arriving is Corrigan (Lee), a wealthy gentleman there to scope out Baldpate as a potential real estate investment.

A long shadow hangs over the stately Baldpate Manor in this Italian billboard poster.

As the night goes on, the true reason behind the Grisbanes' unexpected reunion at Baldpate is revealed. Forty years earlier the fourth Grisbane sibling, Roderick—who was fourteen at the time—brutally murdered a "simple" village girl he'd been having relations with once he discovered she'd become pregnant. Rather than risking scandal, the family covered up the affair and took Roderick's punishment into their own hands, sentencing him to be locked inside his childhood bedroom for the next four decades. His sentence now over, they've returned to release him when the clock strikes midnight. However, when they open his door Roderick is *gone*. Over the next few hours, the guests at Baldpate—including yet more arrivals in the form of troubled young couple Diane (Louise English, a regular on *The Benny Hill Show* from 1978 to 1986) and Andrew (Richard Hunter)—are killed off one-at-a-time in gruesome ways, as Roderick takes his revenge on the family who locked him up so many years ago.

I won't spoil the surprises that come in the movie's second half, because there are many of them and they are actually quite good. *Long Shadows* has not one, but *two* twist endings. (Even M. Night Shyamalan would be impressed.) After a slow start—Christopher Lee and Vincent Price don't show up until halfway through—the movie takes off once its four horror superstars have assembled. After that, the movie's many, morbid murders come fast and furious.

House of the Long Shadows was finished on schedule and under budget. (As Walker told it, Cannon ran out of money three weeks into the shoot and he was forced to front the cast's paychecks himself for the remaining weeks.) The movie's odd pacing can probably be chalked up to Cannon's interference in the editing room, as is so often the case. Part of Walker's contract—drawn up, in typical Cannon fashion, on the back of an envelope—gave the final cut to the studio, who allegedly trimmed the film to lessen its humor, and tried to turn it into a mainstream horror film that would somehow compete with the bloody slasher movies of the day. Price was reportedly so livid about his scenes being cut that he refused to help promote the film, or even speak with anyone at Cannon.

The movie had a somewhat tepid showing in theaters, perhaps due to it being mis-marketed as a straight horror film. If the whole idea of a Gothic, haunted house movie sounds outdated, that's because it absolutely was—Hammer Films, Amicus, and AIP had all ceased production of horror movies by 1983, and few studios were still making this style of film any more. Some savvier fans and critics understood the movie, and saw the film for what it was: a purposefully campy send-up of the Gothic Horror genre, and one in which all four of the top-billed horror greats were obviously having a blast while making it. It's received a kinder appreciation in the years since, and is now considered to be an overlooked gem by many of those who enjoy old-fashioned scares. Armstrong's script, in particular, gives the old horror guard some fantastically fun dialogue to chew on. ("Don't interrupt me while I'm soliloquizing," Price scolds Arnaz at one point—what a wonderful line!)

In the end, *House of the Long Shadows* could still be considered a success for Cannon, even though it never found much of a theatrical audience. The sales of broadcast rights (to HBO) and video licensing (to MGM) more than exceeded the modest $1 million the movie cost to make. More importantly, both to Golan and to horror cineastes everywhere, it succeeded in bringing together these four horror icons on screen for the first, final, and only time.

A videocassette copy of *Young Warriors*, formerly rented by Town Video of Montclair, New Jersey.

Young Warriors,
a.k.a. *The Graduates of Malibu High*

Release Date: August 26, 1983
Directed by: Lawrence D. Foldes
Written by: Russell W. Colgin & Lawrence D. Foldes
Starring: James Van Patten, Ernest Borgnine, Richard Roundtree
Trailer Voiceover: "They're the new American heroes, and the ultimate weapon in the fight against crime!"

Have you ever wondered what would happen if you threw *Death Wish* (1974) into a blender with *Animal House* (1978) and mixed the two together? Cannon apparently tried just that in 1983, and the resulting film was *Young Warriors*.

It wasn't unusual for Cannon to release a movie that seemed to be suffering through some sort of identity crisis. Swerving between tones and genres in a fashion that could give audiences whiplash, *Young Warriors* may somehow be one of the studio's most identity-confused movies.

Young Warriors begins as your standard '80s teensploitation flick. It opens with the film's cool cat lead, Kevin (James Van Patten, son of Dick), collecting his high school diploma by riding his motorcycle up to the podium with a bikini-clad lassie on his back. "These are the Graduates of Malibu High," the on-screen titles read, and you might guess that the film is heading in the direction of *The Last American Virgin* or *Fast Times at Ridgemont High* (1982)—but then, it doesn't. Cue the surprisingly dark theme song:

"In the heart of the city you don't walk the streets alone
'cos some stranger with burning desires is grinding his teeth just to take you on, he's runnin' you down
Blastin' out of the shadows, they take your heart and your reason to live
But you know it's an eye for an eye, and you answer with blood in the streets!
The Young Warriors, they're ridin' through the city!"

The lyrics will make sense by the movie's final act. Honest! *Young Warriors* was composer Rob Walsh's first score for Cannon; he'd do *Revenge of the Ninja* next.

Young Warriors skips ahead three years, and jarringly appears to re-mold itself into a crass, campus comedy. It's suddenly the sort of movie where nubile co-eds are chased naked through a dormitory, students hook up for hanky-panky between the stacks at the library, and a ringing alarm clock is dealt with by launching it through a window with a baseball bat. (The young, nude woman who the boys chase from their bedroom is none other than scream queen Linnea Quigley, famous for her roles in *Return of the Living Dead* [1985], *Savage Streets* [1984], *Night of the Demons* [1988], *Silent Night, Deadly Night* [1984] and many other low-budget, VHS-era horror flicks.)

Kevin and his cronies—now fraternity brothers—live together in one, big house along with their adorable pooch, Butch, who wears sunglasses and a bandana. We get a lot of cutaways to silly reaction shots of the dog as these party animal bros haze a group of poor fraternity pledges. At this point it's the sort of movie where we're given an extreme close-up of a pledge's freshly-shaved rear end as he pinches an olive between his butt cheeks and deposits it into a martini glass.

The first third or so of the movie goes on like this. Then, just as we're settling in and getting comfortable with what we figure is yet another, lesser *Animal House* knock-off, *Young Warriors* throws a glass of ice water in our face. You see, while Kevin and his friends are forcing freshmen to tie bricks to their wieners and toss them out of second-story windows, shit gets super-dark elsewhere.

While Kevin's rowdy cohorts play up to their campus comedy antics, his little sister Tiffany is riding home from her senior prom when all of a sudden her car is run off the road by a group of lowlifes in a black van. She's able to escape the crashed vehicle, which naturally explodes into a giant fireball, killing her date (played by James' brother, Nels Van Patten). Unfortunately, she's unable to elude the despicable thugs, who sexually assault her in a rape scene so disturbing and graphic that it possibly could have made *Death Wish II* director Michael Winner a little bit uncomfortable.

There's no more laughter in the film from this point onward. Tiffany dies from her injuries a few scenes later, which sends Kevin into a downward spiral. He rages against the criminal justice machine much to the chagrin of his cop father, Lieutenant Bob Carrigan, who never really seems overly interested in apprehending his daughter's killer at all. Kevin's pops is a rigid, by-the-books homicide detective played by Ernest Borgnine, who won the Best Actor Oscar for *Marty* in 1955. His bushy eyebrows and unmistakable voice were regularly seen and heard on television—*McHale's Navy* (1962–1966), *Airwolf* (1984–1987)—and in more than a few awesome movies—such as *The Wild Bunch* (1969), *The Dirty Dozen* (1967), *Escape from New York* (1981)—across his 61-year acting career.

Carrigan's partner is played by Shaft himself, Richard Roundtree, a fixture in many classics both cult and otherwise. (He's one baaaaaad motha—*shut yo' mouth!*) Despite their truncated screen time compared to the movie's young leads, Borgnine and Roundtree receive top billing in the movie, because star power. Meanwhile Kevin's mum is played by Lynda Day George of *Mission: Impossible* (1971–1973).

In the days and weeks following his sister's assault, Kevin's behavior becomes erratic. He starts his own investigation into Tiffany's death but only runs into dead-ends and interference from his father. His mounting frustration summits with an extended softporn scene where he and his girlfriend,

Lucy, make love by the light of 100 candles. She's played by Anne Lockhart, who was Lieutenant Sheba on the original *Battlestar Galactica* (1978–1979). Fans of cult, 1980s b-movies will also recognize her from Empire Pictures' *Troll* (1986); she also had a tiny amount of screen time appearing as a murder victim in the Cannon Bronson flick *10 to Midnight* (1983).

Three of our heavily-armed young warriors, from left to right: Stan (Ed De Stefane), Scott (Tom Reilly), and Kevin (James Van Patten).

This soft-lit whoopee somehow provides the jolt inspiration Kevin needed to come up with his master plan: to organize his frat brothers into a gang of armed vigilantes. They're all too eager to get involved—his gang of "young warriors" includes the handsome Scott (Tom Reilly, best known as Bobby "Hot Dog" Nelson on *CHiPs*, 1977–1983), their shaggy dog, Butch, and the awkward, nerdish Fred, played Chuck's son, Mike Norris. Believe it or not, Mike was the first Norris to appear in a Cannon film, a full year before his father became one of the studio's top stars in *Missing in Action* (1984). Mike would later co-star in the studio's *Delta Force 3: The Killing Game* (1991) and do some stunt work on *Hero and the Terror* (1988).

At first they're focused solely on taking revenge on his sister's assailants, but the young vigilantes soon find satisfaction in stopping whatever crimes they happen to come across. This is where the movie basically turns into *Death Wish: College Edition*. Kevin and his vigilante force cruise around in their jeep at night, stopping to gun down car thieves, muggers, and armed robbers in a volley of machine gun fire. There's a car chase, an exploding helicopter, and lots and lots of slow-motion squib action. The bodies pile up on both sides—good and bad—before Kevin and his team begin to question whether they're heroes, or if maybe they're just as bad as the villains they're terminating.

To *Young Warriors'* credit, that's a sobering question that many similar vigilante flicks never bothered asking. We root for Charles Bronson as he blows through baddies in the *Death Wish* films, but we rarely question whether his brand of lawless retribution is necessarily the right way to do things. (It's not—except in movies, where it's the most awesome way to do things.) *Young Warriors* attempts to force the question, as the audience watches Kevin stumble onto the realization that his bloodlust has robbed him of his humanity.

The young warriors wouldn't dream of going out and hunting down criminals to murder without bringing along their adorable canine mascot, Butch.

The grand finale milks the hero's tragic downfall extra hard: as the police close in, Kevin pulls the pin on a grenade, taking out both himself and his lone, surviving frat brother. Who would have guessed a movie that began with zany fraternity pranks and a nude coed chase scene would end in murder-suicide by hand grenade? The movie fades out as an instrumental version of "The Star Spangled Banner" plays on the soundtrack. The somber credits roll over a group photo of the cast in their graduation gowns. It's a downer, yeah, but of all the vigilante movies that Cannon made over the years, it's the only one that explores the character's mental state with any degree of realism.

But, that's a lot of pontificating over a movie which so prominently features a dog that wears sunglasses. *Young Warriors* was the product of filmmaking wunderkind Lawrence D. Foldes, who—by this time, age 22—had already directed two feature films, written four, and produced the cult teensploitation flick *Malibu High*, which had been a modest drive-in hit in 1978. (The movie—about a high school girl who screws her way to the top of her class—had the tagline, "Malibu High: Where the most important subject is *physical education*.")

Young Warriors was originally to be called *The Graduates of Malibu High*. Based on the working title, we have to assume that Cannon initially thought they were buying a sequel to Foldes' prior hit. The released product wound up being a totally unrelated film.

Hercules
Hercules II: The Adventures of Hercules

Release Dates: August 26, 1983 [I], October 4, 1985 [II]
Directed by: Luigi Cozzi (as Lewis Coates)
Written by: Luigi Cozzi
Starring: Lou Ferrigno, Sybil Danning, William Berger
Trailer Voiceover: "From the depths of space comes the strongest man on Earth!"

Sherlock Holmes. Allan Quatermain. King Arthur. Dracula. There are some characters whose existence long predates motion pictures, yet feel as if they were tailor-made for the medium. None perhaps more so than Hercules, the legendary hero of Greek and later Roman mythology. Since the dawn of cinema, more than 40 movies starring the muscle-bound son of Zeus have been released. He's been played by everyone from Gordon Scott to Arnold Schwarzenegger to Dwayne "The Rock" Johnson, but far and away the most famous of cinematic Hercs was Steve Reeves, an American bodybuilder who played the role in two wildly successful, Italian-produced movies of the late 1950s: *Hercules* (1957) and *Hercules Unchained* (1959). These movies spurred a long string of imitation sword and sandal flicks—known as "peplum" in their native Italy—many of which made their way to U.S. television screens in badly-dubbed versions and were eagerly consumed by American children on lazy, Saturday afternoons. One such child was Louis Ferrigno of Brooklyn, New York, who would grow up to be TV's *The Incredible Hulk* (1977–1982).

The first of Cannon's two *Hercules* movies on VHS.

The story behind this muscular Hulk of a man's rise to fame is a truly inspiring one. As an infant, a string of debilitating ear infections left Ferrigno with only 20% of his hearing. This impeded his early speech development, nearly rendering him deaf and mute. To tune out the bullying he took from the mean kids at school, he started weight-training in his early teens, looking to Steve Reeves of the old *Hercules* movies as his inspiration. He was still a teenager when he won his first bodybuilding title, and trained with Arnold Schwarzenegger for the first few years of his professional career. (The competition between these two heavyweights was famously chronicled in the 1975 documentary *Pumping Iron*.) Meanwhile, Ferrigno worked as hard on his speaking skills as he did his biceps. In 1977 he was cast as the green-skinned Incredible Hulk on the TV adaptation of the popular Marvel comic book series, while actor Bill Bixby played his scientist alter-ego, Bruce Banner. Ferrigno's popularity on the show led Cannon to cast him as the hero of their new *Hercules* films, poetically bringing everything full circle. It would fulfill a lifelong dream for a man who was inspired to get so massively ripped by the very same character he idolized as a child.

The film's sales ads weren't very subtle about reminding prospective buyers of Ferrigno's prior role as TV's *The Incredible Hulk*.

Whether you love or hate Ferrigno's two *Hercules* movies, it's hard to imagine any actor more physically perfect for the role. Standing six-and-a-half-feet tall with 23-inch biceps, Ferrigno was half a head taller than his bodybuilder rival, Arnold Schwarzenegger. Where Arnold was lean and chiseled, Ferrigno's appearance packed muscle on top of muscle on top of muscle. For the Hercules role, Ferrigno grew a beard and bulked up even further to an absolutely massive 270-pound frame. In peak *Hercules* form, Ferrigno was the physical embodiment of *strength*. He looked like a guy who could crush a car or, for that matter, throw a bear into outer space.

Hercules, though, wasn't the first film Ferrigno shot for Cannon. That would be Bruno Mattei's *Seven Magnificent Gladiators* (1984), but it wouldn't be released until the year after *Hercules*. The plan was to shoot the two films back-to-back, and so much of the same cast was hired for both movies. The studio opted to shoot *Gladiators* first. The production ran into many problems—you can read about those in that film's chapter—but chief among them was that the movies' two lead actors (Ferrigno and Sybil Danning) got along so poorly that they weren't even on speaking terms through much of the shoot. The final product delivered to Cannon was such a disaster in the studio's eyes that they shelved the footage, fired Mattei from *Hercules*, and replaced him with fellow Italian genre maestro Luigi Cozzi.

Through his early career, Cozzi was best known as a collaborator of Dario Argento's, having co-written the classic 1971 giallo *Four Flies on Grey Velvet*. His directorial efforts received little attention until 1979's *Starcrash*, the biggest (and most entertaining) spaghetti *Star Wars* knockoff. Starring Caroline Munro, Marjoe Gortner, Christopher Plummer, and a young David Hasselhoff, this space epic came out of one of the most comically troubled productions in film history. The resulting film was rejected by the prolific b-movie factory American International Pictures but has gone on to become one of the quintessential cult, camp sci-fi films—and was a box office success. If anyone was well-equipped to make a grand, special effects-driven fantasy film on a grossly insufficient budget, it was Cozzi. Cannon had gone to the right guy for *Hercules*.

One of the premier b-movie sex symbols of the 1970s and 1980s, Sybil Danning was best known for her role in Roger Corman's 1980 science fiction magnum opus, *Battle Beyond the Stars*. (Which, like Cannon's *Seven Magnificent Gladiators*, was another genre-fied remake of *The Magnificent Seven* [1960] which itself was a cowboy remake of *Seven Samurai* [1954].) She headlined many video staples in the mid-80s, from *Chained Heat* (1983) to *Malibu Express* (1985), *Reform School Girls* (1986) to *Amazon Women on the Moon* (1987). Prior to her breakthrough she'd play a terrorist in Menahem Golan's Oscar-nominated, pre-Cannon feature *Operation Thunderbolt* (1977). An established star of the sci-fi and fantasy genres, signing Danning on for *Hercules* must have seemed like a big win for the filmmakers up until the co-stars began to butt heads.

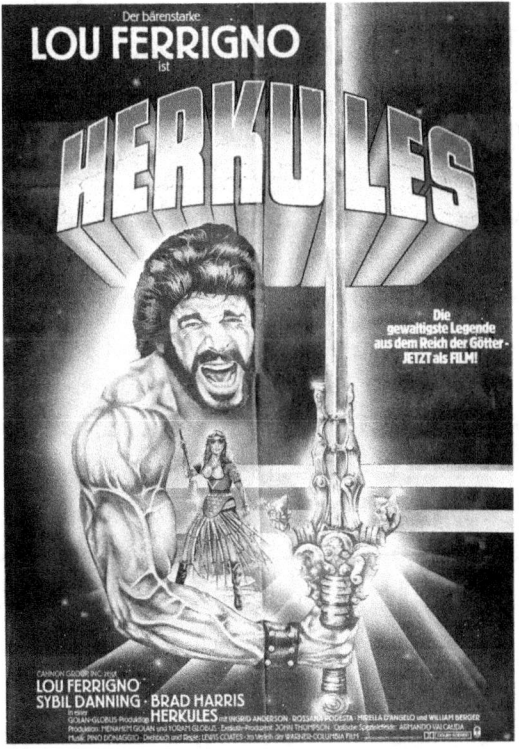

A tiny Sybil Danning is nestled within Lou Ferrigno's monstrous bicep in this illustrated German theatrical poster.

Ferrigno and Danning were given a couple weeks after *Seven Gladiators* wrapped up to let their tempers cool down. In the meantime, Cozzi only had two weeks to write an all-new *Hercules* script, per Cannon's request. The original screenplay reportedly had way too much sex and violence, and Ferrigno wouldn't do the film unless it was kid-friendly. To Danning's loudly-vocalized chagrin, the movie was toned down to receive a PG rating. Danning dragged Ferrigno over the coals throughout the lengthy *Hercules* press tour, which included magazine features in *Starlog* and *Cinefantastique*, a Roger Ebert interview, and a *Playboy* cover story. In many of these, she claimed that she'd been hired to play Hercules' sorceress love interest, but her role was switched to the villainous princess after Ferrigno complained about working with her.

Meanwhile, Cozzi planned for a *Hercules* that was less traditional, inspired more by science fiction than mythology. He pitched his approach to Golan and Globus as *Hercules*, but "like Superman," and they loved the idea, and boy, does this *Hercules* take liberties with its source material. The film effectively opens with a planetarium light show chronicling the origins of the universe. Good and evil is released into existence by the opening of not Pandora's Box, but her "jar," in a flashy, pyrotechnic display of exploding pottery. The fragments create the planets as well as the moon, where the gods in our movie choose to live rather than on the more traditional Mount Olympus.

Zeus (Claudio Cassinelli), his evil wife Hera (Rossanna Podestà), and the goddess Athena (Delia Boccardo) chill out next to a random moon crater. An Italian cult actor, Cassinelli's appearances *Hercules* and its sequel were among his final filmed roles: he was killed in a helicopter accident while filming the action b-movie *Hands of Steel* in 1985. Podesta was a screen siren of the '50s and '60s, most famously playing Helen of Troy in the 1956 film of the same name. Boccardo is best known stateside for co-starring in the ill-advised *Inspector Clouseau* (1968), the much-maligned Pink Panther sequel in which Alan Arkin stood in for Peter Sellers; she'd also appear in *The Assissi Underground* (1985) for Cannon.

As can be quickly gleaned from the gods' lunar pow-wow, the balance of good and evil on Earth has started to tilt in favor of the bad guys. The only thing to do is give humankind a champion: one man with the strength of an entire army, whose sole purpose in life is to give the good people of Earth a fighting chance against evil. Zeus crafts Hercules out of pure light, building first a skeleton and then a disturbing, naked prototype model with a crotch as smooth as a Ken doll's. They can't just send him down to Earth to start kicking evil's ass, no—Hercules' spirit must be sent down from the moon, to the ancient Greek city of Thebes, where it takes possession of the king's infant son. Considering that Hercules' traditional origin story involves Zeus magically disguising himself as a famous Theban general he could secretly pork the guy's wife and sire his son, this is one aspect where Cannon's version of the Hercules story actually improves upon the centuries-old myth.

Unfortunately, Zeus' timing and choice of baby weren't all that great. Hardly a few hours after Hercules' soul has moved into the baby king's body, he's the target of an assassination plot engineered by the evil princess Adriana, played by Danning in a cleavage-baring costume barely able to contain her nipples. She's credited as "Adriana," but everyone in the film clearly calls her "Arianna." For what it's worth, the mythological basis for her character was named "Ariadne," so neither name used in the film is technically correct.

A chambermaid escapes with the infant through a secret passage and is chased to the riverside, where she chucks baby Hercules into a paddleboat before being shot to death by traitorous bodyguards. One of them raises his bow to put an arrow through the infant, but stops. They smarmily quip that the river "will do the job for them." Of course they're wrong, or else we wouldn't have a movie.

And thus, Hercules' epic journey begins . . . as an infant, floating for miles and miles down a river, like a Hulked-out Baby Moses. It's clear that (a) god is looking out for this kid when a gigantic, celestial hand pops up out of the water and catches Hercules' boat right before it topples over a waterfall. Meanwhile, Hera—who disapproves of Zeus meddling in Hercules' misadventures—sends a pair of water snakes with light-up eyes to attack the child. Li'l Herc proves to be not so helpless at all when he squeezes their heads off with his tiny, baby hands.

Hercules' boat washes ashore and is stumbled upon by a kindly couple, who exclaim that that gods must have answered their prayers and sent them the baby they've been unable to have on their own. They raise young Hercules as their child, but mostly seem to keep him around to do the sort of excruciating farm labor that would normally be handled by a team of donkeys, such as pulling a plow or pushing a millstone. Time passes and soon he's a fully-grown Lou Ferrigno, helping his adoptive father clear the land by ripping trees from the ground as if he were plucking weeds. After more than 20 minutes of the film have passed, Hercules finally speaks his first line in the movie. His voice here has been overdubbed an actor who sounds nothing like Ferrigno at all, which is only distracting if you know what Lou Ferrigno *should* sound like. (The actor wasn't aware he'd been overdubbed until he attended the movie's premiere.)

Hercules appears to be living a relatively normal life as his new parents' slave/son until his father, out of nowhere, is fatally attacked by a "bear." The hilariously unconvincing bear costume had previously been used in Joe D'Amato's delightfully cheesy Conan knock-off *Ator the Fighting Eagle* (1982). When the crew realized that the threadbare costume wasn't going to intimidate anyone, especially next to the gigantic Ferrigno, Cozzi convinced Cannon to license b-roll bear footage from the movie *Grizzly* (1976), which was later inserted into the scene.

Hercules gets his revenge on the father-killing bear by punching it repeatedly in the face and then, for good measure, hurling it into outer space, where it dissolves into stars and becomes the constellation Ursa Major. The movie likes to suggest that constellations aren't the result of eons-old star patterns, but crap that Hercules got pissed off at and chucked into space.

Because of Ferrigno's inhumanly massive proportions it was impossible for the crew to find a remotely convincing body double, and so the actor was forced to perform most of his own stunts in the movie. (A stand-in was only used during the water scenes, because Ferrigno couldn't swim.) Ferrigno tore a calf muscle while fighting the bear and had to work through the pain of the injury for the rest of the shoot. During one of the movie's many swordfights, a stunt man missed his cue and was smashed with a shield by Ferrigno, opening a wound that required almost three dozen stitches to close.

Elsewhere, on top of a skull-shaped mountain, we're introduced to Adriana's father, the evil King Minos (William Berger), the movie's main villain. Berger was a fixture of many great spaghetti westerns, including *Sabata* (1969), *Keoma* (1976) and *Face to Face* (1967), and is further remembered by horror fans for the seven films he made with Spanish director Jesus Franco. Aside from the two Hercules movies, he also appears in Cannon's *The Berlin Affair* (1985) and was the father of *Nana* (1983) star Katya Berger. He plays the role of King Minos with delirious, wild-eyed camp—it's one of the hammiest villain turns we've seen in a Cannon movie since *The Apple*.

A sales ad for the second Hercules movie, with King Minos (William Berger) and Daedalus (Eva Robbins) cavorting in the upper corner.

King Minos' weird goal is to prove that scientific knowledge is more powerful than the gods, even though he barely does anything in the film without the help of some sort of magical and/or divine intervention. He's asked by Hera to help kill Hercules, and so he recruits the help of the mad, genius inventor Daedalus. He supplies him with three toy-sized, mechanical monsters that will grow to titanic proportions when they hit Earth's atmosphere, much like one of the Power Rangers' villains-of-the-week.

In mythology Daedalus is traditionally a male character, here played by transgender Italian actress Eva Robbins, who'd previously appeared in Dario Argento's *Tenebre* (1982). Her costume—a silver cape and space corset with a prominent, bulging cod piece in place of a bikini bottom—makes this version of the character more than a little ambiguous when it comes to gender.

Hercules' family farm is attacked by the first of these monsters—a gigantic, robot fly—showing off a fine display of special effects designer Armando Valcauda's stop motion work. *Clash of the Titans* (1981) this film is not, but *Hercules*' special effects are more than serviceable. Anticipating that the stop motion would appear herky-jerky as it so often does, Cozzi cleverly wrote the beasties into the script as machines. That way, their appearing to have robotic-looking movements actually played in the film's favor.

With his parents dead after a combined 45 seconds of screen time, Hercules burns down his hut and resolves to go on an adventure to figure out why he's so freakishly strong. This leads him to the dominion of King Augeias, played by Brad Harris, who was a veteran of many older, Italian sword and sandal movies—he actually played Hercules himself in 1962's *The Fury of Hercules*.

King Augeias happens to be holding his royal games, which Herc walks in on and wins handily. His prize is the opportunity to escort the king's daughter, Princess Cassiopeia (Ingrid Anderson), to Athens. (This was Anderson's first movie role, but as a model she is well-remembered as the object of Peter Cetera's affections in the music video for Chicago's "Stay the Night.") Before they can head along their merry way, though, he's tasked with the least interesting of Hercules' legendary labors: to clean all the horse shit out of the Augean stables in a single day. Easy, peazy: Herc diverts a river to run through the stables. This heroic display of janitorial work really impresses Princess Cassiopeia, and she and Hercules fall head-over-heels in love.

Unfortunately, the good king's flamboyant advisor, Dorcon—Cannon's most dependable actor, Yehuda Efroni—sells the happy couple out to the evil

Princess Adrianna, who kidnaps the good princess and tosses Hercules into the sea. (As Golan and Globus' most frequently-hired character actor, you'll come across Yehuda Efroni's name many times throughout this book. This was already his fifth Cannon movie, and he'd appear in almost 20.)

For the rest of the movie, Hercules dedicates himself to rescuing his beloved Cassiopeia. He is saved from the sea by a withered old crone, who takes Herc back to her fancy cave and convinces him to let her drink his blood like it ain't no thang. This causes her old lady makeup to magically melt away, and she turns into the much more attractive sorceress, Circe, played by Mirella D'Angelo of *Caligula* (1979) and *Tenebre* (1982).

The sorceress claims she can help Hercules rescue his princess if he, in turn, helps her get back her magic medallion—which, no big deal, has been hidden away in the depths of Hell itself. To get there, he must first defeat a stop-motion robo-hydra, cross a rainbow bridge, and then bum a ride across the river Styx from its terrifying, Skeletor-like boatman. Once he's finally in Hell he has to remove the medallion from a magical egg, which tests his capacity for pain by first setting his arm on fire, then freezing it. Despite all the pains he went through to retrieve it, Circe's medallion sadly doesn't possess enough magic to get them all the way to Cassiopeia. Instead, she takes him on a detour into Africa, where the chariot of Perseus is hidden.

Within seconds of teleporting onto the continent they're greeted by none other than the King of Africa himself, King Xenodama. (He is the movie's fourth—and thankfully, final—king we're be asked to keep to track of. Literally half of the movie's cast is the King or Princess of something-or-other.) King Xenodama agrees to hand over Perseus' magical chariot if Hercules can bring water to their dry, desert lands. Once again, this is no big deal for Herc. With the aid of Circe's spells, he grows to a colossal size and uses his incredible strength to push apart mountains, creating a channel coming in from the sea.

When Hercules and Circe find the chariot but no Pegasus to pull it with, their next best idea is to tie one end of a rope around a boulder and the other to the chariot. They climb in, and then Hercules hurls the boulder as hard as he can into outer space. The momentum alone is enough to pull him across the cosmos and through asteroid belts.

Hercules' chariot eventually falls apart in-flight, but luckily it happens right as he's overtop the kingdom where Cassiopeia is being held captive. Circe admits to having romantic affection for Hercules, but she's murdered by a stop-motion robot centaur before you can say the movie ever truly featured a love triangle.

Hercules is briefly captured by the wicked Adrianna, whose plan is to seduce him so that she can give birth to an army of super-men. (Yes, really). Hercules escapes just in time to stop King Minos from slowly lowering Cassiopeia into the heart of a volcano. For some reason Minos believes that if he sacrifices the princess to the mythical phoenix he's captured in his castle, that will somehow prove his scientific superiority over the gods.

In a battle that recalls Luke Skywalker and Darth Vader's final duel from *The Empire Strikes Back* (1980), Hercules picks a swordfight with King Minors on a narrow walkway over the mouth of an active volcano.

In spite of Minos' rainbow-colored, flaming blade and a few slick, pirouette-like sword fighting moves, Hercules wins the duel. He and Cassiopeia flee Minos' castle as the entire evil island explodes and collapses in around them—using a heavy amount of stock footage licensed from the 1961 MGM adventure film *Atlantis: the Lost Continent*. Ironically, *Atlantis* itself was notorious upon its release for being pieced together with large chunks of stock footage from numerous, older movies. (In addition to this and the shots taken from *Grizzly*, *Hercules* utilizes pre-existing battle scenes from another, unidentified gladiator movie.) Safely on a sandy beach with the bad guy's kingdom exploding behind them, Hercules and Cassiopeia share a passionate kiss—and then transform into another constellation in the sky. The End!

Alright, so *Hercules* is no *Jason and the Argonauts* (1963). The plot feels like a jumble of tossed-together ideas, which makes sense when you consider that Cozzi had only ten days to write the script. He also had to come up with enough characters to use all of the actors Cannon was already paying to stay in town after the prior shoot, which explains why there are so many damn kings, gods, and princesses in the film. While the budget was relatively high for an Italian genre production, it was far smaller than the budgets of the special effects-heavy fantasy epics to which American movie-goers would no doubt be comparing it. Factor in its tight shooting window and you can see how much *Hercules* had going against it from the start.

Taking all of that into account, let's appreciate all of the things that *Hercules* does well. Many of the special effects—while old-fashioned even by 1983 standards—look pretty darn good. To make up for their lack of funding, Cozzi's SFX team looked to early cinema for inspiration. Most of the establishing shots of *Hercules*' fantastical locations were hand-built miniatures, not unlike those used in 1927's *Metropolis*. The clockwork monsters Hercules battles were done in much the same manner as the stop-motion dinosaur movies Willis O'Brien made for Thomas Edison back in the 1910s—and, of course, the gargantuan gorilla from his 1933 masterpiece, *King Kong*. Think that's old? The camera trick that Cozzi & Co. used to grow Hercules to the size of a mountain was cribbed straight from Georges Méliès' 1901 silent short, *The Man with the Rubber Head*.

Even the simpler-seeming visual effects—such as swords flashing when they clang together, or King Minos' flaming blade—were complicated, time-consuming affairs in the days before CGI. A lot of blood, sweat, and tears went into *Hercules*' visual effects, and the care they took shows on screen. To the same effect, the sets themselves are quite eye-catching, from the surface of the moon to the Gates of Hell, to the Heart of King Minos' volcano.

There is also the film's original score by Pino Donaggio, which is among the best in Cannon's library. When it was initially announced, *Hercules* was to feature a score by Ennio Morricone, arguably one of the greatest of all time when it comes to film composers. When Cozzi showed him some of the monster footage and asked him to compose something loud and exciting, like the music Bernard Hermann recorded for Ray Harryhausen's monster flicks, the maestro recoiled and asked Cannon to remove him from the project. (He'd still score *Sahara*, *Nana*, and *Treasure of the Four Crowns* for Cannon instead.)

The *Hercules* scoring gig ultimately went to Donaggio, who was hand-picked by Cozzi. A respected composer in his own right, Donaggio was best known for scoring Nicolas Roeg's classic *Don't Look Now* (1973) and many of Brian De Palma's films. His soundtrack is exciting and heroic-sounding, just perfect for this mythical adventure. Cannon were also evidently very happy with Donaggio's sweeping *Hercules* score, as they went on to recycle parts of it again and again for movies such as *Hercules II*, *Gor* (1987), and then *Outlaw of Gor* (1989). Donaggio would get a lot more work from Cannon over the next decade, as they later commissioned him to score *Over the Brooklyn Bridge* (1984), *Déjà vu* and *The Berlin Affair* (both 1985), *The Barbarians*, *Dancers*, and *Going Bananas* (all 1987), and finally *Appointment with Death* (1988).

Cannon cooked up a clever publicity stunt to promote *Hercules*' arrival in movie theaters. Just before release Lou Ferrigno, clad in a toga, rode down Hollywood's Sunset Boulevard in a Roman chariot pulled behind two white horses. En route to a Sunset Strip movie theater—where he purchased a ticket to a preview screening of *Hercules*, and was greeted by a flock of Cannon-supplied maidens—Ferrigno was pulled over by a man in a police officer's uniform and issued a ticket for driving a vehicle without license plates. The stunt worked, and photos of Ferrigno driving his horse-drawn chariot through Los Angeles traffic appeared in newspapers across the country. Unfortunately, many of the outlets soured on the film when they were forced to publish corrections in their following issues, discovering they'd been duped and that the cop they'd reported on was not a cop at all—but in actuality another actor hired by Cannon.

In America, *Hercules* was a more than modest hit with movie-going audiences, bringing home roughly $11 million domestically. Critics, however, had a field day with the movie, poking fun at everything from Ferrigno's over-dubbed performance to the actresses' invariably scanty costumes. The movie garnered five Razzie nominations, with the grand prizes for Worst New Star and Worst Supporting Actress being bestowed upon Ferrigno and Danning, respectively.

Of course, it didn't matter much to Cannon what audiences or critics thought of the film: they were ready to deliver a sequel whether people wanted one or not. The studio had plans in the works to have Ferrigno reprise his role as Hercules even before the first movie ever reached theaters.

The U.S. video release for *Hercules II: The Adventures of Hercules*.

The higher-ups at Cannon were so pleased with Cozzi's rough footage of *Hercules* that they asked the director whether he might also help them salvage their first Ferrigno movie, *The Seven Magnificent Gladiators*, which had been deemed un-releasable and tossed onto a shelf. They presented Cozzi with a proposal: if he wrote a half hours' worth of new scenes they could insert into *Gladiators* to save the film, they'd convince Ferrigno to come back for two weeks of re-shoots. All three parties agreed—Cannon, Ferrigno, and Cozzi—and got to work.

Not long after shooting began, Golan cooked up a far more harebrained idea. If Ferrigno was willing to do two weeks of re-shoots at a reduced fee, why not try to sign him up for *four* weeks at the same price? If Cozzi could shoot thirty minutes in two weeks, their thought was that he the director could conceivably churn out a full hour with twice as much time. After that, they would send their star home and give Cozzi another couple weeks to shoot more scenes with a cheap ensemble of local actors. Doing the math, that could theoretically net them a 90-minute, feature-length movie. With that much material they could just make it a sequel to *Hercules* and forget about *Seven Magnificent Gladiators* altogether.

There was one stipulation: no one could tell Ferrigno what it was they were *actually* filming, because Cannon was only paying him a small fee to do re-shoots, rather than what he would have been owed to star in a second *Hercules* movie.

So, if it seems like *Hercules II*—or *The Adventures of Hercules*, as it was somewhat confusingly titled in most regions—is more haphazard and disconnected than the first movie, there's good reason for that. Cozzi had to scramble to come up with a feature-length script built around scraps of the shelved *Gladiators*, and then give Hercules reasons for being at locations from the altogether different movie. When our hero disappears for sizeable chunks of the movie, it's because Ferrigno wasn't even around for large parts of the shoot. Heck, even when he *was* there he had no idea what movie he was actually shooting.

By this point Sybil Danning had clearly had her fill of Ferrigno and was long gone. Her character had been killed off in the first *Hercules*, sure, but that didn't stop William Berger from returning to play the similarly-deceased King Minos. A few other, minor actors re-appear from the first movie, but otherwise *Hercules II*'s ties to its predecessor are tenuous at best.

The premise, in a nutshell: Zeus's Seven Mighty Thunderbolts have been stolen, and the moon will crash into the Earth if Hercules doesn't collect and return them. The movie really doesn't feature a plot, per se, but a series of wacky fights and psychedelic special effects punctuated with dialogue-heavy scenes of expository mumbo-jumbo. I'm going to attempt to summarize it with a loose play-by-play, which I hope you'll forgive me for—but using any other, linear method to track this movie's action ultimately proved futile.

Hercules II begins with one of the most prolonged opening credits sequences we'll see in any Cannon movie. Seemingly everyone who worked on the film is given their own title card. These are broken up with lots (and lots) of choice footage from the first movie, recycling essentially all of its flashiest shots. A full eight minutes pass before we start into the events of the current movie, which only runs 88 minutes in total.

The story begins with a comely maiden (Cindy Leadbetter) being sacrificed by a flamboyant priest in KISS makeup and a red feather boa. He summons a "fire monster"—made out of blue lightning—which consumes the poor girl, leaving behind a blackened husk that looks like a chicken wing that was left in the fryer for too long. *Hercules II* impressively manages to grab even more footage from other movies than its predecessor; the fire monster here was actually a distorted version of the Monster from the Id seen in 1956's *Forbidden Planet*.

We find out the sacrificed young lady comes from a tribe of women who wear leather- and rivet-studded swimwear, of which we only ever see two more of them: the blonde, semi-psychic Urania (Milly Carlucci) and her brunette bestie, Glaucia (Sonia Viviani of the 1980 Italo zombie flick *Nightmare City*.) Carlucci acted sporadically throughout the 1980s, but ultimately became more famous as a television personality: namely as the host of a popular, televised Italian dance competition.

Tired of sitting around idly as her homies are periodically gobbled up by this fire monster, Urania heads to a papier mache altar in the middle of the woods and prays to spectral figures she address as "little people, friends of Zeus"—fairies, basically. They inform her that they've got bigger problems: the Gods have lost control of the universe's heavenly bodies, which as far as we're concerned means that the moon is about to crash into the Earth. Oh, snap! She'd better find Hercules!

Meanwhile on Mount Olympus, Zeus (Cassinelli again) is irked to find that his Mighty Thunderbolts having gone missing, and pretty bummed about that whole Earth-is-about-to-be-destroyed-by-the-moon thing. After lamenting to Athena—this time played by Lou Ferrigno's real-life wife, Carla Ferrigno, under the pseudonym Carlotta Green—he summons Hercules from a patch of stardust and sends him down to Earth to take back his Mighty Thunderbolts.

While wandering around the woods aimlessly on his pony, Herc is suddenly attacked by . . . a yeti, I guess? If you thought they wouldn't be able to find a costume goofier-looking than the "bear" Herc fought in the first movie, well, you were wrong: this one looks like a cross between the Shaggy Dog and the Toxic Avenger's kitchen mop. It ultimately doesn't matter because the fight doesn't go on long, and Hercules fatally runs him through with a plain, old, wooden stick. The dead yeti-thing transforms into one of the missing thunderbolts which is ridiculously good luck, considering Hercules spent less than five minutes searching for them before he found his first one. If this was any indication, it looks like his quest will be smooth sailing.

Elsewhere in outer space or something, the Bad Gods who stole Zeus's thunderbolts—Aphrodite (Margie Newton from *Hell of the Living Dead* [1980]), Poseidon (*Jason and the Argonauts*' Ferdinando Poggi), Hera (Maria Omaggio, also of *Nightmare City*), and Flora (Laura Lenzi)—are all in a tizzy because Hercules is back in town. The best idea they can come up with to stop him is to resurrect Hercules' greatest enemy, the science-obsessed King Minos, to take another crack at defeating Herc. King Minos—played once again by the wonderfully hammy William Berger, thank goodness—doesn't seem the least bit surprised to find himself returned from the dead and sheepishly agrees to kill Hercules for them.

Back on Earth, Herc randomly stumbles across Urania and Glaucia and the pace finally begins to pick up. *Hercules II* gets a little video game-y in the way that Herc wanders from one boss monster to another, effectively breaking them apart to get at the Mighty Thunderbolts that are hidden inside them like cereal box prizes. First he fends off some "slime people," who look like they're wearing cheap, Swamp Thing Halloween costumes you could buy in the seasonal aisle at Rite Aid. They're chased into the Forbidden Valley—which sounds like a particularly intimidating brand of salad dressing—where they encounter Medusa's better-looking sister, Euryale, played by Serena Grandi (star of the notorious video nasty *Anthropophagus* [1980].) She forces Herc to fight some magical green guys before transforming herself into her snake-haired form for another spiffy display of stop motion animation. After killing her and winning another 'bolt, Hercules walks into the forest lair of a really tall knight who decorates his trees with creepy dolls. Herc kills him, too, in like three seconds, basically by playing a deadly game of peekaboo.

In yet another random magical realm, Minos meets with his partner in science, Daedalus (Eva Robbins again, cod piece as prominent as ever). He's gifted an ancient, magical ice sword that can apparently kill gods, because all of a sudden he's more interested in murdering the deviant deities who brought him back from the dead than his arch-nemesis, Hercules. Minos then goes on a god-slaying rampage, freezing Flora with his ice sword and knocking off several others.

Back on Earth, Urania prays to the Little People again and is given a mysterious, magical leaf, which Hercules eats without hesitation because it seems Hercules is always down to party. It transforms them into psychedelic, glowing sperm and they fly to Atlantis, where a telepathic mermaid queen who lives in a seahorse-shaped castle gives him a magic balm which makes him fireproof. They soon wake up from their acid trip on a beach, where they find a shield belonging to the KISS priest we saw at the beginning of the movie, who apparently kidnapped Glaucia while the two of them were off tripping balls and hanging out with mermaids. Hercules teleports to the cultists' sacrificial altar just in time to save her, killing off the bright blue fire monster with his signature finishing move: punching it into outer space.

Afterwards Urania tries to touch base with the Little People again, but something is blocking her prayers. She pays a visit to the Oracle of Death—a giant foam skull, possibly left over from one of Alice Cooper's stage shows—who gives her a magical potion. This little serum transforms her clothes into a white bikini and sends her into space, where the Little People give her the 411 on the gods' moon problems.

While Urania's tripping on the Oracle of Death's crazy LSD juice, Herc and Glaucia are attacked by a tribe of "women warriors," who are obviously played by men in masks and blonde wigs. (You can tell from their bone structure, the flesh-colored sleeves that mask their body hair, and the way that their costumes cover more than just their nipples, unlike any of the other female characters' outfits in this movie.) They trap Hercules with a magical net and offer him up as sacrifice to their Spider Queen, whom he straight up strangles to death when she takes the form of an attractive lady human.

A foreign lobby card featuring Hercules (Ferrigno) and Glaucia (Sonia Viviani).

The finally arrive at the Temple of Echoes, where the sixth Thunderbolt isn't even hidden inside a monster, but just sitting on a rock. Suddenly, Glaucia betrays Hercules and holds a dagger to Urania's neck. It turns out she's not actually Glaucia, but—get a load of this—an evil clone created by King Minos... *with science*!

Minos reveals he's been hiding out downstairs in the temple, takes a little Bond villain moment with Herc where he painstakingly explains his nefarious plan, and then makes the evil Glaucia clone commit seppuku. Afterwards he goes on his merry little way, leaving Hercules unconscious on the floor instead of killing him or something because, Minos is a gall damn idiot.

Now that Zeus has most of his Thunderbolts back, the Good Gods decide it's finally time they intervene in the affairs of humans. First Zeus kills Daedalus by summoning his own dad, Father Time, who manifests himself as a giant space skull with eyes that spew lightning. (Daedalus? More like *dead*-alus, amiright?) Athena wakes up Hercules and gives him a magical, science-proof shield for his rematch with Minos.

Naturally Hercules' and Minos' final showdown occurs in outer space. It is *literally* their same final battle, shot for shot, from the end of the first *Hercules* movie, except rotoscoped to look like they're made of beams of extraterrestrial light. (You'll be able to tell it's the same fight scene because King Minos can't swing his sword without doing a full, 360-degree twirl.) Remember: Ferrigno wasn't around for one third of the shoot and wasn't even supposed to know they were filming a sequel, so of course asking him to film a scene with King Minos would have been a dead giveaway that they were working on a second *Hercules* film.

Partway into the battle Minos transforms into a line-drawn Tyrannosaurus Rex, and Hercules morphs into a giant gorilla. It makes zero sense until you realize that the makers of *Hercules II* just lifted this scene from the original *King Kong* movie, and then *traced over it*. While Cozzi was never shy about borrowing footage from other movies, taking an entire scene out of arguably one of the most famous sci-fi films of all time takes balls.

The battle ends and Herc comes away with the victory, as you'd expect.

Running out of time as the moon hurtles closer and closer to Earth, Urania reveals that Zeus' final lightning bolt is hidden *inside her heart*. The goddess Hera then tells Urania she's her mother, and Urania begs her to give her the "kiss of death." Hera agrees and—after a tender moment of shoehorned, girl-on-girl smooching—Urania dies, transforming into the final Thunderbolt. Zeus uses his returned powers to blow Hercules up to the size of a planet so that he can catch the moon before it slams into Earth. Humanity is saved!

Hercules may not have been one of the best fantasy movies of the 1980s, but *The Adventures of Hercules* has a way of making it look like one of the best movies ever made, period. The original film had a plot that was loosely strung together at best, while *Herc II* plays out like a feverish acid dream. Any time a character introduces themselves, it sounds less like dialogue and more like someone reading aloud a backstory they made up for their *Dungeons and Dragons* character. The first movie had fully serviceable stop motion effects; the sequel has . . . silly swamp monster costumes and people painted in gray body paint to look like statues.

Ferrigno figured out at some point that he'd been duped into making a second *Hercules* flick, and accepted the fact. (Or, at least, the paycheck.) To hedge his bets against what he could probably already tell would be a stinker, he told interviewers that the sequel would be "slightly more humorous" while promoting it ahead of its release. There were apparently no hard feelings, as Ferrigno and Cozzi both worked with Cannon again on 1989's *Sinbad of the Seven Seas*—which had just as crazy, circuitous a path to the screen as this film. (But more on that movie in a future volume.)

Interview: Filmmaker Luigi Cozzi

A legend of Italian genre filmmaking, writer/director Luigi Cozzi's career began in journalism, working as a correspondent for North American horror and science fiction magazines. He was recruited to co-write the screenplay for the giallo film *Four Flies on Grey Velvet* (1971) by his friend, filmmaker Dario Argento, which led to further work as both a writer and as a director.

His breakthrough film was 1979's *Starcrash*, a psychedelic space epic in the vein of *Star Wars* (1977) that was a box office success and now has a major cult following. He was promptly signed to helm a sequel for Cannon which never came to fruition; instead, he wrote and directed the studio's two *Hercules* movies, and was later brought in to rescue their *Sinbad* (1989), which had fallen victim to a convoluted and disastrous production.

Other films directed by Cozzi include *Contamination* (1980), *Paganini Horror* (1989), and *Blood on Méliès' Moon* (2016). He continues to work with Dario Argento, serving as a second unit director on *Two Evil Eyes* (1990) and *The Stendhal Syndrome* (1996) and overseeing the special effects in his 1985 classic *Phenomena*, in which a young Jennifer Connelly telepathically speaks to insects to help catch a serial killer.

Our hero during a rare moment of weakness in *Hercules II*.

***The Cannon Film Guide*: You started using the pen name "Lewis Coates" early on and kept it throughout your career, including for *Hercules*. Do you remember how you came up with that name?**

Luigi Cozzi: When I was a child at school, I drew famous fantasy movies in a sketchy, comic book form and signed most of them as "directed by Walt Tickney," or "directed by Lewis Coates." Many years later while I was directing *Starcrash*, the movie's producer came to me and said that his American partners didn't want my real name on the credits, because they were convinced that American audiences would not believe that an Italian guy could be able to make a good science fiction movie. So the producer said that I had to give him a pen name of my choice or he himself would have selected an American name for me. At this point I told him that he could use my old, kid-ish "Lewis Coates" nickname.

Later, when *Starcrash* became a major hit at the box office, all producers always wanted me to use this "Lewis Coates" name. I accepted with no problems, because this name belonged to my childhood days and it was me, anyhow. But obviously I do prefer to use my real name, when I can do that.

You were given only days to write the *Hercules* script. Pre-production was similarly quick. What was the biggest challenge in preparing for *Hercules* in such a short amount of time?

Pre-production had been very short for *Starcrash*, more or less just a month, and because of this I was forced not to make as technology-oriented a movie as *Star Wars* was, but instead a fantasy movie like Harryhausen's Sinbad movies. This is also the reason why in it I used the colors in a wild, expressionist way.

Later, when I was going to do *Hercules*, I had to face the same problem: no time for a good preparation. Because Bruno Mattei's *Hercules* had been scheduled to start at the end of July, [Ferrigno] was already in Rome and on Cannon's weekly payroll. But when Mattei's script for *Hercules* was refused by Cannon, I was given just fifteen days to write it anew, because Cannon was paying the actor to stay in Rome just waiting. So it was absolutely imperative to start shooting *Hercules* as soon as possible, not to pay him an overwhelming amount of money due to these delays. Obviously I had written my script knowing this haste. So, thanks to my *Starcrash* experience, we started shooting it from the exteriors, which did not require complicate set build-ups. Only when these were finished we went back to the studios, having given the technicians enough time to put up the interior sets, such as Hell, the Temple with the Egg, the Phoenix Lair, the stables, and so on.

The last time you watched *Hercules*, was there a scene that was your favorite?

At the end of January 2017, I was invited to Madrid where, in one of the main theaters in the city, they showed *Starcrash* and then *Hercules* during the same evening. Seeing these two movies just one after the other on a very big screen, I realized how much they looked alike, with just a difference of experience. In *Starcrash*, for the very first time I was doing many tricks like optical effects, stunts, miniatures, fights, explosions and matte shots in quantity. Consequently some of them were slightly flawed by inexperience, while the same kind of stuff which I later did again in *Hercules* looked much better.

Anyhow, the *Hercules* scene which I liked best is the trip to Hell with Charon, partly inspired by Disney's *Peter Pan*'s skull island.

You were asked to film *Hercules II* without telling Lou Ferrigno that it was a sequel, so that he could be paid for re-shoots instead. Do you recall when he was finally told what movie he was really working on, or how he reacted when he found out?

After we finished shooting here in Italy, Lou Ferrigno went back to Los Angeles. Once there, sometime later, he was informed that Cannon had decided to use the so-called "reshooting" takes apparently made for *Seven Magnificent Gladiators* as part of a totally different movie titled *Hercules II*. They discussed money for a while and in the end Ferrigno accepted their last offer, signed the deal and got paid.

Is any of your work visible in the released version of *Seven Magnificent Gladiators*, or was all of it re-purposed for *Hercules 2*?

After the decision to shoot *Hercules II*, nothing of what had been planned for *Seven Magnificent Gladiators* was made. *Seven Magnificent Gladiators* was left exactly as Mattei had delivered it and the movie simply was shelved. It was taken out of the vaults only a few years later, when Cannon was in crisis and short on movies, and just released as it had been edited by its director.

In the meanwhile my *Hercules II* went into production as a completely brand new, six week movie: four weeks with Ferrigno and two with only the other actors. Lou and his wife were the only ones in the crew who had not been informed about the change.

Under the conditions you were given, it seems as if making the sequel was a Herculean labor of its own kind. Yet, you pulled it off. Looking back on it now, was it a fun challenge as a filmmaker?

Writing *Hercules II* was a very complicated matter, like a jigsaw puzzle. First I wrote a half hour of new scenes planned to be put inside *Seven Magnificent Gladiators*. Then, when the decision was made to do a new Hercules movie, I had to enlarge this half hour that was already written and approved to a full hour. I had to write it in order to be able to shoot with Ferrigno only for a four week schedule, then add to it scenes with all of the other actors to be made during the remaining, two week schedule. A real mess, and this explains why the plot of the finished movie is so episodic.

Furthermore, I knew I had to re-use the music recorded for *Hercules* and could not shoot spectacular scenes, so I decided to rely completely on the special effects. As a matter of fact, for me *Hercules II* was almost an experimental movie. I do really enjoy doing experimental special effects, so I had a lot of fun doing the visuals for *Hercules II* and am proud of what I did technically in it, even if I always knew that story-wise the script had many holes, but it was not my fault.

Interview: Actress Mirella D'Angelo

Mirella D'Angelo played the good-natured sorceress, Circe, opposite Lou Ferrigno in Cannon's fantasy epic, *Hercules*.

At the time she crossed over into acting, teenage D'Angelo was one of the top fashion models working in Europe. This led to her catching the eye of many of the great filmmakers and actors working in Rome and Paris, including Tinto Brass (*Caligula*, 1979), Federico Fellini (*City of Women*, 1980), Jean-Paul Belmondo (*Le guignolo*, 1980), and Dario Argento (*Tenebre*, 1982), the latter of whom would lead her to *Hercules*' Luigi Cozzi, a director she'd with whom she would collaborate a number of times throughout her career.

Hercules shields Circe (Mirella D'Angelo) in this image from *Hercules*, which was confusingly used as a lobby card to promote *Hercules II*.

The Cannon Film Guide: **By the time you made *Hercules*, you'd already worked with Fellini, Argento, and Brass. Can you tell me about your early career?**

Mirella D'Angelo: I started my career as a model. I was a catwalk model from fifteen or sixteen years of age, for Versace and many other designers. Then I was chosen for the cover of *The Sunday Times Magazine* when I was seventeen years old. We did beautiful pictures, they were very striking. English agencies started to look at me, and very quickly I was represented by agencies in London, Rome, Milan, and Paris. And so at eighteen years old I was living in Paris. Then, in the 1970s, there was so much work in the fashion industry. I was working almost every day, and for a time I was one of the two

Italian models—because, at the time, Italian girls weren't allowed to leave the home. [*Laughs*]

My third movie was with Tinto Brass, *Caligula*. I was a model then, in Paris, and it was an intense movie. It was a huge production, with Gore Vidal [as a writer] and so many actors who I loved, like Peter O'Toole. Tinto met me and he said, "I would like you to do a screen test." I said I actually didn't want to do it. I knew he'd auditioned 200 girls for that part, and at the time I was very busy in Paris. The role was mostly about innocence and beauty, and I thought that if he could get that from me from our meeting, then he didn't need the audition. And so I just said, "Thank you very much, I would love to do that role, but I won't do the audition." I thought I would be rejected, but then Tinto chose me even without an audition. And to be honest with you, I really, really loved working on *Caligula*.

At that point, then, I decided it was now time I studied acting, because they kept choosing me for roles without any kind of schooling! [*Laughs*] I went to New York and contacted Susan Strasberg. She was very kind to me. She said, "My gosh, you have already done three movies, so you can start with us." I said thank you, but then I went to a workshop by Frank Corsaro. This director—or teacher, at the time—really impressed me. His pupils were wonderful, and doing great work. I studied with Corsaro for nine months, and it was wonderful.

You became a very busy actor over the following years. Did you audition for *Hercules*?

Luigi Cozzi is very, very close friends with Dario Argento. They have a bookstore together, and Luigi wrote a movie of Dario's. [*Four Flies on Grey Velvet*, 1971.] They've been friends for many, many decades. When I worked with Dario in *Tenebre*, I was called in by Luigi Cozzi for an appointment. That's when he offered me Circe with no auditions! He trusted Dario Argento, who also didn't audition me for his role. I think Dario had spoken wonderfully of me, and so Luigi asked me to play Circe.

When I started as an actress, I had months of work booked ahead as a model. I called my French agency and said I wanted to stop modeling. They asked, "Are you crazy? Why?" Being an actress was about *feeling* things, it wasn't about posing and being beautiful only. I thought that modeling was becoming a distraction to me.

In 1987, Dario called me because he wanted to interview me for a show he was doing called *Giallo*. On this show he had a few minutes where he'd interview different guests; we spoke about *Tenebre*. He was also then producing a series of TV films with Luigi, and I was offered a lead role in one of these small movies for television. [The "L'impronta dell'assassino" installment of the Italian series *Turno di notte*, 1987.] Again, I worked with Luigi Cozzi. I just finished another movie with Luigi, called *I Piccoli Maghi Di Oz* (2018). It was a very fun movie, like *The Wizard of Oz* (1939), where I got to play the headmistress and the Wicked Witch of the West. After so many years it was so much nice to see him again.

Luigi Cozzi is the most gentle man. He's a director that respects you very much. He spoils me a lot, I must say. *Hercules* was the first movie we did together, and he understood my personality a lot. And then when we did the TV movie, he let me do things like change the lines. I'd ask "Can I say this instead?" and he would say, "Yeah, yeah, go ahead." On our latest movie, he came to me and said, "I want you to do this role. I have to concentrate on so many things for this movie, and I know I won't have any problems with you." We work very well together.

Dario is also fantastic—people who don't know him might not think this, but on set he's so kind and sensitive and a very happy person, and he's very scared of all the horror things. [*Laughs*] When you go to the cinema with him to see a horror movie, he just hides behind you because he's so scared.

Luigi strikes me as a very resourceful director. The movies he did for Cannon weren't exactly the easiest productions, with rushed schedules and other issues. Yet, he found ways to pull them off every time.

Absolutely. That's exactly right. It's a combination of his love for the fantastic and his calm, kind, concentrated character. You rarely see him nervous or worried because he has within him this calmness that helps him do the things that he wants to do. I'm sure he's worked under very difficult situations, but his character is always really calm.

He likes to include many special effects in his movies. Especially in some of your scenes from *Hercules*, was it ever challenging to act through those?

The scene where I am an old woman, a witch, at the beginning of *Hercules*, was wonderful to make. [*Laughs*] It was so out of the world for me, I'd never done anything like that. On *Hercules* we had a fantastic makeup artist, he was really good. He did many layers on my face. That makeup was quite elaborate, and very complicated to do every day. We were also shooting during the summer, so it was very hot underneath. But it was very, very well done. When we went from that old face to the young face, we did it with the camera, filming every time another makeup layer would come off. It was like seeing the makeup artist's work. That little scene, I loved it. In fact, when my daughter was little, I used to show it to her. She was always very happy when I'd become young, you know, with the stars in my eyes. [*Laughs*] The children really like that part.

The special effects were with the help of Massimo Antonello Geleng, who was a very good [production designer]. He'd worked with Argento and Fellini, and he worked with us on this. But most of the special effects in *Hercules* were done after we'd finished the action parts. When we did the action we had to imagine certain things, but it was very easy with Luigi because he explains thing to you. It was very easy for me.

How was working with Lou Ferrigno?

Ah, Lou Ferrigno! He's amazing. Ferrigno is a Scorpio man. He was very kind and had passion and sensitivity as a person, but was also serious and didn't want to open up too much, because he was always thinking about his role. I was the Italian one, and I had all of the Italian crew saying to me, "Mirella, tell him to do this! Tell him to do that!" In a way, I got along with the crew and I got along with Lou Ferrigno. For some of the Italian crew, I think he might have seemed too introverted.

Ferrigno was very reserved, but he liked me as a person so we had a good time. For all of his muscles, he was very serious about his training. Every morning he used to eat an enormous quantity of food and would be training his body. I would look at this big muscle man, and he was very rigorous about his body. My experience with him was very harmonious, because I got along with him. We could do what we had to do well.

I remember, once, it was very funny. We were shooting the scene where I fall in love with him and I lose my power as Circe, and so we fell in the water. When we fell in the water, I came out with all of my hair back. All of a sudden Ferrigno saw me with my hair back instead of the fringe, and he went to Luigi and said, "We shoot re-shoot all of the scenes with Mirella because she is so beautiful with her hair back!" [*Laughs*] I said, "No, no. We shot too much with the fringe." But it was funny. He was so passionate for *Hercules* to do well. He was a very nice person to work with.

Hercules embraces the dying Circe (D'Angelo).

You didn't have any scenes with William Berger in this film, but you acted in other movies with him.

Yes! William Berger was wonderful. When I did my first movie [*Terminal*, 1974], he had the lead role. In that film he played a powerful man in crisis, who is questioning his life. And so the first time I met William Berger, it was in this very intellectual, interesting movie. I met him again on another wonderful movie called *Stamboul Train* (1981), by the writer Graham Greene. It was a movie about the Second World War. William Berger and I did two of the leading characters in that story. It was a four-hour movie for television, and directed by Gianfranco Mingozzi, who was the assistant director on *La Dolce Vita* (1960) by Fellini. And then we did *Hercules*, so three movies together. He was another lovely person. He was in all the scenes I wasn't in on *Hercules*, so we were there on different days, but as a person I knew him well. His talent was huge—I'm sure he had loads of fun in *Hercules*.

What was your favorite scene to do in *Hercules*?

As a scene to look at my favorite is, as I said, the one where I change. I also enjoyed playing the old woman—it was interesting to try the movement, and her walk, and all of that. But my favorite scene? I think I like where I am killed, and I say goodbye to Hercules. I think that was a moment where I could put in a little acting, more intimate acting. I accepted Hercules because I loved Circe, but the experience of doing a genre movie like that, I didn't know what it would be. So for me to try to understand what I was doing every day, it was like discovering a new genre. With Luigi's help it was easy, but at the same time I couldn't act the way I was used to. And so, I think I enjoyed that scene, where I could put my feelings into it.

What did you think when you finally saw it, with all of the special effects put in?

The thing is that we're now used to seeing huge movies with incredible special effects. I'm not very much a fan of action movies. For me, I considered *Hercules* a mixture of action and a film for little children. The special effects I couldn't compare because I didn't go to see action movies, but I liked *Hercules*. I'm very happy now to find after so many years have passed that *Hercules* is liked by a lot of people.

A few years later Federico Fellini said to me, "You know, I watched *Hercules*. You have so many amazing close-ups!" [*Laughs*] Fellini really loved the movie!

Recently I went to see *Hercules* with Luigi Cozzi in Rome, it was at an evening of his movies. I am very proud to say that in the Italian version, I am the only actor with my own voice!

One of the greatest pieces of VHS cover artwork ever made.

Revenge of the Ninja

Release Date: September 16, 1984
Directed by: Sam Firstenberg
Written by: James Silke
Starring: Sho Kosugi, Keith Vitali, Arthur Roberts, Kane Kosugi
Trailer Voiceover: "Only a ninja can stop a ninja!"

Revenge of the Ninja was the second film in Cannon's loosely-linked "Ninja Trilogy," connected more or less only by a single, shared actor: action cinema's top ninja, Sho Kosugi. While Kosugi was tasked with playing a secondary villain opposite Franco Nero in the earlier *Enter the Ninja* (1981), the accomplished martial artist was given the chance here to be the film's hero and choreograph all of its wild, violent fight scenes. This is a movie that tops its predecessor not only with a more exciting story, but in kick-ass ninja action. I'll say this up front: *Revenge of the Ninja* is one of the most essential Cannon releases, and couldn't come any more highly recommended.

Menahem Golan was originally slated to direct *Revenge of the Ninja* after helming the trilogy's first successful entry, but other duties at Cannon pulled him away from the project. The job was then given to rookie action filmmaker Sam Firstenberg, who had been working with Golan and Globus in various capacities going all the way back to *Lepke* (1973) and had just written and directed his own debut feature, the drama *One More Chance* (1983), which featured one of the first film appearances for actress Kirstie Alley. Firstenberg would become one of Cannon's most important, core directors, making eight films for them over the next decade.

Firstenberg was hungry to make movies, and wound up being a fantastic choice on Golan's behalf. To begin with, Firstenberg was young and eager—and his relative newness to directing feature films meant he didn't suffer from the crunch of Cannon's tight budgeting like many veteran directors would have. Like the savviest independent filmmakers, Firstenberg squeezed a ton of extra bang from his buck when it came to production value. Second, he approached the project with a level of self-awareness and never took the subject matter more seriously than was necessary. The results are a movie that is intentionally fun and looks far better than its budget would typically allow.

This time around Kosugi plays Chozen "Cho" Osaki, the descendant of a long line of Japanese warriors. In *Revenge of the Ninja*'s absurdly violent, Tokyo-set prologue, we watch a clan of rival ninjas converge on Cho's village and coldly murder his wife and prepubescent son—the latter, with a ninja star straight to the forehead. (That unfortunate little boy is played by Kosugi's youngest son, Shane Kosugi.) We're never told what these other ninjas had against Cho's family, but it doesn't really matter because Cho returns home just in time to ninja-tastically dispatch every last one of them. One of his coolest moves involves catching an arrow mid-flight and then using it to stab the nearest bad guy.

Kosugi cooked up the movie's badass fight scenes alongside stunt coordinator Steven Lambert, who was here overseeing his first major film. Like Firstenberg, Lambert became one of Cannon's regular collaborators over the next decade, coordinating stunts on *Ninja III* (1984), *American Ninja* (1985), and *Invaders from Mars* (1986), and performing them in *Firewalker* (1986), *Delta Force 2* (1990), and others. Away from Cannon he's worked as a stunt man on everything from *Titanic* (1997) to *Indiana Jones and the Last Crusade* (1989) to *Pee-wee's Big Adventure* (1985).

In the movie, Cho appears to bounce back from the massacre surprisingly well. Seconds after the cold-blooded murder of almost everyone he ever knew and loved, Cho's discussing relocating his remaining family—his mother and infant son, the attack's lone survivors—to California and opening up a high-end porcelain doll gallery with his American pal, Braden (Arthur Roberts). Cho and Braden had been hanging out while his family was being casually slaughtered that fateful afternoon.

Revenge was released in France with an impossibly cool title that translated to "Ultimate Violence."

Revenge of the Ninja cuts to a shot of a proudly-waving American flag and, just in case the new setting wasn't made clear from that image, the words "United States" are superimposed across the screen. The movie never states exactly what city it's supposed to be set in; the film was primarily shot in Salt Lake City, as Utah offered very attractive financial incentives to film there.

(Several exteriors and pickups, as well as the Tokyo-set prologue, were filmed in Los Angeles.)

Six years have passed since the events witnessed in the introduction and Cho and Braden have *finally* gotten around to opening their fancy doll gallery. It's conveniently located behind the dojo where Cho trains his martial arts students, including Braden's foxy assistant, Kathy, played by local fashion model Ashley Ferrare, who'd make her second (and only other) film appearance in 1987's *Cyclone*.

Cho has solemnly sworn off the ways of the ninja, which seems like a sensible thing to do given the way that ninjas destroyed everything he held sacred in his life. He even ties a little paper ribbon around the scabbard of his katana to symbolize that it's been sealed off for good. However, his retirement doesn't stop him from keeping his ninja skills sharp and passing them all on to his young son, Kane, who proves to be a capably dangerous little shit-kicker when he adorably beats the living crap out of several schoolyard bullies.

Little Kane is played by Sho Kosugi's other real-life son, Kane Kosugi, who went on to become a well-known martial artist and actor in his own right. Kane was a five-time competitor in the early seasons of *Sasuke*—better known in the U.S. as *Ninja Warrior*—and has appeared in many other films and TV shows, including *Ninja Sentai Kakuranger* (1994–1995)—the basis for the American franchise Mighty Morphin Power Rangers—where he played the English-speaking Black Ranger. As a kid he also appeared with his father in the films *Nine Deaths of the Ninja* (1985), *Pray For Death* (1985), *Black Eagle* (1988), and *Journey of Honor* (1991); as an adult he'd star in films like *Ninja: Shadow of a Tear* (2013) and Takashi Miike's *Terra Formars* (2016).

It's quickly obvious that Cho's "pal" Braden is up to no good, and that Kathy—who attempts to seduce Cho with a sexy, pantsless sparring match—is in on the scheme. When he's left unsupervised in his father's gallery, Kane accidentally breaks open one of the expensive Japanese dolls, which is revealed to be filled with heroin. It turns out that Braden's involvement in the doll gallery is just a front for his Yakuza-connected drug smuggling ring. (It's no brilliant criminal mastermind or anything, but there have to be better drug lord business models than spending six years establishing an art gallery just to smuggle narcotics inside expensive porcelain dolls, right?)

Worried now that his law-abiding, ninjutsu-trained partner, Cho, might find out about his secret criminal dealings, Braden tries to make a deal with a mob boss named Chifano (Mario Gallo of *Raging Bull*, 1980), who could only be more of a funnier Italian mobster stereotype if you dropped a plate of pasta in his lap and asked him to mumble a few lines about making an offer that someone can't refuse. When Chifano refuses to pay for the drugs, Braden does what any sensible, aspiring drug smuggler would do: he becomes a *demon ninja* to take his revenge on the mafia!

The film's sales ad attempted to pack in much of the film's action into one, tiny image.

Oh, ho, ho—*this* is where *Revenge of the Ninja* starts to get really wild. As crazy as *Enter the Ninja* was, it had nothing that compared to demon ninjas. These evil martial artists have deadly magical powers and wear scary, silver masks under their traditional black shozoku. Demon Ninja Braden's powers include, but aren't limited to: hypnosis, short-range teleportation, spontaneously conjuring foam-rubber decoys of himself, and *shooting flames out of his damn hands!*

In his new form, Braden knocks off one of Chifano's associates in a public bathroom during a picnic with his family; he takes out an informant with another throwing star to the eye; he also murders Chifano's nephew and his lover mid-hot tub canoodle. All of these mysterious killings attract the attention of Lieutenant Dime (Virgil Frye), a local police detective. An actor and boxer, Virgil Frye was the father of two famous, small Fryes: Sean Frye, who played Elliot's older brother in *E.T.* (1982), and Punky Brewster herself, Soleil Moon Frye.

Lieutenant Dime assigns Officer Dave Hatcher (Keith Vitali) to the case, who just so happens to be a fellow martial artist and personal friend of Cho's. A highly touted karate champion, Keith Vitali had at this point already been inducted into *Black Belt Magazine*'s hall of fame. (The amount of martial arts talent packed into *Revenge* is truly impressive.) He later went on to co-star in other action films, such as *No Retreat, No Surrender 3* (1990) and *American Kickboxer* (1991).

Hatcher asks Cho to examine the murder weapons. Cho confirms that only a ninja would be capable of such killings, but declines to assist the police any further. Of course, Cho becomes unwittingly entangled in the war between the mafia and the demon ninja.

Chifano sends over a few goons—one, interestingly enough, dressed like a stereotypical Native American from an old Western movie—to smash up the doll gallery and steal Braden's heroin. Cho catches them as they're loading up the loot and an amazing battle unfolds. The ex-ninja makes short work of his three assailants, who try to flee in their getaway van—which Cho chases down (on foot) and leaps onto its roof. The fight continues on top of and inside the speeding vehicle until it crashes, and Cho and the bad guys are thrown through the windshield. They get up and keep fighting—the Indian character doing so with a pair of tomahawks, because of course—until Cho once again hands their asses to them. The last bad man standing climbs into the van and tries to escape. Cho grabs hold of the back of the van and is dragged behind it for a while before finally giving in to exhaustion and letting go.

Stunt coordinator Steven Lambert was Cho's double in this action sequence, and it's a testament to his great talents that he wasn't killed or horribly maimed while filming it. He wasn't wearing a cable while balancing on the van, which, I'll mention, wasn't sped up in the edit, and was *really* moving that quickly. He was actually dragged behind the vehicle (wearing thick, protective pants) as it was throwing up sparks. One of the movie's most complicated action scenes, the whole van-chase-fight sequence took a week to film.

While Cho is indisposed, Braden—in demon ninja form—arrives at the gallery to find his heroin stash has been ransacked. He's discovered by Cho's elderly mother, who puts up a respectable, ninjutsu-style attempt to defend the family dojo before Braden runs her through with his katana. (This fight is especially fun, as they hired a local gymnast to double for grandma when she does flips, making the old woman appear surprisingly spry.) Braden looks up to discover Cho's son, Kane, has been watching the battle unfold through a hole in the ceiling. The little boy manages to elude the demon ninja in the ensuing foot chase.

Unable to catch a break, Cho returns home to find his son has gone missing and his elderly mother has been murdered by a ninja. As he mourns her death at a Buddhist temple, Officer Hatcher informs him that he has a lead on a group of ex-convicts who might know something about the attack on his business. Cho accompanies him along to a local playground where the gang likes to hang out. (As a parent, I probably wouldn't leave my kids to play somewhere that was widely known to be a meeting place for violent criminals.)

They find the four ex-convicts dressed like a cowboy, a biker, a punk, and a break dancer, and sitting at a picnic table. (Factor in the Native America thug we saw earlier and you have to wonder whether *Revenge of the Ninja*'s costume department raided the Village People's wardrobe.) The criminals would rather fight the two skilled martial artists than say whether or not they know anything about the missing dolls, and so another amazing battle breaks out. The *Revenge* crew did an incredible job finding ways to use the playground environment as a weapon: Cho knocks the punk rocker down a sliding board, and Hatcher throws the cowboy into a climbing net. Meanwhile, a group of fearless bystanders gleefully applaud them on just a few feet away.

Braden returns home to find one of his goons—a sumo warrior played by the late, great Professor Toru Tanaka—about to take advantage of Kathy, and kills him. Charles Kalani, Jr. took on the wrestling name of Professor Tanaka and rose to fame in the 1960s while playing a heel in the World Wide Wrestling Federation. He made his film debut getting kicked around by Chuck Norris in *An Eye for An Eye* (1981) and went on to have small but memorable roles in movies such as Cannon's *Missing in Action II*, *Pee-wee's Big Adventure* (1985), and *The Running Man* (1987).

Braden hypnotizes Kathy to go out and try to capture Kane. She finds and corners Kane at the dojo, tries to fight him, and gets beat up by the adorable little kiddo. Just as he is about to run her through with a spear, he decides she isn't worth murdering and spares her life—letting his guard down just long enough for her to scoop him up and whisk him away to Braden's evil lair. Kathy eventually snaps out of her trance and has immediate kidnapper's remorse. She calls Cho to tell him that not only was his son kidnapped by his supposed friend and business partner, but Braden is secretly a powerful and dangerous ninja. (Just when you think you know a guy . . .) When Braden discovers Kathy's betrayal, he imprisons her with Kane in his sauna and then prepares to take out Chifano once and for all.

If you've learned *anything* about ninjas thus far, it's that the only way to stop a ninja is with *another* ninja. Thankfully, this forces Cho to finally remove the symbolic paper ribbon from around his katana and get back to his asskicking roots.

The cover of the Spanish press kit featured Kosugi in the iconic black shozoku.

The demon ninja mounts his assault on Chifano's headquarters, zip-lining into a high floor of the building and picking off his bodyguards with a wide variety of tools from the ninja arsenal. (As with *Enter the Ninja*, Kosugi served as something of an uncredited ninja consultant and supplied many of his personally-designed weapons for the film.) Meanwhile, Cho—now dressed in his own black shozoku—takes an alternate route into the building while eliminating any of the gangsters who dare come between him and his demon ninja target. Along the way Hatcher has the misfortune of running into the demon ninja first and meets his untimely demise, which only further fuels Cho's lust for revenge.

Elsewhere, Kane is able to free himself from his bindings and steal the guard's nunchaku, which he then uses to incapacitate him, like a badass, baby Bruce Lee. Kane frees Kathy—who was bound inside a hot tub, which was retro-fitted as a drowning/torture device—and they head off to Chifano's headquarters to catch up with Cho.

The two adversaries eventually meet on the roof of the skyscraper, where the movie's climactic battle between good (ninja) and evil (ninja) takes place. This movie's extended, action-packed finale makes up the last 20 minutes of the film, ten of which are spent on the roof as Cho and Braden duke it out to the death. Rooftop shooting took ten full days, much of that time spent setting up pyrotechnics and safety rigging. It was all worth it: *Revenge of the Ninja*'s final showdown comprises arguably the best ninja action in cinematic history. The two ninjas square off with swords, throwing daggers, chains, smoke grenades, and kama. The demon ninja breaks out more than a few nasty tricks from his black magic playbook, including teleportation and shooting flames out of his hands, to conjuring a decoy dummy that's dressed exactly like him. Just when it appears Cho can no longer endure the demon ninja's assault, he manages to sneak in a killing blow. Braden's chest sprays a glorious fountain of blood, and he drops dead. (The high-pressure blood spray, along with the shot where Cho's elder son takes a shuriken to the face, were occasionally deemed too graphic and trimmed from several releases of the film.) In the end Kathy and Kane finally make their way to the roof, where father and son are reunited happily ever after.

I really, really, really can't overstate how gratuitously awesome the movie's action-packed third act is. The demon ninja was usually played by stunt man Steven Lambert throughout the movie, including in these final sequences, as the silver mask worn by the character made it easy to swap out actors. Lambert narrowly avoided a fatal accident during the zip-lining scene when his assistant, Don Shanks—the same man who played the Native American thug earlier in the movie—stopped him from riding the line before it had been weight-tested. They sent out several sandbags on the cable, which gave out and fell several stories to the ground below—which is where Lambert would have been, had Shanks not stepped in and saved his life.

For all of its goofily-garbed baddies and kiddie combat, *Revenge of the Ninja* is not only the most consistently fun movie in Cannon's sizeable ninja canon, but one of the best ninja movies of all time. Minute for minute, you'll be hard-pressed to find many other films that feature more action sequences than *Revenge*—in fact, there are so many fights squeezed into this movie that it's a wonder how they found room to include its plot at all. The movie cemented Kosugi's stardom—historically, this was the first time an Asian actor received lone, top billing on a Hollywood feature—and launched Firstenberg's career as an action movie specialist. (Revenge made more than $13 million domestically on a budget of roughly $1 million.) Factor in other exemplary elements such as its top-notch stunt work and Rob Walsh's fantastic score and you've got an essential piece of '80s exploitation cinema.

Director Sam Firstenberg (left) on set with ninja star Sho Kosugi. Courtesy of Sam Firstenberg.

Interview: Director Sam Firstenberg

From 1983 to 1992, Sam Firstenberg—or "Shmulik," as his collaborators fondly refer to him—directed eight films for Cannon, although his relationship with the company's commanding cousins long pre-dates that ten-year span. Firstenberg worked with Golan and Globus for nearly a decade before he helmed his first feature film, serving in a wide variety of roles, from messenger all the way up to assistant director. After a break in the late 1970s that saw him return to film school and complete his first feature-length movie, Firstenberg was hired to direct his first picture for the newly-managed Cannon: the 1983 classic *Revenge of the Ninja*.

With a skill for delivering fast-paced, cinematic stories and wringing exceptional production value from low budgets, Firstenberg instantly became one of Cannon's most trusted filmmakers. His works for the studio include classics such as *Ninja III: The Domination* and *Breakin' 2: Electric Boogaloo* (both 1984), *Avenging Force* (1986), and the first two *American Ninja* movies (1985, 1987). As Cannon's fortunes faded, Firstenberg took on hired work for other producers; several of his notable works away from the studio included the underrated *Riverbend* (1989), *Cyborg Cop* (1993), and *Quicksand* (2002), all of which starred fellow Cannon alumni.

To date, Firstenberg has directed 22 feature-length films. He spends time now giving talks at festivals around the world as one of the living ambassadors of '80s action cinema. These volumes naturally focus on his Cannon output; for those interested in reading further, Marco Seidelmann's book, *Stories from the Trenches*, deep dives into Firstenberg's entire filmography.

The Cannon Film Guide: **Your time with Golan and Globus dates to long before they were running Cannon. Correct me if I'm wrong, but you were one of only four employees they had when they were operating as AmeriEuro?**

Sam Firstenberg: Yes. In Israel, they had a company called Noah Films, like Noah's Ark. It had been around forever, even when I was a teenager the company already existed. This was the 1960s. They produced local, Israeli movies and they tried, even then, to produce American, Hollywood-style movies. They would bring actors in from Italy and America. I didn't know them at that point, when I was living in Israel and they were making movies there. When I met them here in Los Angeles it was 1973, I think. They'd established a company in Hollywood called AmeriEuro Pictures, and I think it was established specifically to produce the movie *Lepke* (1973), starring Tony Curtis. That's when I met them and started working for them.

Were they very different back in those early days, or were they already the same guys they'd be when they were running Cannon in the following decade?

On a personal level, I would say they were there. [*Laughs*] That was them. Menahem Golan and Yoram Globus were the same characters, but the operation was tiny. Small, small, small. It was a really small operation. Of course, then they didn't have the money and the power they'd have during the Cannon years. I guess the ego grew bigger, and they believed they were invincible later, but those two guys were not shy people to begin with. They knew how to push their way through, and they understood the business. They were already in the business—they'd traveled to the Cannes Film Festival ten years priors to this, we're talking 1963. They conducted business their way, right away, from the beginning.

They were certainly outsiders in Hollywood at that time, but in Israel they had been very successful.

In Israel they were *very* famous. Menahem Golan always made sure that his name would be above the title—that his name was more important than the name of the movie. [*Laughs*] It was always on the posters in Israel, "A Menahem Golan Movie," whether he produced it or directed it. They went to a lot of European film festivals, but in the United States not many people knew them. What brought them here to America was a movie they'd made in Israel called *Kazablan* (1973). They were successful selling it to [MGM], but I don't think anyone knew about them when they came here. There was a movie they'd produced—not directed—that was nominated for an Academy Award. They were still very small scale.

You assistant directed and worked on a few of Menahem Golan's movies during this time.
I was here as a student when they came over from Israel. I met Menahem Golan at a party and I started to work with him on *Lepke* doing all kinds of odd jobs, then on another movie called *Four Deuces* (1975) with Jack Palance. And then they had an office! I became their runner. I was running around town on a motorcycle delivering scripts, bringing back scripts, contracts, all of that kind of stuff. Then came a point where they went back to Israel to make the movie *Diamonds* (1975), with Robert Shaw. I begged Menahem to go with him, and be an assistant director. He agreed, and I was made second assistant director. I spent three months working on that movie, and then I came back [to Los Angeles] and finished my studies.

I kept working for them as a runner. Their offices were very, very tiny—only four or five people. And then they acquired the book *52 Pick-up* by Elmore Leonard. They were planning to go back to Israel to produce it with Joe Don Baker, I remember. We went back to Israel and the idea was that I would be the first assistant director, because by then I'd acquired a lot of experience. Elmore came with us to adapt the book for Israel, because they wanted to shoot it there. My job then was mostly to chaperone him around while he worked on the adaptation. I don't know what happened—maybe it was a problem with Joe Don Baker, I don't know—but suddenly it was postponed. While we were preparing they decided not to do it. And so I moved to working on another movie called *Lupo Goes to New York* (1976).

Before they bought Cannon, you returned to school and made your first movie, *One More Chance*. I know you ran out of money while making it. When did it occur to you to pitch it to your old employers?
When *52 Pick-up* didn't happen, I moved from one Israeli movie to another as assistant director. Many, many, many movies: comedies, et cetera. Also one of the biggest movies they produced as Noah Films, *Operation Thunderbolt* (1977). By this point it was 1979 and I was tired of assistant directing so many movies. It was not my goal to be an assistant director. My wife was accepted to study for her PhD in Los Angeles, and I decided to go back to

graduate school. I was accepted at Loyola Marymount University in their film program.

I was the oldest student there—I was already 29—and I had a lot of experience, but I enjoyed school. Part of the program was to make a short film, so we had to write a script. I like crime dramas, and that's something I've always been drawn to. I came up with a story about an ex-con who's getting out of prison and trying to put his life back together. It was a 30-minute script. Then, one day when I'm walking in the corridors, I met another Israeli student: David Womark. He's now a very famous producer. We started to talk, and I told him that I had a lot of experience, and that I'd already made shorts prior to this. (I'd made a 30-minute short called *For the Sake of a Dog* for Israeli television.) I told him, I needed a chance—let me extend this script to 90 minutes. If you're interested you can produce it, and I'll direct it.

In film school you have equipment, stages, and enthusiastic fellow students who'd love to lend a hand and help. The school liked the idea. We were shooting on weekends, on location and building sets on the stages. But these weren't the video days: we were shooting on 16 millimeter. You have to buy the film, you have to develop it, and all of this costs money. The school only provided the equipment, the stages, and the students. Where do we get the money? First we figured we could get student loans, and then all sorts of scholarships, and we sunk that money into buying film and sending it to the lab. But yet, we ran out of money.

Film was the main expense—of course, you have to feed your crew, buy them pizzas during the day, but film is expensive. We eventually figured out that if you develop film, they won't charge you until you pick it up. And so at some point we stopped picking up the film! We'd buy raw material, shot on it, and then took it to the lab but never picked it up. [*Laughs*] That's how we accumulated a large debt to the lab. We had 60 or 70 minutes of the film finished, and then one day we got a call from the lab saying, "Listen, you have so much film here, and you owe us thousands of dollars." Somehow we convinced the lab that if they didn't give us back the film, we wouldn't have a movie and we'd never have the money to pay them back. We told them we'd edit it together, find an investor, and then re-pay them. They agreed, but they knew they had no other choice.

This was maybe 1980, and at that point I'd found out that Menahem Golan and Yoram Globus had bought this New York-based company, Cannon, and moved it to Los Angeles. I picked up the phone and set up a meeting. I said to him, "Here is the movie. It's unfinished. We need money for the lab, and for another 20 minutes." They watched what we had, and they liked the idea. They needed material for the company, it was still their very beginning. They gave us money and we had another week or week-and-a-half of shooting. The deal was that they'd become partners and they'd distribute the movie. We didn't make a lot of money, but it was a good launching pad and that's how I got in with Cannon films.

One More Chance played at festivals, but then it sounds like you perhaps weren't sure how to take the next step in your career until you convinced Golan you were the right director for *Revenge of the Ninja*, and the rest is history. You became known as an action director after that. If it hadn't been for that opportunity, do you think those are the sort of movies you would have made?

No, not at all. Action wasn't in my mind when I set out to become a director. The sort of movies I wanted to make were socially-conscious dramas, maybe crime dramas or other dramatic movies. I was never interested in action. Of course when I was growing up I saw James Bond and other, mild action movies, but I didn't have a special love for them in particular. And so, I don't know where I'd have ended up if not for *Revenge of the Ninja*. [*Laughs*] But I don't think it would have been in action.

Had you been pitching Cannon for work before that?

Well, *One More Chance* was done, and it was accepted to the Chicago Film Festival. We got the second prize, and we were accepted into the Locarno festival in Switzerland. They took it to Cannes, and then here and there they sold it around the world. You could see this movie and tell that evidently the director—who happened to be me—knows how to make a movie, and he can tell a story in a cinematic way. It was obvious. You could tell.

Cannon's 1983 sales catalog gave many potential buyers their first sneak peek at Sho Kosugi in *Revenge of the Ninja*.

I didn't know what to do next. I was working on another script with David Womark, and we were trying to get Cannon interested in it. It was a youth movie, not an action movie. But Cannon had made *Enter the Ninja* and they were about to do *Revenge of the Ninja*. Menahem had directed *Enter the Ninja*, but he did not want to direct *Revenge*. So he turned to me, not in full confidence—because as you said, it was an action movie and I had not made an action movie yet. But he approached me and said, "I have this movie I want you to direct, but the only problem is that it's an action movie and you don't have action experience." So I tried to reassure him, "Don't worry, I can handle the action. I can do it." And Cannon took a chance. They could have fired me after four days if they wanted—it wasn't my project, I was a director for hire. As a hired gun, they could have fired me whenever they wanted. And it turned out okay!

One of the tricks I figured out in how not to be fired is that I told the crew I wanted to shoot an action sequence right away. We set up the schedule so that it's the first thing we did. We were shooting in Salt Lake City, and we sent the action footage back to Los Angeles they'd realize we could do it. And that's exactly what we did. They saw it and decided not to fire me. [*Laughs*] The rest is history.

You've said before that you had never even heard the word "ninja" before working on this movie, and yet you became Hollywood's foremost ninja movie director. Can you tell me about meeting Sho Kosugi, and the crash course he gave you on ninjas?

As you said, I'd never heard the word "ninja" before that. No only me—most of the Western world hadn't heard of ninjas, either. But I wasn't even a fan of martial arts movies. I'd never seen a Hong Kong or kung fu movie. The only thing I knew a little bit about was the samurai movies of Japan, I loved them, Akira Kurosawa, those kind of movies. Those aren't really martial arts, but they were close to the same area.

I was introduced to Sho Kosugi and told he was the star of the movie. In the previous movie he was the villain, this time he was going to be the hero. He realized I didn't know anything about ninjas or ninjutsu. He was really gracious enough, he basically took me under his wing. There was a Little Tokyo neighborhood in Los Angeles, and he took me to one of the book stores there. He told me, "Okay, you need to read this book and this book to even understand what I'm talking about." They were small books about ninjutsu and its history. He showed me all of the weapons, and the things he was doing with them. And then he started showing me some of those movies. There are little theaters here in Los Angeles where they screen kung fu movies, mostly in the Asian neighborhoods. They played the movies with no subtitles. [*Laughs*] And these are usually long movies, 100 or 120 minutes. And I watched them! But the subtitles were not important to me. I had to watch the action, and see what they did with it. Bit by bit, I got to understand what it means.

As a director, I knew I didn't have to be a ninja expert. It was my job to direct the movie, and he was the choreographer, in any case. He was going to choreograph the fights the right way and use the weapons the right way. My job was only to direct the movie. It can be a ninja movie or it can be a James Bond movie: the director's job stays the same, and that's to translate the story in a cinematic and visual way. That's all.

Ironically, like you said, though, I became a director of ninjas. Even today, though, I'm still not an expert on the subject of ninjutsu, but I know enough.

Everyone I've spoken to about working with you has said it was a pleasure, since you're so open to hearing their ideas. Across your career, how important have you found collaboration to be to your role as a filmmaker?

It's extremely important! In my point of view, the director of a film—and I'm not talking about people who write their own scripts and then go and direct them, the auteurs, but about the general role of a director. In Hollywood, 90% of the movies are directed by directors who are given a script and told, "Go ahead. Go direct this script and we'll pay you." In my opinion, an analogy you can draw is to an orchestra conductor. The conductor gets the script, or the music—the music is written by Beethoven, or Mozart, not by him—and he gets 120 players with their instruments and now he has to put it together. He has to make it so it sounds good to the audience. If you give him lousy players, the music will sound lousy. If you give him a lousy score, the music will be lousy. He needs good material. He needs to collaborate with the musicians, and the heads of the sections. He needs to listen to them, and then interpret the music. A director, in a way, is the same. There are maybe more elements—the production elements, the visual elements, art directing, acting, the action, cinematography, sound—but in my opinion a good director is the one who listens to all of the departments. Together it's a cumulative effort. A film is not a one-man job.

There *are* directors who write their film, direct it, film it, and edit it, but even *those* directors still need actors. [*Laughs*] Maybe only in animation can a director do everything by himself.

Collaboration is extremely important to a director if you want your movie to be interesting and full of ideas. The more you listen to people and the more you work with them, in my opinion the better your movie will end up.

Something that pops up in many of your movies are bad guys in eye-catching costumes. I think of the playground thugs in *Revenge of the Ninja*, **the masks that John P. Ryan's goons wear in** *Avenging Force*, **the many, colorful ninjas in** *American Ninja* **or the Viking in** *American Samurai*. **Would you consider this to be one of your trademarks?**

These characteristics you're bringing up in my movies were collaborations with the art departments and the costume designers. The same thing goes for *Electric Boogaloo*. It's very colorful. I work with them, I listen. Again, this is not traditional. In a traditional ninja movie, all the ninjas would be covered in black. We invented the military ninja look for Michael Dudikoff, and all the colors for what we called the ninja school in *American Ninja*. But it comes from my decision when I started those ninja movies that they weren't going to be pure martial arts movies like the ones from Hong Kong, but more like a James Bond action movie with a ninja twist. Once I made that decision within my own mind I was open, I didn't have to stick to the traditional schools of thought! I'm open to listen to my wardrobe designer who comes up to me and says, "Why don't we change it up a little bit?" In general when I direct movies, I encourage my crew to come up with crazy ideas. I always thought that the most interesting, cinematic visuals come out when you're not afraid to push for crazy stuff. And so I always encouraged my crews to come up with ideas. We didn't always have it in the budget and we didn't always execute it—not even every idea *I* had—because, after all, we were making low-budget movies. But, you can see it! It's there. The crazy, far-out ideas are there.

As a director, I would say, "We can compromise on this, but I *really* want to see the guy going through the glass of the van." Let's say that. And so I would give up on something else and juggle all of those crazy, extravagant elements within the budget that we had.

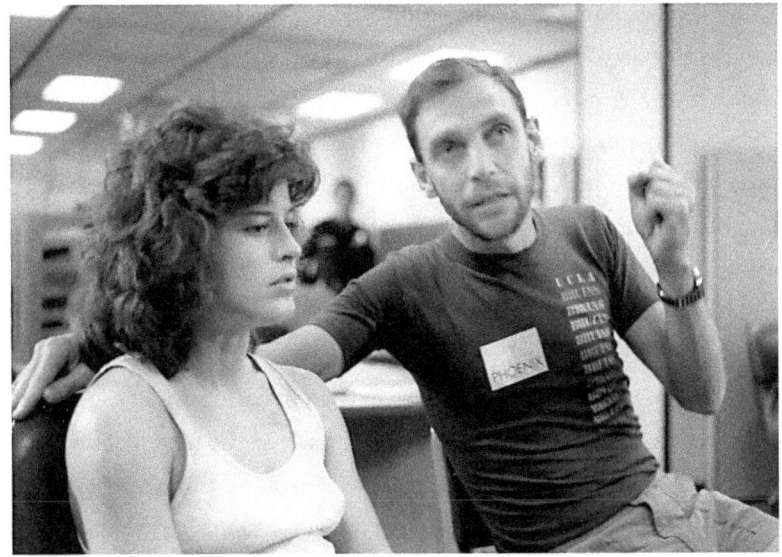

Firstenberg directing Lucinda Dickey on the set of *Ninja III: The Domination*. Courtesy of Sam Firstenberg.

It's hard for me to put a finger on it, but that's probably why you see things like the colorful costumes in the ninja movies. It's because I was open to ideas, and didn't have to stick to traditional rules. We were open to experiment.

I love that, though. In how many other action movies do you remember the lowly bad guys who are only there, frankly, to get kicked around by the hero? These ones stick in your mind because they aren't just your generic thugs. You remember their costumes.

Right, right. When we made the group of the four guys sitting in the park [in *Revenge of the Ninja*], everyone said they looked like the singing group . . . who were they?

The Village People?

Yes, the Village People. [*Laughs*] Those were ideas that weren't necessarily in the script, but came up later when we were working on the production. We'd say, "Let's have the villains look like The Village People." Or, "Let's make the guy who gets the shuriken in his eye be a beggar, or a homeless guy."

Remember, I don't like boring movies. [*Laughs*] I like interesting, exciting movies. How do you make stuff exciting in the kind of movies we're talking about, right? You make crazy, colorful villains. Think of James Bond . . . the villains in those movies are *always* crazy. It's not like *American Sniper* (2014), You don't need to stick to reality. It doesn't have to be accurate historically, or militaristically. Rather, it's fantasy. Let's have fun with it! That's my approach to this kind of film.

How much downtime did you have between shooting *Revenge of the Ninja* and starting on *Ninja III*?

People who don't work in movies have to understand that the director is involved in this type of low-budget movie for maybe nine months. From the minute where he's hired, through development, to casting, shooting the movie, and then editing. The shooting of the movies I made were about eight to nine weeks. And then you'd have post-production, all the way to the end. All of that always took about nine months for me. I would say there was usually a year between shoots, but you're working that entire time in between.

This is probably considered a very tight schedule. Some big-budget Hollywood directors only make a movie once every four years, you know.

I imagine there were scenarios where you were editing one movie while marking up the script for the next one.

That happened to me a little bit. The day we finished *Avenging Force* I was already on a plane to Africa for *American Ninja*. They would have sent me even earlier but I needed to finish the editing. I wasn't able to supervise the post-production on that one because I was already in Africa. It was tight.

You worked a schedule like that for years. Was it as exhausting as I imagine it was?

I was young. I was 29 years old when I made my first feature film. So, I was young and vibrant. But it's true that we worked hard. The shooting day for a director is usually 16 hours. You're on set for 12 hours, but the director comes in early and stays late to review the dailies from the day before. Sometimes there are production meetings about the next day. So, you're usually working sixteen hours a day.

Editing is much more relaxed. But, saying that, I must point out that for me, making movies was like putting a little kid in their most favorite toy store and then paying him a salary to play with the toys. [*Laughs*] That was kind of how I viewed it!

I guess a good thing about directing is that sometimes you're not working. Sometimes I had five months just to play with my daughters. Maybe it was physically exhausting when I was going from one movie to the next, but I can't say I felt it because I was having the time of my life. I was playing with the toys that I loved.

The opening of *Ninja III* is so crazy, and has an incredibly high body count. How much of that was in the script versus how much of it was just cool stuff you came up with working with Steven Lambert and Sho Kosugi?

When we got the script for an action movie—at least, this is how I worked, I can't speak for a big budget action movie—it would have all of the story, the dialogue, and maybe all of the action up until you get to a fight, but then the actual fight sequence or a chase sequence isn't spelled out in the script. Usually it's only half a page. Maybe it says, "Okay, the ninja kills all the policemen, then he dies, and he possesses Lucinda." It's not described move-by-move in the script at all. That's where I start to work with the stunt men, and this particular sequence was more the work of Steven Lambert than of Sho Kosugi because it's not pure martial arts, you know.

So let's say then I start to work with Steven Lambert or another stunt coordinator. I'd say, "Let's build a sequence." This is in pre-production, before we start filming. I like to work with the stunt coordinator or fight choreographer and a storyboard artist, and we take our time. We build a sequence. During shooting, more elements may come up and be added to the sequence, because we aren't close-minded. I don't think we need to shoot the exact way we'd decided. Some exciting idea might come up. We bring in a special motorcycle stuntman, let's say. He says, "Listen, I'm here. Why don't we add this little twist where I jump the motorcycle from this hill to that hill? It will only cost so much." I get together with the producer and we say, "Wow, that's a good idea. We didn't think of it." Then I'd talk to Steve, the stunt coordinator, and we'd say "Let's go for it. Let's do it." And so that adds an element we hadn't thought of before, and it makes the action sequence that much more exciting. So, to answer your question, those sort of things aren't in the script.

I've heard that the idea to have *Ninja III* star a female ninja came from Menahem. Was it 100% his idea to go in that direction?

Yeah. What happened was, we finished with *Revenge of the Ninja* and it was accepted by MGM for distribution. Cannon Films was very excited; they'd never had a movie distributed by a major company prior to this. It was the first movie they successfully placed for major distribution with MGM. The movie was a moderate success, which was not bad for a low-budget movie. It opened at the time on 400 or 500 screens, made money, and was #1 at the box office in New York City. And so they wanted to do a sequel.

I don't know his exact reasoning [for a female ninja]. Cannon was mostly a foreign sales company. Their main business was selling movies to foreign countries. Maybe they found out they needed the hero of their movie to be more Western, more Caucasian, more White, for better sales? I don't know that I'm right. That's just my speculation.

When Menahem Golan approached me and said, "We're going to make a sequel, *Ninja III*. I don't want Sho Kosugi to be the hero this time, but I want something else. Why don't we go with a female?" We already discussed that I didn't take these movies too seriously, I approach them in a light way. So I said, "Wow, what a crazy idea! Let's do it. Let me work with the writer." The writer was James Silke. Menahem didn't have any other ideas. His only idea was to have a female ninja, and she'd be the hero.

It wasn't a completely crazy idea. In the history of ninjas in Japan, there was such a thing as a female ninja. The ninjas were assassins hired to assassinate shoguns, ministers, whatever, for influence or for power. There were groups of female ninjas, also. Here and there in Hong Kong movies you would see ninja women as villains, but never as heroes. So it wasn't a totally crazy idea, but it was 100% Menahem's idea.

The director and his female ninja, Lucinda Dickey.
Courtesy of Sam Firstenberg.

It sounds like he left you alone, for the most part, once shooting began on these movies. The freedom had to have been wonderful, but did it ever make you nervous not knowing whether or not your producers would be happy with what you were doing?

You are correct, but what you're saying is correct about any production, any movie, any studio, any director. It's even worse when you work for a studio. If a director makes a movie for Disney, it's even more nerve-wracking. But as I told you, I had a little trick. With our schedules, we wanted to maximize the resources that we had. The best way to do that was to shoot it action sequence, then drama. Action sequence, then drama. That way the action people had some time to rest and prepare for the next sequence while you go and work with your actors. That's the optimal way to work. So I'd start with a big action sequence and send it back to the office for them to view. I knew that if it was exciting enough, they would leave me alone. [*Laughs*]

But then, you still wouldn't know how [the producers] felt until you showed them a rough cut of the movie. In the case of Cannon, Menahem

Golan would always see the rough cut and say, "Okay, let me bounce some ideas with you. Let's cut this out, or change this thing." At least two times with me he was willing to send me out to shoot additional photography to really fine-tune the story. That was usually they procedure but yes, you're right, there was always the chance that something would not come out perfectly.

You went from *Ninja III* into *Breakin' 2: Electric Boogaloo*. I know you didn't view it as a huge leap, since shooting ninja action wasn't all that different from shooting dance moves. Were you excited for the change of pace? I know you're a fan of old musicals.

I was very excited. It was a great opportunity. The first *Breakin'* was another director, Joel Silberg. I'm not sure what happened, but there was some sort of relationship problem between him and the company. Suddenly they were turning to me and asking, "Will you do it?" I'd already worked with Lucinda Dickey, anyway.

Shabba-Doo, Lucinda Dickey, and Sam Firstenberg behind the scenes of *Breakin' 2: Electric Boogaloo*. Photo courtesy of Sam Firstenberg.

But you're right, I didn't see a big difference from a directorial standpoint. In the outside world a lot of people see them and think, "This is action! This is dance! They're two entirely different things!" But they're not! One has choreographed pieces, and the other has choreographed pieces. Really, they're the same thing. They're movies with choreographed sequences.

I was excited. I love music, and I loved musicals. Wow, what an opportunity. The budget was really good, it was a bigger movie with nine weeks of shooting. And then two weeks into shooting we find out that a big company wanted to buy the movie for distribution—it was TriStar, who were actually Columbia. So, everything around it was so exciting. And the first movie had been a big success. We were making a sequel to a big success.

It was a really fun set, with music from the morning to the evening every day. I was really excited about making a musical dance movie.

I heard that actors and crew members would show up on set even on days they weren't needed, just because they were having a good time. Would you say that *Breakin' 2* was the most fun movie set you were ever on?

Definitely. On the ninja movies with Sho Kosugi, he was a sensei. He had students coming to see him, but martial arts are more limited [in exposure]. Here we had Shabba-Doo, who was a big icon in the dance world. He was big. Debbie Allen would come to set to see what Shabba-Doo was doing. Big dancing names would show up, big names in pop culture and hip-hop. He was connected. We'd also have a lot of kids coming from the street. It was summer vacation time, and they'd hear the radio reports and know where we were shooting and they'd come all the way just to meet Shabba-Doo. It was a big deal. Years later when I made a movie [*McCinsey's Island*, 1998] with Hulk Hogan, it was the same way.

But this was fun. We were shooting in East Los Angeles, where hip-hop culture and street dance was happening. The dancing troupes had a lot of members and as you mentioned, they would show up on the days they were working and the days they weren't working.

We were shooting with playbacks. There were speakers on set and the sound man would play back the music and they would just mimic, move their lips, or dance to it. We had a rule with our sound man. Early in the morning, as soon as we were on set, he would start to play the music right away. And so it was fun: we'd show up every morning and the music would already be blaring on the loudspeakers. We'd be dancing, and we'd have all those fluorescent colors around us most of the day. Something like *Avenging Force* was more challenging from a professional point of view, but here it was fun. People dancing all day long.

You had to be the busiest person on set and didn't get to hang out and party nearly as much as everyone else. Are there any days, though, you look back on most fondly?

What you say is correct: as the director I'm busy all of the time. When we're shooting, of course, I'm there by the camera. When we're not shooting there are a million questions, people approaching me every two minutes to ask "How do we do this? How do we do this?" Even when we are not shooting, I need to stage the scene. I don't remember myself getting to hang out with the dancers and the kids. I don't think I had time for it, nor did I think it was appropriate. I wasn't part of the hip-hop culture.

Setting up Shabba-Doo's dance on the roof of the building is what I remember. I went up with him to the top of the roof to work out the number, and it was quite dangerous. That's what comes into my mind.

You weren't a martial artist when you made *Revenge of the Ninja*, and I assume you weren't a breakdancer when you made *Electric Boogaloo*, either. Did you have a similar collaborative relationship with Shabba-Doo and choreographer Bill Goodson to what you had with Sho Kosugi and Steven Lambert on the ninja movies?

No. You see, Sho Kosugi meant to teach me, to take me by the hand and explain to me what a ninja is. I'm not a dancer, Bill Goodson didn't have to teach me how to dance. I know dancing. Everybody knows dancing and music, but not everybody knows ninjas, you know what I mean? [*Laughs*] By being a human being you're exposed to dance and music. So, no big deal, I don't have to learn anything about dancing and music. And so Bill was doing his own preparation. So was Shabba-Doo. They had a whole language that I didn't understand. But every sequence, every number, before we shot it they'd show it to me.

One crazy idea that Bill Goodson consulted with me about and had nothing to do with Shabba-Doo was the crazy nurses in the hospital. It was completely his idea. He came up to me and said, "Listen. Let's take it one notch up and spice it up. I'll bring in four girls from Las Vegas." Those girls were Vegas dancers! They came in the morning, finished up by around three o'clock, and flew back that evening. Bill said, "These girls are professionals. I'll show them what to do and they'll do it in one take. Don't worry!"

An aerial shot of the gigantic dance finale of *Breakin' 2: Electric Boogaloo*.

You mentioned that TriStar bought the movie only two weeks into production. With such a big deal in place, did that add any pressure for the rest of the shoot?

Suddenly not only me, but the *company* was under more pressure. Yoram Globus and Menahem Golan were under more pressure. They really wanted to impress Columbia. Suddenly they gave us more money and a longer schedule. I know they felt more pressure, but I'm not sure how much of that trickled down to me. I just kept doing my work, that's all I could do, it didn't matter whether it was for Columbia or for Cannon.

There were at least two sequences Menahem came up with while we were shooting. The dancing around the roof and the dance with the doll were not sequences that were set up when we started shooting. He came up with the ideas to add them to the movie.

And then when it came to the editing, there was a big rush. At some point we worked with seven editors to finish the movie. For some reason TriStar moved the release date up and they needed the movie fast.

I get the impression that Menahem was a man of strong opinions, but he could listen to reason when he needed to. Were there many times when you butted heads over an idea, or where you had to stand your ground over something you didn't see eye-to-eye on?

Yes, there were different instances. But it was very good for me to remember that he was very good with these kinds of action movies. These were the movies that he understood how to produce, and make, and sell around the world, so usually his ideas were very good ideas.

Most of the time his ideas were about cutting. He'd cut things out to make the movie more concentrated and precise. He had a rule where he didn't want movies longer than 94 or 95 minutes. By cutting down, cutting down, cutting down, you make the movie more intense. You're cutting out the fat and leaving the meat only. A director doesn't have an objective point of view, maybe because they were involved emotionally in some aspect of the shooting. They remember, "Oh, this was so much fun to shoot, I don't want to take it out of the movie." There's an attachment. But then you realize it's actually not good and the movie's better without it. In this way Menahem Golan was very good, and it was good to listen to him because it would make the movie better and better.

But, sometimes, I would not see eye to eye with him. I had to argue with him. It happened a few times on *Electric Boogaloo*. It was not so much on the action movies. On those he wouldn't argue with me. If I insisted on something he'd say, "Okay, keep it." He didn't care. He'd say, "Let's watch it again when you're finished." But on *Electric Boogaloo* I thought he was wrong sometimes. It was a give and take.

He was a strong-minded individual by all means, you're right about that, but he'd listen to people and their ideas. He was a storyteller, all about the story. If you could convince him with other people's opinions or with another screening that your idea was better for the storytelling, he would go for it.

Kane Kosugi (right) trains under the watchful eye of his father (Sho Kosugi) in this press still from *Revenge of the Ninja*.

Interview: Actor Kane Kosugi

Kane Kosugi wasn't even ten years old yet when he played Kane Osaki, the pint-sized, ass-kicking son of the heroic Cho Osaki in *Revenge of the Ninja*. The real-life son of star Sho Kosugi, young Kane—who was himself trained in martial arts—appeared in a number of his father's films following *Revenge*, including *Pray for Death* (1985), *Nine Deaths of the Ninja* (1985), and *Black Eagle* (1988), before becoming a star in his own right.

In Japan, Kosugi played the black ninja on *Ninja Sentai Kakuranger* (1994–1995), which was one of the shows brought over to America and recut to make the popular Mighty Morphin Power Rangers franchise. He's appeared in the action films *DOA: Dead or Alive* (2006), *Ninja: Shadow of a Tear* (2013), *Tekken: Kazuya's Revenge* (2014), and *2 Guns* (2015). He was also a frequent athlete competitor on *Sasuke*, a Japanese series that was edited and rebroadcast in the United States as *Ninja Warrior*.

The Cannon Film Guide: Your father was a teacher before he went into the movies. At what age did you start training in martial arts?

Kane Kosugi: I was a year-and-a-half old. Basically I think I started walking when I was nine or ten months, and then my parents thought my legs were pretty strong so they decided to start me in martial arts at a pretty young age.

Were martial arts something you naturally wanted to do so young, or was it something that was expected of you?

It was pretty much expected. My brother also trained in martial arts. After school we would always have to go to our classes, and stuff like that. Growing up we didn't mind, but we always kind of dreaded it. We'd have much rather played. It was like, our friends don't have to do this every day, why do we? Growing up we had that feeling, I think.

Once your father's film career took off, what did that do for his dojo business? Were there suddenly a lot more people coming in and looking for instruction?

I think he expanded. He originally had only one, small dojo, but eventually he had two dojos. The thing I think I remember the most at the dojos was that he'd always be selling ninja outfits. Around Halloween we had to help out around the dojo, because he was so busy selling those ninja outfits. [*Laughs*] I think that was one of my first, official, part time jobs.

You grew up in, around, and part of the movie business. At what point did you decide that's what you wanted to do yourself?
Actually I wanted to be an actor after watching my dad's first movie, *Enter the Ninja* (1981). After I saw the movie I thought, "Wow, this is so cool." Watching it at the movie theater, seeing him like that. Even though he played the villain, he still looked really cool to me. And so I thought, "When I grow up, I want to be able to do that." I wanted to be an action actor. I guess he could feel that from me, and so in his next movie he put me in as his son.

Were you and your brother really excited when the opportunity arose to act in *Revenge of the Ninja*?
Yeah! Not only were we able to miss school, we were able to hang out with our dad and meet a lot of people, go to different places. We loved it a lot.

Did your father choreograph your fights in that movie?
Yeah. The parts that I did, my dad was the main choreographer. I remember practicing it a lot at the dojo, and also on set. But for me, because I was doing martial arts from such a young age, it was like second nature. It was more doing it over and over again because I was so young, and the days were so long. But I remember enjoying it a lot.

I know you were so young, so you may not have too many clear memories, but are there any other stories, or things you remember about working on *Revenge of the Ninja* that you're able to share?
I remember our hotel pretty clearly for some reason, I don't know why. [*Laughs*] There was this billiards table in the lobby, or somewhere in the hotel. My dad and a few other crew members would always gather there and we'd play pool after shooting.

Besides that, I remember shooting the fight scenes–that was really cool. And working with [Ashley Ferrare] was nice. She hadn't done any of those action scenes before but she was really good at it. But, just getting to work with my dad. I have really good memories of that.

Young Kane Kosugi features prominently in the Spanish poster for *Revenge of the Ninja*.

You went on after that to do a string of classic ninja movies with your father, like *Pray for Death* and *Nine Deaths of the Ninja*. Can you talk about your life during those years, traveling the world with your father and brother and making movies?

I don't quite remember hearing things from my dad like, "Oh, we have another movie coming up." When there were projects we'd be able to travel. A lot of these projects seemed to take place in the summers, so we didn't miss school much. I remember enjoying it, because just being able to hang out with my dad was a nice experience because he was always busy working.

On *Black Eagle* we go to work with Jean-Claude Van Damme. I remember him being a really nice guy. He was always working out in between takes. Just being able to meet people was really cool. Since I wanted to be an actor from when I was five-and-a-half or six, I always enjoyed the experience and being able to be with my family and travel made it better.

I think back to my own childhood in the '80s and early '90s, when ninjas were everywhere and just the coolest thing in the world. What was that like for you, having been in these movies and being the son of the '80s most prominent ninja? Were you the coolest kid in school?

Yeah, but it was kind of funny. [*Laughs*] I went to the same school for a long time—it was elementary all the way through junior high. All of my friends were kind of used to it. Everyone knew my dad and would watch his TV programs and movies, but during school and all of that nothing really came up about it. No one would say, "Oh, your dad is a ninja." But there were times when we'd go out to watch the premiere of one of my dad's movies, or we'd go out to dinner and people would ask him for autographs. I'd think, "Oh, wow, he's famous!"

Tell me about striking out on your own. You'd made these movies with your father, but it didn't take long after that for you to start landing your own roles, especially on television.

After graduating from high school, I was deciding whether I wanted to go to college in the States, or if I just wanted to focus on my acting career. I was kind of in between and didn't know what I wanted to do. My father gave me this advice, he said "Why don't you go to Japan and study the language and the culture for a bit, since you're half-Japanese? You can go stay there for half a year or a year, and after that maybe you'll know what you really want to do." I thought that was a really good idea. I'd never stayed in Japan for a long period of time, and I figured studying Japanese would help.

Through a few of my father's connections I was able to land a couple roles, even though my Japanese wasn't yet that good. I was lucky to be able to work in Japan. The culture was so much different from what I'd seen in the States at that time. It was the '90s, and in the States there were movie actors who only did movies, and TV actors who mostly only did television. When I got here, there were actors who were multi-talented and did everything. They would do movies and TV shows, and not only TV dramas, but they'd host their own talk shows or variety shows. They'd also sing, or do radio hosting and stuff like that. I thought, "Wow, if I could work here I could learn a lot by doing so many different things. Maybe it will help me as an actor?"

I think one of my first roles was doing *Power Rangers* here. That was really good because it was a year-long series. Going in every day and working with everyone, I was able to pick up Japanese a little bit at a time. It was cool because I got to work with a Japanese crew and stunt guys, and so I was able to learn the Japanese way of doing action.

Little by little I was able to work on a few programs, but then I kind of hit a wall. It had only been two or three years and my Japanese still wasn't up to the level to do TV dramas and movies, or things like that. For two years I wasn't really working, but during that time I was able to learn and train. I was lucky because in those two years I was able to meet Jackie Chan through a friend. He was really nice and invited me to his sets, and so I was able to study and train with him and his stunt team. And then when I came back, I got a few lucky breaks and was able to work in Japan. There was a program that really lifted my career in Japan, and after that I was busy working in a lot of TV shows and movies.

I learned a lot and was enjoying working in Japan, but then my love and my ultimate goal ever since I was a little kid was to try to work in movies, especially in Hollywood and around the world. I was really busy in Japan, with basically no days off and little time to train. When I turned thirty, I figured it was time to try to focus on movies and trying to work in Hollywood. I cut down on a lot in Japan and went back to the States, started looking for an agent and manager and went to a lot of auditions. I worked on a few movies, but then thought I shouldn't only focus on Hollywood, so I went to Asia, China, a lot of different countries to find work there as well. I think I've been lucky to be able to work in so many different places and with so many different people.

Watching some of your more recent fight scenes, like your fight with Scott Adkins in *Ninja: Shadow of a Tear* (2013), it's all up close and you can just *feel* every blow—it's a very different style of martial arts action from the movies your dad did in the '80s, when the shots were pulled back more. Having seen how martial arts movies were made in the '80s and then working in them today, as an adult, what do you see as the biggest differences in how they're made?

It's funny. I have the DVD of *Revenge of the Ninja*, and I watched the movie again after I hadn't seen it in years. I was pretty surprised that it was actually a really cool movie, and even today it still works. I thought the action scenes were really well done. I think during the period when my dad did movies—there was also guys like Bruce Lee, Chuck Norris, and Van Damme in the '80s and '90s, and in Asia there was Jackie Chan and Jet Li. I loved all of those fight scenes. But after it became the 2000s, I think people started using more computer graphics and wires, things like that. That was kind of the big thing.

Nowadays I think the audience is used to watching those things, and the trend is that it's going back to those old days before computers and wires. You've got guys like Tony Jaa, and people want to see more of the action. Nowadays there are so many athletic and talented people in martial arts. People want to see the actors do the actual things more. They don't want to see the editing and quick cuts—the audiences don't get as excited about all of the tricks.

Ninja movies kind of disappeared for about a decade, but they're making a comeback. Do you think audiences were just burned out on them by the end of the '80s, or did the style of action movies change?

After the '80s there were so many ninja movies. You had the ones with my father, the *American Ninja* movies, Ninja Turtles. After a period of time I think people maybe just got tired of it, or maybe they just ran out of ways to tell that story. I don't know. [Ninjas] don't really exist these days, so I think building a new story around them was probably hard.

During the period of time when there weren't any ninja movies, I always thought it would be cool if they had them again. But I think Marvel and all of the superhero movies might have helped revive them, because in a way the ninja is kind of a superhero. They're a Japanese icon.

It sounds like you're interested in every facet of the film industry. Do you think you'd ever want to put together your own ninja film or TV series?

It always pops up in my mind. I'm actually producing a movie right now, as well. For some reason ninja movies always pop up for me, too. The movie I did with Scott Adkins was a ninja movie, and the Power Rangers I did in Japan was about ninjas. It just seems like I always have this connection with ninja movies, even when I'm not thinking about it or hoping for it. I'm always wondering if there's some way to do a project, movie, or something that would be cool. Hopefully one day something will pop up. Ever since I was a kid, it seems like I had this connection and destiny with ninjas.

The Wicked Lady

Release date: October 28, 1983
Directed by: Michael Winner
Written by: Michael Winner, Leslie Arliss, Cordon Glennon & Aimee Stuart
Starring: Faye Dunaway, Alan Bates, Denholm Elliott, John Gielgud
Trailer Voiceover: "It was a time of revelry, and *she* was scandalous! It was a time of violence, and *she* was lawless! It was a time of passion, and *she* was the mistress of deceit!"

Re-making *The Wicked Lady* had long been director Michael Winner's dream project. The 1945 original had starred Margaret Lockwood in the title role of an aristocrat turned outlaw and had made a leading man out of James Mason, who played her partner-in-crime and romantic foil. Written and directed by Leslie Arliss from a book by Magdalen King-Hall for Gainsborough Pictures, the film brought in record-setting audiences for a British feature—its "scandalous" reputation no doubt lending a hand in its ticket sales. (American censors were so alarmed by the many low-cut bodices worn in the film that many scenes had to be re-shot using costumes which revealed less cleavage before it was deemed releasable in the USA.) Michael Winner saw the movie as a youth and it stuck with him long into his prolific directing career.

A VHS copy of *The Wicked Lady* rented by Video Zone of Newport Beach, California.

The notoriously difficult-to-work-with filmmaker had joined the Cannon fold when Charles Bronson refused to do a second *Death Wish* movie with any other director than Winner. That box office hit had won him plenty of good favor with Cannon, who immediately greenlit his pet project, *The Wicked Lady*, when Winner brought it to them with Faye Dunaway already attached to star. (Winner had been close friends with Dunaway's husband, the esteemed British photographer Terry O'Neill.) For Cannon, it was an unmissable opportunity to work with a respected and highly-acclaimed American actor.

Despite hitting a lull in her career after starring in the colossally jeered *Mommie Dearest* (1981)—now considered a cult classic of camp—Dunaway was still not that far removed from her Best Actress Oscar win for *Network* (1977), which had followed nominations for *Bonnie and Clyde* (1968) and

Chinatown (1975). To secure the star's participation, Cannon picked up the film rights to Dunaway's own dream project: Tom Kempinski's acclaimed stage play, *Duet for One*, with the intention that Dunaway would star and her husband, Terry O'Neill, would direct. (Cannon did eventually make that film in 1986, but without either of Dunaway's or O'Neill's involvement.)

The award-winning actress was joined on *The Wicked Lady* by a trio of respected, British thespians. These included Sir Alan Bates, who had been Academy Award-nominated for his role in *The Fixer* (1968), and was well-known for popular movies such as *Zorba the Greek* (1964) and *Women in Love* (1969). Unlike Dunaway, he *would* appear in Cannon's *Duet for One*. Also present was the vaunted stage actor Sir John Gielgud, who had just won the Best Supporting Actor statuette for 1982's *Arthur*. Rounding out the set would be Denholm Elliott, whom cinema fans will recognize as Indiana Jones' recurring, academic pal, Dr. Marcus Brody.

The lauded cast was a major selling point of this full-spread ad from the company's 1983 sales catalog.

To measure up with the talent he had in front of the camera, Winner was able to secure a prestigious cinematographer in Jack Cardiff, who had shot films for Hitchcock, Huston, Welles, and Olivier, as well as two Powell and Pressburger features—*Black Narcissus* (1947) and *The Red Shoes* (1948)—which arguably contained some of the most beautiful use of Technicolor ever committed to celluloid. Cardiff's career had ebbed by the early 1980s, but it did see a commercial upturn: two of his next films were *Conan the Destroyer* (1984) and *Rambo: First Blood Part II* (1985). It takes quite a career leap to go from shooting Bogart and Hepburn (*The African Queen*, 1951) to Schwarzenegger and Stallone.

With all of these lofty names involved in *The Wicked Lady*, one might assume Winner was geared up to make a sophisticated, high-class picture. When one of the first things we see in the film is a farmer banging a milkmaid on a pile of hay, and then the milkmaid being chased through the village, nude, by the farmer's angry wife, it's immediately clear that class isn't what this crew had signed up for. We *are* dealing with the director of *Death Wish 3* (1985), after all.

The movie wastes no time establishing its seventeenth century setting, taking us on a tour through a British countryside dressed with all the subtlety of a renaissance fair. Village minstrels play jaunty tunes; maypoles are danced around; thieves are hunted and hanged by wealthy landowners while Tony Banks' orchestral score swells. As he did with Herbie Hancock in *Death Wish* (1974) and Jimmy Page in *Death Wish II* (1982), Winner recruited a popular artist to compose *The Wicked Lady*'s soundtrack: Banks was the keyboardist and a co-songwriter for Genesis, who would release their biggest hit, "Mama," a month after this film hit theaters.

The servants scurry about the palatial home of Sir Ralph Skelton (Elliott), making preparations for their kindly boss' wedding to the much younger Caroline (Glynis Barber.) Unfortunately for the poor girl, her older cousin Barbara (Dunaway) arrives to be her maid-of-honor but has designs on stealing her rich fiancé. She wastes no time seducing the buttoned-up Sir Ralph, playing the damsel-in-distress and throwing herself off her horse into a pile of leaves where she invites the rich gentleman to ravage her. Barbara barges into the bridal suite where Caroline is being fitted for her wedding dress, announcing that Sir Ralph is in love with her. Though heartbroken, Caroline is surprisingly not bitter about the whole situation. Not only does she volunteer to bow out of her own wedding and let Barbara take her place as the bride, she agrees to stick around and serve as Barbara's maid of honor.

The more cartoonish promotional art used in some ads and seen here on the soundtrack album seemed to portray the movie as a raunchy comedy, although no one seems to have told the cast that's what they were making.

Scene for scene, 1983's *The Wicked Lady* is remarkably faithful to the 1945 version, with most of the dialogue lifted almost verbatim from the original's script. (Leslie Arliss—the first movie's writer and director—was credited as a co-writer on the remake.) The one thing the remake has that the original did not is, of course, tons and tons of topless women. It's as if Winner attempted to fill every possible frame he could with naked, jiggling flesh. Around every corner there seem to be peasants rutting; behind every closed door, a footman soiling a handmaiden. The high level of needless nudity might have been at home in one of the R-rated teen comedies of the era, but it feels wildly out-of-place in a period, costume film featuring this many knights and Oscar-winners.

This aggressive titillation extends through Ralph and Barbara's nuptials, where the hired help throw an orgy while the upper-class guests celebrate downstairs. Barbara becomes considerably less enthralled with her gold-digging marriage scheme when she meets the man of her dreams, Kit Locksby (Oliver Tobias), moments after walking down the aisle—which, we can all agree, is the worst possible time to meet the man of your dreams.

As time goes on, Barbara becomes more and more miserable in her loveless marriage. One night Barbara foolishly bets her mother's brooch in a card game—an item earlier established to be her most cherished possession—and loses it to Ralph's stuffy sister. A guest mentions that a notorious highwayman named Captain Jackson has been looting carriages in their region, which gives Barbara a harebrained idea to disguise herself as a robber and steal back the brooch.

Barbara dresses herself in a black outfit which can most accurately be described as "bad guy clothes," complete with a face-covering mask and floppy, feathered hat. She sneaks out of the estate through a secret passageway, somehow catches up with her sister-in-law's carriage, robs her of her jewelry, and then gets home and changed back into normal clothes before Ralph's sister can return with the bad news.

This little bit of danger spices her life up in a way Barbara never expected, and so she embarks on an honest-to-goodness crime spree. Meanwhile, her husband is tasked with arresting and executing the nefarious brigand as the majority of robberies occur on his land, for reasons more than clear to the audience. Barbara eventually does bump into the *real* Captain Jackson (Bates), who is amused to discover the copycat highwayman that's been impersonating him is actually a highway*woman*. They naturally become lovers, and partners-in-crime.

Barbara (Dunaway) is confronted by the real Captain Jackson (Bates).

The criminal lovebirds attempt to knock over a wealthy caravan but botch the job, and Barbara murders one of her husband's favorite villagers. She accidentally leaves a monogrammed hankie at the scene of the crime, which her scripture-quoting butler, Hogarth (Gielgud), recognizes as hers. Barbara buys herself some time by privately confessing to him her sins and asking for his help in earning God's forgiveness for her wicked ways—then slips him a bit of poisoned brandy, which doesn't kill him as quickly as she'd hoped.

When Caroline—the cousin whose husband Barbara stole—learns her beloved butler is in poor health, she hightails it back from snowy London to visit him. (The foam detergent the crew used to produce the fake snow in this scene was accidentally dumped into Hever Castle's water supply, causing the sinks and fountains all over the estate to issue soapy, bubbly water for long after the crew had left town.) While Caroline was away she unwittingly romanced Barbara's dream man, Mr. Locksby; their tender relationship is conveyed through a moment of spicy, softcore sex by the fireside.

Before Hogarth can tell anybody about his Lady's secret, criminal pastime, Barbara is hilariously and preposterously able to suffocate him to death with a pillow while Caroline, Ralph, and several servants are *in the same room*.

The guilt-ridden Barbara seeks solace at Captain Jackson's hideout, but instead she finds him in bed with another woman—played by *Star Trek: The Next Generation*'s Deanna Troi, Marina Sirtis, in an early role. (Sirtis would work for Cannon and Michael Winner again in *Death Wish 3*.) In a jealous rage, Barbara anonymously rats out Captain Jackson, and he's captured by her husband's men. His public hanging turns out to be the social event of the decade, drawing a huge crowd. Several thousand locals turned up to appear as extras in this scene, having been given advance notice that "a semi-nude whip fight" would be filmed that day.

Many international stills and lobby cards used one of several shots of the topless Sirtis (left) being whipped by Dunaway (right).

And here we've come to *The Wicked Lady*'s most notorious scene. While Captain Jackson refuses to give up the female accomplice who betrayed him, his dying wish is for Barbara to give the girl she caught in his bed—his *true* lover—a small share of their fortune. Barbara gives the grieving woman a pouch of coins, which she throws back in her face. This ignites a catfight between the two women in which a horse whip eventually becomes involved.

Barbara whips Captain Jackson's nubile, young widow until her clothes come off and then continues to whip her naked body as she attempts to flee. (The dress worn by Sirtis for this scene was made of paper, assuring that it would tear sufficiently during their brawl—it still must not have torn enough, because a creepy, behind-the-scenes photo exists of Winner using scissors to cut the dress off Sirtis' body.) Eventually an excited spectator tosses the battered girl a whip to defend herself with, which must have been the 1600s' equivalent of a wrestling fan tossing a metal folding chair into the ring.

Today *The Wicked Lady* is still famous for its notorious "erotic whipping scene," which stirred up quite a lot of controversy ahead of the film's release. James Ferman—the British film censor largely behind the notorious "video nasties" panic of the mid-1980s—demanded that cuts be made to the whip fight before the film could be released with anything less than the British equivalent of an X-Rating.

To battle these censorship requests, Michael Winner asked several of his celebrity friends—including novelists Kingsley Amis and Fay Weldon, filmmakers Lindsay Anderson, John Schlesigner, and Karel Reisz, and *Rumpole of the Bailey* (1978–1982) creator John Mortimer—to publicly defend the film after viewing it themselves. These tastemakers issued statements to the British Board of Film Classification; Anderson called the film "a first-class piece of popular entertainment," and Weldon told them she "would be happy for [her] twelve-year-old son to watch the film." Winner won his battle with the BBFC, and the film was released, uncut, after a short delay, his bout with censors actually drumming up a lot of free publicity and boosting ticket sales. However, it turns out Winner may have duped his famous friends: according to a *Daily Mail* article released after Winner's passing, Weldon alleges she was shown a doctored version of the film—with much of the nudity trimmed from the scene. (This likely made her quote about showing the film to her preteen child embarrassing in retrospect.) Given that Winner edited the film himself under the pseudonym "Arnold Crust," it's easily within the realm of possibility that he could have prepared an alternate version of the movie to show to his respected friends.

In Spain, the film's title was translated to "The Perverse Lady," which is funny but still didn't appropriately reflect the movie itself.

The topless whip fight goes on for a ridiculously long time before it's broken up by the hunky Locksby, whom Barbara is mortified to learn is now engaged to Caroline. The rest of the movie is just a bunch of silliness. Jackson survives his hanging, escapes the gallows and seeks revenge on Barbara. Caroline tells Kit she's in love with Ralph, and Kit confesses that he's in love with Barbara, so the three of them agree to a wife swap. Before they can deliver the good news, Barbara dons her outlaw gear one last time with plans to kill her husband for standing between her and Kit. When Barbara holds up her husband's carriage, ironically it's Kit who pops out and puts a bullet in her, assuming she's the fugitive highwayman and canceling out any hope of an implausibly neatly-wrapped, happy ending. Caroline rushes home to share the news of their new marriage arrangements with Barbara, but finds her cousin dying of a bullet wound. When Barbs confesses her crimes to Kit, he flees in disgust. The credits roll as Barbara dies, alone and unloved, on the floor.

The Wicked Lady seems to have no idea whether it's a serious, costume melodrama or a raunchy sex comedy. (The director himself described it as "a sort of seventeenth century soap opera," and "a cross between *Bonnie & Clyde*, *Dallas* and *Tom Jones*," which is pretty weird mishmash of references.) Watching the film, it feels as if the cast and crew never bothered to discuss its tone amongst themselves, with some actors appearing to play it straight while others make their performances as broad as possible. Unfortunately you can't successfully play for camp if half your cast is taking their roles dead seriously. Dunaway may provide the biggest hurdle for the movie's ass-backwards tone, since she's never the slightest bit funny: every single one of her lines is uttered with either wooden coldness or bug-eyed intensity. It's as if she read the script and saw her character as a Blanche Dubois or Norma Desmond, when in reality the character was much closer to a Cruella de Vil. For such a brilliant actress, this is an absolute turd of a performance—and one very deserving of the Razzie Nomination it earned her in 1984.

This split identity as a drama/comedy extended to the ways in which *The Wicked Lady* was marketed. The theatrical trailer tries to make *The Wicked Lady* look like a classier act than it actually is, touting its high-pedigree actors and posturing it as a historical epic, even having the gall to try to pass it off as a true story. ("This is the lusty, bawdy, epic story of England's most legendary robber," the voiceover announces. "She was the most amorous, adventurous, and treacherous woman who ever lived!")

While the story does have a teensy-weensy degree of historical basis, what's depicted in both the 1945 and 1983 versions is rooted more in folklore than fact. Lady Katherine Ferrers was a seventeenth century British aristocrat. At eight years old—following the untimely deaths of her father, grandfather, brother, *and* mother—she became the sole heir of her family's great fortune and vast tracts of land. Caught on the losing end of the first English Civil War, her husband was imprisoned and her family's wealth dwindled to nothing, and she died at only 26 years old. Urban legends sprung up in the centuries after her death; in these, she is said to have become a highwayman to keep herself financially afloat during her husband's imprisonment. (Her ghost is widely said to haunt the roads near her family's estate.) Though it's a fantastic story, there's not a drop of evidence that supports her leading a criminal career. Moreover, many elements of her popular legend are lifted from the lives of other, real-world highwaymen. "Captain" James MacLaine, an eighteenth century robber, seems the likely basis of Captain Jackson's character. The son of a respected clergyman, MacLaine became known as the "gentleman highwayman" for his courteous behavior during holdups.

Where the trailer tried its best to make the movie look like an awards-worthy historical drama, the U.S. TV spot harbored no false pretenses. Over a wacky, fast-paced electronic soundtrack complete with goofy sound effects, the television commercials played up the comedy and sex and, of course, touted the movie's infamous, erotic whipping scene. ("It was a wicked time filled with wicked people, but the wickedest of all was . . . The Wicked Lady!" the narrator chortles over a 'boi-oi-oi-oi-oi-oing' sound effect. "She really knew how to *whip up* a good time!") The winking "whip up a good time" tagline was used on most of the U.S. film posters.

THE CANNON FILM GUIDE, VOL.1 (1980–1984)

Please turn your book upside-down to see the topless version of the German theatrical poster.

In Spain, the movie's title was changed to La Dama Perversa—"The Perverse Lady." The Dutch poster is even more honest: it takes the U.S. videocassette art and adds a few extra naked people around the border. One German poster, however, is a straight up painting of a woman in an outlaw's mask baring her breasts. Although Miss Dunaway never actually doffs her own corset in the film, this image may be the most honest representation of the movie's contents of all.

The Secret of Yolanda

Release date: 1983
Directed by: Joel Silberg
Written by: Eli Tavor
Starring: Shraga Harpaz, Asher Tzarfati, Aviva Ger
Tagline: "A lusty love story!"

A nomad cowboy wanders onto a ranch, bangs every breathing woman within a 40-mile radius, and then is run out of town for taking advantage of a handicapped stable girl. That's *The Secret of Yolanda*, in a nutshell. And that guy is supposed to be the *hero* of the movie!

This Israeli Golan-Globus Cannon production didn't receive a theatrical release in the U.S., but was shown in a number of English-speaking countries as *Mute Love*, and ultimately released stateside in a poorly-dubbed VHS version as *The Secret of Yolanda*. Normally I've chosen to bypass the straight-to-video international Cannon productions. This is simply because they weren't really intended for American consumption, are getting rather difficult to come by, and because this book is long enough as-is. I'm giving *The Secret of Yolanda* special treatment, however, because it's hypnotically bad, and was assembled by some of Cannon's regular collaborators.

The VHS cover for *The Secret of Yolanda*, perhaps the most obscure film release covered in this volume.

Cowboy Guy (Shraga Harpaz) is an earthy, Joe Don Baker-type, short on social graces but written to be somehow irresistible to women. In the real world he would be considered a wandering hobo, but in the world of this movie he's viewed as a romantic type who "doesn't like to be tied down." Guy strolls onto a horse ranch looking for a job and is immediately given one by the fairly alright-seeming farmer, Benny (Asher Tzarfati, who would play a small role in Cannon's *Hellbound* in 1994). Benny's ailing health has led him to stop giving classes himself and bring on a new riding instructor. During the job interview, Guy makes lewd comments about the riding school's beautiful, exclusively-female clientele, and then startles a horse so badly that a student is thrown from its back—but, whatever! This rascal is apparently the *perfect* candidate for the job.

Guy is given a cot in the dilapidated shack out back, and gets down to business. You see, Guy is a *busy* guy. By his third day on the job—and only halfway into the film's runtime—Guy has bedded multiple students in the barn, on bales of hay, and even on horseback. I never thought I'd say it, but *Yolanda*'s horseback intercourse scene makes Bo Derek's nude ride in *Bolero* (1984) look almost... dignified? Guy and a wealthy tart are even tossed from the horse *mid-penetration* and it hardly slows them down. Talk about focus.

Guy also makes it with the farmer's spiteful, shrewish wife, Micky (Miri Aloni), who falls for him because her husband—the one in poor health—can't give her the affection she craves. Guy is a sex machine, sure, but we're also supposed to believe he has a tender heart, or something like that, because out of all the women he's sexing, there's only one he'd like to be sexing the most: a beautiful, deaf and mute stable girl named Yolanda (Aviva Ger), whom the farmer and his wife have taken into their home like an adopted daughter.

Yolanda seems quite innocent at first, but as we get to know her we figure out that she might be a little—how shall we say?—*freaky-deaky*, if you will. She spends a lot of time creeping around silently, spying on Guy as he indiscriminately plows every woman who dares step foot in the farmyard. When Guy catches her, he chases her into the field, pins her down, and rapes her. It's awful. Yolanda eventually starts reciprocating, and we're supposed to believe that the two have fallen in love. This movie...

Benny takes notice of all the special attention Guy's suddenly giving Yolanda, and tries to intervene—not just because Guy is a depraved sex maniac who'd probably fuck a dead donkey if he thought it gave him a come-hither look, but because Benny truly seems to care about the young, disabled girl. (In the whole film, he's the only one who goes out of his way to speak to her in sign language.) Guy keeps stringing Yolanda along, even after she walks in on him in bed again with another woman. Normally here, Benny would have grounds to fire this horny good-for-nothing before one of the students' angry husbands shows up at the ranch with a shotgun, and so the movie manufactures a dumb horse racing subplot—which Guy has to win, to help make a name for the riding school—to keep him around.

Guy goes on to win that stupid race, and vows to leave town. Benny catches Guy in the barn again, mackin' with Yolanda, and then the poor bastard's wife trots in to admit that she's been bumping uglies with this sloppy, lecherous cowboy, too. They get into a nasty fight, wherein Guy jabs his kindly, ex-employer with a sharp tool and then proceeds to nearly strangle him to death. Only Yolanda's terrified shout—the only sound she makes through the entire movie, beyond orgasmic moans—stops Guy from killing Benny.

The next day, Guy packs up his rucksack and hits the road. Just as he's about to disappear over the horizon, Yolanda runs out of the house with her bags packed and joins him, because the rape-y hobo landing the naïve deaf girl is just the happy ending that nobody ever asked for.

The Secret of Yolanda was originally released in 1982, but didn't hit U.S. video shelves until the following year. It was directed by Joel Silberg who, of course, helmed some of Cannon's best-known movies, from *Breakin'* (1984) to *Rappin'* (1985) to *Lambada* (1990). Screenwriter Eli Tavor co-wrote much of their hit Israeli *Lemon Popsicle* series—the first entry was remade as *The Last American Virgin* (1982)—as well as 1988's *Salsa*. Director of photography David Gurfinkel was their most frequent collaborator of the bunch, shooting well over a dozen Cannon films from *The Apple* (1980) all the way to *American Samurai* (1992).

Over the Brooklyn Bridge

Release Date: March 2, 1984
Directed by: Menahem Golan
Written by: Arnold Somkin
Starring: Elliott Gould, Margaux Hemingway, Sid Caesar
Trailer Voiceover: "Alby Sherman's got problems—he's got problems you can't believe!"

Over the Brooklyn Bridge may be one of the ultimate Cannon movies. It may not be an action flick; it may not star Charles Bronson, Chuck Norris, or Michael Dudikoff; it doesn't even have any ninjas in it, but hear me out. Here we have a film directed by none other than Menahem Golan himself, featuring a stable of actors from the Cannon repertory including Elliott Gould, Shelley Winters, Victoria Barrett and Jerry Lazarus. It was shot by Adam Greenberg, scored by Pino Donaggio, and was filmed in New York City behind union picket lines—yet *still* came in under budget and ahead of schedule. We're really just a Yehuda Efroni cameo or a random shot of break dancers away from winning a Cannon bingo card.

Alby Sherman—played by Elliott Gould, next to be seen in Cannon's *The Naked Face* (1984)—runs a small, Brooklyn lunch counter with his widowed mother, played by two-time Oscar winner Shelley Winters (next to be seen in Cannon's *Déjà Vu* [1985] and *The Delta Force* [1986].) Alby is a middle-aged man with big dreams of shaking the dust of his crummy little town off his feet and opening a fancy-pants restaurant on Manhattan's East Side. Unfortunately, that would cost more money than Alby will ever earn while managing his mother's deli. The only option Alby can fathom is to turn to his wealthy Uncle Benjamin (comedian Sid Caesar), a distinguished purveyor of ladies' underpants.

A well-worn videotape copy of *Over the Brooklyn Bridge*, formerly rented by Primetime Movie of Mountain Grove, Missouri.

Uncle Ben is happy to cut his nephew a check under one condition: that he settles down and marries himself a nice, Jewish girl. There's a big problem with his uncle's proposal, however, and it's that Alby's madly in love with his live-in girlfriend, Elizabeth, a Catholic girl from Philly played by supermodel Margaux Hemingway.

An early sales ad for the film, sold under yet another title that was ultimately discarded.

The fact that *Over the Brooklyn Bridge* went more than three decades without a home video re-release speaks volumes about its place within the '80s comedy canon. Granted, the movie limits its audience. Many of its jokes require a deep knowledge of Jewish stereotypes, and Yiddish slang is dropped left and right without any supplied definition. Originally the film was intended to be titled *My Darling Shiksa*—"shiksa" being a usually-disparaging Yiddish term used to refer to non-Jewish women. Where such a title might have worked for one of Golan and Globus' Israeli comedies, it was no doubt changed once they realized how many American movie-goers would have no idea what it meant.

When the humor isn't overly insular, it is borderline offensive: unkind stereotypes stand in for characters from almost half a dozen different ethnic groups, including Italians, Irish Catholics, African Americans, Puerto Ricans, and the Japanese. The script, from veteran TV writer Arnold Somkin, provides plentiful reminders of all of the outdated slurs your racist grandpa would uncomfortably drop at the dinner table almost entirely unprompted. The film also packs not one, but *two* visual gags involving pee. This is a lowbrow rom-com, to say the least. It's proto-Farrelly Brothers, if you will.

Where *Over the Brooklyn Bridge* does succeed particularly well is in broadly capturing a time, place, and community. Director of photography Adam Greenberg had started working for Golan and Globus in Israel as far back as 1972's *I Love You Rosa*; he shot a total of 18 films for them through 1985, including *The Last American Virgin*, *10 to Midnight* and *The Ambassador* before moving on to lens gigantic studio blockbusters like *Ghost* (1990), *Rush Hour* (1998), and the first two *Terminator* movies.

He catches mid-'80s New York in all of its authentic, seedy glory. The movie was shot all over the city, from Times Square and its blinding mess of bright signage and porno theaters, to the subways with their graffiti-covered trains and token-fed turnstiles. Everything about New York looks downright *dirty*, even the fancy First Avenue diner which Alby so desperately longs to purchase. (Nowadays passersby would likely glance a "B" health code rating card in the window and continue walking.) Alby's bustling, Williamsburg lunch counter—a location which, ironically, would probably now be considered more hip than the one Alby lusted for in midtown—is the sort of place that's been pushed further and further out into the city's boroughs in the decades after this movie was filmed. Quite frankly, it spotlights a New York City that no longer exists. Like other low-budget NYC location shoots from the '70s and '80s—think *The Warriors* (1979) or *Taxi Driver* (1976)—it's great to see such a visually evocative time and place so well-documented on film.

A post-release ad for the movie. Alby (Gould) is "a man with a deli and a dream," forced to choose between opening his restaurant and staying with his darling shiksa, Elizabeth (Hemingway).

For what it's worth, too, the main cast largely approached the shallow script with a great deal of chutzpah. Gould's Alby is a big whiner but still pretty likeable; it's hard to imagine how tough this movie would have been to endure if a lesser actor had been asked to carry it in that role. Both of Gould's movies for Cannon—he'd play a cop next in their *The Naked Face*, shot shortly after this one—came during a career lull midway between twin peaks that came in the early '70s and the late '90s. Gould's breakout had come in *Bob & Carol & Tom & Alice* (1968), which earned him a Best Supporting

Actor nod. Next came a long string of collaborations with the great Robert Altman: *MASH* (1970), *The Long Goodbye* (1973), *California Split* (1974), and *Nashville* (1975). His career then slowed down for a while but had another resurgence in the '90s with notable appearances in *Bugsy* (1991), *American History X* (1998), and the *Ocean's 11* films, as well as a recurring TV gig as Ross and Monica's dad on the hit sitcom *Friends* (1994–2004).

One of the golden age of television's original funnymen, Sid Caesar, was given the chance to show off a semi-serious side as the authoritarian Uncle Ben, who has a near-breakdown at the film's end that is surprisingly effective. Shelley Winters' role is minor, but endearing. Burt Young plays Alby's lecherous best bud, a character who could pass as the brother of hot-tempered Paulie, the role he received an Oscar nomination for in *Rocky* (1976). Make sure you keep an eye on his kids when they're walking along the Coney Island boardwalk—one of them is played by a seven-year-old, uncredited Sarah Michelle Gellar.

The always-wonderful Carol Kane—one of TV and cinema's most consistently good comedic actresses—nearly walks away with the film as the demure, Jewish girl with whom Alby's uncle would like to see him settle down. (Her character is Alby's distant cousin, but that's better than being Catholic as far as his family is concerned.) The supposedly shy schoolteacher invites Alby up to her apartment after a tame date, only to try to seduce him with a tray of narcotics and an aggressive, New Age-y approach to sex.

Even minor members of the cast are at least recognizable, too—by Cannon fans, at least. Jerry Lazarus—who co-starred in *Treasure of the Four Crowns* and would later appear in *Hot Chili*, *Breakin' 2*, *The Delta Force*, *Murphy's Law*, and *Surrender*—shows up as Uncle Ben's spoiled nincompoop of a son. Actress Victoria Barrett receives some lewd objectification in a sexy fantasy sequence; she would become one of Menahem Golan's personal favorite actresses, leading to increasingly large roles in *Hot Resort* (1985), *America 3000* (1986), and *Three Kinds of Heat* (1987). Robert Gossett, making his debut here as Alby's underling at the deli counter, would eventually co-star in more than 150 episodes of the long-running cable drama *The Closer* (2005–2012) and its spinoff, *Major Crimes* (2012–2018).

It's Margaux Hemingway as the patient, doting, Catholic girlfriend who poses such a threat to Alby's Jewish family, though, who casts a sad spell over this otherwise silly romp. The acting career of the famous perfume model—granddaughter of novelist Ernest, older sister of fellow actress Mariel—appeared to be pointing upward when she co-starred in this romantic comedy, only her fourth film. Like her famous grandfather, however, Margaux was drawn to destructive alcoholism. The decade following *Over the Brooklyn Bridge* was marked by heavily-publicized weight issues, frequent tabloid appearances, a *Playboy* shoot, and poor choices of roles. In 1996 she would take her own life by swallowing twice the lethal dosage of a drug she'd been prescribed to treat her epileptic seizures—almost 35 years to the day after her famous grandfather's infamous suicide. Even in the hokey *Over the Brooklyn Bridge* her talent shines through; it's a crying shame that her troubles got the best of her.

A tender advertisement from Cannon's 1984 sales catalog.

As far as the movie itself, *Over the Brooklyn Bridge* does merit a small place in independent film history. Partway into the shoot, labor unions tried to halt production with a strike once it was clear Cannon had no intention of paying their required rates. (Cannon also ran up against labor issues on *Exterminator 2* [1984] and *Grace Quigley* [1985], two other NYC-based shoots from this same period.) Naturally Golan didn't let the picket lines slow him down, and he shot in small, enclosed locations as the dispute went on. He even managed to wrap the shoot a week early in spite of the stoppage. Meanwhile Cannon held their ground, arguing that it wasn't feasible for a low-budget production to pay the same rates as a $50-million dollar film coming from the big Hollywood studios. Their battle eventually led to a new allowance wherein independent and low-budget shoots—at the time, up to a $3 million production—could hire union workers at more affordable rates. Golan would later proudly refer to this as "the Cannon contract."

I try not to dedicate much space to pointing out mistakes in Cannon movies, since they're often quite plentiful and this book is long enough as it is, but there's one laughably large one at the top of *Over the Brooklyn Bridge*. As the opening credits roll, we're introduced to Alby while he leaves his busy luncheonette and bums a ride into Manhattan. This scene gives way to a long, eye-catching aerial shot of Alby's car as it cruises over a bridge, and the movie's title—*Over the Brooklyn Bridge*—is superimposed with big, bright letters over the screen. The problem here is that it's *not* the Brooklyn Bridge they're crossing, but the similarly-structured (and less picturesque) Manhattan Bridge. It's hard to tell whether the filmmakers didn't think anyone would notice or if it truly was a big oopsie on their part, but it's an error that is sure to leave any New Yorker scratching their head.

Sahara

Release Date: March 2, 1984
Directed by: Andrew V. McLaglen
Written by: Menahem Golan (story), James R. Silke
Starring: Brooke Shields, Lambert Wilson, John Rhys-Davies, Ronald Lacey
Trailer Voiceover: "The beauty of a girl. The thrill of a lifetime. The romantic adventure of the year!"

For those who didn't live through it, it can be difficult to grasp just how huge a star Brooke Shields was in the early 1980s. Shields' face (and her trademark, meticulously-manicured eyebrows) were *everywhere* for several years, from billboards and television commercials—she was a spokesmodel for Calvin Klein, Colgate, Aziza Cosmetics, and Wella Balsam shampoo, among others—to movies and magazine covers. By the age of seventeen she'd been on the front of *Vogue, People, Seventeen, Life, Cosmopolitan, Interview, Glamour,* and even *TIME,* who excitedly proclaimed hers "The '80s Look" in 1981. She'd become a bankable leading lady after starring in the romantic teen films *Blue Lagoon* (1980) and *Endless Love* (1981), and a darling of the tabloids, who delighted in pairing her off romantically with the likes of John Travolta and Michael Jackson who, at that time, was *the* biggest star in the whole entire world. By 1984, Brooke Shields was recognized and idolized across the globe:

a bona fide supermodel, usually referred to simply under the mononym of "Brooke." She even had her own, knockoff Barbie doll!

Though, to fully understand Brooke's superstardom, it needs to be given context. Much of her mystique during this era, at the height of her fame, was built upon a foundation of controversy. Not your run-of-the-mill gossip column fodder, no, but a certain . . . *skin-crawling* sort of controversy. Directors, photographers, and ad men almost invariably chose to play up her sex appeal not based solely on her striking appearance, but *because* she was a minor.

The videotape cover for *Sahara*, with art by the great Drew Struzan of Star Wars and Indiana Jones fame. This copy was rented out by Sounds Easy Video of Provo, Utah.

At the tender age of ten Brooke was infamously photographed nude, body-oiled, and in adult makeup, for a spread in the supremely creepy Playboy publication *Sugar 'n' Spice*. These photographs—signed off on by her mother—would come back to haunt Shields throughout her life. After Brooke was a star, her mother tried to sue the photographer for continuing to sell the images, but lost when the judge somehow found the photos—which contained full frontal nudity—*not* to be child pornography. Decades later in 2009, the image made headlines again when a version was pulled from a show at the Tate Modern after police and protestors proclaimed it "a magnet for pedophiles."

At the age of twelve Brooke starred in Louis Malle's highly controversial 1978 film *Pretty Baby*, in which she played a child prostitute and performed in simulated sex scenes with her adult co-stars. Shields eventually had to give a Congressional testimony that body doubles were used in the steamy sex scenes of the R-rated *Blue Lagoon*, which she shot when she was fourteen. She was only fifteen when she appeared in her most famous advertising campaign for Calvin Klein jeans, in which she sultrily whispered her catchphrase, "You know what comes between me and my Calvins? Nothing." (You can draw the implication.) A year later filmmaker Franco Zeffirelli went to battle with the MPAA, who slapped his first cut of *Endless Love* with an 'X' rating, and ultimately was forced to trim down Brooke's sex scenes to come away with an 'R'. She was sixteen.

All of these notorious career stepping stones were engineered not only by manipulative men who recognized the marketable taboo in an underage sex symbol, but by Brooke's hyper-ambitious mother-manager, Teri Shields. Teri had her sights set on stardom for Brooke practically from the beginning. She raised Brooke as a single mother, and had booked her daughter's first modeling gig for Ivory soaps before she was a year old. A successful career as a child model followed: Colgate, Breck Shampoos, Love's Baby Soft fragrances. The latter featured a prepubescent Brooke dolled up in mascara and lipstick, clutching a teddy bear, with the tagline: "Love's Baby Soft. Because innocence is sexier than you think." (Uhhhhh . . .)

Try to picture the ad man who might have come up with that one: Don Draper, with a pedo 'stache, smoking a cigarette and staring off into boardroom space: "She is a child. And what is a child?" He takes a long drag from his cigarette, rattles the ice in his rocks glass. "Sexy. A child is sexy."

Hurl.

Then came the infamous nude photo shoot, the erotic film roles, and a steady stream of controversies. When the court ruled against her attempt to stop distribution of nude photos of her ten-year-old daughter, the judge took the opportunity to lecture Teri about trying to protect her daughter while exploiting her at the same time, telling her she couldn't "have it both ways."

With that portrait painted, let's fast forward to the early '80s. Brooke Shields was a huge star and so, naturally, Cannon wanted her. Shields' two prior movies, *Blue Lagoon* and *Endless Love*, had grossed more than $90 million in U.S. theaters, after all. But then, so did every other studio in Hollywood. To secure the world's highest-paid model, Menahem Golan had to make mother and daughter an offer they couldn't refuse.

An ad from the 1983 sales catalog. In the early 1980s, Shields' face was all it took to sell a movie.

Cannon's winning contract offered Brooke a cool $1.5 million for starring in their movie, and was full of mother-imposed stipulations over things like how Brooke would wear her hair, makeup, and world-famous eyebrows. It was Golan's offer to Brooke's mother, however, that was the true sweetener. Teri Shields, whose famous daughter would soon be turning eighteen and possibly taking a break from work to attend college, would be made an executive producer on the film. This wasn't just the empty title you'd expect for someone who'd never before produced a movie, either: it included a salary of $250,000 plus expenses and an immense amount of creative control, from final approval on the script to casting the actor who would play the romantic lead opposite her daughter. Teri turned down her daughter's other film offers—including, notably, the role opposite Al Pacino in Brian de Palma's iconic 1983 version of *Scarface*, which ultimately went to Michelle Pfeiffer—and put ink to paper, signing Brooke up to star in Cannon's next surefire hit, *Sahara*.

From how things proceeded, it's pretty apparent that Golan had no idea what he was getting himself into. Cannon's co-founder had initially planned to direct the film himself—he had come up with the story and written the first draft of the script, after all—but Teri promptly put the kibosh on that idea. The final shooting script was the result of eight major re-writes, all prompted by Teri. The final screenplay was credited to Cannon regular James R. Silke (*Revenge of the Ninja, Ninja III, King Solomon's Mines* and *The Barbarians*.) As Teri Shields told the *Los Angeles Times*, Golan's original script had "too many rape scenes and too much gore."

Having been booted out of the director's chair, Golan evidently made up his mind to hire a filmmaker already experienced in the sort of sweeping, old-fashioned adventure films that *Sahara* would be imitating. First attached was John Guillermin, who had directed two of the best Tarzan movies—*Tarzan's Greatest Adventure* (1959) and *Tarzan Goes to India* (1962)—and went on to bigger box office blockbusters in the '70s with *The Towering Inferno* (1974), *Death on the Nile* (1978), and the 1977 *King Kong* remake. Something, however, caused the famously temperamental Brit to quit the film just days into shooting—there were very loud whispers that Teri had him fired—and so the producers at Cannon were forced to scramble for a replacement.

Another British director—the six foot, seven inches tall Andrew McLaglen—stepped in and took over. While he may not have had the same box office track record as Guillermin, his resume was no less impressive. He'd come up the ranks from assistant to the great Western director John Ford on *The Quiet Man* (1952), and directed John Wayne in five films, including *McLintock!* (1963), James Stewart in *Shenandoah* (1965) and *The Rare Breed* (1966), and around 100 episodes each of the TV series *Gunsmoke* (1952–1961) and *Have Gun – Will Travel* (1957–1963). If anyone was prepared to run a film crew on a dry, desert landscape, it was McLaglen.

What McLaglen wasn't prepared for were Menahem Golan and Teri Shields. Golan insisted on remaining on set to "supervise," regularly overstepping his boundaries and wrestling away directorial duties. Teri, meanwhile, was intent to exercise the powers she was granted to their fullest extent, going so far as to make last-minute wardrobe changes, fire crew members, and call "Cut!" in the middle of takes so that she could give her daughter her own direction on her acting. *Sahara* is a premier example of the old axiom about too many cooks in a kitchen.

Never was this more on display than in a much-publicized incident where not only Brooke Shields, but also Menahem Golan and a camera operator were almost killed while shooting the movie. During one scene where Brooke's heroine is driving a vintage race car—she was still too young to legally drive, but the crew was granted special permits to allow it—she hit a curb and lost control of the vehicle. As she recounted to the magazine *Interview*, she was only supposed to drive a short distance at a low speed, but Golan—whom she referred to as the film's director, for what that's worth—was sitting in the back seat urging her to go faster and faster. The car overturned and all three were thrown from the convertible. While Shields escaped with no more than a few bruises, she had just narrowly avoided being crushed underneath the automobile. Of course this generated a lot of publicity for the movie, as there are few things gossip rags enjoy covering more than the near-death experience of one of America's sweethearts.

Early sales ads capitalize on the success of Shields' popular teen romance films. "The story of a love as grand as the place they met ... the romantic adventure of a lifetime!"

Meanwhile, Teri spent a lot of her time on set managing not only Brooke—shooting days were scheduled around her daily tutoring sessions—but the many fans and admirers who showed up in droves to gawk, seek autographs, or shower her with gifts. (The eligible sons of many of the Middle

East's wealthy elite were reported to have sent her gold and diamonds to the set, looking for a date.) It was also Teri's job to sort through the many young men being considered for her daughter's on-screen romantic partner. This included many actors, yes—including *Happy Days'* Ted McGinley, who grew a bushy beard to audition for the role of an African sheik, and Vincent Spano of *Rumble Fish* (1983), who turned down the role. (He'd later star in *Maria's Lovers* [1985] for Cannon instead.) She also brought in an odd few non-actors, from the teenage son of Saudi billionaire Adnan Khashoggi to John F. Kennedy, Jr. As Teri told *People Weekly*, "I don't think his mother would let him."

Golan and Globus returned to Israel to shoot their blockbuster adventure film, and their homeland welcomed them back with open arms. With a budget of around $15 million, *Sahara* would be the most expensive film production ever mounted in Israel to that point. Nearly one hundred tons of props and equipment were flown in from Los Angeles for the shoot, which included seven tamed panthers and eleven custom-built race cars. Much of the equipment imported for the movie was purchased with government grant money received by the duo to build a film studio on the West Bank.

Meanwhile, Brooke's personal entourage included her mother and godmother, her best friend, a documentary crew, a personal driver, multiple tutors and bodyguards, her German shepherd, a dog trainer, and many stuffed animals. According to a cover story in *People Weekly*, her dog even had his own hotel room.

Set in 1927, *Sahara* centers on teenager Dale Gordon (Shields), the flapper daughter of a millionaire auto magnate. When her father (Steve Forrest, best known for playing Faye Dunaway's romantic partner in *Mommie Dearest* [1981]) suffers a fatal injury in an off-screen car accident, it's up to young Dale to carry on his legacy and help him bring his final automobile design to market. For some strange reason, though, the only way her late father's business associate will agree to invest is if the car manages to win the Trans-African Auto Race: a multi-day rally across the Sahara desert. Fortunately our plucky heroine just so happens to be a world-class racecar driver. *Unfor-*

tunately, the conservative regime overseeing the race won't allow a woman driver to compete.

This is where Dale has an idea which requires Herculean effort on the part of *Sahara*'s audience to suspend their disbelief: she'll disguise herself as a man and enter the race anyway.

Yeeeeaah.

Why Cannon felt the need to bend over backwards to hire the world's most famous pretty face just to slap a fake moustache over it, we'll never know. (In all likelihood, the absurdity of that image was probably the whole point of doing it.) Needless to say, the renowned supermodel makes for a very unconvincing boy even while donning a fake 'stache, tying her hair up under a hat, wearing a sharp suit, and speaking in a "gruff" voice. For the story's sake, at least, everyone falls for it. Dale is somehow able to maintain this ludicrous ruse until her car has sped away from the starting line. Once they've made it a safe distance into the desert, Dale tosses her hat and lets her chestnut locks flow in the wind, much to the surprise of her gullible competitors.

Brooke Shields, master of disguise.

Along for the ride are two mechanics, String (Cliff Potts) and Andy (Perry Lang, previously of Cannon's *Body and Soul*, 1981). It's all fun and games until they stumble upon the mass grave of maybe a dozen executed gypsies, freshly murdered by a tribe of evil Bedouin nomads. You see, they'd been warned that the course wound through a war zone, but did they listen? No, oh no, they sure didn't, and wound up smack dab in the middle of a tribal turf war. On one side you have a mostly peaceful group led by a handsome young prince, who swear to protect all those living on their land—including gypsies—and who live by a strict code. On the other side you have the clearly villainous tribe led by a ruthless warlord who hunts humans for sport and keeps a menagerie of flesh-eating cats as both pets and instruments of torture.

The leader of the latter tribe—the big bad guy in *Sahara*—is played be the main Nazi from *Raiders of the Lost Ark* (1981) . . . in brownface. (Cue a sad trombone noise.) English character actor Ronald Lacey's skin was darkened with makeup to play the nefarious Beg, which is going to make a lot of modern-day viewers a bit uncomfortable, and for that matter probably wasn't okay with a lot of people in 1983, either. It's not a whole lot better that the leader of the *good* African tribe is played by Lambert Wilson, a French actor and Calvin Klein model who would go on to play the Frenchman in the *Matrix* sequels. (Fun fact: Lambert Wilson had a role in a totally-unrelated, 2005 Mathew McConaughey movie that was *also* titled *Sahara*.)

Also joining the ensemble of miscast White actors was Welsh actor John Rhys-Davies of the *Indiana Jones* and *Lord of the Rings* franchises, who made a bizarre habit of playing Arab roles throughout the 1980s. Cannon clearly had a lot of love for Rhys-Davies, who played the archeologist Sallah in *Raiders of the Lost Ark*, and cast him in three more of their films: *Sword of the Valiant* (1984), *King Solomon's Mines* (1985), and *Firewalker* (1986). His fellow *Sahara* and *Raiders* co-star Ronald Lacey appeared in two more of Cannon releases in 1984 alone: *Making the Grade* and *Sword of the Valiant*.

Of course, whitewashing ethnic roles isn't out of the ordinary in Hollywood even today, but it might have been easier to overlook here had they not hired *actual* Bedouin tribesmen to appear in the film as extras. As it was, these three featured actors stick out among their fellow tribesmen like sore thumbs.

Luckily—I guess?—Dale and her crew are captured by the good guy tribe and not the bad one. It's still not all that great, though, because tribal law states that she automatically becomes the property of the sheik's rape-y Uncle Rasoul (Rhys-Davies), effectively making her a slave to do with whatever he pleases.

Sheik Jafar (Wilson)—who is young and good-looking enough to be an underwear model—develops a big-time crush on the "blue-eyed demon," as some are calling her, and co-opts her as his new bride-to-be. Dale spends a good chunk of the movie being passed around by the various Bedouin leaders, which you can guess doesn't fly well with the strong-willed young lady. She quite frequently gives 'em hell, mounting several varyingly unsuccessful escape attempts. Dreamy Prince Jafar, though, eventually cracks her wary exterior by proving he isn't so bad after all, and can't help his culture's backward customs. Despite sharing some tender moments with him—though nothing nearly as steamy as what the starlet filmed in *Blue Lagoon* or *Endless Love*—Dale sneaks off into the desert, where she's snatched up by the evil warlord Beg. Naturally this means our prince must set off on a daring, action-packed rescue mission to save her.

Thankfully all of the kidnappings, escape attempts, the forced marriage, the romancing, and the bloody tribal war happen so quickly that the ravishing, ever-determined young Dale has time left over to climb back into her car and win the big race by movie's end.

Every single bit of *Sahara* may be unintentionally silly, and there's very little that isn't entertaining. Cannon had lofty ambitions to create one of those grand scale, Hollywood adventure epics—Golan was *convinced* that Brooke Shields would win an Oscar for her role—but the end results were a pulpy b-movie through and through. It was old-fashioned, but in an entirely different sense than they set out for. With an open mind it's a lot of fun, and a good score by the master Ennio Morricone goes a long way in setting the right tone for everything we see on screen.

Also appearing in the film, though in roles of extremely little consequence, are German actor Horst Buchholz (Chico in 1960's *The Magnificent Seven*) playing a competing racer who is secretly an arms dealer for the African tribesman, and Academy Award winner Sir John Mills (*Ryan's Daughter*, 1970). The daddy of Disney darling Hayley Mills and star of many Disney features in his own right, he plays a *Lawrence of Arabia*-like Englishman living voluntarily among the Bedouins.

Golan's story for the film was said to have been inspired by the great, silent-era romantic adventure *The Sheik* (1921), starring Rudolph Valentino, as well as a recent current event. In early 1982, Mark Thatcher—son of the British Prime Minister Margaret Thatcher—had gone missing with two companions while competing in the Dakar Rally, an auto race across the Sahara desert. This was a major news item, and a massive search effort involving three nations' militaries was mounted for the vanished lad. He and his crew were found safe six days after their disappearance. However, they were not kidnapped by warring tribesmen, as Dale is in the film—Mark Thatcher simply hadn't done enough research ahead of his journey and got his ass thoroughly lost in the desert.

Sahara's distribution was handle by MGM who—perhaps sensing they had a clunker on their hands—opted to release the film only west of the Mississippi, where costs to market and advertise a movie were much cheaper than on the East coast. It turns out they were correct to temper their bets: the sweeping, romantic epic handed over to them by Cannon brought home only $1.4 million at the domestic box office, not enough to even recoup the $1.5 paid to its lead actress. The reviews were generally abysmal: Gene Siskel, writing for the *Chicago Tribune*, called it "a shockingly bad film." While that was perhaps a little extreme, few contemporary critics were much kinder.

For her work in *Sahara*, Brooke Shields was nominated for 1984's Worst Actress Razzie. (She lost out to Bo Derek in *Bolero*, another Cannon masterpiece.) Brooke had the more dubious honor of also being nominated—and *winning*—the Razzie for Worst Supporting Actor, as "Brooke Shields (in a moustache)."

in a GOLAN-GLOBUS Production of an ANDREW V. McLAGLEN Film

Sahara

Brooke Shields appearing alongside her Razzie-winning co-star, "Brook Shields (in a moustache)," in a foreign sales ad.

The Worst Actress nomination perhaps isn't fair, since the goofy script gave poor little Brooke very little to work with. Other roles proved that Brooke Shields is a more than competent actress unlike, say, Kathy Ireland, who in Cannon's 1988 movie *Alien from L.A.* proved that she was not just a pretty face, but maybe one of the worst actors to ever work in Hollywood. We'll give the Razzie folks their Worst Supporting Actor nomination, on the other hand. Never for a second in *Sahara* do you believe that *anyone* would actually mistake Brooke Shields for a man, even when she's wearing an awful, fake moustache.

Brooke, for her part, came out of *Sahara* relatively unscathed. She broke from acting for the next four years to attend Princeton University, but remained an uber-famous and highly paid supermodel until making a gradual return to acting in the late '80s. While Brooke eventually fired her mother as her manager, the two remained close. (Teri never did produce another film, however.) After Teri's death in 2012, Brooke penned a memoir titled *There Was A Little Girl: The Real Story of My Mother and Me*, to share her side of their atypical tale. For some odd reason, though, she never once mentions *Sahara* in the book . . .

Breakin'
Breakin' 2: Electric Boogaloo

Release date: May 4, 1984 (I), December 21, 1984 (II)
Directed by: Joel Silberg (I), Sam Firstenberg (II)
Written by: Charles Parker, Allen DeBevoise, Gerald Scaife (I), Jan Ventura, Julie Reichert (II)
Starring: Lucinda Dickey, Adolfo "Shabba-Doo" Quiñones, Michael "Boogaloo Shrimp" Chambers (I & II)
Trailer Voiceover: "Don't be mistaken – you gotta see *Breakin*'!"

Push it to pop it! Rock it to lock it! Break it to make it!

The legend goes that the concept for *Breakin'* came to Menahem Golan when his daughter told him about a group of street dancers she saw performing near the beach. Whether that story is true or not, the breakdancing film he rushed through production in early 1984 tapped into an electrical pulse which had been buzzing within popular culture. For a studio regularly knocked for bandwagon-jumping, *Breakin'* was a rare instance when Cannon was actually breakin' new ground. A valid argument can be made that it was the film which broke hip-hop dance styles into the mainstream.

The three stars of the *Breakin'* franchise: Turbo (left), Ozone (top), and Special K (right), played by Michael "Boogaloo Shrimp" Chambers, Adolfo "Shabba-Doo" Quiñones, and Lucinda Dickey. This video copy was rented out by Golden State Video of San Jose, California.

If neither Golan and Globus nor *Breakin*'s Israeli director, Joel Silberg, seem like the most likely ambassadors of urban American culture, you won't be blamed for scratching your head. *Breakin'* was made to be a traditional Hollywood dance film in the vein of a movie like *Flashdance* (1983), rather than something striving towards any realistic portrayal of the Los Angeles hip-hop scene. Just because the plot is contrived, however, that doesn't mean the dancing isn't legitimate. On the contrary, Cannon hired many of the hottest names in West Coast street dance to appear in their movie.

Brought on initially as a consultant before being asked to star, Adolfo "Shabba-Doo" Quiñones had been a well-known figure in the street dancing community long before *Breakin'* was even a glimmer in Menahem Golan's eye. Through the mid-1970s he'd been the youngest member of The Lockers, a popular dance group who pioneered the "locking" style and helped it spread through their appearances on many national television shows from *Saturday Night Live* to *Soul Train* to Johnny Carson. (Other members included singer-dancer-actress Toni "Hey Mickey, you're so fine!" Basil and Fred "Rerun" Berry of *What's Happening!!* [1976–1979] fame.) After the troupe's dissolution, Shabba-Doo embarked on a solo career with more appearances on stage and television, which eventually brought him to the attention of Hollywood and the producers at Cannon.

Shabba-Doo's co-star would be sixteen-year-old Michael Chambers, better known under his street dancing name: Boogaloo Shrimp. Boogaloo Shrimp started dancing when he was a kid, inspired by the movie *Saturday Night Fever* (1977). As disco faded and was replaced by faster, electric, new wave beats, he developed a style that was more robotic and inspired by the stop-motion animated monsters of Ray Harryhausen movies. Shrimp was one of a reported hundreds of dancers who auditioned for *Breakin'*—and although he was younger than most others, word had gotten around that he was the dancer who had taught Michael Jackson how to moonwalk. The King of Pop had seen Boogaloo Shrimp performing the move when a Los Angeles news program aired a feature about dancers on Hollywood Boulevard. Jackson had Boogaloo Shrimp and a friend summoned to the family's Los Angeles compound to help him perfect the move ahead of its famous unveiling on the *Motown 25* television special in 1983.

Prior to *Breakin'*, Boogaloo Shrimp and Shabba-Doo had already appeared together in the *Breakin' 'n' Entering* (1983) documentary as well as music videos for Chaka Khan ("I Feel For You") and Lionel Richie ("All Night Long")—the latter of which had also been choreographed by Shabba-Doo. What's important to keep in mind is that these two guys weren't unknowns, but stars of the West Coast hip-hop and street dance community. They were joined in the film by a number of other respected Los Angeles street dancers, including Bruno "Pop N Taco" Falcon, Timothy "Popin' Pete" Solomon, and Ana "Lollipop" Sanchez, who played their rivals on the dancefloor. Vidal "Lil Coco" Rodriguez appeared in the film as a kid dancer.

For their female lead, Cannon turned to an outsider of the street dancing world. While Lucinda Dickey may not have had any prior breaking experience, she'd been dancing her whole life. Dickey was the daughter of a dance teacher in Kansas; after taking lessons in her mother's studio from early childhood, she continued to study the art form at Kansas State University. She toured with a dance group for some time and re-located to Hollywood on a scholarship from an elite dance school, Dupree Academy. There, she landed a role as a principal dancer in *Grease 2* (1982). She went from there to *Ninja III: The Domination* (1984)—directed by Sam Firstenberg—which was her initiation into the Cannon family. (*Ninja III* was shot prior to the *Breakin'* movies, but was released in between the two films.) This prior relationship led her to audition for *Breakin'*. Despite having no formal street dance training, her extensive background in other styles naturally helped her to be cast in the movie's lead role.

Israeli filmmaker Joel Silberg was tapped to helm the production. Golan and Globus had produced his films *Marriage Tel Aviv Style* (1979) and *Secret of Yolanda* (1983), but *Breakin'* would be his first stateside film. (He would become Cannon's go-to director for musicals, also handling *Rappin'* in 1985 and *Lambada* in 1990.) At some point during the film's planning stage Menahem Golan caught wind that Orion Pictures was working on their own breakdancing film, titled *Beat Street* (1984), which was being shot in New York with East Coast b-boys and was scheduled to be released that upcoming summer. He wouldn't let himself get beat to the box office, and so he rushed Cannon's movie into production. Shot in only 21 days, *Breakin'* hit theaters on May 4, 1984—a full month ahead of Orion's *Beat Street* (which had been filmed the previous year!)

The film's production was so rushed that this two-page *Variety* advertisement proclaiming that the movie was "now shooting"—which ran only *eight weeks* before *Breakin'* was in theaters—couldn't even be bothered with capturing the stars' likenesses.

The movie itself is extremely fun and full of energy. When we meet *Breakin'*'s leading lady, Kelly (Dickey), she's busting her butt waiting tables at a burger joint so that she can afford classes from Franco (Ben Lokey), one of the hottest young names in choreography. After class, one of Kelly's classmates takes her down to Venice Beach to meet his friends, Turbo (Boogaloo Shrimp) and Ozone (Shabba-Doo), a pair of highly talented street dancers. She watches them break it down for a while, and then joins in for a spell of freestyling. They're as impressed by her moves as she is by theirs. A friendship is sparked, and they even give her a street name: "Special K."

Kelly's teacher, Franco, turns out to be the Harvey Weinstein of dance instructors. He gets a little too hands-on after class one day, and Kelly has no choice but to drop out. She tries her damnedest to land a gig as a solo dancer, but all of her auditions come to nothing. Her best friend, Adam (Phineas

Newborn III), comes up with an idea to pair Kelly's refined jazz dance training with Ozone and Turbo's fresh street moves. While Turbo and Ozone have no interest in becoming professional dancers, they *are* interested in schooling some fools down at Radio-Tron, a club where b-boys battle for dominance in head-to-head dance-offs. If they want to win, they'll need a girl in their group.

What entails are a few dance battles, many training montages, and quite a bit of awkwardness when a platonic, pseudo-love triangle forms between Ozone, Kelly, and her supportive agent, James (Christopher McDonald). Eventually our heroes—newly self-christened "The T.K.O. Crew," after their street initials—land an audition for the biggest dance production of the decade.

To get into the show, their unique blend of skills must first be pitted in a high-stakes dance-off against those of Franco's highly traditional, hoity-toity troupe. Ever the evil choreographer, Franco nearly has them disqualified from their tryout sight unseen, but the T.K.O. Crew's passion and nonconformist style blow open the stodgy, old judges' minds. Cut to the film's grand finale, wherein the T.K.O. Crew star in "Street Jazz," a full-blown stage production which becomes the smash hit of the dance world.

Breakin' is not exceptionally heavy on plot, but these sort of films rarely are. It's all about connecting a series of energetic, eye-grabbing dance segments, and *Breakin'* has many of those. The sequence the movie is most often remembered for is Turbo's famous "broom dance," a magical little number that sees Boogaloo Shrimp popping, locking, moonwalking, and making a broom appear to levitate over the sidewalk he'd been sweeping moments earlier. (While a fishing line can be seen quite plainly in the newer, high-definition releases of the film, it does not diminish the magic of this scene a bit.) This number was dreamed up by Boogaloo Shrimp and the movie's choreographer, Jaime Rogers, who had been a dancer in the Best Picture winner *West Side Story* (1961). It was inspired by the scene where Fred Astaire dances with a hat rack in the film *The Royal Wedding* (1951).

Breakin' was released internationally in many countries as "Breakdance," as the contracted slang of the American title wouldn't have made sense to many non-native English speakers. This Italian theatrical poster was painted by Sandro Symeoni.

If your eyes aren't glued to the colorful dance performances in the foreground of *Breakin'*, it's probably because you were watching someone you saw dancing *behind* our fleet-footed heroes. This particular movie must go down as having some of the most distractingly famous background extras of any film, ever. If you watch the scene where Kelly first meets Turbo and Ozone down near the beach, one member of the crowd gathered to watch the dancers is future Cannon star Jean-Claude Van Damme! Don't worry, you won't miss him: he's wearing a spandex tank top and shorts, getting down almost as excitedly as the breakers he was supposed to be cheering for. (In an interview for *The AV Club*, Van Damme said he even did back flips during this scene in hopes that it would help him be noticed. As you'd expect, those proved too distracting and were cut out of the final product.) Van Damme's roommate at the time, fellow martial artist-turned-actor Michael Qissi—who would play his future *Kickboxer* (1989) nemesis, Tong Po—appears briefly as a passerby in the same scene.

Later during the first dance battle at Radio-Tron, the rapper—or "Rap Talker," as he's credited in the film—emceeing the main event is none other than future hip-hop superstar and *Law & Order: SVU* actor Ice-T making his first big screen appearance. Before his music career took off, Ice-T appeared in three movies for Cannon: *Breakin'*, *Breakin' 2*—in which he plays the same role but wears a studded, leather bondage suit, like something out of a *Mad Max* movie—and *Rappin'*. (Ice-T rap-narrates a plot recap at the end of the film, as well as *Breakin'*'s raptastic theatrical trailer.) One spectator in the Radio-Tron scenes is actress Lela Rochon, who was married to Shabba-Doo at the time and would later star in movies like *Any Given Sunday* (1999) and *Waiting to Exhale* (1995).

Even *Breakin'*'s secondary cast is pretty recognizable. Playing Kelly's agent is Christopher McDonald in an early role. While his 200-plus film and TV credits include such acclaimed films as *Requiem for a Dream* (2000), *Thelma & Louise* (1991), and *Quiz Show* (1994), McDonald will probably always best be remembered for playing the dastardly pro golfer Shooter "I eat pieces of shit like you for breakfast!" McGavin in *Happy Gilmore (*1996). The super-slimy

Franco is played by Ben Lokey, a professional dancer who was no stranger to Hollywood productions, already having credits in *Staying Alive* (1983) and *Sgt. Pepper's Lonely Hearts Club Band* (1978) to this point, but most notably he played one of the zombies in Michael Jackson's landmark "Thriller" music video.

While Phineas Newborn III may not have made many appearances on screen post-*Breakin'*, his character here—Adam, whom Kelly more frequently addresses as "cupcake"—was a very uncommon sight for a mainstream film released in 1984. Not only was Adam an openly gay character with significant screen time, but a Black one. In that sense, *Breakin'* was remarkably progressive.

"The explosive dance of the Eighties!" The Spanish poster was painted by Enrique Mataix.

"Hip hop! Hip hop! Hip hop! Hip Hop! Hip Hop! More than a musical comedy... a revolution that comes from America!" The French theatrical poster, where the film was released as "Break Street 84."

Breakin' hit theaters on the first weekend of May in 1984, on a rather ambitious 1,069 screens. To perhaps everyone's surprise, it was a massive hit. Debuting at #1 nationwide, it beat out fellow new release *Sixteen Candles* and knocked popular 1984 hits such as *Police Academy*, *Romancing the Stone*, and

Splash from their long-held spots atop the box office rankings. It managed to keep up its hot streak in theaters for seven straight weeks—an unprecedented feat for a Cannon movie—while the *Breakin'* soundtrack peaked at #8 on the Billboard Charts, a space it shared with all-time classics like *Born in the U.S.A.* and *Purple Rain*. The soundtrack album eventually went platinum on the strength of its lead single, "Breakin'... There's No Stopping Us" by Ollie & Jerry, which itself was a top ten hit over the summer of '84.

Reading through vintage reviews of *Breakin'*, it's clear that more than a few critics couldn't wrap their heads around the movie's runaway success. More than one newspaper columnist was surprised to find lines outside matinee screenings in places unexpected, from Pittsburgh to New Orleans. The movie resonated with audiences across the country, many of which unto that point had very little exposure to hip-hop and hip-hop culture. *Breakin'*'s authenticity was a big boost in that regard: everything from the dancers to the music were straight out of the local, Los Angeles scene. Even the clothes worn by Turbo and Ozone came from their personal wardrobes.

For a company which usually seemed to be two steps behind the times, Cannon had finally struck a hit while the iron was hot. *Breakin'* was a bona fide pop culture phenomenon. When all was said and done, the movie brought in more than $38 million at the domestic box office, which made it Cannon's all-time most successful U.S. release. (Not to mention their most profitable: *Breakin'*'s shooting budget was only around $1 million.)

And so, of *course* there was going to be a *Breakin' 2*. Cannon was so confident about this that they advertised it at the end of the first *Breakin'*'s credit roll.

The high-ups at Cannon wisely figured that breakdancing wouldn't hold the public's captivation indefinitely, and so they wasted no time putting the sequel into motion. The stars of the two movies barely had a moment to catch their breaths, going from the set of *Breakin'*, to promoting the film at Cannes and around the world, and then on to *Breakin' 2* almost immediately afterwards.

A script was commissioned from screenwriters Julie Reichert and Jan

Ventura, who'd written a screenplay for the first *Breakin'* which ultimately went unused. Sam Firstenberg was brought on as director, having just done bang-up jobs knocking out the Cannon classics *Revenge of the Ninja* and *Ninja III* in rapid succession. While he'd never directed a musical before, Firstenberg saw plenty of similarities between shooting martial arts action and choreographed dance numbers.

The American poster and video art featured our breakdancing heroes hovering over a glowing, neon sneaker, which was also an electrical plug.

Breakin' 2: Electric Boogaloo was written, filmed, and edited at an unbelievably breakneck speed, to finally be released in December of 1984—a mere *seven months* after the first *Breakin'* movie hit theaters. Some might say that the movie was rushed; I would argue that they were riding high on their momentum. To any viewer, though, it's clear that *Breakin'* and *Breakin' 2* are very different movies. The first is an enthusiastic, can-do dance film just dripping with austerity. The second is an unbelievably insane, full-blown musical: as over-the-top as the most far-fetched of Hollywood's Golden Age productions, and it is absolutely *wonderful*.

When *Breakin' 2* opens, Kelly appears to have put her Special K alter ego on ice to pursue a more serious, yet unfulfilling, career as a Las Vegas-style, chorus line dancer. Her parents unsupportively wish she would give up her dreams, quit dancing, attend Princeton, and marry a pompous law student named Derek. (She's not interested because, as she puts it, Derek's a "nerd.") We also learn here for the first time is that her family is absurdly wealthy. The mansion which was used for Kelly's parents' home was situated next to Muhammad Ali's estate in Los Angeles; the boxing legend once dropped by set to perform magic tricks for the movie's cast and crew.

Wanting to clear her head after an argument with her old man, Kelly heads downtown for some hang time with her old friends Turbo and Ozone. Their professional careers appear to have cooled similarly to Special K's, but they've charitably channeled much of their downtime into building up a youth outreach center known as "Miracles."

It's only about a minute into the T.K.O. Crew's happy reunion when the proverbial acid kicks in. If you were to try to pinpoint at what exact moment when the *Breakin'* series goes from an implausibly grounded story of aspiring dancers to a psychedelic fever dream, well, this is it, folks. One of Turbo and Ozone's adopted street kids begins rapping out of the blue, and the entirety of their downtown Los Angeles neighborhood suddenly goes *absolutely freakin' nuts*.

Ozone, Turbo, and the kids lead Kelly on a dance-march across town to their beloved youth center. As they go, literally every*one* and every*thing* they pass magically starts breakdancing. A mailman backflips off a lawn to bust a move; a meter maid stops writing a ticket to get in on the groove. Electrical contractors shake their money-makers while hanging from telephone poles, construction workers step into a synchronized routine, and an elderly grandmother jumps and flails like a wild woman. Hell, even an *empty car* miraculously bounces to the beat. Anyone who sees the old T.K.O. Crew boppin' down the road starts to dance as if possessed by a sort of pop-lockin' Lucifer.

Their black magic parade eventually leads them to the brightly-colored, graffiti-covered youth center known as Miracles. (The building is a historic cultural center called Casa Del Mexicano in the Boyle Heights neighborhood of Los Angeles; as of this writing, it hosts lucha libre wrestling matches and swap meets.) Inside the massive Miracles building, troubled kids learn to dance, box, juggle and mime, which is all it takes to keep them out of gangs and off drugs. It's a cause to which Ozone has fully dedicated himself, teaching dance classes and lending a hand wherever and whenever needed.

If you've seen pretty much *any* film involving a wholesome gathering place for wayward youth, you'll know right away that an evil developer is lurking nearby, licking his lips at the thought of bulldozing it to erect a shopping center in its place. You'll also understand that the *only* possible way our dancing heroes have any hope of saving their community center is to raise an impossible-seeming amount of money by staging a big-ass fundraising show. It's been a reliable, stock plot of Hollywood musicals since little Judy Garland and Mickey Rooney ruled the screens, and if you've seen one (or ten), you'll be able to guess where it's all heading within the movie's first ten minutes. The predictable plot is really a non-issue, however: like its predecessor, *Electric Boogaloo*'s story is only here to usher us from one dance number to the next.

The sequel also supplies its heroes with love stories to help fill the moments between dance routines. It's not really clear how much time was supposed to have passed between the two movies—all we can figure is that it was more than the seven months which passed in the real world, given that the characters went their separate ways after the success of *Street Jazz* and somehow established a thriving community center. Now Ozone and Kelly are semi-dating, judging by the intimacy they share at the start of *Breakin' 2: Electric Boogaloo*, but Ozone also has a jealous ex to contend with. (She's played by Sonny Bono's then-wife, Susie Coelho.) Meanwhile, Turbo falls head-over-heels for a Latina girl named Lucia, who doesn't speak English but can obviously communicate with Turbo via the universal language of dance. The actress, Sabrina Garcia, reportedly had a very soft voice, which is why her lines are so obviously dubbed on screen.

Kelly eventually makes a hard call and gives up a big role in Paris so that she can stay with her friends and help them save Miracles. In the end, the T.K.O. crew and the Miracles kids put on a massive dance performance in front of the community center. Kelly's parents are so impressed with her mettle that they cut a check that's just big enough to keep Miracles out of the evil developer's hands. The end! Now, let's talk about all of the wonderful wackiness that gets us from Point A to Point Z.

If there's a single dance number which *Breakin' 2: Electric Boogaloo* is best remembered for, that would be Turbo's famous "ceiling dance." Made weightless by his feeling of youthful love for Lucia, Turbo launches into an impromptu dance routine which sees him popping, locking, breakin' and moonwalking around the shack he shares with Ozone. He dances up the walls, and even upside-down on the ceiling. It's an amazingly fun moment, and might have been memorable enough had he performed the moves on the floor— Boogaloo Shrimp's dancing is that infectious—but he looks here as if he's legitimately defying gravity.

Like the broom dance in the original *Breakin'*, Turbo's footwork on the ceiling echoes a similar trick from the Fred Astaire film *The Royal Wedding*. In both movies a set was built on a gimbal, which allowed the entire room to be rotated on its axis; meanwhile, the camera rig was turned simultaneously, requiring its operator to do his job upside-down. (As far as I was able to find out, no one threw up while shooting this scene.) The effect is what you see in the movie: the viewer retains their orientation, while the dancer appears to cut a rug up the walls and on the ceiling. The only moment where it doesn't fully work is when Lucia wanders into the room and doesn't lose her mind watching her beau boogie upside-down in the rafters. To maintain the appearance that Shrimp was dancing on the ceiling, the poor girl had to be strapped upside-down to the wall, with her hair pinned to her shoulders to keep it from falling while pretending to watch him from the floor.

The gimbal rigging the *Breakin' 2* team used in this scene had originally been built for Wes Craven's influential *A Nightmare on Elm Street* (1984), which had filmed earlier that same year. (You'll see it in Tina's death scene where she rolls around on the ceiling, as well as in the famous "blood geyser" scene where Johnny Depp—in his movie debut—gets eaten by a bed.)

In another scene of *Electric Boogaloo*, Ozone gives Turbo tips on how to woo a woman by demonstrating his most romantic dance moves with a life-size doll version of Kelly. (Yeah, the Kelly effigy is a bit weird. *Why* exactly do they have one of those in their shack?) As the boys tango with the doll and pass it back and forth, it morphs between being a doll, Kelly, and Shrimp's girlfriend, Lucia. The scenes is actually a really cool and creative piece of editing.

Speaking of Ozone, Shabba-Doo finally gets his own solo number on the roof of Miracles. It's a great spotlight for his talent as a dancer, if perhaps a bit more suggestive than you might expect from a PG-rated dance movie. There's also a memorable rematch between the villainous dance crew, Electro Rock, and the T.K.O. gang. After catching them vandalizing the youth center, the T.K.O.s chase their rivals to their hangout place underneath a Los Angeles overpass. Seeking revenge after their dancefloor rivals vandalized the youth center, the competing crews pair off and attempt to out-dance each other with moves that must have taken days to choreograph and lock down. The whole, silly "fight" scene makes *West Side Story* look like *Boyz n the Hood* (1991) in comparison.

Oh—and have I mentioned that one of *Breakin' 2: Electric Boogaloo*'s primary side characters is a *mime*?

Believe it or not, that's still not the weirdest thing you'll see in *Electric Boogaloo*. A bit of drama enters the film when a crew of surveyors show up at Miracles to plan out their upcoming demolition of the local children's hopes and dreams. Turbo mischievously steals the workers' lunch box and then leads them on a chase across Boyle Heights. He takes a bad tumble down a set of stairs, landing himself in the hospital and in a coma—on the eve of their big fundraising show, no less!

Ozone, Kelly, and half the Miracles gang pay the unconscious breakdancer a visit. A kiss from Lucia is all it takes to revive poor Turbo, and his pals are so overcome with joy that they start dancing—and as you know, when these guys start dancing, so does everyone else within a 100-foot radius. They bop down the hospital halls as patients emerge from their rooms, leap out of their wheelchairs and do flips over their walkers to get in on the groove. It's as if all of modern medicine doesn't hold a candle to the healing power of breakdancing. Laboring mothers wander out from the maternity ward and start high-kicking in sync A quartet of foxy nurses—played by showgirls flown in from Las Vegas—strut past the emergency room as surgeons drop their tools on a dying patient to go dance with these salacious ladies. (The patient flat lines.) Then, the grand pinnacle of crazy shit happens: there's a blip on the electrocardiograph, and then another, and then another. The patient—left for dead by his doctors only minutes earlier—slowly sits up and begins to dance on the surgical table.

Yes, that's right. The magic of breakdancing brings a man *back* from the *dead*!

The movie makes no bones about its utter absurdity: *Breakin' 2: Electric Boogaloo* is a high-flying, neon-colored fantasy. Accept that, and it's a ridiculous amount of fun. This comes across most during the movie's big, concert finale, which I'm sure The Guinness Book of World Records team could confirm features the most fluorescent clothing that's ever appeared in a single film scene. Ice-T takes the stage to rap about the movie's plot, and soul singer Carol Lynn Townes performs the movie's theme song, "Believe in the Beat." Hundreds of extras are squeezed onto the street in front of Miracles—at least a third of them wearing matching, white Pepsi hats, oddly enough—cheering and dancing along with the performers onstage. Even the wicked Electro Rock squad are able to put aside their differences with Ozone's crew and take the stage to help out a good cause. Everything is so bright and infectiously cheery—from the song, to the beaming crowd, to the blindingly fluorescent color scheme—that you may want to get up and dance along.

Breakin' 2: Electric Boogaloo was the first of two Cannon films distributed by the newly-launched TriStar Pictures. (Their next and last would be *Lifeforce*, in the summer of '85.) The company no doubt hoped to repeat the success of the first *Breakin'* film, but the public had long since reached peak breakdance exhaustion months earlier. *Breakin' 2* debuted at #10 at the box office on its Christmas '84 opening weekend, and only proceeded to drop from there. After six weeks in theaters, the movie had brought in just over $15 million domestically. That made it a resounding success compared to most Cannon releases in the U.S., but it was a far cry from the $38 million *Breakin'* had banked that summer.

When it failed to match its predecessor's ticket sales, Cannon correctly chalked it up to a waning public interest in breakdancing, rather than the movie's inherent craziness. The studio proceeded with an unofficial, spiritual sequel the following summer. That urban musical was titled *Rappin'*, and you can guess which "craze" they were looking to cash in on there.

As time went on, the stars of *Breakin'* remained best-known for their roles in these films. Both Shabba-Doo and Boogaloo Shrimp continue dancing to this day; the former reunited with Cannon for 1990's *Lambada*, in which he co-starred and choreographed the dance numbers. (That one was also helmed by *Breakin'* director Joel Silberg.) Boogaloo Shrimp would channel his signature, robotic style of dance into playing the Robot Bill in *Bill and Ted's Bogus Journey* (1991) and the Urkel-Bot on multiple episodes of *Family Matters* (1989–1997). Notably, he also choreographed *The Simpsons*' animated "Do the Bartman" music video in 1990; the track was ghost-written by Michael Jackson, who hand-picked Shrimp for the job as payback for sharing his moonwalk knowledge all those years earlier. Lucinda Dickey started a family shortly after *Breakin' 2* and only made one more film—the 1988 slasher *Cheerleader Camp*—before embarking on careers outside of the movie business.

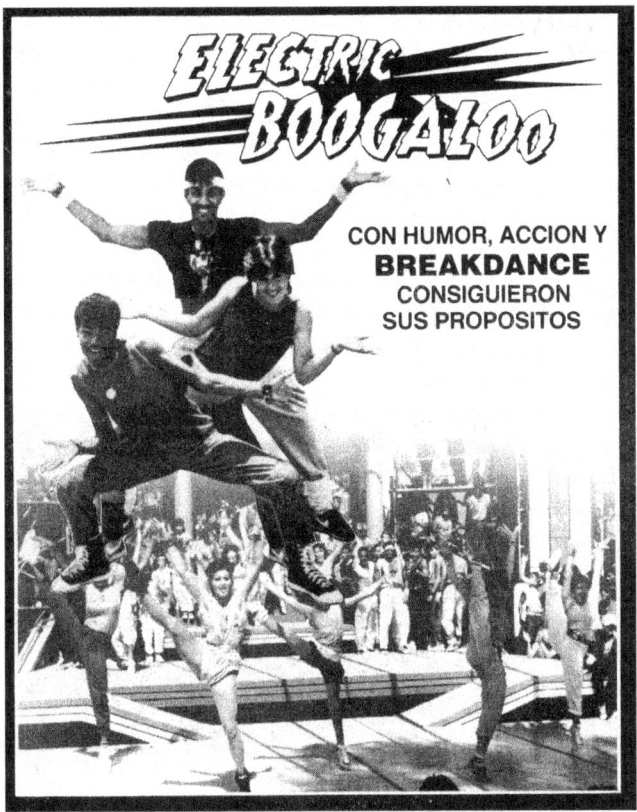

"With humor, action, and breakdance they got their purposes." An ad for the film from Spain.

Breakin' 2's greatest lasting legacy was, of all things, its subtitle. In the decades since the film's release, "Electric Boogaloo" has become the tacked-on punchline title for any sequel, movie or otherwise, which can be considered relatively unnecessary. For example: if I were to joke about there being a fake sequel for the movie *Sophie's Choice* (1982), the only acceptable name for it would be *Sophie's Choice 2: Electric Boogaloo*.

Some of the earliest riffs on this jocular naming convention appeared in the early '90s, as jokes on the TV series *Mystery Science Theater 3000*. By the early 2000s, however, it had proliferated across the Internet; nowadays, it wouldn't be out of the ordinary to see a newspaper article about a political candidate's re-election under the headline, say, "Mayor's Campaign II: Electric Boogaloo." It's gotten so common that a Google search for "2: Electric Boogaloo"—even when you omit entries containing the word "Breakin"—yields more than 500,000 results. At this point, people are in all likelihood more familiar with the snarky, "Electric Boogaloo" sequel naming joke than the movie which spawned it.

When you think about it, thought, that's really not a bad legacy at all, considering that Menahem Golan only slapped the nonsensical phrase onto the title because he liked the way it sounded.

Turbo (Michael Chambers) cozies up with Lucia (Sabrina Garcia) in a Spanish lobby card for *Breakin' 2: Electric Boogaloo*.

Interview: Michael "Boogaloo Shrimp" Chambers

Breakin's youngest star was Michael Chambers, a teenage dancer from Los Angeles who was better known under his performing name: Boogaloo Shrimp. Although he was only sixteen when the film was shot, Chambers had already been dancing on a professional level, having appeared in music videos for Lionel Richie's "All Night Long" and Chaka Khan's "I Feel for You." As impressive as that was, his biggest contribution to pop culture to this point had happened behind the scenes: working with Michael Jackson ahead of his famous *Motown 25* (1983) performance, teaching him b-boy moves and helping him master the moonwalk.

In the early 1980s, Chambers was featured performing the move on a television documentary on Los Angeles' vibrant hip-hop culture. Jackson saw the program, and reached out to Chambers and another featured dancer. The two were summoned to the Jackson compound, where they met the family and started working with Michael on his moves. Though Chambers never received credit for this early contribution to Jackson's signature style, the pop star eventually payed him back by requesting he work as choreographer for the *The Simpsons*' "Do the Bartman" music video, which Chambers that time was credited for.

The *Breakin'* movies made the young Boogaloo Shrimp into an '80s dance icon. Both films made use of Chambers' unique dance style, dubbed "liquid animation" after it was inspired by the stop-motion animation method of the great special effects maestro Ray Harryhausen. As his career went on, Chambers moved into the special effects area of the film industry himself. His robotic moves made him perfect to play the Robot Bill in *Bill & Ted's Bogus Journey* (1991), and helped him land a recurring role as the Urkelbot on the sitcom *Family Matters* (1989–1997), a staple of ABC's Friday night TGIF lineup throughout the 1990s.

Chambers' legacy and career are the subject of *The Boogaloo Shrimp Documentary* (2019), directed by Taylor Golonka. Chambers continues to dance to this day, and passes down his knowledge and footwork to pupils through private workshops. [The below is an excerpt from an interview published by *Under the Radar* magazine in 2019.]

The Cannon Film Guide: You've said that disco, animation, and science fiction movies inspired you and your friends to start dancing. But in reality, you were at ground zero for West Coast hip-hop culture. At the time, could you tell that you were part of something special, or that it would have such a big impact on pop culture?

Michael Chambers: On the West Coast it seemed every city had its group of dancers so, yes, it was an amazing time to get recognition for your dance skills and meet and work out with other dancers to improve and master your unique, personal style.

You were still so young when you starred in *Breakin'*, but you also already had a lot of experience making music videos and hanging out with huge stars like Michael Jackson and Lionel Richie. Were you totally over camera shyness by the time you starred in your first movie?

For the record, I was not hanging out with big stars, it was all work related. I joined the Screen Actors Guild and Actors Federation for Television and Radio Artists unions. By performing on the Redondo Beach pier and dance contest, I had built my confidence. But if you look closely at the "All Night Long" music video and Chaka Khan's "I Feel For You," I was concentrating on my dance steps and did not look into the camera or smile much.

Were you skeptical at all when you were first starting out on *Breakin'*? I can't imagine two Israeli producers, Menahem Golan and Yoram Globus, felt like the obvious people to bring street culture to the silver screen.

I was not raised to be racially biased, so it was a job opportunity and it was not like many people were employing street dancers in lead roles. So my agent, Vaughn Hart, suggested it would be a good career move to go to the audition and the rest is history. I had no idea that it was not just my dance skills, but my improv comedy and personality that helped me carry my character and made audiences laugh in between the dancing.

***Wild Style* (1982) had already come out, which focused on New York b-boys. When you were making *Breakin'*, did you feel any pride or pressure in knowing that you guys were representing the West Coast scene you'd come from, which a lot of the country would be seeing for the first time?**

Not at all. We on the West Coast were very aware NYC had great b-boy dancers. Director Topper Carew had made a documentary before the *Breakin'* films called *Breakin' 'n' Enterin'* (1983) which featured the best of the best in Los Angeles, as well as a young Ice-T and Egyptian Lover. The best thing that happened at that time to hip-hop was a fusion of East Coast interpretation and West Coast. New York's fashion and lingo were different than California's, as well as the dance styles. Here on the West Coast we popped, locked, and boogalooed, robotic styles. New York style was called electric boogie and b-boying was Boogie Down Bronx.

Your *Breakin'* character, Turbo, seemed kind of shy, except when he was dancing. I've read that they re-wrote the script a bit as they got to know you guys. How much of yourself back then do you see in Turbo?

They had a script but decided to hang out with us and see how we really spoke, learning street terminology at the same time. I admire the writers and the Golan/Globus team because they allowed me to improv most of every scene with my dialog, and there were many rewrites to make it work.

***Breakin'* was a huge hit. Can you describe your experience during the height of *Breakin'* mania? Were you getting approached by fans everywhere?**

It was a bit overwhelming and sometimes frightening. I remember my schooldays friends and I went to our favorite hangout, Del Amo Fashion Center, in Torrance, California, and the film was playing. The security had me wait until the theater lobby was cleared to leave. Also, some fans found out where I lived. My mother and father told me when I woke up in the morning that fans were waiting across the street to get an autograph. It was fun, but I felt like still a normal guy and came back to the areas where I grew up: the South Bay of Los Angeles and the East Los Angeles disco/funk party areas.

You went to being of an icon of the 1980s to playing a part in several zeitgeist moments of '90s pop culture, from *Bill & Ted* to "Do the Bartman." You even played the Urkelbot on *Family Matters*. Is it true the cast and crew had such a good time with you that they wrote more Urkelbot episodes just to get you back on set?

Well, after the media labeled my dance art as a passing fad and people started saying my character was a NYC wannabe reject, I realized I wanted to do other projects that highlighted my signature dance style. So I told my agent at the time, Julie McDonald, who was Paula Abdul's agent as well, that I wanted to go up for special effects parts since I was influenced by Ray Harryhausen's stop motion characters to help create certain dances, and my style of liquid animation dance.

Michael Jackson and I had worked out during the Victory Tour in 1983. He filmed the session and was able to master what he learned at that time. I have to admit it hurt a bit not getting credit on paper for my work with him, so when the Bart Simpson project came up I specifically asked Mr. Jackson if I can be credited for my work and my agent, Julie McDonald, got the contract and to this day I am on the record for working with Mr. Jackson, who wrote the song "Do The Bartman" for *The Simpsons Sing the Blues* (1990). I was very pleased because the mystery of who was teaching Mr. Jackson now started to unfold, since I was listed as the choreographer.

The director, Rich Correll, and the producers of the *Family Matters* TV show were very happy with the ratings, so they called me back for a second episode. Also, there were plans for me to be in a third, which was Steve Urkel going to the Epcot Center and donating the Robo-nerd to the science center, but the effects artist, Kenny Myers, told me they could not reach an agreement with his work, and they cancelled my job. So it was a tough time trying to provide for myself and my family.

So many of your friends, colleagues, and admirers appeared in *The Boogaloo Shrimp Documentary* to talk about your legacy. How did it feel listening to them talk about your achievements?

I was humbled and very thankful, since most people would sum up my career by the two *Breakin'* films.

The documentary makes it clear it wasn't just your dance moves that made you a star, but a lot of smart, forward thinking. If you hadn't become a professional dancer, what do you think you would like to have done as a career instead?

Like my father, I would have found a regular nine to five and joined a production team with an upbeat company, and been a better father when given the chance.

The Spanish theatrical poster for *Electric Boogaloo*.

Interview: Screenwriters Jan Freya and Julie Reichert

At the time they wrote the screenplay for Cannon's *Breakin' 2: Electric Boogaloo*, neither Julie Reichert nor Jan Freya had previously worked in movies. (The latter was credited on the movie as Jan Ventura.) Yet, their script resulted in one of Cannon's wildest and most well-loved sequels, and added the phrase "Electric Boogaloo" to the pop culture lexicon.

After *Breakin' 2*, Freya worked as a psychotherapist and, later, as the dean of students at a holistic health college. She went into business as a highly sought-after editor of theses and dissertations, and has returned to the arts through painting.

In 2011, Reichert released her directorial debut, *Warrior Woman*, about a cancer survivor who helps her student escape an abusive relationship. She instructs medical students in narrative writing, and co-founded the Taos Writing Retreat for Health Professionals.

***The Cannon Film Guide*: *Breakin' 2: Electric Boogaloo* gave you your first film credits of any kind. Were you involved with the film industry in any way leading into *Breakin*?**

Julie: I was not involved in the film industry except as an interested moviegoer. What got me into this was my friendship with Michael Ventura. He's someone I'd known since I was a kid, basically, and he was involved in the movie biz. He gave me the script to a movie that I had seen, and it was mindblowing to see the words on the page and be able to remember the images. This, of course, was before you could run out and get a movie script. And so I was interested in movies, but I was more of a prose writer at that time. I was more interested in trying to write a novel.

Jan: I was married to Michael Ventura, who was a film reviewer for *LA Weekly* and had also written screenplays. I was writing film reviews for *High Performance* magazine, and so we were in that milieu a lot. Personally, I have a Masters in fine arts, and had made films as a student. I did film, performance art, and installation kinds of work, and so I had studied film a lot. However, I'd never been involved in a real, professional film—just on the periphery.

Julie: Michael was working on a Cassavetes documentary [*I'm Almost Not Crazy: John Cassavetes – The Man and His Work*, 1984] and found out that Cannon was looking to do a breakdance movie. He thought that his wife, Jan, and I would have a good time doing that. He didn't have the time to do it, but thought that we could and so we just jumped in.

Jan: You know, Cannon would make a trendy film—or a schlocky, trendy film—and then they would turn around and give money to someone like Cassavetes. They funded *Love Streams* (1984), and then funded Michael's documentary about the making of *Love Streams*.

Julie: To me, it was great that this exploitation movie-making, money-making machine, Cannon Films, would support a John Cassavetes movie and not make any demands on him. I really, really appreciated that about them.

Jan: So, Michael was editing at Cannon and somebody came down the hall and said, "Anybody want to write a breakdance movie?" He just spoke up and said, "I know someone who can do that!" Julie had been his friend since childhood and had moved out to Los Angeles, and he was thinking of us two teaming up. It was pretty nepotistic, actually. [*Laughs*] But he knew that we could do it, and they hired us to do it.

Was it written entirely on spec? You hadn't had any meetings with producers?

Julie: No, no. It was one of those things that was like, "They really want to make a breakdance movie. Maybe if you write a script by, like, next Tuesday, they might use it."

Jan: The first one we wrote didn't get taken, and they actually had to take the script of one of the producers. It was one of Golan's or Globus' nephews, or something like that. They felt obliged to take the script that he had written, but they asked us to do the sequel and we wrote another screenplay for that.

What can you tell me about that original, unused script?

Julie: It was a more integrated story than the one we wound up with when we did *Electric Boogaloo*. It also plays in Venice Beach. Basically, the story was that there was this street kid who was a breakdancer, and he encounters this young woman who was a gymnast. It was about their relationship, pretty much, and how they each influenced each other. She wound up giving him some new moves from gymnastics, and he gave her the heart that was missing from what she was doing with gymnastics. It was mostly the back-and-forth between them, but there were also various friends, complications, and love interests.

What kind of exposure had you had to hip-hop and breaking at the time?

Julie: Our exposure was simply as interested observers. People dancing at Venice Beach, and here and there. We were in California at the time, so we would see people breakdancing. I seem to remember that we had some kind of written matter on breakdancing, a book or a pamphlet, or something like that. Beyond that, it was just what we observed.

Jan: I had a son who was about eight years old and was interested in breakdancing, so I knew about it. But, no, I really didn't know much.

They chose to go with another screenplay for the first film. When it became a hit, they rushed out a sequel and came back to the two of you to write it. How did you get involved?

Julie: They called us out of the blue. I don't know why they didn't go with us originally, but we just got a phone call where they asked, "How would you like to write the sequel?" And we said "Okay!" There was a back-and-forth for a little while, where we weren't sure if it was going to be another, separate breakdance movie—in which case, we could heavily draw on our original script—or whether it would be an actual sequel using the same characters.

Do you recall how much time you had to write it?

Jan: I don't know for sure, but I would say it was a matter of months. Two months, maybe. They were pretty lickety-split over there. [*Laughs*]

What sort of guidance were you given from anyone at Cannon?

Jan: We interviewed Shabba-Doo and Boogaloo Shrimp and maybe a couple other people. We just talked to them about their experience with breakdancing, and we got a lot of the lingo from there. That was one of the main things we wanted: the talk. Of course, we couldn't put in any of the swear words. [*Laughs*] We got so frustrated with that, so we started writing in phrases like "Oh, baloney" and they used them! Of course, they wanted kids to see the movie, so we couldn't use the swear words—which were, like, every other word when we were interviewing the stars.

Julie: The producers would call and they would have all these harebrained ideas that we'd have to try to incorporate, or talk them out of. That happened frequently. We got to a point where we had to put our foot down and say "No," we can't do these things or we'd have no script. It was an interesting process.

When you're doing a script and make changes, they'll use different colors of paper. You'll have yellow pages, and blue pages, things like that for the new scenes. The production coordinator on the movie—a lovely young woman named Stefani Deoul—made a habit of wearing a sweatshirt that was the color of the page for the day. She started running out of colors. [*Laughs*] Unfortunately I don't have the colorful script anymore.

Were you able to reuse much of your first script for the second one?

Julie: A little bit came over. We borrowed some characters.

Jan: It was a different kind of story. I think in our first script we had more focus on the rich girl and her being drawn into the breakdancing, and the socio-economic contrast of that.

The first movie is a more traditional dance movie, while the second one is a big spectacle. It often gets compared to the old MGM musicals.

Jan: That's what I always say. It's the old sort of musical where they just say, "Let's do a big show, right here!" [*Laughs*]

Julie: Part of that came from the script being so disrupted all the time: sometimes you would just have to insert a musical number because you didn't know what else to do.

Did any of those old movies inspire you at all?

Jan: We never admitted it, but they probably slipped in there without us thinking of it. That was part of our upbringing, watching so many hours of those old musicals. I watched some of the 1950s ones in theaters, and the older, 1930s ones were on TV when we were kids. I think we probably associated on-screen dance with those.

Did you spend much time on set?

Jan: A lot. We were really welcome to be there, and it was a lot of fun. They really filmed it in East L.A., especially around the big, domed building that used to be a mosque, which looks out over downtown Los Angeles. I remember going to a few of the cast parties, too. We were welcome to be on set any time, we had a free pass.

Julie: We could just come in whenever we wanted to. I went a bunch of times, sometimes with Jan and sometimes on my own. It was really fun. Everyone was actually having a good time.

Do you recall the first time you saw the finished movie, and what you thought?

Jan: Oh, yeah. [*Laughs*] I think I have a photo of us standing under the marquee. We saw it in Westwood. We took Michael, and my son went with us. It was a lot of fun.

The sexy, dancing nurses—played by Vegas showgirls—were a surprise addition to the movie.

Julie: There were certain things we saw and were like, "What?" For example, they made a big deal in the beginning about how this had to be a G-rated movie, and so we couldn't use any street language, which was a challenge for us. It was difficult to have dialogue that sounded remotely like people would actually be saying those things while being careful about the language. And so there we are, concentrating and focusing on that, but then the producers add in those "foxy nurses." Nurses in short skirts and tight outfits doing a Rockettes kind of thing. We were working our butts off to keep things wholesome and then they put in those buxom nurses for no reason! [*Laughs*]

Jan: They jazzed it up with the sexy nurses dancing in the hospital—we didn't write in any sexy nurses. [*Laughs*]

Did those scenes surprise you when you saw them on screen?

Jan: I think that one did, mostly.

Julie: We were also disconcerted about a character we had in there, but in the movie he was a mime in white makeup doing pantomime, and it was so different than the character we had imagined. But going to the set and seeing a lot of stuff happening there prepared us to see the movie, I think.

Jan: Otherwise it was pretty true to our script. We had story meetings with them every once in a while. We'd go into the office and they'd have read the script, and they'd have these harebrained ideas. [*Laughs*] Menahem would jump up and go, "I've got it! We'll make it into a *Romeo and Juliet* story! It will only take a few changes! Julie and I would look at each other, because we knew—we'd accommodated a lot of their ideas already—and we'd shout them down. "No! You can't do that—not at this point!" And they'd go, "Oh, okay." It was a fun ride. They were pretty flexible guys. They knew they could jazz it up and make it colorful, all of that stuff. Make it look spectacular.

Julie: We went to see it the day it opened, in the afternoon. It was really great to see it, actually. Really nice. Going from day one where you're writing words on a page, and then seeing it enacted. There's a magic in that.

Over the decades it's become a true cult movie.

Jan: It really has. It just astounds us, because the residuals keep going on and on. I think Julie told me the first time she heard of it being on videocassette, it was from somebody who had seen it in Kathmandu! It must have been pirated, or something. We weren't even aware it was even on videocassette yet.

Julie: It's astounding to me how many people have an emotional response to it. It's nice to be part of something that's become a cultural icon, in a way. People who were of a certain age when the movie came out love it.

Jan: It's really got worldwide appeal! Even nowadays, every once in a while I'll mention it and people would just go, "Ah! I love that movie! I saw it with my sister when I was three!" or, "That's my favorite movie!" I went back to graduate school for psychology and one of my professors was totally head-over-heels in love with that movie.

I think it has a spirit to it. It's a real innocent, fun spirit. Maybe it's a schlocky movie and kind of formulaic, but the spirit in it really came through. Most of them were real kids who came up from the streets, and so that part was real.

Julie: I live in Albuquerque, and my husband and I do tango. The old part of town has a gazebo, and a couple times a month the local tango group will dance out there. For a while, after we folded up for the night, there would be a group of young people who would use that gazebo to breakdance. One time my husband couldn't contain himself and had to tell them I was the writer on that movie, and everyone knew what it was. That felt good. Here I am, an old lady, and they're these young kids, and it was nice to feel that connection.

Making the Grade

Release Date: May 18, 1984
Directed by: Dorian Walker
Written by: Gene Quintano & Charles Gale
Starring: Judd Nelson, Dana Olsen, Jonna Lee, Andrew Dice Clay
Trailer Voiceover: "The comedy that hits higher education below the belt!"

This would be a near-forgettable campus comedy were it not for a pair of auspicious debuts. *Making the Grade* features the first starring role for eventual Brat Pack-er Judd Nelson, and was the movie that unleashed Andrew Dice Clay upon the world.

Palmer Woodrow the Third (Dana Olsen) is the spoiled, good-for-nothing son of a millionaire industrialist. He spends his days drinking and hanging out with his friends instead of getting his education, but his attitude changes when he learns that daddy will cut him off unless he buckles down and finally graduates from school. Does that sound a little like *Billy Madison* (1995) to you? It's nearly the same setup.

While *Making the Grade* may have been Olsen's only major role as an actor, he made a career for himself as a screenwriter, penning Joe Dante's *The 'Burbs* (1989) starring Tom Hanks and the big-screen version of *George of the Jungle* (1997).

A tattered, ex-rental copy of the campus comedy *Making the Grade*.

To ensure his son's success, Palmer's father has enrolled him in the snooty Hoover Prep, an all-boys private academy. However, Palmer's not going to let a year of school cramp his style—he has other plans to fly off to Europe and canoodle with Parisian girls. He comes up with a wild scheme to hire someone to pose as him and take his place while finishing out his senior year.

Where will he find a schlub desperate enough for cash to take him up on his offer...?

This brings us to Eddie Keaton (Nelson), a rough-and-tumble street kid who has run afoul of his shady bookie, Dice (Clay), who has threatened to break his legs if he doesn't miraculously come up with the thousands of dollars in gambling debt he's accrued. Eddie manages to elude Dice's goons in a zany foot chase which coincidentally takes him through the country club where Palmer and his best friend Rand (Carey Scott) are pondering Palmer's prep school plight.

The two strike a deal: Palmer will hand over $10,000 and the keys to his red Porsche in exchange for a Hoover diploma at the end of the school year. Eddie will pretend to be Palmer, and Rand will keep an eye on him to make sure he doesn't act out of line. It's clear on his arrival at Hoover that the cocky, uncouth Eddie is going to have a hard time blending in with the well-to-do yuppies at his new school. To make matters worse, Eddie falls for Tracey Hoover (Jonna Lee), the lovely granddaughter of the school's founders, which puts him at odds with fellow senior Bif (Scott McGinnis), the academy's alpha asshole. (McGinnis is most familiar as Mr. Adventure in *Star Trek III: The Search for Spock* [1984]; Lee starred in the sci-fi television series *Otherworld* in 1985.)

If you *think* you know where the movie is ultimately heading, chances are you're probably correct. The plot plays out in predictable ways, but this sort of movie's always more about showing the nutty hijinks our heroes get into than telling a story that audiences haven't seen before.

At Hoover Prep, Eddie has a hell of a time maintaining his ruse, especially as he commits such zany gaffes as wearing non-preppy clothing and breakdancing at a formal ball. Matters are further complicated by a series of unexpected drop-ins, the first by Palmer's girlfriend Muffy, who has no idea that her beau is off carousing across Europe. Eventually, Palmer and Dice make their way to Hoover as well and just sort of hang around the campus keeping an eye on Eddie. The lazy millionaire's kid wants to make sure Eddie earns his diploma—as does the crooked bookie, who knows that Eddie's success is the only way he'll ever see any of the money he's owed.

An early ad for what would become *Making the Grade*. The title was no doubt changed to avoid confusion with Chuck Vincent's sex comedy, *Preppies* (1984). In even earlier ads, the film was known as "The Last American Preppies."

Is it starting to feel crowded in here yet? Well, there are yet more characters who become entangled in the madcap, rags versus riches tomfoolery. Among the good guys is the school's friendly physical education instructor, played by Walter Olkewicz of *Twin Peaks* (1990–1991) and *Grace Under Fire* (1993–1998). We also have Nicky, a hot dog vendor from Eddie's hometown in Jersey who somehow winds up at Hoover—he's played by famous, melting, *Raiders of the Lost Ark* (1981) Nazi Ronald Lacey, who also had roles in *Sahara* (1984) and *Sword of the Valiant* (1984) for Cannon.

There's also the token chunky classmate named Blimp, played by Dan Schneider—who co-starred as the goofy, geeky Dennis Blunden on ABC's *Head of the Class* (1986–1991). He also had notable appearances in *Better Off Dead* . . . (1985) and Cannon's own *Hot Resort* (1985) before he made a fortune as a wildly successful producer of tween television programming. He had his hand in creating the Nickelodeon series *All That*, *iCarly*, *Zoey 101*, and

Henry Danger—the latter of which he co-created with his *Making the Grade* co-star, Dana Olsen. Things *do* come full circle!

Playing for the villain's team you'll find Bif's loyal lackey, Skip, played by TV's angel of death, John Dye, of *Touched By An Angel* (1994–2003). Hoover's headmaster, Mr. Harriman, is played by Gordon Jump, best known for playing Arthur "Big Guy" Carlson on *WKRP in Cincinnati* (1978–1982) and his long tenure as the Maytag repairman in TV commercials. For a movie that's really not an ensemble comedy—Judd Nelson is the film's clear-cut lead—there are a *ton* of characters of which to keep track. Yet, the famous and semi-famous faces among its cast are the only things which make *Making the Grade* stand out more than 30 years after its release.

Making the Grade wasn't Judd Nelson's first film appearance, but it was his first starring role—and he's got a cool-as-ice screen presence which shines through the lackluster material he's given to work with. He'd soon be put to much better use over the next couple years in '80s classics like *The Breakfast Club* (1985), *St. Elmo's Fire* (1985), and cinema's crowning achievement, *Transformers: The Movie* (1986).

As the story goes, Cannon's first choice to play Eddie Keaton wasn't Nelson but future superstar Jim Carrey. This would have been a full six years ahead of *In Living Color*'s premiere in 1990. *Making the Grade*'s casting director approached Carrey about the role following a performance at The Comedy Store in Los Angeles, but Carrey declined. However, Andrew Dice Clay—who at this point still just Andrew Clay, no Dice—had been performing as his "Diceman" character on the same bill with Carrey, and they were so impressed with him that they specifically re-wrote the bookie role in *Making the Grade* to fit him in. Clay parlayed his vulgar shtick into roles in *Pretty in Pink* (1986), *Casual Sex?* (1988), and the eventual starring vehicle *The Adventures of Ford Fairlane* (1990), in spite of a sexist standup act that made him a lightning rod for controversy during the height of his popularity.

Making the Grade was co-written by Cannon regular Gene Quintano, who wrote and co-starred in *Treasure of the Four Crowns* (1983) before penning both Allan Quatermain movies, and Charles Gale (who went on to write 1991's *Ernest Scared Stupid*.) Filmmaker Dorian Walker went on to direct the nutty *Teen Witch* (1989), and not much else.

In the end, *Making the Grade* is no *Animal House* (1978) or *Fast Times* (1982). In a classic case of Cannon counting their chickens before they hatch—or box office receipts before they've come in—the last few frames of the film proudly announce that the two main characters, Eddie and Palmer, will soon return in a sequel titled *The Tourista*. That follow-up movie, of course, never happened.

From left to right, Tracey (Jonna Lee), Bif (Scott McGinnis), Eddie (Judd Nelson), and Blimp (Daniel Schneider), in a posed publicity photo for *Making the Grade*.

Interview: Actress Jonna Lee

Jonna Lee made her mark as Judd Nelson's objet d'affection in Cannon's *Making the Grade*. This led to a great deal more work throughout the decade, most notably in a recurring role on TV's *Otherworld* (1985) and appearances on classic 1980s sitcoms such as *Silver Spoons* (1982–1987) and *Growing Pains* (1985–1992). In 1988 she starred in the high-profile television movie *Shattered Innocence*, a fictionalized story inspired by the life and death of famed pornographic actress Shauna Grant.

By the end of the 1980s, Lee had grown tired of acting and eventually left Hollywood behind to pursue her truer passions as a visual artist. Today she still resides in the Los Angeles area and is well-regarded for her work as a sculptor.

The Cannon Film Guide: **Can you tell me about how you got started into acting?**

Jonna Lee: I was the "accidental actress." I was never interested in acting. I never took theater in school or performed in a play, it was completely out of my mindset. I got my start on the set of *Zapped!* (1982). My boyfriend was working as a stand-in and told me to come to the set with a pretty dress. I showed up. They gave me a silent bit. I made $250! *Huge* for a seventeen year old who had been working at the library for $5.80 an hour. I went home, told my mom that I was turning down my scholarships and was going to be an actress. It didn't go over that well, but my Mom said "Give it a year, dear," and I did, and it very weirdly worked.

I really only started learning the craft of acting shortly before I went to college. I was not a terribly good actor as far as that went, but I was spot-on at being a professional. I always knew my lines, could hit a mark, and did my best to be friendly with the rest of the cast and crew.

This was your second feature film in Hollywood. Can you tell me what it was like to be a young actor searching for work in the 1980s?

I think it was like any other job search, and any other social situation. There were always the scumbag directors and producers lurking in the shadows, but there were also wonderful, caring people who tried to nurture anyone who came in the door. We all—my fellow actors and myself—met both. There were always the "mean girls" who wanted to degrade everyone who was in competition with them, but the majority were warm and wonderful women who I would see week after week during the interview process. We would celebrate when one of "us" got a role, no matter who had been auditioning for it.

I am really glad neither one of my kids had any desire to go into the business. In general it is heartbreaking. I was just super, super lucky. From the day I got my SAG card in 1982, until my second year of college in 1991, I never had any other job except as an actor.

I've heard Cannon was a company that young actors kept tabs on, as they were hiring a lot of new talent. Was that the case for you?

This goes back to my being a fairly out-of-touch actor. I did not own a television until the late 1980s and I did not—and do not to this day—really watch TV. I was aware of Cannon and that they could "make" stars, but they were not known for their warmth and support. I think they were basically looking for new, hot, and fast products that they could market in their next film and then move on. It was not like the studio system of old where personalities were nurtured and grown. I think when they found a hot product they ran with it for as long as the public was interested.

Can you describe your audition process for *Making the Grade*?

I still have *no idea* how I got this film. It was pretty crazy. I went to an audition. I read. There was no one else there. I left on a plane either the next day or two days later to shoot in Memphis! I don't completely remember, but I think we filmed the last scene of the movie *that* day. It was whirlwind crazy. They had already been filming for a bit, so it was very disconcerting to show up on a set where everyone had already gotten to know one another.

Judd's career took off after this movie. Working with him here, did you get a sense that he was bound for bigger things?

I love and respect Judd in every way. He interviewed for *The Breakfast Club* (1985) while we were filming. He had an astonishing focus and I knew that he would do well. I am still looking forward to the day he finds a vehicle to truly shine in.

Do you have any favorite memories or stories from your time making the film?

The trees! During our breaks Judd and I used to climb the wonderful trees around the campus we were shooting on. I remember sitting in said trees with my brand new, yellow Walkman playing "Burning Down the House" as loud as it would go. And eating grits and drinking tea with lemon and honey every morning with [Russell Williams], the sound guy. We were the only two who didn't get sick and we swore it was the tea and honey.

We also had to chew ice when it was freezing out so our breath didn't show during the "spring" and "summer" scenes. The warehouse where we shot the love scene was freezing cold. It was the single, most unromantic setting in history. Also, it is quite astonishing how *every* member of the crew suddenly finds a reason to be on set when there is a "love scene." Did I mention it was really, really cold?

We played "quarters" on the floor of the elevator at our hotel. Hey, it was the '80s, we were young!

We had a police escort through Memphis, flashing lights and everything. The band struck up "Hello Dolly" at Blues Alley when I walked in the door! I guess there hadn't been much filming there at that time so Memphis treated us *great*.

I was really annoyed that they wouldn't let me work with the horse that Judd was supposed to get on during the filming. The poor thing was freaked out by the cameras and kept rearing every time he would get on its back. I rode all my life and started getting paid to work out other peoples' horses when I was thirteen. I *knew* I could have him calmed down in fifteen minutes but no one would let me. Then in the scene where we were cantering through the field, the horse bolted with Judd's double. So, I ended up having to race after them so I could grab the reins and get him stopped. It was an odd day. After watching me ride, some people at the barn invited me to go on a fox hunt—a humane, dragged hunt, no actual foxes involved—which I really wanted to do but I wasn't allowed because of insurance concerns. Oh, well.

The end of the film has a plug for a sequel entitled *Tourista*, which was ever made. I'm wondering if you knew anything more about it—what it was going to be about, or whether your character was going to return?
I think all of us were a little shocked at seeing that at the screening. I never know anything about it and obviously it never went anywhere.

From what I understand, later on you decided to pursue another passion of yours, which was sculpting. Can you tell me how you developed your interest in the visual arts, and the thought process which led you to change your focus at that point in your career?
I have been drawing and painting for as long as I can remember. My Mom is an *amazing* artist but she didn't pursue it as a career until later in life. When I was filming in Norway in 1986, I started going to a figure drawing group. It was so wonderful. I really started looking at modern and contemporary art and fell in love. I bummed around Scandinavia and Europe for a bit and went to every gallery I could find.

In 1988, the writers' strike hit literally the day after *Shattered Innocence*, a TV movie that I starred in, came out. I had a lot of meetings with some great directors but literally nothing was being made. During that huge lull I started looking back at some of my journals. The year 1987 was great for me, acting-wise, but I kept seeing the same line written in my journal: "Awesome audience tonight, I just wish I could be painting," or "Great day on the set, I really wish I had the time to paint."

When the strike was over I got a couple more jobs, I think just to make sure I was leaving on my own terms, then I decided to go to college. The timing was perfect. My manager, who had been with me from day one of my acting career, wanted to go back into the fashion industry. We were each dreading telling the other that we wanted to quit, since neither one of us wanted to let the other down. We were both *so* excited to be embarking on something new.

At Otis College of Art and Design, I figured out why I was dissatisfied with painting: I am a sculptor!

Do you find art more fulfilling to you than acting?

Art is so much more fulfilling. I always felt a bit like I was faking it as an actor. I didn't really start learning the craft until maybe 1986. Right when I stopped acting was when I was really learning to fully develop a character. I've now studied art and know my craft, and am pretty innovative. I have a great group of fellow artists, mostly female friends from grad school who I have surrounded myself with and work with regularly. But sometimes I do miss the intense comradery that you find on a film set.

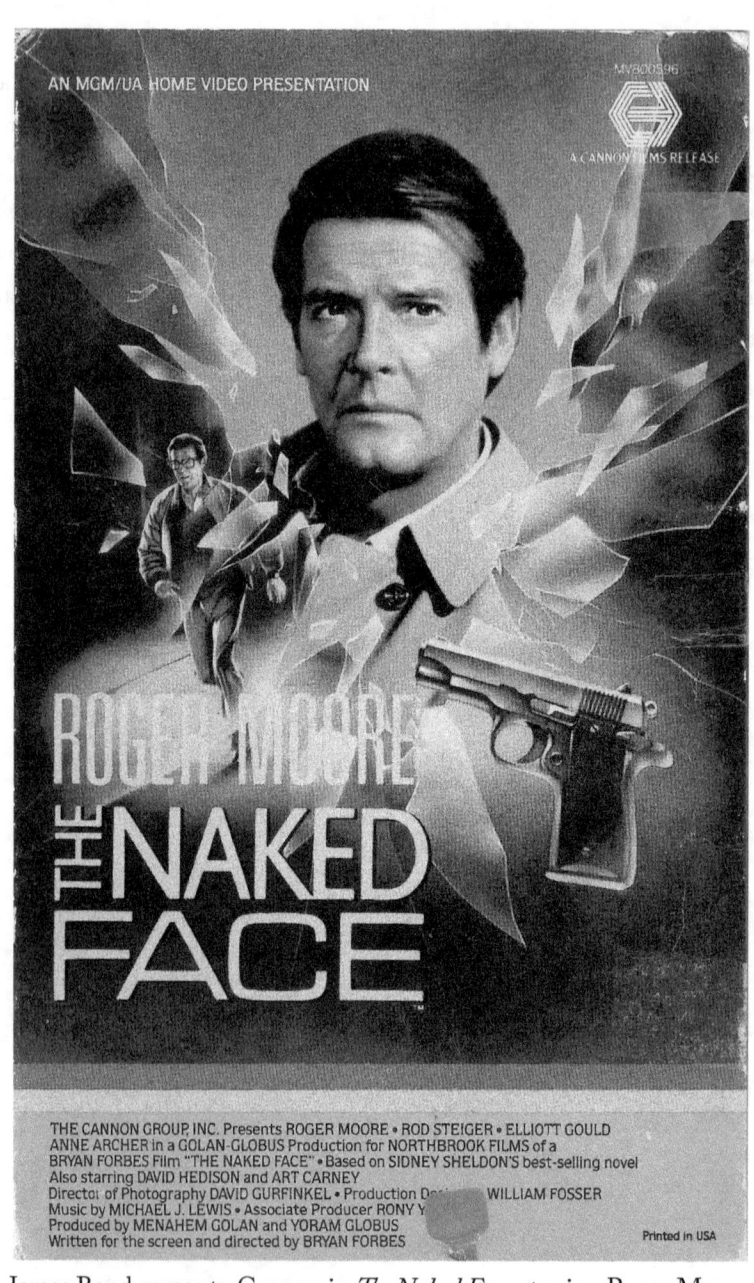

James Bond comes to Cannon in *The Naked Face*, starring Roger Moore.

The Naked Face

Release Date: June 15, 1984
Directed by: Bryan Forbes
Written by: Bryan Forbes
Starring: Roger Moore, Rod Steiger, Elliot Gould, Anne Archer, Art Carney
Trailer voiceover: "Beneath the cold exterior of the city beats the heart of a murderer . . . Roger Moore is the doctor who shares his patients' darkest secrets!"

You have to imagine it's not as easy as it looks, being the face of a character beloved by millions. Sure, you've got your untold wealth, international celebrity, fast sports cars, swift sailboats, and palatial homes in exotic locales. Still, there has to be a nagging feeling when you think about all of those fans lining up time and again to see the latest entry in your character's popular franchise. Do they really love *you*? Or do they only love the guy you play on screen?

The other problem such actors almost surely run into is typecasting: the tendency for filmmakers to cast them in roles that resemble their most famous on-screen persona. Some actors recognized this as part of their appeal and embraced it—the Cannon Group leaned heavily on some of those guys over the 1980s. Charles Bronson played a loose-cannon cop and/or off-the-rails vigilante not only in Cannon's three *Death Wish* sequels, but also the studio's *10 to Midnight*, *Murphy's Law*, and *Kinjite: Forbidden Subjects*. They got Chuck Norris to play the ultra-specific role of a middle-aged badass lured out of retirement for one last mission in all of *Missing In Action*, *Braddock: Missing in Action III*, *Invasion USA*, and *Delta Force 2: The Colombian Connection*.

An early sales ad pitched the film on Moore's recognizability alone.

Frequently-typecast actors often become eager to get out from under the shadow of their iconic character, and will occasionally sign on to smaller, or lower-budget movies when it gives them the chance to show audiences they can play a different sort of role. Of course this created opportunities for Cannon. By the late 1980s, Christopher Reeve was so closely associated with playing Superman that the role of a dishonest reporter in *Street Smart* (1987) had to have seemed pretty appealing to him. You can also look at poor Adam West, who took on roles as a cross-dressing movie producer in Cannon's *Happy Hooker Goes Hollywood* (1980) and a loopy extraterrestrial in *Doin' Time on Planet Earth* (1988), presumably because it meant he wouldn't have to put on the Batman costume.

This leads us to Roger Moore, who fought an uphill battle against typecasting throughout his career. Starting with 1973's *Live and Let Die* and finishing with 1985's *A View to a Kill*, the actor played cinema's most famous secret agent, James Bond, in seven films over the course of 12 years. (Coincidentally, Moore's first and last Bond movies featured what this author considers the series' best theme songs, by Paul McCartney and Duran Duran respectively. Sorry, Shirley Bassey!) While Moore continued to make other, non-*007* movies in the midst of this run, the greater public only saw him as one man: Bond, James Bond. We mean that quite literally: hardly *anyone* in the U.S. went to see the movies where he wasn't playing the suave, British superspy. Out of the 13 non-Bond movies he made during those years, only one—1981's *Cannonball Run*—could be considered a hit.

Moore himself was key in bringing *The Naked Face* to the screen. At the pinnacle of his *Bond*-age, Cannon approached Moore about making a film with them. Given that Moore was paid $4 million plus a 5% share of profits for 1983's *Octopussy*, and then $5 million plus shares for 1985's *A View to a Kill*, which he made immediately after *The Naked Face*, it would seem like Cannon was punching above their weight class. (His Bond fees were more than the studio was spending on entire movies during this era.) But Moore was game and suggested an adaptation of *The Naked Face*, the 1970 debut novel by Sidney Sheldon.

Sidney Sheldon had penned more than two dozen films and Broadway shows, from the 1940s through the 1960s, before going on to create the successful TV sitcoms *The Patty Duke Show* (1963–1966), *I Dream of Jeannie* (1965–1970), *Nancy* (1970–1971), and *Hart to Hart* (1979–1984). Eventually he very successfully transitioned to writing thriller novels. Global sales of his 21 books earned him the rank of seventh best-selling fiction author of all time, ahead of writers such as J.K. Rowling, Dr. Seuss, and Stephen King. (*Yowza!*)

Moore had another request for Cannon, and it was that they hire his old national service buddy, Bryan Forbes, to direct the film. Forbes and Moore had served together in an entertainment unit in Hamburg shortly after WWII; an actor turned filmmaker, Forbes was best-known for his 1975 film adaptation of *The Stepford Wives*. Cannon agreed, and so contracts were signed and announcements were made in all of the trade papers.

In *The Naked Face*, Roger Moore plays mellow-mannered, Chicago psychoanalyst Dr. Judd Stevens. He is one of the windy city's top shrinks, commanding a cool $50 per hour for his talk therapy sessions. One day he suddenly finds himself the target of an anonymous killer—or killer(s). One of his patients turns up dead, stabbed to death in the streets after borrowing the doctor's raincoat. That same evening somebody breaks into Stevens' office and brutally murders his secretary. It becomes clear quite quickly that it's Stevens they are after. The attempts on his life continue: Stevens is run down in an alley with a motor scooter, and two assailants disguised as doormen try to murder him in his own apartment.

Enter homicide detectives McGreary and Angeli. The former is played by a wildly over-the-top Rod Steiger as a hot-tempered police lieutenant who speaks only in blustery accusations and homophobic slurs. A superb actor whose career stretched back to the 1950s, Steiger starred opposite Marlon Brando in *On the Waterfront* (1954) and in classics like *The Big Knife* (1955), *Oklahoma!* (1955), and *The Pawnbroker* (1964). Other film appearances included *Doctor Zhivago* (1965) and *In the Heat of the Night* (1967), for which he won his lone Academy Award for Best Actor. Steiger had reputedly gone under the plastic surgeon's knife just before filming *The Naked Face*, and his own face does look noticeably different than it did in roles shot a few years earlier.

We learn that Dr. Stevens appeared as a professional witness in the trial of the man who shot and killed the lieutenant's previous partner, and as a result of Stevens' testimony the killer received a life sentence on an insanity plea instead of the electric chair. Lieutenant McGreary is still pissed off about this and determined to pin the murders on Stevens in any way he can. His new partner, Angeli—Elliott Gould, fresh off Cannon's *Over the Brooklyn Bridge* (1984)—seems to be the more sensible of the two cops, aware that they have no evidence against Stevens and that someone is clearly trying to kill the doctor, rather than the other way around, but who could it be . . . ? Perhaps one of Dr. Stevens' unstable patients? That seems possible. Or perhaps it's the brother of Stevens' wealthy, deceased wife, who happens to be in line for a small fortune if something were to occur to the good doctor? That seems less likely, but it can't be ruled out, either.

A film noir-flavored, Spanish advertisement for *The Naked Face*.

The relative unhelpfulness of the Chicago P.D. leads the doctor to hire a private investigator, chosen at random from the yellow pages. The private eye, Morgens (Art Carney), is an old eccentric working out of a home office filled with cuckoo clocks, but he's still sharp. Carney is best-remembered for playing Jackie Gleason's coworker, Ed, on *The Honeymooners* (1955–1956), and for his Oscar-winning performance in 1974's *Harry and Tonto*. His brief, oddball role in *The Naked Face* is one of the movie's highlights.

Morgens saves Stevens' life when he finds and disarms a car bomb—only to be murdered by the doctor's unknown enemy and strung up on one of his beloved cuckoo clocks. Yet, the dead detective's brief digging around was enough to clue Stevens in that his pursuer is a member of the Chicago mafia.

In a well-executed twist, the supposed "good cop," Angeli, is revealed to be corrupt and in the pocket of the mob. He leads Stevens into a trap set by the mafia. As it turns out, the Cosa Nostra were the ones after him the whole time; one of Stevens' most comely, flirtatious patients, Ms. Blake—Anne Archer of *Fatal Attraction* (1987) and *Patriot Games* (1992)—was hiding the fact that she's married to the local crime boss, and now her husband is worried that she's been giving away the family's secrets to her therapist. (In actuality, the doctor knows nothing about her husband's line of work.) The mobsters beat the crap out of Stevens while their boss delivers an evil, flowery monologue, and tosses the crooked Angeli into a trash compactor so that no witnesses are left behind. Fortunately, the blowhard Detective McGreary—who was actually the *good* cop all along—shows up in the nick of time, shoots the mob goons and saves Stevens' life.

As far as giving Moore a role that was different from his famous James Bond screen persona, *The Naked Face* was pretty effective. Our leading man spends a good deal of screen time running away, hiding from bad guys, and getting slapped around, all of which are particularly un-Bond-like behaviors. The movie's performances, on a whole, are good—even Steiger's overemphatic scenery-chewing is endearing, in its own way—but the film suffers from a hefty amount of clunky dialogue. Forbes adapted the screenplay and retained many lines directly from the novel, including many that really only worked on paper. There are also some very dated, early '70s attitudes towards psychiatry and homosexuality, which were probably starting to feel a little backwards by the '80s, let alone when you're viewing the movie today.

The biggest problem with *The Naked Face*, though, is that the tension doesn't progress as it should. Rather than building with each attempt on Stevens' life, the events practically feel disconnected. (This thing happens, and then this thing happens, and then ...) *The Naked Face*'s rushed schedule could be to blame for the film's lack of flow. When Moore's aging mother fell ill in the U.K., Forbes allowed the actor leave the shoot to visit her at her bedside.

Rather than suspend production in response—which would have cost more money—Cannon instead slashed several weeks from the shooting schedule and forced the crew to bang out scenes in less time than was needed.

To its ultimate credit, *The Naked Face* does have one of the best, most brutally random endings ever. As Dr. Stevens visits the cemetery after the film's violent finale, he is met by Ms. Blake, his former patient and the ex-wife of the now-dead mob capo. They flirt overtop the grave of Stevens' dead wife, and Ms. Blake asks him out on a date. As they walk away, arm-in-arm, a gunshot rings out, and Ms. Blake crumples to the ground. (It's implied that a mafia sniper took her out.) Stevens kneels down over Blake's dead body, looks just slightly off-camera, and then screams the word "Bastards!"

Freeze frame. Roll credits.

Who knows why this sudden, absurdly cold-blooded little closing scene necessary, but my goodness is it funny. So, so, so unintentionally funny.

The Seven Magnificent Gladiators on VHS.

The Seven Magnificent Gladiators

Release Date: August 3, 1984
Directed by: Bruno Mattei
Written by: Claudio Fragasso
Starring: Lou Ferrigno, Sybil Danning, Brad Harris
Tagline: "Are they enough to stop an ancient reign of terror?"

Ah, *Seven Samurai*. Akira Kurosawa's 1954 classic about seven misfit rōnin who come together to protect a farming village from bandit raiders routinely lands atop prestigious lists which attempt to rank the greatest cinematic works of all time. To this day it stands as an epic, stunning piece of moviemaking and storytelling, but the wider impact it's had on cinema extends far beyond the film itself. It has been remade innumerable times over the years, most famously as John Sturges' 1960 Western *The Magnificent Seven*, which swapped out samurai for gunslingers. That version spawned three sequels, a television series, and inevitably a remake of its own. Naturally Cannon would welcome a film with *Seven Samurai*'s tried-and-tested story formula into their release slate. That movie was *The Seven Magnificent Gladiators*.

This film was the first of four produced by Cannon Italia that starred TV's Incredible Hulk, Lou Ferrigno. It was shot back-to-back with *Hercules* (1983) in the summer of '82; although *Gladiators* was shot first, it was released a full year later than *Hercules*. It was initially announced under the name *Hercules and the Seven Magnificent Gladiators*, but at some point it was decided that this wouldn't be another Hercules movie and the hero's name was changed. Thus the big, capital "H" that Ferrigno wears on his belt buckle may be a little misleading, but here it stands for "Han," the name of the wandering barbarian he plays in *Gladiators*.

The Seven Magnificent Gladiators takes *Magnificent Seven*'s storyline and gives it a mystical, mythical spin. The set-up occurs in a country village adjacent to some spectacular ruins somewhere in Ancient Rome. Even more spectacular than the ruins is the black, leather outfit worn by the villainous Nicerote (pronounced "knee-cha ro-tay"), an evil demi-god who raids the village on an annual basis. He's played by peplum veteran Dan Vadis, who wears a black leather skull cap, a Dracula cape, and what looks like a leather-studded bikini.

"Peplum" is the term for the Italian sword-and-sandal movies which reached the height of their popularity in the 1960s. Vadis appeared in at least half a dozen of these, including two turns as Hercules himself: in 1964's *Hercules the Invincible* and in *The Triumph of Hercules* that very same year. Stateside he's best known for playing baddies opposite Clint Eastwood in *High Plains Drifter* (1973), *Every Which Way But Loose* (1978), and *Any Which Way You Can* (1980).

This mustachioed madman has been granted powers of near-immortality by his blind, witch mother, who lives in this very same village, wears an incredibly tall hat, and is starting to regret bestowing such powerful magic on her maniac kid. When two teen boys try to defend the village from his latest raid, Nicerote flips out and executes all of the village's young men of fighting age. Once he's departed and the smoke has cleared, a group of the village's most comely young women get together and decide they've had enough. The ladies set off to Rome with a magic sword that can defeat their immortal oppressor, if only they're able to find a hero burly enough to wield it.

Fortunately, a super-jacked barbarian named Han (Ferrigno) happens to be passing through Rome at that very same time. He handily bests the

Emperor's champion in a chariot race, but refuses the ruler's command that he slay his defeated opponent following their competition, and so the now ex-gladiator, Scipio, becomes Han's loyal best bud. The Emperor—clad in a dopey pope hat and twenty pounds of fake gemstones—is played with gloriously levels of camp by Israeli actor Yehuda Efroni, an actor who appeared in more Cannon films than any other. (His escort is played by Mandy Rice-Davies, previously of *Nana*, 1983.) Meanwhile, Scipio is played by Brad Harris, who—alongside Ferrigno, Efroni, and Sybil Danning—is one of the actors who was held over from this production to also appear in *Hercules*.

"The seven best and the magic sword. They destroyed an army and became legends." The German theatrical poster for *Seven Magnificent Gladiators*.

Finding themselves fugitives of the throne, our two muscle-bound gladiators cross paths with the village maidens. They conclude that Han is the hero of their prophecies when he's able to wield their magic sword without it setting him on fire, a grisly fate which beset every other chud who was brave enough to try picking it up. Han agrees that he'll help them solve their evil warlord problem—but to do so, he'll need some additional help.

From here on out the movie follows *The Magnificent Seven*'s storyline pretty faithfully, with Han and Scipio bouncing from one place to another, collecting whatever plucky badass happens to be around and bringing them over to their cause. Naturally they number seven when all is said and done. This total includes a duplicitous gladi-ette named Julia, played by Sybil Danning in cleavage-enhancing armor. (This wasn't Danning's first twist on Kurosawa's heavily-recycled movie plot: she also starred in Roger Corman's 1980 sci-fi epic *Battle Beyond the Stars*, which was basically *The Magnificent Seven* but in space.) With this tough-as-nails septet finally in place, Han and crew travel back to the countryside to take down the evil Nicerote and his army in a pair of violent showdowns.

The Seven Magnificent Gladiators has neither the stop motion animation nor the occasionally laughable special effects that Cannon's two *Hercules* movies are known for. The closest we come are a few lighting effects each time someone unworthy takes hold of the magic blade, and an impressive pyrotechnic display when Nicerote finally meets his maker. This may actually have worked in the movie's favor, as the plot itself holds together more than its sister features. The simple, straight-forward storyline carries logically through the film; unlike the *Hercules* movies, the *Gladiators* plot does more than just link together splashy special effects scenes.

There are a few, telltale signs which give away the production's thriftiness, particularly the small number of extras. The Emperor's grand chariot race appears to have been attended only by a handful of interested Romans, and the movie's major battles have fewer combatants than your average Chuck Norris bar brawl. However, many of the shooting locations were actual, two thousand-year-old ancient Roman ruins, so it's not as if the money-skimping here lessens the production value as much as it would most other films. For a movie which needed to be shot quickly and at a low cost, Cannon wisely turned to a team who were finely tuned at doing just that.

The early sales ads for the film boasted some pretty top-notch sword and sandal-style artwork.

As with many of Cannon's Italy-based productions, the studio hired from a pool of the nation's most experienced grindhouse filmmakers. *The Seven Magnificent Gladiators* was helmed by Bruno Mattei, a collaborator of exploitation icons Jesus Franco and Joe D'Amato. He churned out a handful of hardcore women in prison and Nazisploitation films through the 1970s, and then linked up with screenwriter Claudio Fragasso, the eventual director of a frequent worst-movie-of-all-time contender, *Troll 2* (1990). Together the two made a string of explicit, low-budget nunsploitation, sex, and horror movies which included *Hell of the Living Dead* (1980) and *Rats: Night of Terror* (1984).

Cannon for some reason saw fit to hire the director of *Porno Holocaust* (1981) and the writer of *Women's Prison Massacre* (1983) to head up their PG-rated fantasy adventure, and *The Seven Magnificent Gladiators* was born. Surprisingly, their decision didn't result in the sort of inappropriate-for-children train wreck you might expect it to yield. The only titillation to be found here is Danning's skimpy body armor and an out-of-nowhere, girl-on-girl bikini wrestling segment which, trust me, is *tame* by Mattei's standards.

Although it lifts wholesale from *Seven Samurai* and *The Magnificent Seven* (and takes tiny swipes from *Raiders of the Lost Ark* [1981] and *Conan the Barbarian* [1982]), *The Seven Magnificent Gladiators* is a rather worthy homage to the popular peplums of the 1960s. Is it cheap-looking? Sure. Is it fun? Hell and damn yes.

It's also fun that can be enjoyed by gladiator fans of all ages: the violence is practically blood-free, like the sort you would have seen the old Steve Reeves *Hercules* flicks from the '50s and '60s. Lou Ferrigno, bless him, was intent on making his big screen appearance something that could also be enjoyed by the same, young kids who followed his adventures as The Incredible Hulk. Thus, explicit sex and violence were a no-go, and Ferrigno—poised to be Cannon's next big star—held enough sway over the studio to make such demands. And so the romance we get here is rather chaste: Danning and Harris do a little flirting, the other magnificent gladiators are paired off with village wenches for innocent canoodling, and Han occasionally makes eyes with a local beauty named Pandora (played by the star's real-life wife, Carla Ferrigno.)

While it's cheap and cheesy, *Gladiators* will usually be good fun for anyone who chooses to watch it. However, the same can't be said for the people who made it. As co-stars, Ferrigno and Danning did *not* get along while making *Gladiators*.

We only get Danning's side of the story, as she was the only one who vocalized her complaints about her co-star—and indeed, she was *very* vocal about how much she disliked working with The Hulk. She trash talked him on talk shows, in a *Playboy* interview, and in a nasty, 1983 *Action Films* magazine cover story titled "Sybil Danning vs. Lou Ferrigno: Battle of the Sexes." The actress alleged sexism and vanity on Ferrigno's part. According to the article, Ferrigno was uncomfortable sharing screen time with a female gladiator and repeatedly coerced the director to reduce her role in fight scenes, or to move her character into the background. (Although we only have Danning's point of view to go on as to the reason, it's true that her character is given very little to do during the movie's many battles, and hardly participates in the action herself.) Danning said that it got so bad that some of her scenes, such as the sequence where she goes toe-to-toe with a man in a tavern drinking contest—which mirrors a scene in the first Indiana Jones film—had to be filmed in secret, when Ferrigno wasn't on set.

By the time *Gladiators* had wrapped its six week shoot, Ferrigno and Danning weren't on speaking terms, which was a big problem considering that they were under contract to start filming *Hercules* together two weeks later. The way Danning puts it, their mutual disgust with one another is the reason her role in *Hercules* was changed at last minute, from the hero's love interest to the movie's antagonist.

Unimpressed with the movie's rough cut, Cannon deemed *Gladiators* unfit for release, and exiled it to the backburner for a full year while *Hercules* got underway. Later on Golan and Globus recruited their *Hercules* director, Luigi Cozzi, to film new, replacement scenes with Ferrigno and a group of Italian actors with hopes of salvaging *Seven Magnificent Gladiators*. Instead they used those scenes to make a *Hercules* sequel without telling their lead actor. For that crazy story, though, you'll need to turn back to our chapter on the *Hercules* series . . .

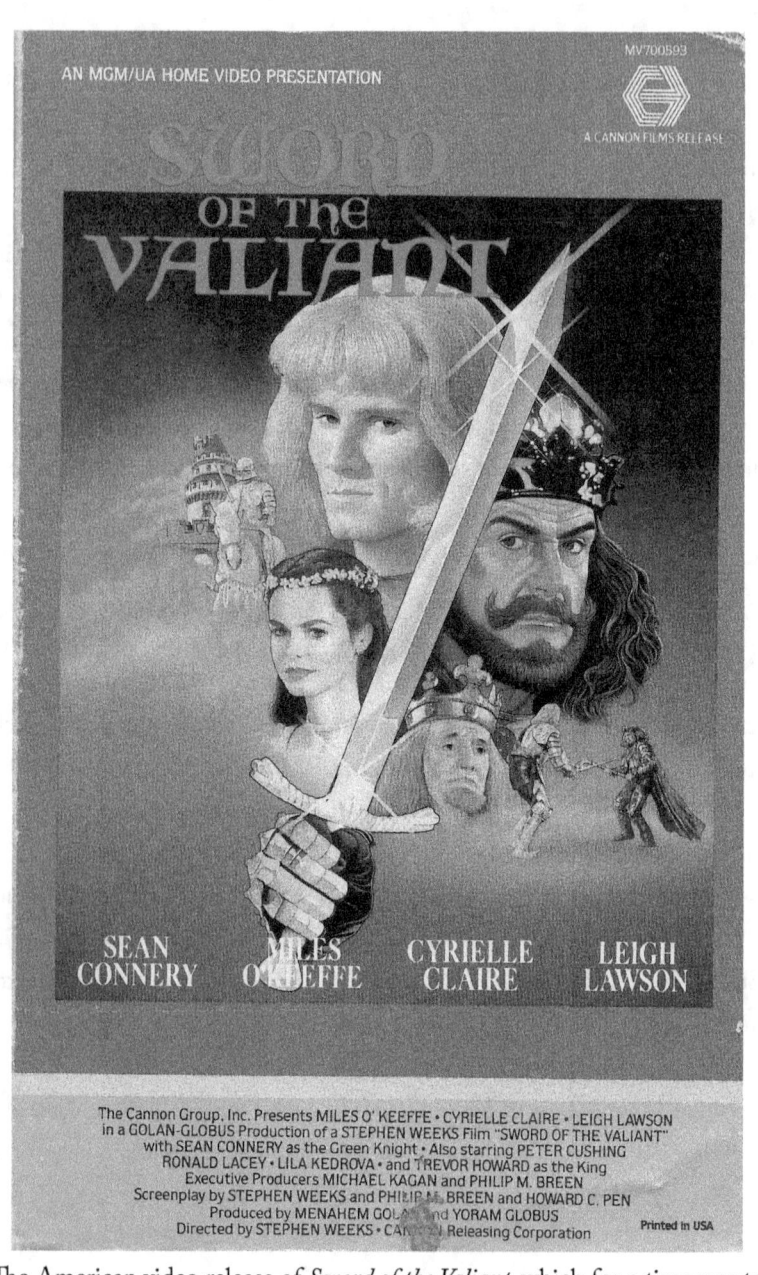

The American video release of *Sword of the Valiant*, which for a time was to be called "Clash of the Swords."

Sword of the Valiant:
The Legend of Sir Gawain and the Green Knight

Release Date: August 17, 1984
Directed by: Stephen Weeks
Written by: Philip M. Breen, Howard C. Pen, Stephen Weeks
Starring: Miles O'Keeffe, Sean Connery, Cyrielle Clair, Peter Cushing, John Rhys-Davies
Trailer Voiceover: "Sean Connery throws down the gauntlet of challenge... Sir Gawain accepts, and sets out on a dangerous adventure marked by combat and the promise of death!"

In the early '80s, there were few movie stars who were bigger than Sean Connery. While he was, of course, best known as James Bond, his star power was enough to carry multiple movies per year for two solid decades leading into Cannon's *Sword of the Valiant*. You figure it must have been very exciting for Golan and Globus to lock him up as the star of their upcoming, medieval fantasy film. So what if he was only available for a few days between shooting scenes of his seventh Bond film, *Never Say Never Again* (1983)? They could work around that.

Oddly enough, *Sword of the Valiant* was director Stephen Weeks' second time filming this particular Arthurian legend. The movie is technically a remake of his earlier 1973 film, *Gawain and the Green Knight*, which starred singer Murray Head of "One Night In Bangkok" fame. The original film was not a hit—with critics, or with audiences—so we're left scratching our heads in regards to how or why this second version came to be.

Both films are inspired by the famous, fourteenth century poem, and for the most part retains only its basic premise. In the poem, a mysterious, green-armored knight wanders into Camelot and bizarrely challenges any knight who dares to try to lop off his noggin with a single swipe of an axe. As return payment for the first axe swing, they must allow him to return the blow in the event that they fail. Only Sir Gawain accepts the wager, but he fails to kill the stranger. In a moment of measured mercy, the Green Knight generously gives Gawain one more year to enjoy his head while it's still attached to his shoulders. It's a morbid poem, sure, but that's apparently the sort of thing that entertained people living in the 1300s.

On to *Sword of the Valiant*. We're introduced to the fresh-faced Gawain as he does some shirtless blacksmithing. (For safety's sake, shouldn't he be wearing, like, an apron or something?) He's played by Miles O'Keeffe, best known at this point for playing Tarzan to Bo Derek's Jane in the erotic, softcore re-interpretation of *Tarzan, the Ape Man* from 1981.

"How Much O'Keeffe is in this movie?" "Miles O'Keeffe!" Any other *Mystery Science Theater 3000* (1988–1999) fans in the house? O'Keeffe's second film in the sword-and-sandal Ator trilogy, *The Blade Master* (1982), a.k.a. *Cave Dwellers*, went on to be one of the fan-favorite episodes of the long-running movie-riffing show.

The story goes that Stephen Weeks' first choice to play Sir Gawain was Luke Skywalker himself, Mark Hamill, but Golan and Globus pushed for O'Keeffe instead. While Hamill would have probably made a more convincing young knight, he almost certainly would not have provided the chiseled beefcake that O'Keeffe brings to the table. Even more distracting than Gawain's lack of protective wear, however, is his hilarious, blonde wig. He looks like the Dutch Boy paints mascot was gene-spliced with He-Man's Prince Adam; even Zooey Deschanel's stylist would agree that his bangs are a little too much.

We next see Gawain—now fully clothed—at the Camelot Christmas party, where King Arthur is going through some serious holiday blues. (He's played by English actor Trevor Howard, known for *Brief Encounter* [1945] and *The Third Man* [1949].) King Arthur calls a stop to the feasting so that he can whine about how un-knightly his knights have become, complaining about how none of them go out questing or doing other badass shit anymore. Before Arthur can finish his little hissy fit about how much his knights suck these days, though, the Green Knight (Sean Connery, hooray!) busts through the castle's front door, Kool Aid Man-style, as a bunch of leaves blow in behind him.

The theatrical poster really showcases the cast's fabulous hairstyles.

If the bright red suspenders, boots, and space bikini he wore in 1974's *Zardoz* prove anything, it's that Connery has never been too shy to wear a silly costume. The get-up he dons in *Sword of the Valiant*, however, sets a new benchmark for spectacularity. His shiny armor appears to have been spray-painted green from head to toe, while Connery himself appears to have been spray-tanned an orangey bronze. He wears a large, unruly wig and a fake hobo beard, both of which have been tossed with more glitter than a first grader's holiday craft fair project. On his head he wears a leaf-shaped crown topped with green antlers and holly berries. For some inexplicable reason, a large hole has been cut out of his breastplate, leaving a carpet of Connery's chest hair visible for all the world to see.

Oddly enough, no one is the least bit concerned that this flamboyantly-dressed wood spirit has sashayed into their impenetrable fortress. They don't even seem all that surprised when he proposes a crazy game, one that involves taking turns attempting to remove one another's head with his axe. (Basically roshambo, but with decapitation.) Whiney, old King Arthur gets especially pissy when no one volunteers to murder this stranger in their court. Finally, Gawain steps forward—still a lowly squire—and requests the honor of killing the eccentric old man. Impressed by his can-do attitude, King Arthur knights Gawain on the spot.

The newly-minted Sir Gawain takes the axe. Connery pops a squat. Down comes the hatchet, and off comes the head. This seems to play out the way you'd expect it to, until . . .

On the cold, stone floor, the Green Knight's severed head begins to laugh. To the filmmakers' credit, this scene is effectively creepy, even with a fake-looking, animatronic head. Or, perhaps it's creepy *because* it's an animatronic head? (Welcome to the Uncanny Valley. I hope you enjoy your stay.)

The *finally* stunned crowd watches in horror as the Green Knight's body calmly retrieves his head, and then places it back on his shoulders. The Knight takes back his axe, but pauses before returning the decapitating blow to Gawain. Deciding he's too young yet to lose his life in a wandering stranger's psychotic murder game, the Green Knight gives Gawain a year to "grow his beard" before he loses his head—that is, unless he can solve the following riddle in those twelve months' time:

"Where life is emptiness, gladness. Where life is darkness, fire. Where life is golden, sorrow. Where life is lost, wisdom."

Because the riddle sounds like four lines stolen from vague, poorly-composed fortune cookies, Gawain's future looks pretty bleak. At least King Arthur is happy, though, because honor has been restored to his kingdom. He gifts Gawain his suit of ceremonial armor and wishes him the best of luck on his quest. Unfortunately for the rookie knight, just what exactly that quest entails isn't entirely clear. So, Gawain sallies forth with a trusty servant named Humphrey (Leigh Lawson) and hijinks naturally ensue.

Once Sir Gawain has left Camelot, the movie appears to have as little grasp on what's going on as the audience does. Our hero stumbles from one episodic adventure to the next, hunting a unicorn, having dinner with a witch, making rainbows appear in the sky with the toot of a magical horn, and learning how to more easily urinate through his armor with the use of a can opener. You see, *Sword of the Valiant* takes a sudden, unexpected "humorous" twist once the action moves away from the castle. It's especially jarring considering how serious and unfunny the film's opening scenes are. (Well, except for Connery's outfit, which is the funniest thing in the whole movie.)

None of what happens is of much consequence until he encounters the Black Knight, who stands guard over a kingdom hidden by sorcery. (The Black Knight's voice sounds an awful lot like Megatron's in the original *Transformers* cartoon, primarily because of the weird, electronic flange effect it's filtered through.) Gawain defeats the Black Knight in combat and is then led to his secret castle, where guards attempt to arrest Gawain for murder. He escapes, but only because a beautiful princess slips him an invisibility ring. Believe me, the chain of events seems just as random when you're actually watching the movie.

Gawain and Princess Linet (Cyrielle Clair) sleep together, but he later awakes to find her arguing with the crusty old Lady of the castle, played by Academy Award-winner Lila Kedrova, about whether or not he's qualified to be the new guardian of their kingdom. (Kedrova won Best Supporting Actress for 1964's *Zorba the Greek*.) At first the Lady is reluctant; the black knight was her husband, see, and so hiring his killer as his replacement is an understandably touchy proposal. Her attitude changes as soon as she sees what a toned slab of meat Gawain is. The old woman decides that if the young knight is to be spared for his crimes, he must marry her instead of the princess if he's to become the kingdom's new champion.

An early sales pitch featuring 100% fewer silly wigs.

Obviously this won't do for Gawain and his princess, who have fallen madly in love over the course of the few lines of dialogue they've shared. They attempt to run away together but are quickly discovered; although Gawain's able to singlehandedly beat up every guard in the castle, he's only able to slip away in the end with more help from his magical invisibility ring. Back in the real world, the Green Knight—remember him?—is peeved to find out that Gawain is cheating at his game by using a magical ring, even though he never really spelled out any clear rules saying that he couldn't do that.

Meanwhile, Gawain runs around having more silly adventures, buying gems from a traveling friar, seeking advice from a sagely dwarf (played by David Rappaport, one of the stars of Terry Gilliam's *Time Bandits* [1981]), doing battle with the black knight's ghost, and mercilessly smashing a talking frog, all before he's suddenly teleported back to Princess Linet's lost kingdom. For some reason, everyone there has been frozen in time and is now covered in cobwebs. He whisks the bewitched princess away from the castle, which breaks the spell.

While gathering firewood, Gawain bumps into his squire, Humphrey, who has apparently been wandering the woods searching for him since we last saw him, more than 30 minutes earlier in the movie. While these two old pals catch up on each other's misadventures, Princess Linet is kidnapped by a villainous prince, because Sir Gawain is just the worst knight ever and can't even protect this poor girl for any longer than five minutes.

The princess becomes the unwilling prize in a power struggle between three brilliant character actors. Her captor, Prince Oswald (Ronald Lacey), desires the beautiful young maiden for himself, but his elder advisor (the great Peter Cushing!) believes that his father, Baron Fortinbras (John Rhys-Davies), should get first dibs on her. All three of these actors have been written about extensively in this book already. Lacey, of course, is best known for playing the melting Nazi in *Raiders of the Lost Ark* (1981) before making appearances in Cannon's *Sahara* and *Making the Grade* (both 1984). Cushing was a horror icon who became famous starring in many of Hammer's Dracula and Frankenstein movies, and who later co-starred in a little-remembered movie called *Star Wars* (1977). He previously appeared in Cannon's *House of the Long Shadows* (1983); in poor health, *Sword of the Valiant* was his penultimate film role. Rhys-Davies, of course, co-starred in *Raiders of the Lost Ark* with Lacey, and then in *Indiana Jones and the Last Crusade* (1989) with Sean Connery. *Sword of the Valiant* was one of four films he made for Cannon, which include *Sahara*, *King Solomon's Mines* (1985), and *Firewalker* (1986).

Back in the movie, Gawain and Humphrey mount a rescue mission. Not only does it fail, but Princess Linet appears to have been burnt to a crisp in a blaze that erupts amidst all of the chaos they caused. (Again: Gawain is the worst knight ever.) He spends the next several months pouting by himself in the woods, until eventually he's taken in by Fortinbras' less sadistic rival, Sir Bertilak. Gawain is pleasantly surprised to find Linet living in the kind baron's castle, as it turns out she was rescued—off-screen—by Bertilak and then granted her freedom. (Ugh, whatever.)

This particular artwork did a great job of making the film look a lot more exciting than it actually was.

With his borrowed year now at an end and the riddle seemingly unsolved, Gawain resigns to ride off and meet his grisly fate at the hand of the Green Knight. He's given a white horse, a new suit of shiny armor, and a pretty, green sash by Linet, and is sent along his way. En route to his certain demise, he once again inexplicably bumps into his trusty squire and a band of loyal followers, who accompany him along his journey. Even more inexplicably, they run into Prince Oswald and his men and a battle ensues in which Gawain gives the wicked prince the (strictly metaphorical) spanking he deserves.

The Green Knight finds Gawain on the battlefield. They ride off together to the Green Chapel, where Connery teases Gawain for not solving his riddles, and then again for flinching when he raises his axe. Before the Knight can strike the fatal blow, Gawain ties Linet's green sash around his neck. When the axe comes down, it passes straight through Gawain, leaving him fully intact and his head still firmly attached to his shoulders. (Weirdly, Gawain isn't the least bit surprised that the sash saved his life, even though he was never given any indication that it had magical properties.) Seeing an opening, Gawain stabs the Green Knight, who mumbles some poetic nonsense about the seasons changing and then crumbles into dust.

Our hero goes off to meet his princess. Alas, she informs him that she, too, had been living on a borrowed year, and that they must part ways. He professes his love and promises he'll never leave her; she invites him to touch her cheek. When he places a hand upon her face, she transforms into a bird and flies away. Tha-tha-tha-tha-tha-tha-that's all, folks! (What just happened?)

Sword of the Valiant was shot in the autumn of 1982, but the movie sat on Cannon's shelves for two years before being released with little fanfare in late 1984. The film reviewed poorly, and many dismissed it as another one of the cheapo, sword-and-sorcery films which had flooded video store shelves in the wake of 1982's *Conan the Barbarian*. In a contemporary review for *Time Out*, the critic compared the film's production values (unfavorably) to those of *Monty Python and the Holy Grail* (1975). Yowch.

You can blame the ridiculous wigs or the lack of budget, but one of the biggest problems with *Sword of the Valiant* is that it's a movie where so much happens but so little of it matters or makes sense. Gawain is the most passive of heroes, simply stumbling from one fantastic setting to another on a quest that's barely defined. Obviously, "Decipher the crazy tree-knight's freeform poetry—or DIE!" isn't the clearest objective for an adventure, but that might have been overlooked if Sir Gawain had kept himself occupied with cunning or courageous acts. He rarely does either, spending most of the movie pouting around the medieval, English countryside. When he does find himself in an interesting predicament, he always takes the cheapest way out. (*cough, cough* *magic ring* *cough*) In the end, it isn't even Gawain who solves half the riddle to which he spent a full year and the entirety of the movie questing for its answer. One line is actually figured out by Linet, and another is explained to him by the Green Knight himself!

In summary, Gawain is an awful hero. Thank goodness Sean Connery chose to go Full Forest Sprite in this movie, because that's really the best reason to see it.

Love Streams

Release Date: August 24, 1984
Directed by: John Cassavetes
Written by: John Cassavetes & Ted Allan
Starring: John Cassavetes, Gena Rowlands
Tagline: "The most beautiful love story of our time."

In the spectrum of American arthouse cinema, few names resonate as loudly as John Cassavetes'. An unwavering maverick from the beginning until the end, some have credited him as a founder of the independent film movement in the United States.

A New York City boy raised by Greek immigrant parents, the young, brash Cassavetes—who'd by this point already quit two colleges—enrolled in the theater department of the American Academy of Dramatic Arts, supposedly because he thought it would be a great way to meet pretty girls. While he presumably did meet lots of women within that community of budding thespians—including his future wife and fellow student, Gena Rowlands, whom he married in 1954—he also discovered he had a natural knack for acting. It wasn't long before Cassavetes started landing film and television roles, including a starring turn opposite Sidney Poitier in *Edge of the City* (1957) and the lead role on a short-lived P.I. show called *Johnny Staccato* (1959–1960).

The strangely psychedelic cover art for the VHS release of *Love Streams*, which had more than 20 minutes of runtime hacked away from the film.

Along the way Cassavetes became disenchanted with the way Hollywood made movies. He imagined a world where films weren't made only by major studios, but individuals. He compared that train of thought to the way Off-Broadway functioned alongside Broadway Theater, feeling there was room for both to not only exist simultaneously, but thrive. After he went off on a tangent about this on a promotional radio appearance, he was surprised to receive checks from donors who wanted to help him get his vision off the ground. Bringing together an almost entirely amateur crew, Cassavetes spent three years filming and re-working *Shadows* (1959), a movie about a young, light-skinned Black woman who passes for White in 1950s New York City. The film was a sensation, and one of the first independent productions to garner mainstream attention.

The copy that ran with early sales ads, such as the one above, seemed to pitch the movie as a heartwarming comedy—which it certainly wasn't.

The early acclaim for *Shadows* landed Cassavetes a pair of Hollywood directing jobs, but he found work within the studio system to be miserable. He continued taking on-screen roles, including an Oscar-nominated supporting turn in *The Dirty Dozen* (1967) and playing Mia Farrow's untrustworthy husband in the classic *Rosemary's Baby* (1968). He funneled the paychecks he brought home for his acting into financing his own independent features, which usually featured many of the same faces. The Cassavetes stable included such fine actors as Peter Falk, Seymour Cassel, Val Avery, and Gena Rowlands, who each appeared in five or more of the dozen films Cassavetes directed in his lifetime. Rowlands earned Oscar nominations for her performances in two of her husband's films: 1974's *A Woman Under the Influence* and 1980's *Gloria*. Cassavetes himself received nods for Best Director with *A Woman Under the Influence*, and for Best Screenplay with *Faces* (1968). Many great filmmakers would eventually cite him as an inspiration for their own work, from Martin Scorsese to Robert Altman.

Now, such an illustrious biography begs only one question: why the *heck* was Cassavetes working for Cannon?

The interest, it turns out, was mutual.

From the beginning, Golan and Globus had visions for Cannon which were far grander than the cheap genre movies the company had been known for before they took over—and which they had more or less continued to produce in force for their first few years at the helm.

Although he's best remembered as a begetter of schlock, Menahem Golan was a ravenous fan of cinema whose tastes ran the gamut from lowbrow crowd-pleasers to the highest of art. While the heads of Cannon were experts at making the sort of cheap, exploitation flicks they could easily sell for a profit, there was a strong desire to produce movies that were about more than just ninjas and happy hookers. There was a level of prestige which Cannon would need to achieve before they would be included in the same conversations as the MGMs, Foxes, and Warner Brothers of the world. With dreams of olive branches and Academy Awards, Cannon put out calls to many of the world's most renowned cinematic auteurs. It can be assumed that—at least this early on—most of these frou-frou *artistes* simply shrugged them off. Cassavetes, on the other hand, was one of the first prestigious filmmakers to take the Go-Go Boys seriously.

For all of the respect he'd earned in arthouses and abroad, Cassavetes wasn't a director with whom studios were exactly rushing to collaborate. His films were almost intentionally non-commercial; on top of that, word had gotten around that he could be difficult to work with. While making *A Child is Waiting* (1963), one of his first studio jobs, Cassavetes was so hard on his star, Judy Garland, that the two of them had to be physically restrained during one especially heated altercation. After discovering that the studio had re-cut the film before releasing it without his consent, he reputedly struck his producer in the face.

Cassavetes was nothing if not ferociously independent: any outside meddling with his vision might be met with stubborn backlash. His directorial style, which called for loose schedules which allowed his actors time to explore their characters—and for Cassavetes' daily script revisions—was a poor match for a studio's rigid shooting calendar. One time after a successful test screening was met with applause, Cassavetes is said to have gone back and re-edited the movie so that it would receive a less positive reaction but better match his artistic vision. Needless to say, studios had a hard time giving money to a filmmaker with such blatant disregard for their bottom line.

Cassavetes was desperate to make another movie on his own terms, and needed the financial backing of a studio willing to not interfere in his methods. Cannon, desperate to reverse their reputation within the industry and make themselves more attractive to other auteurs, were willing to bend over backwards to meet Cassavetes' demands. Even without a final script to show Golan and Globus, ink was put to paper and Cassavetes had a deal to make *Love Streams* for Cannon.

From Cassavetes' perspective, his contract with Cannon must have been among the best he could have hoped for. He was given a budget of around $2 million, far more than he'd ever had at his disposal with his self-financed pictures. He was also guaranteed final cut, which was important to him after films such as *A Child is Waiting* had been taken out of his hands and re-cut by their distributors before release. Lastly, he asked for and received 13 weeks to shoot the movie. This final bullet point is all the more incredible when you consider that the grand majority of *Love Streams* was set in one location, which also happened to be Cassavetes' own home. Any other Cannon director would have been given two weeks to wrap the same material.

Cassavetes' plan had ostensibly been to adapt the stage play of the same name written by his longtime friend, Ted Allan, though the play and Cassavetes' film bear only a passing resemblance to each other. He had staged the play as part of a trilogy in Los Angeles in 1981, to mixed critical reception and a personal financial loss. (In true Cassavetes fashion, he had poured $200,000 of his own money into renovating the theatrical space he was using, and then priced tickets so low that it would be impossible to recoup his investment.) Jon Voigt—who'd later receive a Best Actor nomination for his role in Cannon's 1985 tour de force, *Runaway Train*—had starred in the stage version opposite Gena Rowlands. When Voigt demanded that he be the one to direct the film version of *Love Streams* or he'd walk away from the project, Cassavetes had no choice but to step into the role himself.

In *Love Streams*, Cassavetes plays a character named Robert Harmon. He's a writer—a very wealthy one—and well-known enough that strangers sometimes recognize him from television appearances. The novels he writes are varyingly described as being about women, and being about sex. Robert himself admits he only likes women, and bears a bitter disdain for other men. True to his word, he seems to only keep company with women, and many of them. When we meet Robert, his Los Angeles mansion is overflowing with women. (Are they prostitutes? We have to assume. He writes them checks, yet they appear to maintain at least semi-permanent residence.) Even outside his home, we only ever see him in pursuit—or procurement—of yet more beautiful women.

Robert woos a much younger nightclub singer (Diahnne Abbott of *Taxi Driver* [1976]), only to face plant—literally and figuratively—on her doorstep in an alcoholic stupor. We get the impression that he has always run into trouble with booze, and never had much respect for the women he did welcome into his life. When one of his ex-wives arrives at his door asking him to watch his own eight-year-old son, Albie—a boy whom Robert hasn't seen since birth, and is in all regards is a total stranger—Robert greets her with outright hostility. As for the child, Robert has little idea how to relate with him other than to treat him almost as a peer: he pours the eight-year-old a Heineken, and then dumps him off in a Las Vegas hotel room while he goes out for a weekend of whoring.

Gena Rowlands stars as Sarah Lawson, an elegant but unstable woman of wealth. Her first scenes are set in the midst of divorce proceedings, where she sits in a cramped conference room opposite lawyers, her teenage daughter, Debbie, and her soon-to-be ex-husband (played by Seymour Cassel, another of Cassavetes' repertory players.) It's obvious that Sarah loves her family very much; perhaps *too* much, if that can be said of one's love for a husband and child. Sarah is quite evidently ill, speaking casually of time spent voluntarily institutionalized, and collapsing in a heap at the mere suggestion that her influence within the familial unit has turned toxic. Her love for her family is an all-consuming obsession: it's unclear whether she still perceives of herself as an individual outside of her position as a mother and (ex) wife. Her husband has had enough, and her erratic behavior is rapidly alienating their daughter, of whom she loses custody early in the film's runtime. Suddenly finding herself cut loose to the wind, Sarah does not know how to function on her own.

Sarah shows up at Robert's door just a day after his long-lost son. From their very first embrace, it's apparent that she may be the only woman that Robert has every *truly* loved. Their relationship is—to put it mildly—weird, but tender. They've clearly known each other for a long time, and look upon one another with utter adoration. However, this doesn't stop Robert from whisking Albie away for that aforementioned weekend of drinking and whoring on the Las Vegas strip, just moments after she arrives. When Robert returns the neglected (and traumatized) Albie to his worried mother, he's rightfully beaten and bloodied by the boy's outraged stepfather. It's then that Robert stumbles home to finally share in a quiet moment with Sarah.

It's not until almost three-quarters of the way into the film that *Love Streams* reveals the nature of Robert and Sarah's relationship: they're brother and sister. The film never attempts the faintest explanation as to what sort of childhood could have resulted in two such attractively dysfunctional adults. Indeed, it can hardly keep the two of them in the same place—the siblings are frequently dispersing to pursue their own desires. (Sarah goes out to incompetently pick up men at a bowling alley; Robert, oddly enough, treats himself to a night of champagne and dancing with his latest girlfriend's shut-in mother.) Their unexpected reunion does give them the one thing they each so desperately need in that very moment: someone to love with all of their heart.

"An Extremely Painful, Agonizingly Funny Brother-Sister Act." Yet another rather misleading sales ad, this is one of the few pieces of marketing material which gave away the nature of its leads' relationship.

Love Streams plays out over an unspecified number of days, but a relatively brief period in its characters' lives. Describing it as light on plot might be overstating how much story is actually there. On the other hand, it's a supremely fascinating character study rendered with two of the most enigmatic performances ever committed to celluloid. It's a film that's intentionally vague, but so ripe for interpretation that it's near-impossible to stop thinking about.

The movie can be read on numerous levels, starting with its clever title. On first consideration, *Love Streams* is usually translated as a noun followed by a verb, i.e., love *streams*, as in how Robert gives himself without direction to so many different women, or how Sarah pours her heart out continuously to her husband and daughter. It may also be an adjective followed by a plural noun, as in reference to a line said by Sarah, who describes the love between two people as being like a stream that never stops running. ("Oh, it stops," responds her shrink, played by Rowlands' actual brother.) When you say the title aloud, however, only then does its real brilliance reveal itself. When spoken, *Love Streams* sounds remarkably like the words "love's dreams," a phrase both beautiful and extraordinarily apropos, given Sarah's—and eventually Robert's—numerous, feverish fantasies.

Throughout the movie we're treated to brief scenes of Sarah's frequently disturbing dreams and hallucinations. After one pathetic attempt to reconnect with her husband, who isn't having it, she dreams of running him and her daughter over with an automobile, killing them both. In one particularly maddening burst of manic behavior—and the film's only completely improvised scene—Sarah imagines herself trying to make her husband and daughter laugh by using an arsenal of dime store novelties, from a water-squirting corsage to a set of wind-up, chattering teeth. In the movie's finale, she dreams they're all part of a grand opera; it's a hyper-stylized moment of fantasy that is frankly jarring amidst the movie's otherwise strident naturalism.

These scenes are all clearly defined as dreams, but Robert and Sarah's reality itself blurs that line, particularly after the two finally come together. In perhaps the film's most memorable sequence, Sarah resolves to fix her brother by buying him "a baby," as she describes it. (Until she elaborates that the "baby" is small and fuzzy, you can reasonably wonder whether she's talking about buying an actual, human infant.) The next morning she visits an animal shelter and returns to Robert's home with nothing less than a full menagerie of critters, including a duck, a goat, a mean-looking dog, and two miniature horses, all of which rode back with her inside a taxi cab. She leads these animals—as Robert watches, dumbfounded—through his front door and releases them into his back yard. These creatures become a fixture of their environment for the rest of the film.

The movie's ending is as baffling as it is unforgettable. Awoken refreshed from a state of being near-comatose, Sarah makes up her mind to depart in the height of a thunderstorm, even while Robert's begging her to stay. Powerless to stop her and suddenly appearing very lonely, Robert lounges in his study, the ever-present glass of liquor in his hand. He stares silently off-screen, off-handedly remarking about headlights outside his window, and out of nowhere begins to laugh like a maniac. This strange, frightening shot continues for an uncomfortable and lengthy amount of time. He finally asks someone sitting out-of-frame, "Who the fuck are you?" It then cuts to a naked man, who sits in a chair opposite our main character. This man, whom we've never seen before, cracks a grin, and then transforms into Robert's newly-acquired canine. We realize, then, that Robert is hallucinating, and we're being made privy to his point of view. It's a piece of cinematic surrealism that would not have been out of place in a film by Luis Bunuel or Federico Fellini.

Cassavetes never bothered to explain the significance of the naked dogman that closed out his penultimate feature, and shockingly few of his critics have attempted to do so themselves. *Love Streams* is not a film concerned with answers. Once you know more about the backstory of this particular work and can try to peer into its filmmaker's mental state at the time, only then can you begin to understand what unfolds on screen.

At some point not long into *Love Streams'* production, Cassavetes was told by doctors that he would not live until the end of the year. Only 53 years old, decades of hard drinking and long hours had left his liver completely shot. He chose not to reveal the grim news to his cast and crew, which was mostly comprised of his closest friends and family, instead barreling onward as if nothing was wrong. He knew that *Love Streams* would likely be the last film he'd ever make, and he was resolved to go out on a statement.

It had been a normal part of Cassavetes' process to rewrite his screenplays as he went, revising dialog and amending scenes as the actors inhabited their characters during shooting. With *Love Streams*, however, Cassavetes threw out almost half the script less than midway into production. As he filmed, he truly had no idea where these characters were going, and didn't care.

Cast and crew came around to figure out that Cassavetes was no longer making the movie they'd signed on for and, to their credit, stuck with him. Diahnne Abbott, who plays the singer Robert tries to seduce, was meant to play a much larger part in the movie's second half, only to find her scenes almost entirely excised from the shooting schedule. (As a consolation, Cassavetes let her write her character's goodbye scene.) While the locations stayed the same, the dialogue was re-written up to the moment it was shot, while the director-star and his fellow players figured out the directions they would take their characters. Because the schedule negotiated from Cannon was so lenient, the shooting became more experimental as it went on, with Cassavetes demanding sometimes dozens of takes of the same shot so that he would have a wealth of choices in the editing room. Neither actors nor filmmaker had any idea which takes would make their way into the final film.

The resulting film clocks in at 141 minutes and moves at an almost dreamlike pace. Cassavetes had consciously tossed continuity to the wind while editing, inserting scenes into the film out-of-order from where they arrived in the script. (Most notably, his character opens the movie with wounds to his hand and head that aren't sustained until later in the film's runtime.) Cannon, whose films normally came in at around the 95-minute mark, begged him to trim it down to at *least* two hours, so that they could squeeze more screenings out of each print. Cassavetes wouldn't budge and didn't have to, as his contract gave him final cut. Given his fatal diagnosis and the knowledge that *Love*

Streams would probably be the last film he would ever make, he wasn't going to let his movie be compromised for any reason.

It wasn't until the film won accolades at international festivals that Cannon finally figured out how to market it: with laurel wreaths.

Love Streams played very well on the European festival circuit, going so far as winning the Golden Bear (the equivalent of "Best Film") at the 1984 Berlin International Film Festival. In the United States, however, the response was dramatically more subdued. Critical response was neutral to warm, largely concluding that the film succeeded in spite of the things they didn't yet appreciate about Cassavetes' filmmaking style. (Like much of the director's later work, *Love Streams* wasn't regarded as a consensus masterpiece until after his death.) It was released on August 24, 1984, to low attendance in limited cities. The cash-strapped Cannon had little money to give it much of a marketing push, and after the quiet turnout it was pulled from release. MGM did release the film on VHS—with some oddly psychedelic cover art—as part of their distro deal with Cannon, but butchered the film by chopping out more than 20 minutes of its runtime for videotape. (Cassavetes' final cut clause only applied to the theatrical release of the movie and had no stipulations over the video release, it turns out.) The director's cut went little-seen for almost 30 years, until the movie was re-issued on Blu-ray and DVD.

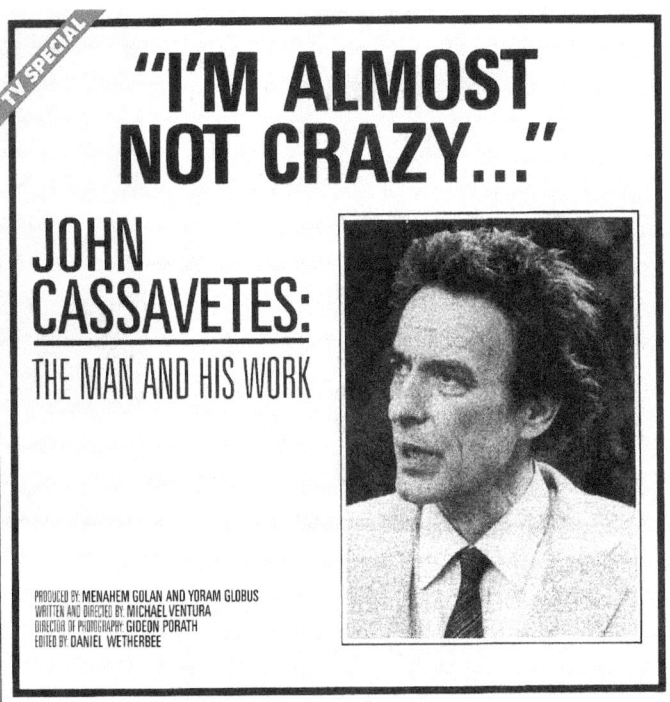

An ad for Michael Ventura's documentary about the making of *Love Streams* from Cannon's 1985 catalog. The documentary itself wouldn't be widely seen until years later.

As for Cassavetes, he outlived his prognosis by about five years. *Love Streams* was indeed his last on-screen performance, but not the final movie he directed—though, perhaps he wished it had been. (He was hired to replace director Andrew Bergman on *Big Trouble* [1986], a studio film he had not written himself and had such a bad experience making that he mostly disowned it through the few remaining years of his life.) Cirrhosis eventually took his life in February of 1989, at the age of 59; he left behind dozens of unproduced screenplays and other writings. Like so many other great artists, his true genius wasn't universally appreciated until after his passing. While he spent the last decade of his abbreviated life unable to get his many, varied projects off the ground, he is now regarded as one of the most important figures in American independent cinema.

Interestingly, the making of *Love Streams* is perhaps the most-documented of any Cannon release. Author, filmmaker, and newspaper critic Michael Ventura was invited on set to chronicle the film's production; he'd act as a frequent sounding board for Cassavetes, and the footage he shot would later be edited into a Making Of-style documentary for Cannon. The resulting, hour-long film, *I'm Almost Not Crazy: John Cassavetes, the Man and His Work*, was not released until 1989, in the wake of the director's passing. (Ventura later published an equally compelling book, *Cassavetes Directs – John Cassavetes and the Making of Love Streams*, extrapolated from his daily notes taken on set, and it reads like a novel.) The documentary is a fascinating glimpse into the director's style and filmmaking philosophy. Like the crew, Ventura was unaware of the director's illness; from the behind-the-scenes footage, you can see what an incredible job Cassavetes did in hiding it. Menahem Golan makes an appearance in the documentary, pleading with Cassavetes to deliver him a rough assembly to show his investors at MGM. Golan also glowingly compares the director to Ingmar Bergman, which shows the amount of respect he had for Cassavetes' work.

Bolero

Release Date: August 31, 1984
Directed by: John Derek
Written by: John Derek
Starring: Bo Derek, Andrea Occhipinti, George Kennedy, Ana Obregon
Trailer Voiceover: "Once in a while, a film dares to be different; dares to be daring; dares to be *Bolero*! ... A movie so daring, we can only show you where the ecstasy begins."

In the early '80s, Cannon poured millions of dollars into a 1920s-set erotic adventure film about a wealthy, virgin heiress (Bo Derek) who travels the globe in search of tall, dark men to deflower her. She hightails it to Spain and comes romantically in between a matador and his 14-year-old gypsy girlfriend, gets kidnapped by an Arab sheik, and eventually cures her boyfriend's bull-gored penis with the help of a naked horseback ride. While to a normal person that may not seem like a *great* investment, at the time it wasn't a totally insane idea, either. To understand *Bolero*, you need to be able to appreciate who Bo Derek was in the early 1980s: perhaps the most famous naked person in the world.

Chances are that while our younger readers are at least *aware* of Bo Derek—either from her role in the David Spade/Chris Farley romp *Tommy Boy*

(1995), or for appropriating cornrows as a hairstyle for White women—I figure it's likely some background info is in order.

Bolero on Betamax, from a private collection. The film did very well on home video, for all of the reasons you can probably surmise.

Born the daughter of a Hollywood hairdresser, the future Bo Derek—birth name Mary Cathleen Collins—spent her teen years as a beach bum, having dropped out of school to become a full-time sunbather on Los Angeles' coastal sands. At the young age of sixteen, this comely, sun-kissed teen caught the eye of washed-up actor turned low budget filmmaker, John Derek.

Derek was thirty years older than her and at the time married to his third wife—*Big Valley* (1965–1969) and future *Dynasty* (1981–1989) star Linda Evans—but that didn't stop the two from falling madly in love. John Derek left his wife and ran away with the teenage Bo to Europe. (This wasn't his first time at the rodeo: twenty years earlier he left his first wife, Pati Behrs, to run away with teenage future Bond girl, Ursula Andress.) The couple's stated reason for crossing the Atlantic was that they planned to make a movie there—but another reason was because Bo was still considered a minor in California, and John could possibly face statutory rape charges if they had stayed at home.

The first film John and Bo made together would eventually be titled *Fantasies*, about a teen girl who becomes romantically attracted to her brother while living on an island with their skeevy, overly-touchy grandpa. If the heavy incest theme wasn't creepy enough, young Bo's nude scenes—filmed when she was still a minor—were another sticking point for distributors. That film didn't see wide release until 1981, after Bo had become famous.

John Derek and his Bo-to-be finally married in 1979; she was 19, he was pushing 50. This was when John gave his young wife a movie star makeover: Mary Cathleen became "Bo," and bleached her hair to its now-famous blonde color. After an appearance in the *Jaws* knock-off *Orca: The Killer Whale* (1977), Bo was cast opposite Dudley Moore in the 1979 comedy *10*, about a middle-aged man who become obsessed with a beautiful young lady whom he deems to be the "perfect" woman. The film was a massive hit, going on to be one of the top grossers of its year. The movie's most famous scene is a fantasy sequence in which Moore's character dreams of Bo Derek in a red swimsuit, running over a sandy beach in slow motion, her blonde hair tied into cornrows. This is the image that, even today, most people will conjure at the mention of the name Bo Derek. If not from the movie *10*, they might know that image from the posters of the scene that were tacked up in garages, dorm rooms, and lockers all over America.

While *10* made her as a sex symbol, it didn't necessarily make her a movie star. Her next movie, *A Change of Seasons* (1980), in which she played a co-ed caught in an affair with her professor (Anthony Hopkins), was a bomb. Rather than allow Hollywood to dictate his wife's career, John and Bo set to work on *Tarzan, The Ape Man* (1981): a sexy reimagining of Edgar Rice Burroughs' famous adventure tales. Originally set to be called "Me, Jane," the story took a distinctive focus on Jane and her awakened sexual passions at the hands of jungle's savage "White ape." (The movie's original Tarzan—boxer Lee Canalito—was fired early in the shoot and replaced with his stunt double, future b-movie icon Miles O'Keeffe, who is written about extensively in this volume's chapter on the Cannon fantasy film *Sword of the Valiant* [1984].)

Starring and produced by Bo and directed and filmed by John Derek, the studio MGM—who produced a string of Tarzan movies in the 1930s—gave the Dereks carte blanche to shoot their vision of the Tarzan origin story. While it doesn't feature any explicit sex, the movie *does* find every conceivable reason it can to allow the camera to linger on our virginal heroine's naked body. She bathes in a jungle river, is stripped and showered by nude tribeswomen, gets body-painted white for a ceremonial de-flowering by an evil tribal leader, and at one point has her nipple licked by a chimpanzee. (Yep.)

The movie didn't feature any full frontal male nudity, either, but boy does it squeeze in its phallic symbols, from a big, shiny cannon that Jane's father eagerly polishes at crotch level, to a rubber python which our ape man wrestles for several minutes straight, to the banana that a monkey tosses Jane and she predictably, and *quite* suggestively, eats. The Edgar Rice Burroughs estate was understandably appalled by the Dereks' treatment of their beloved stable of characters and took the couple to court. (The judge ruled in Tarzan's favor and ordered that several scenes needed to be removed; considering what was left in the movie, I shudder to think of the horrors that were left on the cutting room floor.) Once you factor in an extremely weird relationship between

Jane and her dad that suggests an incestuous attraction, it's a wonder how this fascinating, train wreck of a film went on to rake in $35 million in ticket sales, making it the second highest-grossing R-rated film of 1981.

"An erotic masterwork." The German poster for *Bolero*, like those from many other foreign territories, wasn't shy about advertising the movie's contents.

Although they made a crazy amount of money with their smutty *Tarzan*, the big studios weren't exactly rushing to sign either of the Dereks' services. Critics viewed the movie as little more than an awkward spectacle to showcase Bo's nude body, which it was. Many described John's direction as incompetent, or panned Bo's line delivery for being as statuesque as her figure. The film was nominated for an impressive six Razzies the following year, with poor Bo netting the award for worst actress (in a tie with Faye Dunaway's infamous "No wire hangers!" performance in 1981's *Mommie Dearest*.) All the while, Bo had become a favorite subject for the trashier supermarket tabloids, and the butt of jokes by comedians like Joan Rivers, who was at the time a frequent guest host of *The Tonight Show*.

Perhaps most damning, the Dereks had earned a reputation among the studios for being difficult to work with. Their next project was announced to be a film called "Eve and that Damned Apple" and was briefly attached at Universal before fizzling away into nonexistence. Two years is a long time in Hollywood; time was ticking by, and Bo's career was going nowhere fast. Enter Cannon.

Cannon first approached the Dereks with a pitch to remake the Biblical epic *Samson and Delilah* (1949), which the couple shot down without a second thought. (We have to assume that they intended for Lou Ferrigno to play the role of the muscular Samson, and I can't tell you how sad I am that we never got Cannon's sexy reimaging of the Old Testament story.) John and Bo Derek countered with an idea for a film about two young women who travel the world on the hunt for exotic men, and Cannon took their bait. The company gave the Dereks a deal even better than the one the couple had to shoot *Tarzan* for MGM, promising them full artistic control of their feature.

Named after the sultry ballet composition by French composer Maurice Ravel—the same piece of music to which Bo famously made love to Dudley Moore's character in *10*—the movie would be a full-blown Derek production: written, directed, filmed, edited, and photographed by John, and starring and produced by Bo. Cannon was to effectively remain hands-off as the couple shot *Bolero*—or "Bo-lero," as it's hyphenated in many boastful production ads—in Morocco and Spain over the summer of 1983. At first the trade press reported that it would be a remake of a 1934 dance film of the same name, which starred George Raft and Carole Lombard. Oh, ho, ho, ho, no. No, it was not.

This 1983 sales ad described the movie as "high camp from the desert to Spain as Bo Derek roars through the Twenties and sheds the trappings of girlhood ... she finds love and lust and plays it all for laughs."

In the 1920s-set *Bolero*, Bo Derek plays a virginal (heh) orphan named Mac who—upon her graduation from a posh, English university—becomes, in her words, "an excessively rich little bitch," as her dead daddy's last will and testament leaves her with gobs and gobs of money. Lusting after old Hollywood stud Rudolph Valentino following a screening of the silent classic *The Sheik* (1921), Mac and her bestie, Catalina—Ana Obregon, previously of Cannon's *Treasure of the Four Crowns* (1983)—decide they'll travel to Morocco so that Mac can live out her dream of losing her virginity to a real-life sheik of her very own.

Before she leaves school, however, Mac doffs her top and traipses nude across the lawn, mooning her professors as the student body cheers and her family chauffeur, Cotton, makes his best attempt to protect the liberated young lady's modesty with a blanket. After her decency is finally restored, she apologizes to Cotton for embarrassing him. He tells her he wasn't embarrassed, no. Actually, he tells her he was "amazed by how much you've changed since the last time I've seen you without any clothes. I think you were three, or four. You've grown *well*." (Creepy sexual undertones from the heroine's father figure seem to be a running theme of John Derek's directorial filmography.)

Cotton is played by Oscar winner George Kennedy, who nabbed the supporting actor trophy for his role in *Cool Hand Luke* (1967). He's well-remembered for his recurring appearances in the *Airport* and *Naked Gun* franchises, and would return to Cannon to play a Catholic priest trapped aboard a hijacked plane in 1986's *The Delta Force*.

Mac and Cat fly off to Morocco on their sheik hunt with poor, old Cotton in tow. They wander the Kasbah for a few minutes before they stumble on their unsuspecting prey. (*Bolero*'s Moroccan sheik is played by blue-eyed English model Greg Bensen, an actor no more Arab than Rudolph Valentino. This was his only film role. Surrounded by locally-hired extras, he and Bo Derek appear Whiter than the desert sands.) Dressed in a dreadlock-like hairpiece of beaded crystals and little else, Mac wastes no time making the young, pretty sheik her indecent proposal: "I've come all this way to give you something you may not even want. My virginity!"

The sheik eagerly accepts and the two fly off together in his aeroplane. He complies with all of Mac's silly, romantic demands—sweeping her off her feet on horseback, seducing her in a tent in the desert—but fails to live up to the highly-romanticized expectations set by her beloved Valentino movies. Her biggest disappointment comes in bed, where he strips her down to nothing and drizzles her torso in a sticky concoction of milk and honey. Halfway into licking it off her belly—this is shown in *extreme* close-up and nauseatingly drawn-out slow motion—he passes out face-down on her stomach, having hit the hookah a little too hard beforehand.

Disappointed, the prowling pair of Mac and Cat promptly give up on the whole sheik fantasy and zip off to another place where they've heard the men are dark and sultry: Spain. Once again Mac falls madly in love with a man mere seconds after the setting's establishing montage. This time her objet d'affection is Angel, a horseback matador—or *rejoneador*—who isn't popular with audiences because he refuses to kill the bulls. (The American Humane Association surprisingly gave *Bolero* their stamp of approval, assuring that only the animals' dignity was harmed during filming of this movie.) Mac resolves to herself that the unsuspecting Angel will be her next conquest, and that all of his fiery, Spanish lovers be damned. Angel is played by Italian actor Andrea Occhipinti, who had starred in a number of spaghetti genre flicks, including Lucio Fulci's slasher *The New York Ripper* (1982) and his sword and sorcery movie *Conquest* (1983), as well as Lamberto Bava's giallo *A Blade in the Dark* (1983).

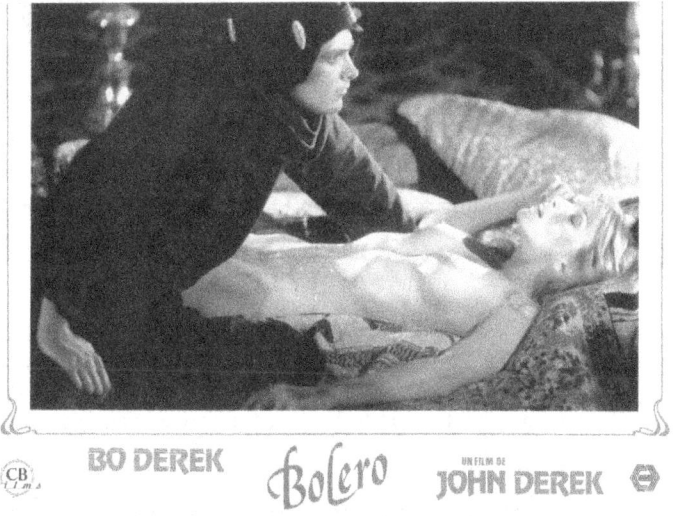

Mac (Derek) and her sheik (Greg Bensen) share a fleeting moment of sticky passion.

Mac and Angel's courtship is as quick as you'd expect, given our heroine's method of straight up throwing her sex at dudes. She gets close to him with the help of his feisty, underage gypsy girlfriend, Palomo, played by Olivia d'Abo, who went on to play Kevin Arnold's big sis, Karen, on *The Wonder Years* (1988–1993) for four seasons. Only 14 years old when shooting *Bolero*, d'Abo does an extended and wholly unnecessary bathing scene with full frontal nudity—a creepy-crawly little detail which didn't fail to escape critics' scrutiny.

While I can't claim to have any expertise in horseback riding, that probably isn't appropriate riding wear that Bo Derek has on in this promotional photo.

For a while Angel plays hard to get, but Mac's seduction tactics are similar to a hostile corporate takeover: after buying out his entire winery, Angel has no choice but to pay attention to her. He finally caves and agrees to help her with that virginity she's so eager to rid herself of. When Angel enters the bedroom he finds Mac standing on the bed, waving her arms and howling with a sheet hung over her head like she's a member of the Peanuts gang in the *It's the Great Pumpkin, Charlie Brown* (1966) holiday special. He asks Mac why she's dressed as a ghost. Her response: "I thought you should be as scared as I am!"

"You are a *ghost* that is *afraid*?" he asks, incredulous.

"That's about to wet its pants!" Mac oh-so-seductively clarifies.

Before they can get down to business, there's one more bit of awkward foreplay as Mac asks Angel to lie down on the bed. She leans over him and slowly extends her tongue what appears to be five or six inches from her mouth, into his ear. After that off-putting display, there are five solid minutes of graphic pelvic thrusting as fourteen-time Oscar-nominee Elmer Bernstein's flowery, orchestral love theme swells to suffocating volumes. (Most famous for his theme song for 1960's *The Magnificent Seven*, Bernstein only composed *Bolero*'s love scenes; his son, Peter Bernstein, wrote the rest of the movie's score.)

And just like that, Mac's mission to lose her pesky virginity is over. There is still more than 40 minutes' worth of runtime to fill, however, so a bunch of new subplots are introduced. Cat gets her own love story (and love scene), as does Cotton! One of Angel's jealous, jilted ex-lovers shows up at the sauna and tries to kill Mac with a knife, but Mac and Paloma are able to wrestle her out of the room. (They're topless while doing so, of course.) At another point, Arab men in black robes sneak into the estate and kidnap Mac. It turns out her sheik has decided he can't live without her, and plans to fly her home to Morocco where he'll force her to become his bride. Mac is able to shimmy free of her ropes and escapes by jumping out the sheik's plane without a parachute. As the movie suddenly cuts to Mac giggling about the whole incident the next day, we have no choice but to assume she landed safely on a pile of blankets somewhere.

The main subplot for *Bolero*'s third act, however, is more directly linked to Mac's never-ending quest for ecstasy. Just days after their first and only lovemaking session, Angel has the extreme misfortune of having his dick gored in a fluke bullfighting accident. While doctors tell him he'll never make whoopee again, Mac won't accept their diagnosis. As Angel hides in his room mourning his loss, Mac marches in with a promise to accomplish what modern 1920s medicine can't. Pointing an accusatory finger at him, she spits:

"That *thing* will work again," and then, with a confident smile and a big, fat thumbs up: "I guarantee it!"

The methods in which Mac goes about treating Angel's shredded genitals are holistic in nature, to say the least. Mostly she dedicates herself to becoming a skilled bullfighter in the hopes that his watching her stick flags onto the back of a bovine will somehow make his mangled penis erect once again. In one of the dually most uncomfortable-looking and least sanitary scenes you'll see in any movie Cannon ever produced, Mac attempts to seduce Angel by riding a horse bareback—and completely naked.

This Spanish lobby card captures the magical scene in which Bo Derek cures her lover's gored genitals with some naked horseback riding.

Ultimately, Mac proves that doctors don't know shit, because her crazy idea actually works. After watching Mac in her first fight against a live bull— you'll notice here that her horse's mane is braided into cornrows, like Bo Derek's famous hairdo in *10*—the two lovebirds go back to the house and will his boner into being. There's another several minutes of emphatic humping in a foggy fantasy realm that looks like somewhere an evil sorceress might call home in a Conan the Barbarian movie, and *Bolero* ends with Mac and Angel's wedding.

Had it been released like any other dirty movie or snuck into arthouse theaters as an "erotic film," *Bolero* would have received a few bad reviews, been seen by interested adults as a filthy curio, and then simply disappeared until it inevitably resurfaced on late-night premium cable alongside other softcore films of similar quality. Instead, the high-profile kerfuffle that unfolded between Cannon and the Dereks in the pages of trade papers and gossip magazines in the months before the movie's release, however, giftwrapped for *Bolero* the sort of publicity that money can't buy. Both sides got downright *nasty*.

Mac and Angel (Andrea Occhipinti) make love in a foggy fantasy realm.

Cannon and the Dereks clashed over copyright, contracts, casting, and money even before shooting began. It all boils down to a case of he said, she said, and so the account presented below is what I've been able to piece together from the numerous articles about their spat which were published over the course of 1984. It does sound as if Menahem Golan had a bit of buyer's remorse over the contract, and regretted signing over so much power to the duo. Attempts to win back things like screenplay rights and the final cut angered the Dereks; Cannon's withholding of finances as leverage downright infuriated them. When John Derek threatened to badmouth the company to every journalist at the Cannes film festival, Cannon capitulated and sent over the money. Things were smoothed over ... for a bit.

Just three days into shooting, the Dereks fired lead actor Fabio Testi, who was originally slated to play Bo's bullfighting amour. According to Golan, it was because Bo didn't like him—and because he was a former lover of Derek's ex-wife, Ursula Andress. According to the Dereks, it was because he had herpes. To keep Testi from suing them, Cannon had to promise him his full salary and a role in another movie. (He'd star opposite Robert Mitchum and Rock Hudson in *The Ambassador* in 1985.) Over the course of the shoot and to Cannon's frustration, the Dereks fired roughly half of their crew—or, let go of "dead weight," as John put it. Aggravating the duo further, the Dereks were forced to put expenses on their personal AMEX cards when Cannon's payments to vendors repeatedly arrived late. In normal cases, the most audiences would have heard about these matters was that the movie "had a troubled production." Rarely does the bulk of showbiz dirt reach the public—but in *Bolero*'s case, it did. All of it, and so much more.

The first, outward signs that trouble was bubbling in softporn paradise came in the form of a leaked memo from Cannon, in which several high-ups at the company expressed grave concern about *Bolero* after privately screening a rough cut for studio executives. The letter explained how the audience broke into "uncontrollable fits of laughter" only fifteen minutes into the film, and started loudly making fun of the movie as it played. This telex—which was meant for the Dereks' eyes only, and contained such descriptive phrases as "completely insufferable," "unreleasable," and "a total embarrassment"— somehow found its way into the hands of the *Los Angeles Herald Examiner*, who printed it. (Uh oh.)

This set off a bomb, and the private war being fought between Cannon and the Dereks was suddenly thrust out into the open. Cannon wanted the film recut, but John Derek—practically waving his contract, which gave them full control—refused, as altering the movie from the version he submitted would be a compromise to his artistic vision. The sticking point, it seems, was not the stuff that made the crowd laugh and jeer, but the movie's abundance of sex. When the company screened *Bolero* for the MPAA, they were told it would receive a "probable X." Cannon wanted this smoothed down to where it might receive an 'R' rating, and thus greatly increase the number of theaters that would be willing and able to book the movie.

The Dereks, livid, told the press that Cannon had encouraged them to make the film as sexy as possible, and had been "eager" to receive an X-rated *Bolero*. Whether or not that was true, the 'X' would be a problem for MGM, who were distributing Cannon's movies at the time. No major studio had put an X-rated movie into theaters since *The Last Tango in Paris* in 1972. This led the studio—who were reportedly fed up with the quality of material Cannon had been feeding them, anyway—to drop *Bolero* entirely and usie the film as an excuse to finally terminate their relationship with Cannon.

Now, most independent film companies would be reeling after having their entire distribution arm unceremoniously severed, but the plucky Cannon found a bright side to the situation. MGM may not have been able to release an X-rated movie, but there was no reason they couldn't do it themselves. No longer being asked to tame their steamier bits, it seems as if the Dereks were once again appeased. Like before, however, that would be short-lived.

Cannon prepped more than 1,000 prints for a summer release which, at the time, was the biggest-ever for an adults-only film. Just before *Bolero* was scheduled to hit theaters, Bo Derek appeared on the cover of the July issue of *Playboy*. The magazine published an entire spread of photographs taken of her while shooting the movie. While this would normally have been considered a major press coup so close to a movie's release, Cannon instead took the Dereks to court, claiming that the photos belonged to them as part of the movie's marketing materials and had been sold by John Derek without their permission. Just weeks before release, Cannon sued the Dereks again for withholding publicity stills that could be used to promote their movie. The Dereks countered that photo usage was a violation of their creative control. The judge ruled in Cannon's favor, stating that a movie's marketing was unrelated to the creative act of making the film.

By this point it was clear that Menahem Golan and the Dereks had not been on speaking terms for quite some time. They let their lawyers act as middlemen while exchanging heated insults through newspaper and magazine articles. If this all sounds very ugly, trust me: it was much worse when it played out in real time.

In one particularly nasty *Chicago Tribune* feature written by Jeff Silverman, John Derek calls Golan a "usurper," a "difficult egomaniac idiot," "an ignoramus," and "a ------- pig." (By the number of hashes, and the context and frequency of his hashed-out curses, we can assume John called him "a fucking pig.") Meanwhile, Bo refers to the producer as a "lying hypocrite" while accusing someone at the Cannon offices of stealing nude photographs from her bag, duplicating them, and then using them in the *Bolero* press kit. In that same piece, Golan paints John Derek as a stubborn artiste who can't be reasoned with: "Who can work with such an ego?"

Bad blood be damned, Golan's hopes clearly remained high for *Bolero*. He maintained that Cannon had a surefire hit on their hands through all of the back-and-forth trash talking. The Dereks' confidence, on the other hand, may have been fading.

"It's not the best picture in the world," John Derek admitted to the *Chicago Tribune*. "Compared to the other shit [Golan] has done, this is an absolute ------- Rembrandt." (Again, that's probably "an absolute *fucking* Rembrandt.") This is from a feature that ran only *five days* before the movie opened in theaters!

After all of the loud bickering over the movie's potential MPAA rating, Cannon finally opted to release *Bolero* without any rating at all. (They still capitalized on the film's controversy by misspelling the movie's tagline on certain posters: "An Adventure in e*X*tasy"—the 'X' being double the size of other letters.) This was a sneaky way of getting around the policies of theater chains, many of which were restricted from screening X-rated films. Cannon also promoted *Bolero*'s unprecedented wide release with a major marketing blitz. When some outlets refused to run ads for a dirty movie, Cannon simply doubled their spending in the places that would.

The film's reviews were absolutely brutal, ripping on everything from the film's ridiculous premise, to Bo's cringe-worthy performance, to John's laughable script, to the sex scenes that somehow lacked titillation despite being the main focus of the movie. In response, the Dereks doubled down on the defense they used after the film's fateful "private" screening for MGM executives, claiming that the movie's intense awkwardness was intentional on their part. "It's just a silly bit of fluff," John told the *Los Angeles Times*. "The film is meant to be corny," Bo continued. (They also went on and on about how mean the movie critics were for picking on them.) Intentionally goofy or not, this was a far cry from the "very lovely and commercially sexy" film Bo was quoted describing it as a few months earlier, or the "The Hottest Erotic Film of the Century," as it was marketed by Cannon.

It turns out that none of this stopped people from going to see *Bolero*, and the movie had an impressive opening weekend. Despite an acerbically negative review from *Variety*, Cannon took out a two-page ad in the publication proudly boasting that "BO is BOx-office," and boldly touting the movie's $4.5 million gross over its first four days. It went on to bring home nearly $9 million in U.S. theaters, and more abroad. The film was an even bigger hit in the channels where softcore films traditionally make their money, with the initial videocassette release selling more than 60,000 units in pre-orders alone and HBO coughing up $2 million for the cable rights. (Understandably, it's far less embarrassing to watch Bo Derek's naked horseback riding movie in the privacy of your own home.)

In spite of all of the nasty, negative publicity surrounding the film—or more likely, in large part *because* of it—*Bolero* has to be considered some level of a success, especially when you consider how hilariously awful it is, even by Cannon's lowered standards. In the course of watching their movies over and over again for the purpose of writing this book, *Bolero* was one of the few that felt like a chore to get through. I think that says a lot.

Bolero won a record-setting six Razzies in 1984, including Worst Picture, Worst Actress, Worst Director, Worst Screenplay, Worst New Star (d'Abo), and Worst Musical Score. It was nominated for three more, including d'Abo for Worst Supporting Actress, Occhipinti for Worst New Star, and Kennedy for Worst Supporting Actor—the last of which lost to "Brooke Shields with a Moustache" in Cannon's very own *Sahara*. (*Bolero* held the record for most Razzies until 1995, when *Showgirls* "won" seven awards.) In 1989, *Bolero* was one of five films nominated for the Golden Raspberry Awards' Worst Picture of the Decade. It didn't win, but Bo Derek *did* take home Worst Actress of the Decade.

Bo Derek, winner of the coveted Worst Actress of the Decade award.

Bo didn't appear in another movie for six years, until she and John made their final film together. Released in 1990, *Ghosts Can't Do It* made *Tarzan* and *Bolero* look like *Gone With the Wind* (1939) and *Casablanca* (1942). In this mind-numbingly unfunny sex comedy, Bo Derek's billionaire sugar daddy (Anthony Quinn) kills himself after a heart attack wrecks his ability to make love to his stunning young wife. (Quinn's character is said to be thirty years Bo Derek's senior. I wonder where the Dereks found that inspiration . . . ?) He returns to her as a ghost who only Bo can see and hear; the rest of the movie involves the two of them plotting to kill a hunky, tropical lothario so that the dead husband's ghost can possess his body and they can get back to, you know, doing it. (Because Ghosts *can't* do it. Get the title now?) As in the Dereks' prior films, Bo spends much of its runtime needlessly nude. *Ghosts Can't Do It* is a spectacularly bad movie worthy of an entire book of its own; nowadays, it's most notable for its Razzie-nominated supporting turn from future President Donald Trump, who plays a business rival of Derek's dead husband.

Exterminator 2

Release Date: September 14, 1984
Directed by: Mark Buntzman, William Sachs
Written by: Mark Buntzman, William Sachs
Starring: Robert Ginty, Mario Van Peebles
Trailer Voiceover: "The gangs are back on the streets . . . So is Ginty – burning with a vengeance!"

If you're not already familiar with this violent, vigilante franchise, I know what you're thinking. You're looking at that sweet, VHS cover art and thinking that this is probably another one of those *Terminator* (1984) knock-offs which rapidly multiplied—like jackrabbits in a bunny bordello—throughout the action and sci-fi shelves of your local video store in the latter half of the 1980s. With a name like *Exterminator 2*, it has to be, right? But no, no, no. In actuality, *Exterminator 2* was released a full month before the first *Terminator* movie. Its predecessor, *The Exterminator*, came out four years earlier. If anything, James Cameron's hallowed series about time-traveling android assassins was beat to the punch with this similarly-titled but otherwise radically different series.

The cover art for *Exterminator 2* on VHS. Now, *this* is how you get someone to rent your movie.

Despite looking a lot like it *should* have been a Cannon movie, the series' first film, *The Exterminator*, was put out by Avco Embassy in 1980. The movie centered on a Vietnam vet named John Eastland who—after witnessing one of his old war buddies crippled by street thugs—decides he'll clean up the streets of New York City with his own brand of vigilante justice. This included torturing a bad guy with a flamethrower, feeding two more to hungry rats, lowering another into an industrial meat grinder, and other similar, ultra-extreme measures. Notable for being so unbelievably violent, *The Exterminator* was shredded by critics—a number of whom wrote it off as a somehow more vicious *Death Wish* (1974) knock-off—but the movie was lapped up by enthusiastic, presumably sadistic audiences, bringing home an admirable worldwide gross for a low-budget exploitation feature.

EXTERMINATOR 2
Starring Robert Ginty
Directed by Mark Buntzman

Jimmy Long is back as the outlaw hero from "The Exterminator." Continuing in the same vein, Long fights evil in his special way with a weapon all his own.

For some reason, the film's sales ads consistently boasted that "Jimmy Long" was back as the Exterminator ... except that wasn't the name of the character, or the actor who played him.

The Exterminator's success did not escape Cannon, who scooped up the rights to make a sequel. No one had necessarily been clamoring for a second *Death Wish*, yet Cannon had one of the biggest successes of their run by gambling on *Death Wish II* (1982). If it had worked for one ridiculously violent vigilante movie, then why not another? Deals were made. The original film's writer and director, James Glickenhaus, had moved on from the series, and so the reigns to the sequel were passed along to its producer, Mark Buntzman.

To say that *Exterminator 2* had an atypical production history would be an understatement of monumental proportions. Cannon gave the rookie director less than two weeks' prep time before his offices were cleared out to make room for the team working on *Grace Quigley* (1985). Location shooting began in New York City immediately after this. Scheduling problems and budget inadequacies were only two of the many difficulties faced by the movie's *first* director—but more on that in a bit.

Exterminator 2 picks up shortly after the events of the first film. It's clear that little has changed: the Exterminator—as he's come to be known—is still doing his thang, exterminatin' crooks off the streets of New York. Robert Ginty reprises his role here as John Eastland, the 'Nam vet who has had-it-up-to-here with crime and will stop at nothing to rid his city of its seediest citizens.

The friendly-faced leading man had become unexpected action hero by this point in his career. Robert Ginty was a Shakespearean actor and musician who had studied at Yale and had once played drums for Jimi Hendrix. He made a name for himself as a screen actor appearing in Hal Ashby's *Coming Home* (1978) and on TV's *The Paper Chase* (1978–1979), but it was his role in *The Exterminator*—which he himself considered to be unnecessarily violent—that would define his career. From that point on, Ginty would become known mostly for appearing in down-and-dirty, occasionally direct-to-video action features with titles like *Code Name Vengeance* (1987), *Warrior of the Lost World* (1983), and *Maniac Killer* (1987). He'd also land another starring role for Cannon with *Three Kinds of Heat* (1987). Ginty moved behind the camera later in his career, directing episodes of TV's *Charmed* (1998–2006) and *Early Edition* (1996–2000), as well as a hip-hop musical version of *A Clockwork Orange* on stage in Paris, which we have to assume was one of the best pieces of theatre ever staged. Sadly, he passed away from cancer in 2009, aged only sixty years old.

It becomes evident early on in *Exterminator 2* that in spite of our vigilante's best efforts to murder every singly bad guy he could find, New York City *still* isn't a very safe place to live. In the very first scene we watch some hoods gun down the elderly, husband and wife owners of a liquor store. Unfortunately for these cold-blooded killers, The Exterminator—now disguising his identity behind a welding mask—appears suddenly as they attempt to make their getaway and slow-motion barbeques them with his trusty flamethrower.

While the flamethrower only made a memorable cameo in the first *Exterminator* film, it was featured very prominently on the movie's poster, and thus became the weapon most associated with our anti-hero. Given how much it's put to use in the sequel, however, you can argue that it deserves the movie's second billing.

Exterminator 2's fashion-forward villain, the evil X (Mario Van Peebles, center).

One thug manages to escape being flambéed and reports back to his big brother, X, a dangerous gang leader who's none too happy about his boys getting roasted. The mono-lettered X is played by Mario Van Peebles in one of his first starring roles. The son of influential indie filmmaker Melvin Van Peebles, he'd originally auditioned for the role of the Exterminator's best friend. Mark Buntzman decided that the young Van Peebles had so much charisma that he might outshine Ginty if he was asked to play the buddy part, and so instead cast him as the movie's villain. It was a smart move, as Van Peebles' ferocious performance is one of the film's highlights. (His villainous turn was so good, in fact, that the bigwigs at Cannon didn't believe he'd ever play a believable good guy; Van Peebles had to lobby hard for himself to play the good-natured John Hood in the company's 1985 musical comedy *Rappin'*.)

X runs a New York City-based youth crime syndicate that is dozens of members strong and heavily armed with assault weapons. He dresses like a Mad Max villain with a flat-top hairdo, flips around like a Ninja Turtle, has a roller-skating right hand man, and delivers fiery speeches to the band of adoring hooligans who live with him in an abandoned subway tunnel. Flamboyantly evil, this guy has more in common with a Batman villain than a common street thug. Van Peebles was allowed to design his character's costumes himself; he described his fashion inspiration for the movie as "*The Road Warrior* meets Grace Jones."

Exterminator 2 gives us the opportunity to get to know our vigilante's softer side. When he's not busy torching bad dudes he's romancing a stripper named Caroline (Deborah Geffner of *All That Jazz* [1979]), who aspires to be a Broadway dancer.

We also meet his best friend, a garbage man named Be Gee, played by Frankie Faison, an actor best known for his roles as Commissioner Burrell on HBO's *The Wire* (2002–2008) and as Hannibal Lecter's caretaker in *Silence of the Lambs* (1991), and who appeared in other cult classics such as *Cat People* (1982), *C.H.U.D.* (1984), *Maximum Overdrive* (1986), *Manhunter* (1986), and *Do the Right Thing* (1989) An old war buddy from Vietnam, Be Gee offers his friend a job at his garbage company, unaware that he spends his nights setting robbers and rapists on fire.

X has a very roundabout scheme to take over New York's underworld by sticking up an armored bank truck, and then using that money to buy drugs from the mafia. His gang's tactics are ruthless. They paint a big, neon pink "X" across the truck driver's chest—subtlety isn't their strength—before tying him to the subway tracks like they're the moustache-twirling villains of an old, Hanna-Barbera cartoon. Later, they kidnap a woman off the street and test out their mob-sourced heroin on her. (During the kidnapping scene, watch the background for a movie theater plastered in *Revenge of the Ninja* [1983] posters—Cannon was always savvy about cross-promoting their films..) Naturally the Exterminator won't condone to such criminal tomfoolery, and sets his targets on these dangerous goons.

Our good guy's and bad guys' paths continuously crisscross throughout the movie. Be Gee happens to pass by the armored car, mid-heist, and heroically plows his garbage truck through the baddies. The Exterminator eventually incinerates X's little brother, earning himself an arch-adversary for life. At one point, a few of X's thugs assault our hero and his girlfriend as they casually enjoy a breakdancing performance in Central Park. They go so far as to annihilate her legs with a baseball bat, which completely dashes her dreams of ever dancing on the Great White Way.

If you thought the Exterminator was pissed off before, well, buckaroos, you ain't seen nothin' yet. He has a surprisingly easy time talking his best bud into joining him on a murderous revenge mission—it so happens that ol' Be Gee has a stockpile of heavy artillery he's been saving for just such a rainy day, or something. The pair kidnap one of X's peons and get him to cough up his boss's whereabouts after nearly crushing him to death in the garbage truck's trash compacter. The Exterminator shows up just in time to spoil X's drug deal with the mafia, but poor Be Gee is gunned down in the process. As if the filmmakers had to make sure the Exterminator was a man with truly nothing left to lose, X figures out his secret identity and revenge-murders his injured girlfriend.

Exterminator 2's primary selling point is its action, and the movie's finale delivers that out the wazoo. The Exterminator squirrels himself away in an abandoned factory, where he uses a welding torch and all of the machine guns Be Gee was hiding to turn the garbage truck into a badass death machine on wheels. This includes pop-out assault rifles, bulletproof armored plating, and a heavy-duty plow for mowing through other vehicles—like X's leather S&M outfits, it's something that would be totally at home in a *Mad Max* movie. Having gotten away with bad guys' drug deal loot, all the Exterminator has to do is sit back and wait for the surviving gang members to walk into his trap.

Part of this sequence was shot in the abandoned Washburn Wire factory in Harlem, which had closed its doors in 1976. Other parts were shot in a building on a California industrial lot. As I'm sure confused matters, James Cameron was shooting *The Terminator* simultaneously—right next door, in fact—in the same industrial park. You have to wonder how many crew members from *Exterminator* got confused and accidentally wandered onto the set of *Terminator*, and vice versa.

Don't let me understate this: *Exterminator 2*'s ending is as cool as all hell. X and his crew roll into the factory in their muscle cars, armed to the teeth with Uzis and bazookas. The Exterminator lays waste to them all in spectacular fashion—the whole sequence is capped off with an amazing, slow-motion take where five brave stuntmen were set on fire simultaneously. This leads to a final, tense showdown between X—his face now painted with his fallen comrade's blood—and the Exterminator, who is once again wearing his welding mask, as they stalk one another across the building's elevated walkways and throughout the abandoned machinery. The ending is (literally) explosive.

Exterminator 2 has a lot of good things going for it. The action is insane, whether the Exterminator is crisping up bad guys in slow motion or running them over in his garbage truck hell machine. If there was an Academy Award specifically for stunt guys being set on fire, this movie would have run away with it. Van Peebles' crazed performance as X has an irresistible, demented charm. While Robert Ginty's screen presence may scream "everyman schlub" more than "vigilante anti-hero," he's affable enough to carry the scenes that don't revolve around flashy pyrotechnics shows. Plus, David Spear's all-synthesizer, *incredibly* '80s-sounding score sets the perfect tone for the setting and time period. (The music that plays over the Central Park breakdance scene has a "Rockit"-era Herbie Hancock flavor to it.)

All of this said, it's difficult to shake the feeling that something about the film seems *off*. There is a disconnect between some of the scenes and much of the film's logic begins to crumble under the slightest scrutiny. There's a certain, hard-to-place *wonkiness* about the movie. As the end credits start to roll, we're presented with a mysterious card which reads "Additional Scenes

Directed by William Sachs." This gives us our first clue about the turbulence this film overcame behind-the-scenes.

After running over budget and behind schedule, Cannon saw a rough assembly of the footage Mark Buntzman had completed and were dissatisfied with the product they'd invested in. Desperately wanting to salvage the movie, Golan sought the help of filmmaker William Sachs, a man well-known around Hollywood as a highly skilled "fixer."

Time and again, Sachs had been brought in by producers to save a faltering production or to clean up another director's work. Sachs' first film doctoring gig came on 1970's *Joe,* starring Peter Boyle and Susan Sarandon, which had coincidentally been the old Cannon's biggest, pre-Golan and Globus hit. He also did work on the notorious *Leprechaun* (1993) and more than 20 other films he wasn't credited for. In addition to these, he directed his own eclectic variety of films, most famously the sci-fi comedy *Galaxina* (1980), starring murdered *Playboy* Playmate Dorothy Stratten, *The Incredible Melting Man* (1977), *Van Nuys Blvd.* (1979), and the Cannon comedy *Hot Chili* (1985), which had its own messy production that you'll be able to read about in the next volume of this series.

The biggest issue with *Exterminator 2* when Sachs took over was that there reportedly wasn't enough footage to put together a full-length movie. Normally this wouldn't have been a big deal, but Robert Ginty had moved on to another project and his contract wouldn't allow for him to be released to film additional scenes. On top of that, Cannon wasn't going to pony up extra money to do any more shooting in New York, so any new footage would have to be filmed in Los Angeles.

Let's review, purely for the sake of understanding just how shitty a job was laid before Mr. Sachs. The director was tasked with finishing a movie that was only half done; he had to do it *without* his lead actor, who played the movie's titular hero; and he had to somehow recreate the movie's gritty, New York setting in Los Angeles.

Sachs had to get *really* creative.

Parsing through the pre-existing the footage, Sachs came across the scene where Robert Ginty wears a welding mask while assembling his garbage truck killing machine. He located an outtake where Ginty removed the mask after "cut" was called and that gave him an idea.

Sachs asked Ginty's stunt double to put on the welding mask and an old army jacket, and then filmed a whole bunch of new scenes featuring the "disguised" Exterminator setting bad guys ablaze. Using that single outtake and some clever shots—such as showing the character putting on the mask in shadow form—Sachs was able to almost seamlessly blend together the footage of Ginty with that of another actor playing his role in newly-shot footage. In real life, Ginty hated the mask and had only worn it for the one scene.

It's easy to delineate between most of Buntzman's original footage, and the footage added by Sachs: if you see Ginty's face, it's from the former, but if he's wearing the welding mask, it came from the latter. This explains the almost surreal way in which the Exterminator suddenly appears throughout the movie wherever dirty deeds are being done. Some parts don't blend together so well—such as when the garbage truck turns a corner in New York City and comes around the other side in what is clearly Los Angeles—but overall Sachs' ingenious thinking paid dividends.

When you *know* you're watching Robert Ginty's body double, some of the scenes can be unintentionally funny. Take when the Exterminator discovers his girlfriend's been murdered, for example. We get the following shots, all of which creatively hide the fact that neither of the movie's headline actors appeared in them: fingers punching a number into a payphone; a close-up of a ringing phone on a nightstand; a man holding a phone, his face obscured by opaque glass; a naked woman, face-down on her bed; the Exterminator's back, standing in a phone booth; the back of the Exterminator's head, as he pounds the phone with his fist; him again as he's sprinting into his girlfriend's apartment building and up the stairs, shot from behind or overhead so as not to show his face; finally, the Exterminator (or his back, at least) reacting, startled, to find a red "x" painted on her apartment door. Smash cut to the Exterminator prepping his garbage truck for a murder spree. Sachs was able to squeak out the film's most dramatic scene without either of its lead actors by using some of the same creative obscuring techniques that, say, TV directors regularly use to hide an actress's pregnancy, or were used in *Austin Powers* (1997) to hide Mike Myers' wiener.

Even though the lead actors didn't make the trip from East to West Coast, the movie's biggest star—the Exterminator's revenge-on-wheels garbage truck—does appear in both directors' sequences. When it was discovered that Los Angeles garbage trucks looked nothing like the ones New York, the production had one driven cross-country to take part in the newly-filmed scenes.

Exterminator 2's unstoppable garbage truck, before Eastland upgraded it into a motorized murder machine that would have made "Mad" Max's knees shake.

Of course, some of the scenes and footage shot by Buntzman didn't survive into the theatrical version of the movie. Glimpses of these scenes can be seen in the trailer, which had already been cut together and released before Sachs took hold of the production. This includes a nightclub explosion which would have happened during the armored truck robbery scene, and an extended showdown between the Exterminator and X. The entire ending, in fact, was changed. In the original version, the Exterminator's girlfriend survives and in fact saves his life when she shows up at the factory and guns down the nefarious X herself. Additionally, some of the more graphically violent scenes—such as the old couple being gunned down in the liquor store robbery—had to be trimmed for the film to receive an "R" rating from the MPAA.

A German poster for *Exterminator 2*. Credited with directing "additional scenes," it was William Sachs who gave John Eastland his famous welding mask and flamethrower when he was tasked with fixing the film for Cannon.

THE CANNON FILM GUIDE, VOL.1 (1980–1984)

Given all of the strife and messiness that occurred behind the scenes, it's downright stunning that *Exterminator 2* came together as well it did. It's in no way one of the greatest action movies of the 1980s, but it's highly entertaining. We have Buntzman to thank for turning a NYC garbage truck into one of cinema's most badass war cars. We owe Sachs our thanks for doubling down on the action, and for getting the movie to where it could be released at all. Considering that the movie had two directors, the main cast had left midway through, and that the original script had been tossed out the window, this movie has no business being as thoroughly enjoyable as it is.

Those of you who enjoy searching lesser-known movies for famous—or at least, familiar—faces should have a hoot with this one, too. John Turturro has a blink-and-you'll-miss-it role as a guy shouting from a parking lot as the garbage truck passes by. (It was his second film appearance, albeit as a background extra.) Arye Gross of TV's *Ellen* (1994–1998) and *Castle* (2009–2016) plays one of X's goons, as does the unmistakable character actor Irwin Keyes (who'd later appear in *Death Wish 4*). Director Mark Buntzman himself makes a Hitchcock-esque cameo as a gang member and the elderly mafia boss was played by his father, David Buntzman.

Interview: Director William Sachs
In the late 1960s, a young filmmaker by the name of William Sachs walked into the offices of a New York film production company called Cannon and tossed a canister containing one of his short films onto the front desk. They hired him on as an assistant editor, where he worked on a number of the studio's low-budget and imported films.

Over the years he'd go on to direct films such as the controversial festival darling *There Is No 13* (1974), 1950s sci-fi throwback *The Incredible Melting Man* (1977), teen comedy *Van Nuys Blvd.* (1979), the children's fantasy film *Spooky House* (2002), and the science fiction parody *Galaxina* (1980), which famously starred *Playboy* Playmate Dorothy Stratten, who was tragically murdered by her estranged husband on the eve of the film's release date. (Crown International Pictures chose to pull the release to avoid appearing as if they were cashing in on her death.) Sachs also directed Cannon's *Hot Chili* (1985), but like many of his prior films, the final product was meddled with by producers with whom he didn't see eye to eye. Throughout this time, he also built a very successful career as a highly sought-after film doctor.

Sachs' first work as a movie "fixer" happened to be the pre-Golan and Globus Cannon's greatest success: *Joe* (1970). Working as an assistant editor for the company, Sachs was promoted to the movie's helm when the film's original director, future *Rocky* (1976) director John G. Avildsen, was fired. Sachs renamed the movie and brought its title character from the background to the forefront. The movie was launched to critical and commercial success, becoming one of the top-grossing films of the year on a budget of just over $100,000, and launching the careers of actors Peter Boyle and Susan Sarandon. Sachs declined a co-director's credit on *Joe*, feeling that post-production supervisor better fit his role on the film. However, word of his doctoring abilities got out, and Sachs went on to be recruited to fix more than twenty similarly "unsalvageable" films, including the infamous horror comedy *Leprechaun* (1993) and, of course, Cannon's *Exterminator 2*.

The Cannon Film Guide: **The success of *Joe* must have been a nice calling card for your services as a film doctor. A few of your other, early projects were for the first, pre-Golan and Globus incarnation of Cannon, but can you tell me how you landed work for other studios?**

William Sachs: After *Joe*, they told me I could share director's credit and I said, "Nah, it's not my movie." I'd just gotten out of film school, so I was into the whole purity of it all. But then they never gave me the bonus that they'd promised me, so I quit. I got offered a job to go to Rome to buy Italian movies, and then make them "not Italian" for American TV. They weren't buying Italian Westerns anymore, so I would do things like put a title at the end of a movie that said, "The Producers Thank the People of Sedona, Arizona," or something like that, even though it had been shot in Spain. [*Laughs*] I would also change the credits to more American-sounding names, which was then part of the deal when you bought them. I would put my cousin as one thing, or a friend of mine as the director of photography. I re-dubbed the whole movie and changed the dialogue to fit the mouths better. I did about twenty movies, and one of those instances was where I met my wife. We're still married, so I came out ahead. [*Laughs*]

You were making your own movies over the years, even as you were doing fix-up jobs on other people's films. Did the fix-up jobs ever get in the way of your own projects?

Well, yeah. As I fixing *Exterminator 2*, I could have directed one of the Chuck Norris movies—I can't remember which one. They wouldn't let me do both. Cannon was kind of like a house of cards, where nobody knew completely what was going on. But I did lose the chance to do a Chuck Norris movie. I think Joe Zito wound up doing it.

That would happen, though, and schedules would kind of get screwed up. I have to tell you, though, I liked fixing the movies, even if I didn't get credit. It was like a challenge or a game that I had to beat. And honestly, on my own movies, I never really had full control, except for on *There Is No 13* (1974) and *Spooky House* (2002). With the fixing jobs, however, I seemed to have more control. Because they screwed up and were desperate, they would let me do what I wanted. [*Laughs*] It was actually more fun because of that. To me, if I can't go with my gut, I don't feel like I can do a good job. That's why I don't like some of the movies where I couldn't do what I wanted to do.

It's interesting that you approached these jobs as challenges needing to be conquered. Did you ever encounter a film that was beyond repair?

I have to tell you, I fixed *Servants of Twilight* (1991) for Trimark, which was based on a Dean Koontz book. I did a big job on that one. I changed the ending and had Bruce Greenwood being strangled from inside his neck, and we had great fun doing that scene. Then they offered me another movie and it was so bad that I turned it down. They actually kept offering me more and more money, and after four times I finally said, "Okay, I'll do it." The movie was so bad that finally I thought, "Well, maybe I can make it a comedy." And that movie was *Leprechaun* (1993). [*Laughs*] I actually turned down *Leprechaun* three times, that's how bad it was. My kids' voices are actually in it:

my son cries from inside a box, and I think my daughter sings "Twinkle, Twinkle Little Star."

I enjoyed doing the fixing jobs, I really did, but then I never really got credit and other people did well because of it. Like with *Joe*. It was kind of a mixed bag.

Can you walk me through how you wound up working on *Exterminator 2*? I know you were on set during filming in New York, serving in some sort of producer's capacity.

From the beginning, Cannon was worried about the director, who was actually a decent guy. They asked me to go and help him and they'd give me a co-producer's credit or something. I knew it would go wrong when we had our first meeting at the Mayflower Hotel in New York with Bob Ginty. He'd come in with pages of ideas, but Mark wouldn't listen to them. That started it. He didn't even want to hear his ideas. He said, "I'm the director, I'm going to make the decisions." But then, he couldn't make the decisions.

There's a little rule I have. If somebody says, "Where do you want the camera?" I usually have something prepared, but if for some reason I can't do that, I just point and say "There!" and that's usually right. I really believe in going by your gut. If afterwards you realize you made a mistake, you say "No, let's move it over there—I changed my mind." And that's fine.

If they asked Mark Buntzman where he wanted the camera, he would stand there. He wasn't prepared. Then everybody would circle around him and give their opinion on where it should be. It was just chaos. Eventually someone would just put it somewhere.

You know Mario Van Peebles' character, X? He was called "X" because Mark had never decided what his name should be, and had just put an "X" in the script. [*Laughs*] And so the character became X. He just couldn't make a decision and it all ran away from him. At some point Cannon asked me to take over, and I wouldn't do it because I was friends with Mark. Somehow they talked him into asking me to do it, and so I did it.

The whole ending chase around the steel plant? That was one of my parts, those ten minutes or something. And then the last shot is one of my favorite shots I ever did, with the Exterminator walking down the tunnel. I had the DP put a white sheet up and shine every light we had through it, so he kind of vanished into it. He became almost transparent, or skeletal. And then the very first credit that appears was "Additional Scenes Directed by William Sachs." [*Laughs*] I had them add that.

William Sachs (left) rides the crane while filming the factory scenes of *Exterminator 2*. Courtesy of William Sachs.

You had to relocate from the East Coast to the West Coast between the original shoot and your scenes. How much time elapsed between when the New York shoot ended and yours began?

Not much! It was almost immediate. The problem was with the teamsters. We started with one or two in New York, and then we got up to something like forty-two and they had to move. I did my first film in New York and the teamsters were great, so I don't know. Maybe Cannon pissed them off. I always liked the teamsters, but I don't know what happened.

The biggest problem was that I didn't know what to do, because we'd already spent one-and-a-half times the budget and had only shot forty-five minutes of the film. Changing Los Angeles into New York wasn't a problem. We just painted the curbs and threw garbage on the ground and suddenly downtown Los Angeles was New York City. [*Laughs*] We got permission to bring the garbage truck over because we couldn't find one here.

Adding the plow to the garbage truck was my idea, I'd suggested it to Mark before we even began. The flamethrower idea came because when were ready to shoot, Ginty wasn't available and he was the star of the whole movie. They said, "Well, you can't have him." I thought, okay, that was my challenge. How do I do half of a movie with a star who wasn't there?

There was one shot from the original movie where he was welding the truck, then he lifts the mask and you can see his face. So I got the idea for a secret vigilante who wears a welding mask. I changed the little torch into a flamethrower, since that was cooler.

I have two signs that I put on the wall in my production office, and one says "Use every problem to an advantage." I think it made the movie better not having him, even though he was a friend of mine, but the whole concept of the flamethrower is what they used to sell the movie, and we wouldn't have had that had he been there. The other sign says, "This is how it *should* be done. Now, how else can I do it?"

***Exterminator 2* led to a lot of back-and-forth with the MPAA over its violence.**

Yeah, with the one scene at the beginning, where the old couple is shot during the robbery. What happened was we had squibs on the actor, and the pistol that fired was in the same frame as the squibs. For some reason, magic happened and all the squibs went off at the right time. The DP, Joe Mangine, leaned back from the camera and said it was the most realistic thing he'd ever seen in his life, and he was a veteran from Vietnam, I think.

I thought it was fantastic but the MPAA freaked out. The said, "You can't use that shot!" But it was such a great shot that I fought it. Afterwards I felt really bad because I started thinking about it. It's fun to shoot wild stuff, with the blood and explosions, but then I thought about the impact on the audience and started feeling, well, maybe it is really nasty that this old guy dies. But at the time you don't think about that because you're all caught up in the magic of cinema. But that was so real, so visceral that it started making me think.

I've read that James Cameron was shooting *Terminator* (1984) next door to your set.

Yes, at the same steel plant!

Was that ever confusing for the crews, keeping track of which set was *Exterminator 2* and which was *Terminator*?

The only confusion was when somehow I accidentally got a bill for either $3,500 or $35,000 for blowing up a gasoline truck. [*Laughs*] It was sent to Cannon in my name, but it was *Terminator* that blew up the gas truck, not *Exterminator*. It was a big plant and we were there on the same days, and somebody must have mixed us up. But, it got sorted out.

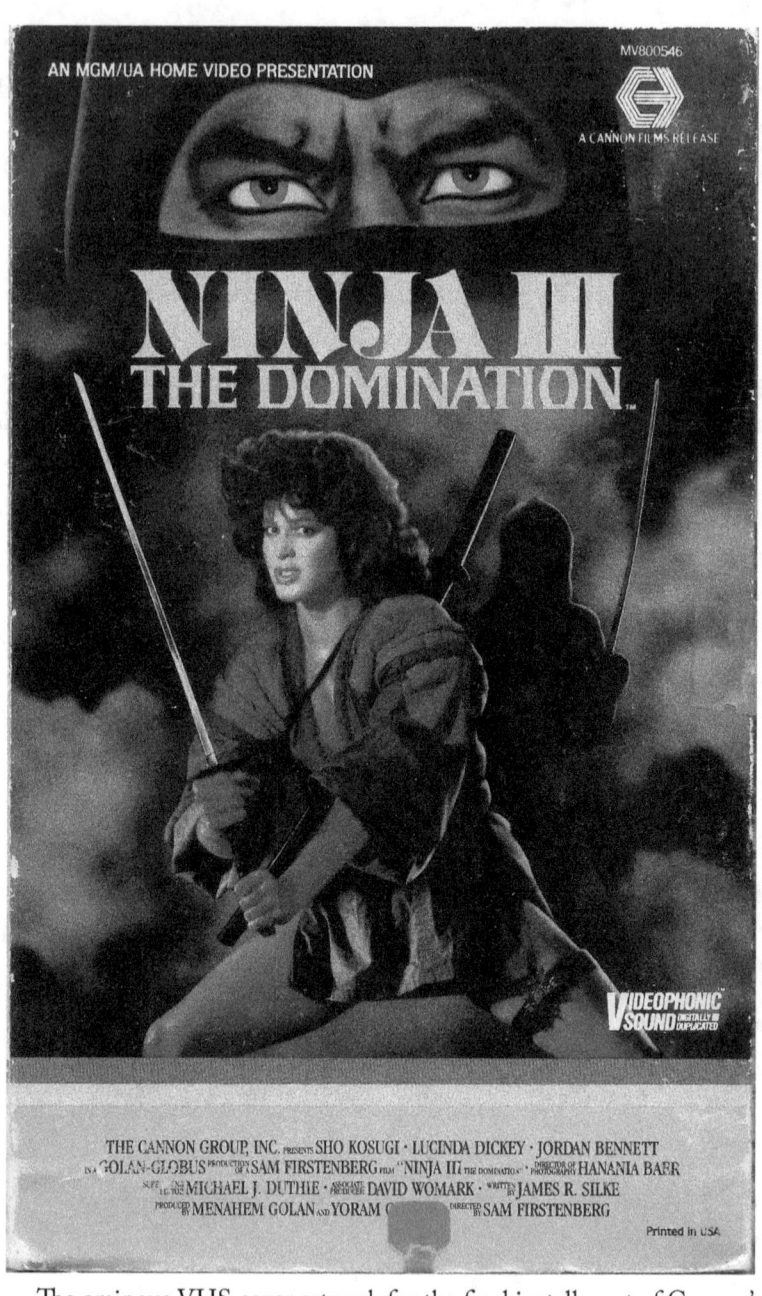

The ominous VHS cover artwork for the final installment of Cannon's first ninja franchise.

Ninja III: The Domination

Release Date: September 14, 1984
Directed by: Sam Firstenberg
Written by: James R. Silke
Starring: Lucinda Dickey, Jordan Bennett, Sho Kosugi
Trailer Voiceover: "An epic struggle of superhuman strength and supernatural forces!"

Ninjas. Aerobics. A V8 juice bath. An exorcism. A demonically-possessed arcade cabinet. Sho Kosugi in an eyepatch. Death by head-stab. Death by exploding handgun. A hot tub triple homicide. Dancercise! And to open the movie, an epic, ten minute, golf course-set martial arts massacre. All of these elements and more come together to make *Ninja III: The Domination,* one of the wildest films Cannon ever made, which says a lot considering this is the same studio that gave us *The Apple, Breakin' 2: Electric Boogaloo,* and *Lifeforce.* (Plus *America 3000,* and *Bolero,* and *Treasure of the Four Crowns,* and *Hercules II: The Adventures of Hercules,* and ... I could go on and on.)

Christie (Lucinda Dickey of *Breakin'*) is just your average '80s girl living in suburban Phoenix: a phone company lineman by day, and a part-time aerobics instructor, also by day. At night, though, her body is possessed by the soul of an evil ninja, transforming her into the ultimate killing machine.

How does a good girl like Christie find herself in a situation like this, you ask? Well, let's give a little background. You see, the movie opens with a sharply-dressed Asian man (David Chung, who also appears in *Missing in Action 2* [1985]) wandering into a cave and retrieving a cache of ancient ninja gear he'd hidden there some time ago. In the next scene he wanders onto a nearby golf course and just murders the hell out of everybody there.

We're never given any insight into what this bad ninja had against these golfers but, man, they don't even stand a chance. He crushes a golf ball in his hand to intimidate them, shoots a blow-dart into an adversary's pistol and makes it explode, and even one-hand deadlifts a golf cart to keep his victims from fleeing. Security guards stumble across the dead bodies and call the police, who send in a chopper, a bunch of cruisers, and even a few cops on motorbikes. What entails is some of the raddest, most over-the-top action stunt work you'll see in any film in this book.

The ninja—while standing on top of a speeding cop car—punches *through* the metal roof to kill a guy; flips a police car and a motorcycle into a lake; and leaps from a treetop to a *hovering helicopter* to eliminate everyone inside. It's *insane*. The stunts here are all the handiwork of coordinator Steven Lambert, who performs most of them himself. Keep in mind, this was all done for real: no dummies, no green screens. (That guy is awesome.)

After leaving more than 20 dead bodies in his wake, the ninja is finally overwhelmed by the police, who take him down with lethal force. They have to shoot him, like, three dozen times before he finally drops. Before they can confirm the kill, though, the pesky ninja escapes with the aid of ninjutsu magic ... and wanders down the road, bleeding to death, until he comes across Christie fixing a telephone pole. When she tries to help him he hypnotizes her, gifts her his katana, and then dies. Unbeknownst to her at the time, the black ninja's soul has possessed her body!

The black ninja's spirit will not rest until he's had his revenge on each and every cop who had a hand in his death, which means taking control of her body whenever one of the off-duty officers can be conveniently assassinated. This scenario would be awkward enough on its own, but Christie's new boyfriend just so happens to be one of the offending officers. At first Christie pretends to not like cops, but after the very persistent Billy Secord (Jordan Bennett) enrolls in one of her aerobics classes, she begins to fall for his straight-forward charms.

In Italy, the movie was released as "Trancers"—not to be confused with the 1980s Empire Pictures film franchise about a time traveling cop.

This Italian poster emphasized the possession aspect of the movie, depicting a mysterious shinobi laser-zapping his way into our heroine's brain.

By the way, the earworm pop tune you hear playing in Christie's aerobics class is "Body Shop," by Dave Powell. The song was commissioned by Cannon for *Ninja III*, but they definitely got their mileage out of the track by recycling it for the soundtracks of *Breakin' 2* (1984), and *Hot Resort* and *Hot Chili* (both 1985).

After class, Billy "arrests" Christie for beating up some attempted rapists behind her gym—it's his cheeky way of finally getting a date with her. It works. Within minutes, they're back at her apartment and she's pouring a can V8 juice down her chest and enticing him to lick it off. Their relationship blooms quite swimmingly, but Christie soon finds herself mysteriously compelled to get out of bed in the middle of the night. Fog fills the room, strange lights emerge from her closet and cabinets, and her furniture moves about as if it had a mind of its own. Before long, the full-size arcade machine she keeps next to her bed is projecting a laser show directly onto her face, and the black ninja's sword comes floating out of her closet on the end of a fishing line and lands in her hands. She wakes up later from a fugue state to learn that a cop has been killed—murdered by an *anonymous ninja*.

Her boyfriend starts to get suspicious, and for several good reasons: one of his co-workers dies each time Christie has of her mysterious blackouts; an evil-looking, white streak has suddenly appeared in Christie's hair; plus, she keeps a freakin' katana in her closet. At first he takes her to a shrink, who finds nothing out-of-the-ordinary with her except for an odd preoccupation with Japanese culture. Billy decides it's time to get Christie some real help, and takes her to see a Japanese mystic—James Hong of *Missing in Action* (1984), *Blade Runner* (1982) and *Big Trouble in Little China* (1986) fame—for a good, old-fashioned exorcism. (A distinguished, Chinese American character actor, Hong is one of the most prolific performers to have ever worked in Hollywood, with more than 400 [!!!] screen credits dating all the way back to the 1950s.)

Billy and the mystic chain Christie up between two pillars and begin the exorcism ritual, which goes poorly. Rather than rid herself of the ninja demon, Christie goes full Linda Blair, growling in an otherworldly voice, spitting smoke into the exorcist's face, and spinning head-over-feet on her chains like a buzz saw. The black ninja's spirit proves itself too powerful for your everyday exorcism. The old man confirms what anyone who's seen the first two films in Cannon's ninja trilogy already knows:

Only a *ninja* can stop a *ninja*!

It turns out Christie's in luck, because on a direct flight from Japan to Phoenix is none other than Mr. Ninja himself, Sho Kosugi. His character, Yamada, has come to the United States in pursuit of the black ninja, who killed his sensei, or father, or some other elderly man of great importance to him—the flashback isn't entirely clear on that detail—and chucked a shuriken into his left eye. (His character wears a sweet eyepatch made from the handguard of a katana.) We get a bunch of great scenes of him tracking down the black ninja, non-lethally beating up hospital security and morgue technicians to identify his nemesis' corpse.

The movie's pre-sales art combined high-flying ninja action with cutting-edge 1980s fashion.

After Christie blacks out and kills, like, a dozen more cops, she and Sho Kosugi's good ninja finally collide. They square-off in an abandoned house—where Yamada jumps through a ceiling like he's a Super Mario brother—

which eventually leads them to a final showdown in an old, martial arts temple that was rather curiously built in the middle of the Arizona desert. Yamada is able to expel the black ninja from Christie, but the spirit flies back into its dead body and mind-controls all of the temple's monks to turn on Yamada. The penultimate battle is the predictably awesome matchup of Sho Kosugi versus half a dozen kung fu monks and a zombie black ninja.

Yamada and the black ninja take it outside for a picturesque death match on the edge of a cliff. Next to the rooftop battle at the end of *Revenge of the Ninja*, this is the best Sho Kosugi fight scene in any Cannon movie. Christie lends a hand by running the black ninja through with his own sword, and Kosugi delivers the coup de grace with a knife-stab straight to the top of the head. The black ninja's body vanishes like Obi-Wan Kenobi's and our heroes live happily ever after, demon-free.

The Spanish poster for *Ninja III*, like many other pieces of Cannon artwork used for marketing in Spain, was painted by Enrique Mataix.

Italian poster artist Sandro Symeoni took a few . . . *liberties* . . . with Lucinda Dickey's wardrobe.

Save for its absolutely bonkers opening, *Ninja III: The Domination* doesn't quite match the nonstop, ninja action of *Revenge of the Ninja*, but certainly deserves the cult audience it has earned over the years. If it somehow wasn't clear by this point in the chapter, *Ninja III* is *super* weird. It's a combination of martial arts and *Exorcist*-inspired supernatural antics that somehow works, against all odds. It's also *very much* a product of the 1980s, from the fashion, to the ninjas, to the gratuitous aerobics scene, to the knock-off Patrick Nagel painting so prominently displayed in Christie's apartment. One of the cops Christie murders is even played by an '80s TV staple: John LaMotta, who was the Tanners' nosy neighbor, Trevor, on *ALF* (1986–1990). (LaMotta was a frequent collaborator of Sam Firstenberg's, having appeared in his directorial debut *One More Chance*, as well as in *Revenge of the Ninja*, *Breakin' 2*, and *American Ninja*.)

Ninja III: The Domination once again paired *Revenge of the Ninja*'s director, Sam Firstenberg, with a screenplay written by James R. Silke. Although *Breakin'* hit theaters before *Ninja III*, this one was actually filmed before *Breakin'* and launched Lucinda Dickey's career with Cannon. Firstenberg cast Dickey in *Ninja III* because he thought her dance and gymnastics training would translate well to her playing a ninja-possessed aerobics instructor. He'd direct her again, of course, in *Breakin' 2: Electric Boogaloo*.

It may seem strange that Sho Kosugi—the movie's top-billed actor, the premier movie ninja of the era, and the clear-cut star of Cannon's original ninja franchise—doesn't appear until more than half an hour into the film. The film's premise—primarily that it would portray a *female* ninja—was handed down from Cannon head Menahem Golan, and was reportedly a major sticking point for Kosugi, who hated the idea and thought it wasn't believable. The idea that the girl would be *possessed* by a ninja (and thus, not an actual ninja herself) was reputedly worked into the script so that Kosugi could buy into the premise. At the time, Kosugi was also filming the short-lived TV series *The Master* (1984), starring Lee Van Cleef and Timothy Van Patten, which is another reason for his limited screen time in *Ninja III*.

This was followed by a dispute over Kosugi's contract, which was the final nail in the coffin for the Cannon-Kosugi collaborations. The star bid the studio farewell, going on to star in a handful of ninja-related films for other companies. Highlights from his post-Cannon credits include *9 Deaths of the Ninja* (1985) from *New Year's Evil* director Emmett Alston; the immensely awesome *Pray for Death* (1985), written by and co-starring James Booth, who'd also pen Cannon's *Avenging Force* (1986), *American Ninja 2* (1987), and *American Ninja 4* (1990); and *Black Eagle* (1988), in which Sho Kosugi would star as the American hero pitted against a villainous KGB agent played by a young Jean-Claude Van Damme.

Kosugi's departure led Cannon to rethink their ninja film strategy. Sam Firstenberg was charged with handling the reboot. The resulting film, *American Ninja* (1985), launched a lengthy series of its own, and Michael Dudikoff's career as an action star. The rest is history . . . and can be read about in our next volume.

The German theatrical poster for *Ninja III*, where it was retitled "The Reign of the Ninja." That's actor David Chung in the photo, but Steve Lambert performed the actual stunts during the movie's wild opening scenes.

Interview: Stunt Coordinator Steven Lambert

After a rough-and-tumble childhood on the streets of Brooklyn, young Steven Lambert moved to California where he found focus in martial arts—and where Hollywood eventually found him. Approached by a casting director at a karate tournament, he was recruited to get kicked around by Chuck Norris in 1978's *Good Guys Wear Black*. It was there he discovered the world of movie stunt work, and became part of a rising wave of stunt men with backgrounds in martial arts.

Lambert's first coordinator job came on Cannon's *Revenge of the Ninja* (1983), which was followed in rapid succession by *Ninja III: The Domination* (1984) and *American Ninja* (1985); in all three films, Lambert spelled practically every ninja who appeared on screen. (In *Revenge*, he the demon ninja whenere the character wore the silver mask throughout the film, as well as Sho Kosugi's cowboy assailant in the playground fight scene.) Over the next half-decade, Lambert continued to work for Cannon on *Behind Enemy Lines* (1986), *Invaders from Mars* (1986), *Firewalker* (1986), *Barfly* (1987), and *Delta Force 2* (1990).

The prolific stunt man also counts many non-Cannon classics among his more than one hundred film appearances, having also worked on *Pee-wee's Big Adventure* (1985), *Remo Williams: The Adventure Begins* (1985), *Rambo III* (1988), *Indiana Jones and the Last Crusade* (1989), *Ghostbusters II* (1989), *Total Recall* (1990), *Army of Darkness* (1992), and *Ocean's Eleven* (2001).

His memoir, *From the Streets of Brooklyn to the Halls of Hollywood*, was published in 2019 and goes into great detail about his life and storied career (and includes numerous tales of his time with Cannon). If you're interested in an unfiltered look behind the scenes at the job of a hard-working Hollywood stunt man, it's a book well worth seeking out.

The Cannon Film Guide: You were already an accomplished martial artist when you got into the movies, having started training when you were only nine years old. What inspired you to pursue martial arts at such a young age?

Steven Lambert: I was born in Brooklyn, New York. When I was a kid I was very small and very thin-framed, and very much a street kid. Any kind of confrontation I got into, I never won it. I would always stand up, though, I would never give up. When I was about nine years old I was walking with my mother and father, on our way to have some pizza, and I saw a karate studio. Looking in the window, I was fascinated. My father put me in there. Six months to a year later I went back, and it was closed up. [*Laughs*] It went bankrupt! They never told us what happened, but the doors were closed. But, that was my first taste of martial arts and I really enjoyed it. Not only physically, but mentally I had grown from it.

That's how I found martial arts. It was a Japanese style, I don't remember specifically which style it was but I do remember it was a karate studio. Back then you never saw things like that! Where did this thing come from? It was like walking into a foreign country.

My father and grandfather were movie buffs. I'd seen a lot of old movies. I remember to this day there was an old movie with James Cagney [*Blood on the Sun*, 1945] where he does karate and jiu-jitsu in it, you know, fighting the Japanese. I remember my father and grandfather watching this with me, sitting in front of a black-and-white TV. I was so fascinated with it.

You eventually moved out to California. Your break came when you got paid to fight Chuck Norris in *Good Guys Wear Black* (1978), years before his tenure with Cannon. How did that come about?

I was tricked into moving to California. I was told we were going on a summer vacation and from age thirteen on, I lived in California. I came across a Kung Fu place on Van Nuys Boulevard. Again I looked in the window, at all these people in black uniforms and using weapons. I was fascinated. I convinced my parents to sign me up.

As I got older, I would compete in tournaments. But after a while, you know, there's no more fooling around. You couldn't make money at tournaments, there were only trophies. So I hit eighteen, nineteen years old and I had to start looking for a job. I'd decided I'd compete in my last tournament, one that was put on by the Black Karate Federation. I took second in three divisions: weapons, fighting, and hand forms. Afterward some casting people came over to me and said, "Hey, Chuck Norris is doing a film. We'd like you to fight him."

I knew nothing about the movies but, my god, every guy my age had seen the stuff he'd done with Bruce Lee in *Way of the Dragon* (1972). I kind of hemmed and hawed, but they offered me cash. The money they offered me, it would have taken me three weeks to earn that. So I said yeah! I went to the set at the time they told me, and I saw all the stunt guys fighting and going through windows. All of a sudden I got the bug. I said, "Oh my god. I did all of this stuff in Brooklyn, New York. That was part of living on the streets!" [*Laughs*]

I fought Chuck on a conveyor belt at LAX, you know, where the bags come in. He hit me a couple of times, kicked me onto conveyor belt and I fell off it. That was it. I was done. But I asked, "What are all these guys doing? How do I become that?" They were stunt guys.

What was the main thing you needed to learn to go from competitive martial arts to movie martial arts?

I was lucky I met some people who were very established in the movie business. Back then—I'm talking about 1976 and 1977—there were no martial arts stuntmen. There were no people like James Lew, myself, Rick Avery, Michael Vendrell . . . these were well-known martial artists, but we were all kids, so to speak. We all came in at the right time. All of these professional stuntmen had never seen anybody like us. A regular stuntman would need a pad to jump one story down, but because of our leg training we didn't need that pad. We were able to give the camera shots they'd never seen before. Because the stunt coordinators would get the credit, we made them look like a million bucks—so we were used, *a lot*. Because I was twenty-one and looking like I was sixteen, I was used for a lot of junior high, high school characters.

Now there are millions of stunt guys who are trained as martial artists. Back then, though, there were none. We were very lucky, and came in at the right time.

I bet Cannon was a company that came to you guys a lot, purely based on the number of action movies they put out.

Well, *Enter the Dragon* came out in 1973, but then for years the only martial arts movies were Hong Kong movies, Sonny Chiba—you know, *The Street Fighter* (1974)—and *Wild, Wild West*, the TV show, with Robert Conrad. [*Laughs*] There was a long time where people enjoyed those movies but American-wise, there wasn't much of it. But then Cannon comes along and they made *Enter the Ninja* (1981).

When that came out they didn't have much distribution for it, but Menahem believed in it. He wanted to do another one. That was going to be *Revenge of the Ninja* (1983). I didn't come on to that picture initially—one of the guys I'd come up with, Michael Vendrell, had heard of Cannon and got an interview with Sam Firstenberg and [producer] David Womark. They were going to use him, but a couple of days later he got an offer to do a TV show called *Buck Rogers* (1979–1981). A TV show could go ten years, but a movie only goes eight weeks—which would *you* rather do, you know? Anyway, he called me up and asked if I wanted to do this movie called *Revenge of the Ninja*. I said sure. He put my name in, I went up and met Sam and David, and the rest is history. That's where our friendship began. We had an hour and a half meeting where they grilled me.

God bless Menahem and Cannon Films, because they weren't into giving out much money. They needed a guy who had the talent but could also give them a break. So, when I went into the meeting with Sam and David, I told them I could double the good ninja, the bad ninja, the enemy ninjas, I can do this, I can do that. I'm one person and I'll do all of that on one contract. Normally if a stunt guy goes in, every time he doubles somebody he gets a separate contract. What I offered them was not only my physical talent, but something that was magical to Cannon's ears. They were all about money. It was like, "Look what we can get all from one guy!" [*Laughs*] Instead of hiring seven guys they could hire one guy. It was tremendous savings, and they loved that.

Lambert tries on his ninja costume for the first time on set of *Revenge of the Ninja*. Courtesy of Steven Lambert.

You brought a lot of your own ideas to the movie, too.

When they gave me the script, all of the action pages were empty. For example, the scene with the van—I doubled Sho Kosugi through that whole sequence—all it said in the script was that there was a van chase. None of it was written. So I had to scout locations and creatively come up with ideas. I'd then bring Sam and our cameraman to the location and go over it with them. Sam would make his minor changes, and that's how it worked.

As a stunt coordinator, or action director or second unit director, I had to understand how to put a scene together from beginning to end, including the shots with the actors. The script would say something like, "The van takes off and Sho pursues it," and I had to come up with everything in between. Then Sho would come in on the day and make his minor changes based on the situation. I would put him in the stuff that wasn't as dangerous. Sho was a very athletic guy and a great martial artist, but he didn't know much about stunts and you have to be careful around that, because some martial artists think they're stunt guys, too. There's a tremendous difference.

That's one of the coolest action sequences in the movie.

It was my first big movie. I'd done other, little things—stunt coordinators had hired me to put together their martial arts scenes—but that was my big chance.

Everything we did in that movie was more or less for real. You know, in martial arts you learn five things, and all five of those are also very useful in the stunt business. Those things are timing, coordination, distance, focus, and power of the mind. I knew I had all of those. I had the utmost confidence. I would do things that people would say were impossible, and that would drive me.

When I did *Revenge of the Ninja*, I was competing with myself. It was like a dream come true, and I was a kid in a candy store. It was like the door had opened for me. Bless Sam Firstenberg, because everything I came up with, he loved it, and Menahem Golan loved it. Sho Kosugi loved it. We worked so beautifully as a team.

I did eight or nine pictures for Cannon. I became part of the family there.

You clearly impressed them—they hired you right away to come back for *Ninja III: The Domination*. Was the process on that one similar to the one on *Revenge*?

After *Revenge of the Ninja*, everything changed. Menahem brought me into the office and we had a wonderful conversation. He was very happy with the work that I did. From then on they would invite me to parties, dinners, and gatherings. It was a beautiful thing. Again, I'll say I was so lucky because that doesn't usually happen to a person. Because it felt like I was part of their family, I didn't feel like I had to worry about work. They kept calling me and offering it.

Sam Firstenberg called me up to do *The Domination*. I went over to Cannon and picked up the script, we talked for a bit, and he asked me to call him back after I'd broken down the script. Well, I read it and I kind of scratched my head. I didn't understand it. [*Laughs*] I said, "With the utmost respect, this is kind of weird." I didn't understand the possessed ninja, especially when it was a telephone repair girl. It was a completely different movie, at least in terms of the script. I couldn't even being to understand it, because *Revenge of the Ninja* had made them so much money and Sho Kosugi became a big star. Why, then, would you go from a guy to a girl? I was confused. But, Menahem had decided that: "I have another brilliant idea! I will make the ninja a girl!" And that's how that happened. Sam tried to convince him not to, as did a number of other people, but you couldn't move the king, you know?

I imagine those ninja movies were a lot of fun for you. You could wear so many different costumes, and get so much more screen time than in other movies.

I had my own section in wardrobe on all three ninja pictures! [*Laughs*] I'll tell you this. In *Revenge*, Arthur Roberts played the silver masked ninja, but the only two scenes he was in were in the beginning, when he puts the mask on, and at the end when I had Sho Kosugi split it in half. That's it. Those are the only two shots where he was the silver masked ninja. All the rest, it was me.

When I got to those movies, part of my job was to train the actors. Obviously I didn't have to teach Sho Kosugi much, but Arthur Roberts didn't know anything. He was a wonderful man, nice guy, but physically he was a mess. When I brought him on camera, Sam and Sho looked at me like, "What is this?" They didn't want to give me money to bring in a stunt double, and Arthur Roberts was twice the size as me. I'm 5'9", and Arthur Roberts is 6'1". So they're scratching their heads, and then Sam suddenly says to me: "You're doubling him in all the stunts. Why don't you go ahead and play him?" That's how that happened. He always has a mask on, and with martial artists you don't see the size difference because they're always squatting.

When we started on *The Domination*, Sam asked me, "So, what girl are you going to bring in to double the lead?" And I said, "What do you mean, bring in? You're looking at her." [*Laughs*] Back on *Revenge* and *The Domina-*

tion, I had only been in the business for a few years. I wasn't going to let anyone else take that opportunity—*I* wanted to do it! That was my thought process. I didn't care if it was a guy a girl, and in those days there were no laws: a guy *could* double a girl. These days, you can't. It's illegal. But in those days it didn't matter, because there weren't as many women in the Screen Actors Guild who could do it, so that's why there were no rules against it.

When *The Domination* came out, I took four or five friends to see it. You know that scene where she's climbing up the telephone pole? Well, that's me. The close-ups are her, but the wide shots were me. So I turned around to my friends and I said, "Boy, doesn't she move her rear end real nice?" And they go, "Oh, yeah! She's the girl next door." And then I told them, "You idiots, you're talking about me." [*Laughs*] Lucinda used to tease me a lot. She said, "If you're going to double me, you need to move your rear end more."

She came from a dance background, rather than martial arts. How was she as a pupil when you had to train her for scenes where she couldn't be doubled?

She was wonderful. For instance, when she comes out of the dance class and has to fight those guys, I was able make it very basic and simple. When you're stunt coordinator, you often need to sit down with your actors and figure out with you have. Her being a dancer, I was able to give her martial arts moves that were similar to dancing. Her attitude was wonderful.

Interview: Actor Jordan Bennett

Jordan Bennett made his mark within Cannon history playing Billy Secord, Lucinda Dickey's cop boyfriend in *Ninja III: The Domination*. Throughout the film he aids her in seeking help for her demonic ninja possession, and is on the receiving end of cinema's first (and only) V8 Juice seduction scene.

While *Ninja III* was his only starring role on the big screen, Bennett is an accomplished singer and musical theater actor, notably starring in *Cyrano: The Musical* on Broadway and as Jean Valjean in the debut Los Angeles run of *Les Miserables*. He now travels, performing concerts and musical comedy shows around the country and aboard cruise ships.

Officer Billy Secord (Jordan Bennett) tries to stop a rampaging ninja in a press photo from *Ninja III: The Domination*.

***The Cannon Film Guide:* You have an educational background in music and political science. What led you into acting?**

Jordan Bennett: I was always a born performer. I was actually given scholarships to three different law schools, but I decided not to go. I got my start in the Catskill Mountains of New York. Do you know about the Catskill Mountains?

I know a lot of comedians came up through there.

Well, not any more. It was kind of like a cruise ship on land, where entertainment and food were the basic draws. People used to go there from New York, there were a lot of good hotels. Many great comics started there. Also, a lot of great performers started there, too. I started there, and I learned a lot—at the time, you could go into any hotel and watch somebody's show and no one would stop you. I saw a lot of great stuff.

You must have found your way to Los Angeles from there. Some of your early TV credits include *Emergency!* (1972–1977) and *The Waltons* (1972–1981).

First I went to New York and did theater, and then I moved to Los Angeles, which was a crazy place to live. As I say in my live show, I was cast in those long-running, hit shows as a recurring character, and after I was cast they all got cancelled. [*Laughs*]

What do you recall about your audition for *Ninja III*?

Oh, boy, I still remember the casting lady, her name was Julie Selzer, if I'm not mistaken. She called me in and I read, and then she brought me in to Menahem Golan. He was a *very* colorful character. I think my favorite story about Menahem Golan—and I don't remember if he told it to me, or I heard it from a third party—but he made a movie called, I think, *Under the Brooklyn Bridge*.

With Elliott Gould.

Right! Well, they had made the poster for the movie, and it had a picture of the wrong bridge. They said, "This is one of the most iconic bridges in the world, you have to change the poster!" And his response was, "Eh, a bridge is a bridge." [*Laughs*]

Ha! That movie does open up with a beautiful shot of the Manhattan Bridge.

So he won out! Why spend money re-shooting? It's a bridge.

From the moment you read the script, could you tell the movie was going to be as wild as it is?

I hate to denigrate screenwriters, but from the script I could tell that it had awful dialogue. I'm kind of brash, and I remember coming in every morning and giving Shmulik [Firstenberg] yellow-page re-writes that I'd done of the dialogue. A lot of which was used. Because the original dialogue, a lot of it you couldn't use. But it was a very fun set, and I had a lot of fun working with Lucinda.

She went on to star in all of their biggest movies for a space of, like, twelve months.

We had a lot of fun together. I remember shooting in Phoenix. She was an electrical worker, or a telephone worker. There's a truck that they used for her character, and I remember going out with her a couple other people from the crew. We stole the truck, and went out for a night in Phoenix. [*Laughs*] It could have been really bad, because if you ruin the main vehicle for a movie it creates a lot of problems for continuity.

Can you describe Sam Firstenberg, as a director?

I loved working with Shmulik. He had strong ideas but he was certainly willing to listen to mine. If he thought they sucked, he would tell me they sucked. If he thought they were good, he would incorporate them. Sometime he would shoot one of my ideas just to see if it worked. He was very accommodating, and on a low budget film you don't want to waste film on something you might not use. One of my favorite ideas, which they actually used, was the V8 Juice.

I was *just* going to ask you about that! That's a scene that everyone remembers about that film.

They wanted Lucinda to do a semi-nude scene, and she refused. I just wanted to do something different and kinky, and there was V8 Juice sitting on the craft services table. So, I thought we should incorporate it and she was game for it, as well. We just thought it was kind of different. [*Laughs*]

Absolutely—it's one of the most memorable moments from *Ninja III*.

If I'm not mistaken, after the movie came out we heard from the V8 company, and they'd sold a lot of extra cases of juice from that unsolicited product placement.

When you think back on it, do you have a favorite day of shooting?

I'd have to say it was one of the scenes shooting with Lucinda in her loft. There was a scene that was deleted. She had an old video arcade machine, and when I first walked into her loft I saw myself in her arcade machine. I'd asked Shmulik if I could have a mirror and they didn't have one, but I noticed that I could see my reflection in the arcade machine. And so when I came in, I looked in the machine and started doing this little strip-tease. But it was deleted!

You did Carl Reiner's *Bert Rigby, You're A Fool* (1989) after that, but then it looks as if stage took precedence over film at that point. You have so many great clippings from cool theater productions, like *Les Miserables*.

How can you beat working with a legend like Carl Reiner? He's one of the greatest comedy minds of the Century. I did *Les Mis* in Los Angeles. It's an incredibly difficult part, playing Jean Valjean, requiring a big vocal range. Even when you're not onstage the character is aging, so you're in makeup—there's not a lot of time to rest. I was a little short for the character, so I had to wear lifts in addition to everything else. It was an incredibly rewarding role, but absolutely exhausting.

Now you're a performing musical artist: you've released CDs, and you've taken your live show all around the world.

And I'm doing a new thing now! My first roommate when I moved to Los Angeles was Robert Picardo. He's done a lot of things, but he was on *Star Trek: Voyager* (1995–2001) for seven years. We hadn't worked together in forever but we've remained friends for a long, long time. He thought it would be fun to do a show together since he also sings a bit, and so he wrote this show—which is more like a musical than a regular, cabaret show—which is incredibly funny, and I did all of the musical arrangements. It's called *The BFF Show*. It's been so much fun.

The VHS release for the first *Missing in Action*: the movie that made Chuck Norris a household name.

Missing In Action
Missing In Action 2: The Beginning
Braddock: Missing in Action III

Release Date: November 16, 1984 (1), March 1, 1985 (2), January 22, 1988 (3)
Directed by: Joseph Zito (1), Lance Hool (2), Aaron Norris (3)
Written by: James Bruner (1), Steve Bing, Larry Levinson & Arthur Silver (2), James Bruner & Chuck Norris (3)
Stars: Chuck Norris, M. Emmett Walsh (1), Chuck Norris, Soon-Tek Oh (2), Chuck Norris (3)
Trailer Voiceover: "A decorated war hero, ex-prisoner of war, an American on a mission. One man who couldn't forget the Americans who were left behind . . . America had no more heroes, until now!"

Carlos Ray Norris—or Chuck, as he's better known—was born in Oklahoma, just north of the Texas border, in 1940. The son of an alcoholic auto mechanic, his parents divorced when he was a teenager, and Chuck and his brothers relocated to the South Bay area of Los Angeles with his mother. At eighteen,

Norris enlisted in the U.S. Air Force and was stationed in South Korea. During his four years in the service he became interested in the Korean martial art of Tang Soo Do, diligently working his way up the ranks all the way to black belt. Upon returning home in the early 1960s, Norris applied his learning by opening a chain of karate schools across southern California. He continued to improve his skills, winning the Professional Middleweight Karate championship in 1968 and holding down the title for six consecutive years.

He landed several small roles in Hollywood movies during this time, but it was his larger involvement in the martial arts world that led to a friendship with Bruce Lee. The future megastar kung fu actor cast Norris as his alarmingly hairy sparring partner in his 1972 feature *Way of the Dragon*, and that splash with stardom led to more and more opportunities for Norris to deploy his famous high-kick to the faces of bad guys on the silver screen. Early-career highlights include the 1977 vigilante truck driver movie *Breaker! Breaker!*, the 1980 Chuck Norris versus ninja terrorists movie *The Octagon*, and *Lone Wolf McQuade* (1983), in which he plays a renegade Texas Ranger at war with a nefarious drug lord. (*McQuade* was the inspiration for *Walker, Texas Ranger* [1993–2001], Norris' long-running, syndicated television series which debuted a decade later. Orion Pictures owned the rights to the McQuade character, and so Cannon—who produced the TV pilot—had to create the new Walker character for the show.)

In all of his starring roles, Norris shied away from what he called "chop-socky filmmaking," or kung fu films where punches and kicks flew constantly, left and right. By mixing in machine guns, explosions, and car chases with his karate chops and roundhouse kicks, Norris was able to avoid being pigeon-holed as purely a martial arts actor. In spite of ongoing critical derision for his wooden acting skills, Norris' profile grew with each role. By the time the mid-1980s had rolled in, this middle-aged karate instructor had become one of Hollywood's most unlikely action heroes. At 44 years old, Norris starred in *Missing in Action*—which was not only his biggest box office success, but one of Cannon's.

The maverick movie studio inked Norris to a lucrative, multi-year deal, and before Cannon closed its doors in 1994, they had made ten films and one TV pilot together. These movies were exemplary examples of the trends and tropes in action movie filmmaking of their era, defined by over-the-top violence and fiery, slow-motion explosions. They featured invincible heroes with hard-sounding names like "Frank Shatter" and "Matt Hunter," who could drop comic one-liners that were as potent as their punches. The *Missing in Action* series introduced us to Colonel James Braddock, a one-man, two-fisted wrecking crew and the North Vietnamese army's worst nightmare.

Italian painter Sandro Symeoni dedicated so much real estate to rendering Chuck's biceps and machine gun that he almost ran out of room for his head at the top of the poster.

By the 1980s, America was hardly a decade removed from the Vietnam War, and the conflict was still fresh in the public's mind. This was especially so for Chuck Norris, who had lost his younger brother, Wieland, to the war in 1970. He made it a point to seek out a project he would be able to dedicate to his brother's memory. After reading J.C. Pollock's novel, *Mission MIA*— which published in 1982, and featured a P.O.W. rescue plot similar to those that would become prevalent in action movies over the following years— Norris turned to his old colleague, screenwriter James Bruner, with an idea to make a film about the prisoners of war that were potentially still being held in Vietnam. (Bruner had previously written Norris's underrated, rogue cop thriller *An Eye for An Eye* [1981] and would later pen several of his biggest movies, including Cannon's *Invasion U.S.A.* [1985], *The Delta Force* [1986], and *Braddock: Missing In Action III* [1988].) Their spec script was shopped around Hollywood under the title *Missing in Action*.

After running into brick walls with a few of the bigger studios, Norris hooked up with The Cannon Group, who it turns out were very eager produce a movie named *Missing In Action* with him as the star. The martial artist was surprised to find out, however, that it wasn't the *Missing In Action* script he had been pitching all over Los Angeles, but another screenplay with the same name—this one by Arthur Silver, Larry Levinson, and teenage millionaire Steve Bing, who had inherited $600 million on his eighteenth birthday and left school to pursue a career in Hollywood.

Now, stay with me here, because this is where things start to get complicated. Norris and Cannon went ahead with the Silver/Levinson/Bing *Missing in Action* script and hired producer Lance Hool to direct it. The cast and crew had barely set up shop on the island of St. Kitts in the Caribbean before it became evident that Cannon's excitement for their new action star couldn't be contained by a single film. A sequel was greenlit to start shooting as soon as production wrapped on the first one, and screenwriter James Bruner was flown down to the island to start writing it. Fortunately the plots of the two *Missing in Action*s lined up well enough that Bruner only had to re-tool the original screenplay that he'd workshopped with Norris, and then re-submitted it to Cannon.

With their second *Missing in Action* scheduled to start shooting in the Philippines in a matter of weeks, Cannon still needed a director. We could assume here that Golan and Globus simply looked at that weekend's box office returns and gone from there. *Friday the 13th: The Final Chapter* had premiered at #1 on April 13, 1984, raking in an admirable $11 million in its opening weekend. That Monday morning Cannon put in a call to the film's director, Joseph Zito. By Tuesday, he was signed on to direct the second *Missing in Action*.

A pre-release sales ad for *Missing in Action*, which would actually become *Missing in Action 2*. Still with me? Good.

Lance Hool's and Joseph Zito's *Missing in Action* movies were shot back-to-back, and post-production moved very quickly. Hool's film was then presented, by Cannon, to Warner Bros. Pictures, who had first option to distribute their films at the time. The famed studio took a look at Cannon's violent, little film and swiftly passed, deciding it was unfit for them to release. What would have been a major stumbling block for most film releases, however, wound up being one of the best things that could have happened to Cannon. Golan and Globus, having viewed Zito's finished sequel, correctly concluded that it was the better of the two movies. In a smart decision, they flipped the order of the two films. They released Zito's sequel first, as *Missing in Action*. Then they gave the origin story the slightly confusing, new title *Missing in Action 2: The Beginning*, reclassifying it as a prequel and scheduling it to be released the following year.

It's not as if Lance Hool's *Missing in Action 2: The Beginning* was a glaringly bad movie, but Zito's film is far more exciting, and a much better way to introduce a new action hero and potentially launch a franchise. Cannon's decision paid off, as Chuck Norris' Braddock character not only resonated with audiences, but led the box office over its November 1984 opening weekend. This was on its way to a cool, $22.8 million domestic gross, making it the second-biggest success in Cannon's history. The franchise that Warner Bros. rejected turned into one of Cannon's biggest hits.

Set in current-day 1984, *Missing in Action* introduces Norris' James Braddock character as a tortured individual. (As in, mentally and emotionally tortured—not the physical sort of torture, which he'll endure plenty of in *MIA 2* and *3*.) He is suffering from nightmares of his time as a prisoner of war in Vietnam, where he and his fellow captured servicemen of the 101st Airborne were held under the tyranny of a sadistic camp warden. He was able to escape—and bring an end to the North Vietnamese troops who unjustly imprisoned him—but even a decade later the memories still haunt him. When he sees a news report about the possibility of other P.O.W.s still being held in Vietnam, it sets him over the edge. He puts a call in to the United States of America, letting them know that certified badass Colonel James Braddock is back in action.

Braddock's flown to Ho Chi Minh City (formerly Saigon) under the guise that he's part of an American delegation there to discuss the war's MIAs with the current Vietnamese regime. In reality, he's there as a one-man investigation team enlisted by his country to find out, once and for all, whether Vietnam still has P.O.W.s by any means necessary. Minutes after entering a press conference for the delegation, he's ambushed by a corrupt Vietnamese officer, General Tran, who slanders Braddock in front of the gathered journalists and accuses him of committing war crimes of his own. Little does the General know what a huge mistake he made by pissing Braddock off. Our bearded hero sneaks out of the embassy that night and into the General's very own bedroom. He holds a knife to the general's neck, coercing from him the location of Vietnam's secret prisoner of war camp.

Another sales ad for *Missing in Action* using a photo and plot description from what would become the prequel.

Braddock is kicked out of the country, but that all plays into his big plan. He hops a plane to Thailand, where he looks up an old friend. He combs the streets, karaoke bars, and brothels in one of Bangkok's seedier neighborhoods as hip-hop music recycled from Chris 'The Glove' Taylor's *Breakin'* soundtrack contributions plays in the background, eventually finding his old war buddy, mid-fisticuffs, in one of the area's sleazier establishments. Jack Tucker, or "Tuck," as Braddock knows him, now works as a boatman and gun runner. (He's played by M. Emmett Walsh of *Blade Runner* [1982] and *Blood Simple* [1985] fame.) Braddock hires out Tuck's skiff for a ride back to Vietnam, and enlists his aid in securing some heavy weaponry—machine guns, explosives, a bullet-proof pontoon, and even a helicopter—for his daring rescue mission.

From here on out it's all Chuck Norris with his guns a-blazing. He's able to con Tuck into accompanying him on his dangerous recovery operation, and the two of them head deep into the South Asian jungles to bring back the long-lost American boys. Bad guys get shot up—lots and lots and lots of bad guys—as Braddock dishes out sweet, unflinching, patriotic justice to all of the Vietnamese soldiers who refuse to abide by the Geneva Conventions. The movie ends with Braddock's helicopter landing outside the P.O.W. delegation from the beginning of the film. Our hero bursts into the room full of senators, politicians, and journalists with his rescued American soldiers in tow. Who's doubting the existence of P.O.W.s now, huh?

The New York Times called the movie "a simple, bullet-riddled, crowd-pleasing action movie," which is a very astute assessment. *Missing in Action* sold more tickets for Cannon than any of their other film but the wildly successful *Breakin'*, and it's easy to figure out why. As far as '80s-style action heroes go, James Braddock is 100% legit: the sort of hero that American audiences have been eagerly flocking to ever since Dirty Harry first asked some punk whether or not he felt lucky.

Not only is Braddock a great shot and good with his fists, but he's a quick thinker; in one of the movie's best sequences, Braddock sneaks out of the Saigon compound by staging a tryst with one of the female delegates. (Even she is fooled: when he meets her in her room, she catches him removing his clothes, assuming it's for some sexy-time—only for him to surprisingly put on an all-black uniform more suitable for espionage.) He sneaks out of the window only to sneak back in and under the covers before the Vietnamese soldiers find their General dead and come knocking. For Norris—who never does romantic scenes too convincingly, anyway—this screenplay and the role itself feel tailor-made for him. When Braddock wants a better deal on the souped-up gunboat he's buying, he simply asks for it down the barrel of one of the dealer's own machine guns.

And then there's the action, which kicks off right in Braddock's opening nightmare sequence and never really lets up. There are sneaky, ninja-like infiltration scenes, car chases, and of course a ton of slow-motion gunfire and explosions. Not only is our seemingly-invincible hero dealing swift justice in a flurry of bullets, but he's dishing out his punishment to bad guys who are practically begging for it. *Missing in Action*'s villains are almost preposterously evil, almost sneering as they lie to television cameras about the missing soldiers they're holding hostage. The film has been accused of jingoism, but its bad guys are so overtly villainous that it seems clear to most viewers that they weren't intended to be real people, but fantastical constructs of pure, unfiltered evil.

There's even comic support on behalf of M. Emmett Walsh. Despite his incessant complaining about being hooked into Braddock's suicide mission, he proves a heroic ally—even going so far as to heroically sacrifice his own life in the line of action. The movie's finale is tense, exciting, and wholly worthy of applause.

The money moment comes when a Vietnamese baddie nails Braddock's boat with a rocket launcher, sending Tuck and our Hero flying into the river. As the villains jump around, laugh, and slap each other on the backs, Braddock erupts from the water holding an M60 and guns all three of them down in gratifying slow-motion.

Crowd-pleasing? You bet it is. After *Missing In Action*'s success, much of the crew—including its writer, director, and high-kicking star—were reunited to do the even bigger, wilder *Invasion U.S.A.* the following year.

Also of note: a certain "J. Claude Van Damme" receives credit for stunt work on this film, marking his second bit of bit work for Cannon after he appeared as a background extra in *Breakin'*. (There will be a lot more to say about him in later volumes, I promise you.)

Missing In Action 2: The Beginning landed in theaters in March of 1985, less than three and a half months after the first movie. The title no doubt confused many movie-goers, but remember: this film was shot first and intended to be the first in the series, before its higher-quality sequel took its place. If you recall the flashbacks he suffered through in the first movie, Colonel James Braddock was held as a prisoner of war in Vietnam, where he was tortured, humiliated, and forced to confess to war crimes he didn't commit. *Missing In Action 2* shows us how he managed to escape from imprisonment back in the 1970s

Missing in Action 2: The Beginning lands on VHS, chronicling the events in James Braddock's life that led up to *Missing in Action*.

The movie opens with the mission in which Braddock and four of his brothers-in-arms are captured. Pursued by North Vietnamese soldiers, their escape helicopter takes a critical hit and the men bail, one-by-one, as the chopper plummets toward a crash-landing. (Braddock waits until very last to save himself, naturally.) As each man leaps into the lake below, we get a freeze-frame portrait stating their name and rank, which is immediately stamped over with the words "MISSING IN ACTION" in thick, red letters. As far as character introductions go, *MIA2*'s are pretty damn cool.

The film suddenly makes itself quite topical, as we're treated to real-life footage from the national funeral held in Arlington Cemetery on Memorial Day of 1984, when President Ronald Reagan addressed the nation at the interment of an unidentified Vietnam casualty in the Tomb of the Unknown Soldier. A snippet of Reagan's speech is used to emphasize the voiceover narration, which ties the ceremony back to rumors that American soldiers were still alive and being held prisoner in Vietnam a decade after the war's end. This jarring interlude's purpose seems to be to add some real-life credibility to the violent Chuck Norris film which unfolds afterwards.

A French billboard poster for *Missing in Action 2*.

We fade to an establishing shot of a jungle prison; a title card simple reads "Vietnam." This is during the War again, presumably sometime in '73 or '74. Based on their unkempt hair, unruly beards, and battered psyches, it appears the Americans have been held prisoner for quite some time now. This is where we meet the camp's ruthless leader, Colonel Yin (Soon-Tek Oh). This was Soon-Tek Oh's second film with Norris; the Korean-American actor and martial artist had previously appeared alongside him in *Good Guys Wear Black* (1978).

The theatrical poster for *Missing in Action 2* captured a similar tone to the original, action-packed, smash hit movie.

Colonel Yin is attempting to exploit a loophole in the Geneva Conventions by claiming the American soldiers are not being held as prisoners of war, but as war criminals. He uses this as an excuse to torture and humiliate our good guys until their bodies and souls are broken. Yin makes things worse among the imprisoned men by suggesting that he'll release them all on the condition that their leader, Braddock, confesses to committing fabricated war crimes. (If you know Braddock from the first *MIA* movie, you'll know that there is no way in hell he's going to do that.) Yin's ploy works, however: one of Braddock's men has already turned against him, and the others are getting closer every day.

One of best ways to look at *Missing In Action 2* is to compare it to a vinyl record: there's clearly an A-side to it, and then a B-side. The film's first half is a grim, grueling chronicle of the terrors and tribulations our five P.O.W.s were made to endure. After almost an hour of this, the record flips and Braddock escapes. The rest of the movie is the blood-spattered rescue of his fellow brothers-in-arms, and Braddock's personal vengeance on the enemies who put them all through so much suffering. The first half of the film is intended to make you wince; the second half, to make you hoot and cheer.

The first half of the movie can feel like an endurance test. We hear plenty of threats and see many guns held to soldiers' heads. They're told that their wives have declared them dead and remarried, and forced to watch as letters from their loved ones are set aflame. At one point, Braddock is hung upside-down by his ankles and a burlap sack containing a hungry rat is closed around his head. (The joke winds up being on the rat, which Braddock bites to death.) Braddock's breaking point comes when one of the men is burned alive while he's powerless to do anything but watch. By the time the second half arrives, it's no wonder that Braddock has wholesale murder in his eyes.

For what it's worth, the first part of the movie feels like a prolonged setup for the second, so that once Braddock finally makes his move you won't question his motives for unleashing full scale Chuck-justice, and blowing up Vietnamese soldiers left and right. After you've spent nearly an hour watching these assholes abuse our boys, you're gonna be A-OK with their indiscriminate destruction. With a combination of smart thinking, automatic weaponry, and some good ol' karate, Braddock quickly dispatches almost every bad guy and rescues his surviving comrades.

The movie's finale is justifiably the part most people remember from the film. After safely evacuating his friends, we see Colonel Yin crawl out of a trap door in his burned-out headquarters. Thinking he may have gotten away with his life, Yin hears a door unlatch—and turns around to see Braddock slowly emerge from the shadows. Yin makes a final, foolish attempt to save himself: he challenges Braddock to a one-on-one fight to determine once and for all "who is the better man." They drop their guns and boot heels start flying. While Yin is no slouch in the martial arts department, he's not Chuck Norris, either. As Braddock lands each decisive, devastating blow, he dedicates it to one of the P.O.W.s he lost. ("This is for Nester!") He leaves Yin in a crumpled, bloody pile on the floor of the hut. As Braddock walks away from the prison camp for the final time, we see him pull a remote control from his pocket. "This is for me," he says, pressing the red button and detonating the C4 he rigged under Yin's camp headquarters. A fiery, slow-motion explosion swells behind him. It's pretty freaking awesome.

Braddock (Norris, right) has his final showdown with the wicked Colonel Yin (Soon-Tek Oh, left).

Missing in Action 2: The Beginning is not a bad film, but it's easy to see why Cannon favored *Missing in Action* to be released first: it had more of the excitement expected from an '80s action adventure. Braddock spends much of this movie selflessly accepting his torture and humiliation before he finally turns the table on his captors. It's not until the final 40 minutes that we see anything close to the heroic violence of the first *Missing In Action*.

Missing in Action III on home video. The film was released four years after its two predecessors.

Because *Missing in Action* established James Braddock as a prototypical action hero, audiences would presumably be eager to come back for more, and they did. *Missing in Action 2: The Beginning* brought home nearly $11 million from the U.S. box office, making it another major success for Cannon. That it only made half of what its predecessor did probably had a lot to do with moviegoers' exhaustion and the short, three-month gap between the release of the first film and its sequel.

Critically it didn't fare as well. In a mixed review, *The New York Times* poked fun at the prequel-sequel element: "If [*MIA2*] does too well, we will undoubtedly be seeing a Part 3 covering his high school years." Once again, some complaints of jingoism—even racism—were levelled against the franchise for its portrayal of the Vietnamese. However, it seems pretty clear within the film that the atrocities were unique to this one, fictional prison camp at the behest of its mad leader, Colonel Yin, rather than being intended as a depiction of the North Vietnamese people as a whole.

Braddock's fellow P.O.W.s are played by Steven Williams (who played Captain Fuller on *21 Jump Street*, 1987–1991), Cosie Costa (who had a small part in Cannon's *10 to Midnight*, 1983), John Wesley, and Joe Michael Terry. Character actor and former pro wrestler Professor Toru Tanaka—previously seen in Cannon's *Revenge of the Ninja* (1983)—turns up as one of Colonel Yin's right-hand men. The soundtrack is by Brian May—not Queen's Brian May, but the film composer—who recycles a few little snippets from his score for *The Road Warrior* (1981).

While *Missing in Action 1* and *2* came together swiftly and with few issues, the production of *Braddock: Missing in Action III* was beset with problems and marred by tragedy. Joseph Zito was the first slated director but reputedly left over creative differences with Chuck Norris and the brass at Cannon. Other directors came and went, each layering their own re-writes over James Bruner's script. The buck eventually stopped on Aaron Norris, brother of Chuck, who stepped away from his usual stunt coordinator role to sit in the director's chair for the very first time.

Filming began in the Philippines in the early summer of 1987. On May

30, a helicopter hired by Cannon from the Filipino Air Force to film aerial shots developed engine troubles while passing over the Manila Bay. The aircraft plunged into the water below, killing four Filipino soldiers on board and injuring five others. In a macabre coincidence, the crash occurred on the same day a "Not Guilty" verdict was handed down to filmmaker John Landis and his associates when they stood trial for the manslaughter of an adult and two children killed by a helicopter crash during the shooting of *The Twilight Zone: The Movie* (1983). In an even more macabre coincidence, this would not be the only time people would die in a Filipino helicopter crash while shooting a Cannon film starring Chuck Norris and directed by his brother. (See 1990's *Delta Force 2: The Colombian Connection*.) It wasn't even the first time a helicopter crashed and killed someone while shooting a Cannon movie, either: a pilot was killed when his chopper went down in Alaska en route to a location for 1985's *Runaway Train*. In total, ten people died in Cannon-related helicopter crashes. In spite of the tragedy, filming on *MIA3* continued on schedule.

The idea was that *Braddock* would be a direct sequel to the first *Missing In Action*, both tonally and chronologically. The film is primarily set in 1988, save for a chaotic prologue that occurs in 1975. We open during The Fall of Saigon, as American forces work frantically to evacuate all personnel while the city is under attack. Colonel James Braddock is there, having presumably returned to action after escaping the prisoner of war camp sometime in '73 or '74. (If we've learned anything from this franchise, it's that it's impossible to keep Braddock *out* of Vietnam.) He now has a Vietnamese wife, who isn't at the embassy when she's supposed to meet him for their ride out of town. Instead, she runs back to her apartment to pack a suitcase for America. She gets caught in the fleeing throng on her way to the embassy, where a street urchin steals her purse containing all of her relevant documentation. It could have been much worse, however: minutes after leaving her home, it takes a direct hit of artillery fire. Braddock gets there just in time to see medics carrying out the corpse of his wife's friend, which has been burnt to a crisp—but because the dead woman happened to be wearing his wife's bracelet, he simply accepts that it was her and drives away with a blank stare on his face. (Keith David—of *The Thing* [1982], *Platoon* [1986], *Road House* [1989], and many other movies—has a brief cameo here, as a soldier working the gates of the American embassy.)

"He fights for everyone who can't fend for themselves." The German poster for *Missing in Action III*.

We then jump ahead to current-day 1988, courtesy of an editorial juxtaposition of helicopter blades and a ceiling fan that's straight out of *Apocalypse Now* (1979). Braddock is getting drunk solo at a swanky D.C. bar, presumably to drown out the death howls of the dozens and dozens of Vietnamese soldiers he killed in the first two *Missing in Action* movies. He's confronted by a kindly priest—played by Cannon repertory man, Yehuda Efroni—who tells him that he met Braddock's wife while doing humanitarian work in Vietnam, that he has a twelve-year-old son, and that they're both living under terrible conditions because she had worked for the U.S. military during the war. Braddock refuses to believe that his wife is still alive based on a two-second look at a crispy corpse wearing a bracelet, so the priest gets under Braddock's skin in the most effective way possible: he tells Braddock that there's nothing he could do to help them.

In a botched attempt to convince Braddock that the priest was out of his mind, CIA spook Littlejohn (Jack Rader) accidentally confirms that Mrs. Braddock is, in fact, still alive. He's told that the CIA has no plans to help her escape, but you can tell by the look in Chuck Norris' eyes that he has other ideas. As he's walking out of the CIA offices, Littlejohn orders Braddock not to step on the agency's toes. That's when Braddock turns around and delivers the movie's best line:

"I don't step on toes, Littlejohn. I step on necks!" (Cue dramatic music.)

You could guess from the very existence of a third *Missing in Action* movie that Braddock would be heading back to Vietnam for yet another high body count rescue mission. It's obvious that the filmmakers were trying to recapture some of the magic from the series' wildly successful first movie. When we next see our hero, he's flying to Bangkok to meet with an old friend-turned-expat arms dealer to stock up on weaponry. If you recall, the last guy to fill this role in Braddock's life—Tuck, played by M. Emmett Walsh—sacrificed himself to help the P.O.W.s escape in *Missing in Action*, but apparently Braddock is friends with more than one guy who does this sort of thing for a living. Before the new guy, Mik (Ron Barker of *Hanoi Hilton* [1987]), can hand over the assorted assault rifles, grenade launchers, and military-grade vehicles that

Braddock ordered, the CIA shows up to pursue our hero on an exciting chase scene through the strip clubs, alleyways, and Buddhist temples of Thailand. Not only does Braddock have to contend once again with the Vietnamese military this time around, but with America's Central Intelligence Agency.

Braddock sneaks into Vietnam by parachuting out of an airplane and into the sea alongside a jet-engine-powered Ski-doo that's painted to look like a Stealth bomber. (It's something I'm sure even James Bond would kill to get his hands on.) This may have had something to do with the popularity of Chuck's rocket-launching motorcycle from *The Delta Force* (1986), because *Missing in Action III* features a few cool pieces of what can only be described as "fantasy firearms." Besides the jet ski, the most notable piece of his arsenal is an assault rifle with seemingly unlimited bullets, and which comes with an attached RPG and spring-loaded bayonet. At one point Braddock runs an enemy soldier through with the blade, and then launches him through the wall with a rocket, which is topped off by the bad guy's body straight up exploding. Moments later Braddock uses the same weapon to shoot more soldiers, then blow up several watchtowers and an enemy APC without ever pausing to reload, or even wipe sweat from his forehead.

Braddock (Norris) wielding his custom, rocket-launching machinegun with spring-loaded bayonet, one of action cinema's deadliest weapons.

Make no mistake: *Missing in Action III* is Chuck Norris in full superhero mode; the first *Missing in Action* practically looks grounded in reality next to this one. Though it's hard to imagine that Aaron Norris would have landed this directorial gig had his brother not been the studio's biggest star, his background in martial arts and stunt work really shines here. The action in *Missing in Action III* features the right amount of the hand-to-hand combat—or, more accurately, the foot-to-face combat—which fans flocked to in Chuck Norris' early film career, combining it with the over-the-top gunplay that defined the '80s action boom and Norris' Cannon oeuvre so far. By this point in his career, Norris' movies tended to lean more toward one style of action or the other; *Missing in Action III* finally finds a sweet spot right in the middle of the two.

Braddock stashes his guns and meets the priest at his religious mission he set up to aid the half-Asian, half-American children of U.S. soldiers and the mothers they left behind in the war. Braddock is promptly reunited with his wife and introduced to his son for the first time. The joyous family get-together doesn't last long, though, as Braddock is captured by an evil Vietnamese General named Quoc, played by prolific Asian-American character actor Aki Aleong. At that point Braddock's long-lost wife is unceremoniously executed (bye, again!) and he and his son are taken captive. Our hero is tortured for a long while inside a Bond villain-like contraption designed by Quoc, but he eventually escapes (sans shirt) and frees his boy. The downside of this, though, is that the first place the evil Quoc thinks to look for Braddock is at the priest's mission. Not finding the American super-soldier on hand, the General decides to make all of the Amerasian children his hostages, and thus bait for Braddock.

Rather than his usual captured G.I.s, this time around Braddock has to save adorable little kids from a prison camp. For the last 40 minutes of the film, the action and excitement barely let up. Braddock launches a one-man assault on the Vietnamese military, breaking necks left and right, spraying bullets everywhere, and blowing up half of the buildings we see with C4. This shit is just crazy, and the way the bad guys react—by panicking and screaming "Braddock! Braddock" into their radios as everything explodes around them—you can just tell that this bearded, middle-aged killing machine is a terrifying legend among Vietnam's most villainous circles. These bad guys have clearly been kept awake with nightmares about Braddock ever since they were small, and it's no wonder because by this point in the franchise he'd single-handedly killed more than 100 of them.

Braddock and his priestly pal (Yehuda Efroni, left) go to superhuman lengths to rescue an orphanage's worth of abused children.

Once Braddock finally finds the kids, he then has to get them safely out of the country while the evil Quoc pursues him in a heavily-armed attack chopper. This extended chase scene—which is worth the movie's price of admission alone—starts in a hijacked truck, moves to a stolen plane, and then ends in a final showdown right on the border between nations. (The U.S. military shows up, but they can't cross into Vietnam to help Braddock—so they stand on the other side of the bridge connecting the countries and proceed to loudly root for the old veteran, as if they were attending a professional wrestling match.) The whole finale to the movie is ludicrous, but wow, it's so much fun. There's even a Mexican standoff between *three helicopters*, and a wonderfully Chuck Norris-y moment when an injured Braddock asks his young son to help him lift his machine gun and point it at the sky so that he can headshot a helicopter pilot. Just, *wow*!

The Spanish theatrical poster for *Missing in Action III*.

All of this insane violence has a message behind it, too. As we get a long, aerial shot of Braddock and company crossing the bridge to freedom, text pops up to remind the audience that there were a supposed 15,000 Amerasian children still in Vietnam at the time of the film's release. (The closing credits song, "In Your Eyes (Freedom)," is by Ron Bloom, and is so unapologetically patriotic that it sounds like something Trey Parker and Matt Stone would have written for *Team America: World Police* [2004].)

The Italian poster for *Missing in Action*, where the movie's title was translated to "Rumble of Thunder."

From a pure action standpoint, *Missing in Action III* delivers in spades. The movie's big issue is that whenever Chuck Norris isn't kicking and/or shooting somebody, he's required to act, and that was never his strong suit. *Braddock* calls for a few super-emotional beats, which wind up feeling more awkward than tender. When Braddock discovers the charred corpse of what he believes to be his wife, his expression is less of anguish than of mild boredom. When Braddock has a heart-to-heart with his long-lost, twelve-year-old son, it sounds as if he's delivering a public service announcement. But really, no one really comes into an '80s action movie—especially an '80s action movie produced by Cannon and starring Chuck Norris—looking to have their heartstrings pulled by Oscar-quality acting. They're there to watch people get kicked and/or exploded, and we get a *lot* of that here.

Braddock: Missing in Action III flopped with both critics and audiences and brought the series to a close for Cannon, but don't let that deter you. Let's put it this way: if a scene where Chuck Norris drives a truck full of orphans across an exploding bridge as a helicopter fires missiles at them sounds like something you want to see, then *Missing in Action III* is exactly your type of movie.

As far as Norris' Cannon trilogies go, the *Missing in Action* series trumps *Delta Force* on the basis of consistency alone. If you prefer your wild Chuck action distilled down to a single film, *Invasion USA* provides all of this franchise's lovable lunacy but without any of the filler.

Interview: Screenwriter James Bruner

James Bruner's longstanding, collaborative relationship with Chuck Norris naturally made him a screenwriter that Cannon would turn to time and again. After writing Norris' 1981 *An Eye for an Eye*, Bruner penned a Vietnam P.O.W. rescue script at the martial arts star's request. When that story finally (and rather circuitously) found its way to silver screen via Cannon, the resulting film—1984's *Missing in Action*—became one of the studio's all-time biggest hits.

Following the success of *Missing in Action*, Bruner wrote three more of Norris' best movies for Cannon: *Invasion USA* (1985), *The Delta Force* (1986), and *Braddock: Missing in Action III* (1988). He was also brought in on numerous occasions for script doctoring assignments, including credited work on *P.O.W. The Escape* (1986) and uncredited work on *American Ninja* (1985). He was also hired to co-write an unproduced screenplay for *Delta Force II* when *Death Wish* director Michael Winner was attached, and penned the script for a *Delta Force* television pilot that Cannon was to produce for CBS until the deal fell through.

In 2007 Bruner released his directorial debut, *Hollywood Dot Com*. In recent years, he and his wife—his frequent writing partner, Elizabeth Stevens—have branched out into children's books and adult thriller novels.

The Cannon Film Guide: **What are some of the early movie experiences from your life that steered you toward screenwriting?**

James Bruner: I'm going to give away my age—because I'm only 29, like everyone else in Hollywood—but the first movie I remember ever seeing in a theater as a little kid was Kirk Douglas in *The Vikings* (1958), and it remains one of my favorite films of all time. I probably have all of the dialogue memorized. I grew up in Milwaukee and I had polio when I was a kid, so I couldn't I couldn't play sports or anything. My mom got me into reading books and playing with toy soldiers, all of that stuff, and I got really interested in history. My parents were great about taking me to the movies. For instance, another one of my favorite movies of all time, *Lawrence of Arabia* (1962), I remember seeing the road show version as a little kid. Same thing with *Spartacus* (1960). Another one of my all-time favorite movies was Errol Flynn in *The Adventures of Robin Hood* (1938). Now, that one I didn't see in first run. [*Laughs*]

In those days I could take the bus downtown and for a dollar, or whatever it was, see movies. I used to go all the time, but I never really thought much of it as far as being able to do anything with it later on in life. That was pre-Internet, pre-digital, and Hollywood felt so far away from Milwaukee. I went to University of Wisconsin-Madison, and I took film courses where we made movies on Super 8 and watched all the old Ingmar Bergman movies. They pretty much put me to sleep. I got a degree in history. That was my background in film until I kind of literally fell back into it.

From what I understand, your first paid writing gigs were for gaming magazines. How did that come about?

I did a lot of wargaming, and then my friends I used to play *Dungeons and Dragons* back when it was just one, little pamphlet. We used to get graph paper and we'd draw out the dungeons and create the whole scenario. It was super-imaginative. I liked wargaming, too, World War II, and things like that. There were a couple magazines that were published in those days on that topic, and I wound up writing articles for three or four of those. For my history classes, we'd have to write papers and I'd find really obscure things I could research the heck out of. Then, I'd find ways to turn those papers into wargaming articles.

I wound up writing a few articles for Gary Gygax. He was in Lake Geneva, which wasn't far from where I was. He had, of course, created *Dungeons and Dragons*, but he also had a little wargaming shop. They had a magazine called *The Dragon*, and I got hired to write some articles for it. It was fun, and one of the side benefits was that I got to play a little bit of *D&D* with Gary down at the shop, and it was cool to sit there for an afternoon with the guy who had created the whole phenomenon.

How much do you think that background in creating worlds and characters for roleplaying influenced your work as a writer?

That's a really insightful question. I hadn't thought of it, but I really think that's a good point. I played roleplaying games back in high school and college, and even the regular war gaming with miniatures could be very creative. I had a lot of toy soldiers when I was a kid. I couldn't go out and play with the other kids a lot, and so I had these really big armies. We had a room where I'd set up these big campaigns, and play out the whole scenarios.

Going into roleplaying, you had to create things. The *Dungeons and Dragons* booklet gave you guidelines, but you had to come up with what the world looked like, what you'd encounter, the ultimate goals. And so you have a good point—I'm sure that did contribute considerably to writing and being able to create characters and situations that were unexpected.

Most people go to Hollywood to get into the movies, but it sounds more like you wound up in Los Angeles almost by accident. Getting into the film industry wasn't your intention?

No, no. As I said, I'd never really thought of it. Not even in my wildest dreams. Before the Internet, Hollywood was more of this Holy Grail sort of thing—you could look at it from afar, but you couldn't get close to it or even really think about it. I ended up out here because I finally got sick of school. I got my degree in history and I couldn't get any sort of job. I tried to get jobs at museums all over the world, but nothing happened so I went back to school. I got fed up with history, switched to business, and went three semesters toward my MBA but I couldn't get past accounting. My mind just didn't work that way.

I had a cousin-in-law up in Seattle that was hanging sheet rock. His partner had quit and he needed help, and it paid really well. I went out there, but it was not working out. I had another cousin-in-law who was in Los Angeles, and had a business doing industrial videos, or slide shows, telling companies how to operate machinery or sell products. He'd read my war gaming articles. He told me, "I know you can write, and I know you can take pictures. Why don't you come down here? I want to expand my business." So, I moved down here.

That wasn't really working out or paying the bills. I did some odd construction jobs. I thought about moving back to Wisconsin, but I had this casual friend who said to me, "You told me about all of those articles you wrote. Why don't you write a screenplay for a movie?" She said, "I've got a cousin who works for Warner Bros., and I'll get him to read your script." I thought, I love movies and I love writing, this sounds great. The issue was that I didn't know how to write a screenplay! I'd never even seen one. I had no idea what one looked like.

I went back to visit my father in Wisconsin. I went to the library and, lo and behold, there was a book about screenwriting called *How to Write Screen-*

plays. It was written before World War II. I took it off the shelf and, literally, the pages fell out. No one had taken it out in 40 years. I studied the book, and luckily the format was still basically the same.

I loved Westerns, so I figured I'd write a Western. I started working on this thing while still doing construction jobs during the day. By the time I finished it, though, I'd lost track of my friend, so I had no connection to the industry anymore. But, I had a completed screenplay.

This was the pre-Information Age—getting information about anything was near-impossible. I'd seen on TV or something that people in Hollywood had agents, and agents were located in Beverly Hills. So, I literally drove up from the beach and found a phone booth in a Beverly Hills parking lot that had a yellow pages in it. I looked and there were actually agencies listed. I thought, "Oh, that's easy!" I dialed the phone and said, "Hi, I've got a screenplay." [*Laughs*] After twenty or thirty calls, I got somewhere down into the D's and actually got hold of an agent who said, "Okay, send it in and I'll let you know." I got a nice rejection letter about six weeks later. They said, "It's pretty good for your first attempt, but it's a Western and nobody wants Westerns. Write something contemporary."

In college I was taking martial arts, and I got just below a black belt. I had that background and I had an idea for an action movie that would combine martial arts and guns. If you're familiar with some of John Woo's early work like *Hard Boiled* (1992), it was a little like that. I was kind of ahead of that curve. I wrote a script, and once again I didn't know what to do with it. Being dumb, I never thought of going back to that original agent.

I'd looked into making my own movie at one point while I was going through this process. I went down to a little equipment rental house on Hollywood Boulevard, one of the cheap ones, and started asking questions. I met a guy who was an aspiring cameraman and we hit it off. I was telling him about the script that I'd just finished, and he knew an actor that had actually been in a movie and had dialogue. I asked, "Do you think your friend would read my script and give me some pointers?" And he said, "Yeah, yeah. I'll see if he'll read it." This guy's name was Mel Novak. He'd just done a movie with Chuck Norris called *A Force of One* (1979).

Mel Novak read it and called me up. He said, "You know, Chuck Norris is looking for another script and I think this one would be pretty good. I want to send it to him." This was in January. In March I got a call back from Mel, and he said, "Chuck likes the script, but it's kind of short." It was only 72 pages, or something. And so I fleshed it out and sent him the new version, but I didn't hear anything back.

For my main job at the time, I worked at one of the first mini storage facilities in Los Angeles. At night they would turn loose about four or five Doberman Pinschers on the property to keep people out. My job was to go over to the place when they opened at seven o'clock in the morning to pick up all the dog poop so their customers wouldn't step in it. That's what I was doing at the time. I'll never forget it: it was a Sunday night in June, I had $8.43 left to my name, with a car payment due and a rent payment due. I'd run out of odd jobs. Mel called and said, "Chuck and I are going into AVCO Embassy tomorrow, they want to make the movie." [*Laughs*] I was like, "What?"

And that went on to become *An Eye for an Eye* (1981)?

Yeah. I was still literally learning as I go about how things worked. I met Chuck and his brother, Aaron, once in person as we were making the deal and so on. There was going to be a rewrite, and so I started calling the head of the story department every week asking, "So, when do you want me to start?" They always told me to just hold off, hold off. After about a month I called back and they said, "Oh, the rewrite is done." And again I was like, "What?" They paid me for it, but they didn't have me do it. That was really disappointing. And then I was supposed to go work on the movie as an associate producer, Mel Novak and I had that credit. He didn't want to go on location and told them no location work, so I didn't get the chance to go on set and meet anybody, or actually learn how movies are made, so on and so forth. That was disappointing as well, but at least I got paid for it.

You met your wife on that film though, right?

Yes. The best part was that there was a cast and crew screening at MGM.

Even though I didn't end up working on the film, I knew a couple of the stunt men on the movie. They introduced me to this beautiful girl at the screening; they'd set up a kind of blind date and didn't tell us. They told me her name was Elizabeth Stevens, that she was an actress and a singer. She was friends with all of these stunt guys. They used to come over and mow her grass, she'd make spaghetti, and they'd play penny poker. They decided that we'd hit it off. She didn't know I'd written the movie—luckily, she liked it. We got married four years later, and we just celebrated our thirtieth anniversary.

Norris' and Bruner's *Missing in Action* was the second movie in the series to be filmed, but it was the first to be released.

What happened, too, was Elizabeth's daughter—my stepdaughter—was taking Tang Soo Do from one of Chuck Norris' senior students. She used to see Chuck at different belt testings. He liked to hang out with her and shoot the breeze, so they knew each other casually in that way.

An Eye for an Eye had come out and done very well at the box office, but I was still waiting for the phone to start ringing. Meanwhile, I'd written a few spec scripts and so on. I'd thought, "I wrote a hit movie. People are going to want me to write other things, right?" But a year goes by and nothing happens.

Elizabeth got invited by the director of *An Eye for an Eye*, Steve Carver, to a screening of the trailer for *Lone Wolf McQuade* (1983). Chuck was there with his brother, Aaron. After the screening, Chuck came up to her and said, "Hey, are you still going out with that guy, James Bruner, who wrote *An Eye for an Eye*?" She said yes. He said, "I'd like him to write something else for me. Can I have his phone number?" He had an idea to do a movie about M.I.A.s in Vietnam, so that's where all of that started.

Did he call you and say, "I want a script about M.I.A.s, just run with that," or did he have more guidance for you on the subject?

He had read a book called *Mission M.I.A.* by J.C. Pollock, who ended up becoming a good friend of Elizabeth and mine. It was about a mission to rescue M.I.A.s and so on, and he wanted to use an idea like that as the basis for a movie. Chuck's brother, Wieland, had been lost in Vietnam, and he wanted to do something to memorialize him, but also the guys who made it back and were treated so poorly when they came home.

I worked with my friend, Jim Monaghan, who is an ex-green beret. He helped me with a lot of the technical stuff in the script. We wound up writing a screenplay with Chuck's input, Aaron's input, and so on. What we wound up with has basically the same story as what was in *Missing in Action*. Chuck was taking it around town looking for someone to finance it, but it was a bigger budget than the movies he'd done. I think it was $10 to $12 million dollars, which back in that day was huge, especially for a Chuck Norris movie. So, we weren't having much luck getting any financial backing.

Chuck called me up one day and he said, "I've got this producer who's interested in *Missing in Action*. I don't really have time to meet with him. Can you have lunch with him and check him out?" I said yeah, okay. I went to Malibu and had lunch with this guy named Lance Hool. He'd produced a couple of things at that point. Nice guy. He took the script and said he might have some ideas for it. I didn't hear anything for a while, and then I get another one of those calls from Chuck. He says, "Lance and I are going in to meet with this new company called Cannon Films. They want to do *Missing in Action*. Our meeting is at 10:00, I'll call you after the meeting and let you know when we're starting." Noon rolls around. Then one, two, three o'clock in the afternoon. I started wondering what happened. I got a call from Chuck around four, and he said he walked into the meeting—this was the first time he met Menahem Golan—and Menahem handed him a script called *Missing in Action*, but it wasn't the script I wrote! It was written by some other guys. Menahem told him, "We want to do this movie. You will star in it." He made him a big offer. He made Chuck read the script on the spot. He had to say yes or no right there, and he said yes.

Chuck said to me, "I'm sorry. They want to do this one, but they're at least going to buy your script. You'll at least get a payday." I found out later what happened was that Lance had set up a meeting at Cannon, then found out they had another project called *Missing in Action* that they liked and wanted to do. It had a much smaller budget than the script I wrote. They'd also found out that Cannon had not optioned the script, and so he went and optioned it. When he walked into the meeting with Menahem and Chuck, he owned the rights to the script, which meant that he'd direct it and produce it. I was pretty depressed about it. I'd put a lot of work into it and was very excited. It was nice to get a payday, but that's not the same as getting a movie made.

They went down to Saint Kitts in the Caribbean to make the movie. It was part of a tax deal or something, I can't remember what it was. I get a call from Aaron Norris, who had come back to Los Angeles to pick up some equipment or something. He told me Cannon liked what they were seeing and wanted to do a sequel, and that Chuck wanted me to write the sequel to the movie. He said, "You've got to get on a plane and get to Saint Kitts. They want to film a trailer for the sequel when they finish principal photography on Lance's movie, so you need to write something they can shoot." I went down there, and I took our original script and wrote something that encapsulated it for them to shoot. Luckily cooler heads prevailed and they never shot that, because it would have been stupid. [*Laughs*]

For the sequel, I took the original script and pared it down considerably.

There were a lot more characters in the original, and I had to tailor it to the background of the first movie. They had another director, Joe Zito, do my script, and they went to the Philippines and shot it. They come back to edit it, and all of a sudden it comes out that they're going to release the second film, the one I wrote, as *Missing in Action*.

I found out what happened eventually. At the time, Cannon had a first look deal with Warner Bros., and they'd looked at the Lance Hool *Missing in Action* and passed. Cannon wanted to get into distributing their own films, and they looked at Joe Zito's *Missing in Action* and thought, "We're going to put this out ourselves." They already had a release date. Warner Bros. was upset later because they'd never shown them the Joe Zito movie. They would have taken that, and it would have been a different story. It came out and it was #1.

Obviously in retrospect that strategy worked. At the time you heard they were swapping the two movies around, did you ever imagine that it would work out as well as it did?

Well, I'd seen a lot of the footage and filming for the Saint Kitts *Missing in Action*, and I'd also seen footage from the Zito version. A lot of this is probably an ego thing, but I thought that if they released the Kitts one first, there wasn't going to be a sequel. They'd dump the sequel. I just didn't think the other one was that strong.

I went to Hollywood Boulevard to see the [Zito] *Missing in Action*, and people were standing and cheering at the end. That was very satisfying as a filmmaker, and it continues to play very well to this day. I just don't think that it would have worked the opposite way, but part of that is probably hindsight, too. Not that I had any say over it, anyway!

I can tell you a funny story. Chuck hadn't seen the movie, and I hadn't seen the movie. We'd only seen bits and pieces. I was doing a location scout with Joe Zito for *Invasion USA* and Chuck was shooting a movie called *Code of Silence* (1985) in Chicago. We stopped there to see Chuck, because Joe wanted to show him the final cut of *Missing in Action*. It was Chuck, Aaron, me, Joe Zito, and Mike Emery, who was Chuck's manager, the guy who took care of a lot of his business stuff. The movie's over and I've got goosebumps—it was this tiny, little screening room. Chuck's manager turned to me afterwards and he says, "Well, I don't think it will hurt his career." [*Laughs*] He thought it was a complete bomb!

After his first *Missing in Action* script became a bit hit, Cannon brought Bruner back to write several more films, include *Missing in Action III*.

Epilogue

Cannon brought 1984 to a close on a remarkable high. Between *Missing in Action* and *Breakin'*, they had scored two of the biggest hits they'd ever have. Their work with John Cassavetes on *Love Streams* had earned them credibility as serious filmmakers, and they had even managed to spin the disaster that was the public *Bolero* fallout into a win for their financial returns.

Golan and Globus used this success to effectively double down on their production rate. The mid-1980s—covered in the second volume of this series—saw Cannon release their most ambitious slate of movies ever. Not only did they spend significantly more money on their budgets, but their jaw-dropping 1985–1986 schedule saw the company juggle more film shoots than even the major studios would think feasible.

Up next . . . *The Cannon Film Guide: Volume II*, starring Chuck Norris, Charles Bronson, Michael Dudikoff, Sylvester Stallone, and Dolph Lundgren, and featuring *American Ninja*, *The Delta Force*, *Over the Top*, *Masters of the Universe*, *Lifeforce*, *Invasion USA*, *The Texas Chainsaw Massacre 2*, *King Solomon's Mines*, and many, many more. Don't touch that dial.

Acknowledgments

I'd like to express my deepest gratitude to the many people who lent support throughout the years as this book was coming together. Among them I'd like to say thank you to the countless interview subjects and other Cannon alumni I've spoken with over the years for generously sharing their experiences with me. To Ben Ohmart and BearManor Media, for publishing this book. To Oisin McGillion Hughes, for lending his incredible artistic talents as seen on the cover of this volume. To the League—Zach Hollwedel, Jon Maynard, Shawn Hazelett, Jennifer Chang, and Anne Rumberger—for their many notes, and for being patient while I talked about nothing but Michael Dudikoff movies for several years. To my mother and mother-in-law, for helping with the kids when I most desperately needed time to write. To Robert Kidd, for not talking me out of the idea like I had initially asked him to. To Alex Segura, for setting such a good example. To Jeremie Damoiseau, author of *The Punisher 1989: The Untold Story of a Cult Classic*, for not only a motherlode of Cannon ephemera, but for sharing helpful contact information. To Paul Talbot, author of *Bronson's Loose: The Making of the Death Wish Films* and *Bronson's Loose Again!*, for penning two definitive volumes on cinema's greatest badass—my writings on Bronson are only drops in the bucket compared to his exhaustive research. To Michael J. Weldon and Danny Peary, as well as

Mike McPadden and david j. moore, for being the pioneers and the torchbearers of the cult film guide, respectively. To Keith J. Rainville of the website Vintage Ninja, who since 2009 has stood guard over the ultimate repository of forbidden shinobi knowledge. And to Mark Hartley, whose documentary *Electric Boogaloo: The Wild, Untold Story of Cannon Films* not only proved there was still interest in the studio, but inspired a new generation of movie fans to dive into their filmography.

Most of all I wish to thank my wife, Sara, for being so absolutely loving and supportive of everything I've done, even when it meant me staying up to watch *10 to Midnight* for a fifth consecutive time instead of coming to bed. And to my daughter, Vera, and son, Lyell, each of whom watched the entirety of the *Ninja* and *Missing in Action* trilogies, respectively, before the age of 12 weeks.

The author, age six, channeling his inner American Ninja.

About the Author

Austin Trunick is a Connecticut-based author and filmmaker. He serves as the film editor for the nationally-distributed music and entertainment magazine *Under the Radar*. His writings on movies and pop culture have appeared on *Mental Floss* and *Consequence of Sound*.

THE CANNON FILM GUIDE, VOL.1 (1980–1984)

Index

Numbers in **bold** indicate photographs

10 to Midnight 108, 115, 118, 179-196, **180**, **181**, **182**, **183**, **185**, **187**, **189**, **191**, **192**, **193**, **195**, 210, 306, 370, 484, 508
52 Pick-Up 176, 190

Abbott, Diahnne 400, 405
Ackland, Joss 52, 53, 58
Adams, Edie 8
Adkins, Scott 283, 284
Aleong, Aki 489
Alfonso, Kristian **138**
Ali, Muhammad 89, 91, 92, 94, 337
Alien from L.A. 323
"All Night Long" 327, 344, 346
Allan Quatermain and the Lost City of Gold 165, 361
Allan, Ted 395, 399
Allen, Debbie 273
Allen, Steve 65
Aloni, Miri 301
Alston, Emmett 61, 63, 79, 454
Altman, Robert xviii, 43, 151, 308, 398
Ambassador, The 81, 159, 184, 306, 422
America 3000 101, 202, 308, 447
American Cyborg: Steel Warrior 29
American Ninja x, xi, xiii, 73, 75, 76, 118, 248, 258, 266, 268, 283, 454, 455, 456, 494, 505

511

American Samurai 266, 302
Amis, Kingsley 293
Anderson, Ingrid 222
Anderson, Lindsay 293
Andress, Ursula 411, 422
Anthony, Tony 161, 163-164, **165**, 170
Antin, Steve 131, **132**, 133, **133**, **135**, 143, 149
Apple, The xvii, xix, **40**, 41-60, **42**, **44**, **46**, **49**, **51**, **53**, **55**, **57**, 221, 302, 447
Appointment with Death 115, 226
Archer, Anne 369, 374
Archerd, Army 8
Argento, Dario 216, 222, 234, 235, 238, 239, 240, 242
Arkoff, Samuel Z. xxiii
Arliss, Leslie 285, 289
Armstrong, Michael 197, 200, 201, 205
Arnaz Jr., Desi 197, 201, 202, 205
Assassination 102, 114, 179
Assissi Underground, The 218
Astaire, Fred 41, 330, 339
Atlantis: the Lost Continent 224
Ator the Fighting Eagle 220
Aumont, Jean-Pierre 171, **172**, 176
Avenging Force 115, 258, 266, 268, 274, 454
Avery, Rick 458
Avildsen, John G. xxvi, 440

Baldi, Ferdinando 161, 163, 164, 170
Balsam, Martin 110
Band, Richard 38
Banks, Tony 288
Barbarians, The 226, 315
Barber, Glynis 288
Barfly 456
Barker, Ron 487
Barrett, Victoria 303, 308
Barron, Dana 115
Bates, Alan 285, 287, 290, **291**
Battista, Lloyd 161
Beat Street 328
Behind Enemy Lines 456
Behm, Marc 67, 72, 121, 125, 171, 172
"Believe in the Beat" 341-342
Bennett, Jordan 447, 449, 463-467, **464**
Bensen, Greg 416, **417**
Benton, Barbi 67-68, 69, 70, 72
Berger, Carin 176
Berger, Debra 176

Berger, Katya 171, **172, 173**, 174, 175, 176, 178, 221
Berger, William 174, 213, 221, **221**, 228, 230, 243-244
Bergman, Andrew 407
Bergman, Ingmar 408, 494
Berlin Affair, The 221, 226
Bernstein, Elmer 419
Bernstein, Peter 419
Beswick, Martine 3, 7, 12
Better Off Dead 136, 141, 146, 360
Big Trouble 407
Bill & Ted's Bogus Journey 345
Bill & Ted's Excellent Adventure 110, 136, 141, 347
Bing, Steve 469, 472
Black Eagle 79, 250, 278, 280-281, 454
Blood on the Sun 457
Bloodsport xviii, xix
Bloom, Lindsay 8, 12
Bloom, Ron 492
Blue Lagoon 311, 313, 314, 321
Boccardo, Delia 218
Body and Soul 26, 38, 65, **88**, 89-95, **93**, 320
"Body Shop" 450
Bolero 167, 301, 322, 409-426, **410**, **413**, **415**, **417**, **418**, **420**, **421**, **426**, 447, 505
Boogaloo Shrimp **326**, 327, 329, 330, 339, 342, **344**, 344-348, 352
Boogaloo Shrimp Documentary, The 345, 348
Booth, James 454
Borgnine, Ernest 207, 209
Bowers, George 89
Boyle, Peter xxvi, 435, 440
Braddock: Missing in Action III 370, **483**, 484-493, **486**, **488**, **490**, **491**, 494, **503**
Brass, Tinto 238, 239, 240
Breakin' x, xviii, 272, 302, 325-335, **326**, **329**, **331**, **333**, **334**, 336, 337, 339, 342, 344-347, 348, 350, 447, 454, 476, 478, 505
"Breakin'...There's No Stopping Us" 335
Breakin' 'n' Entering 327, 346
Breakin' 2: Electric Boogaloo xi, 45, 166, 258, **272**, 272-274, **275**, 308, 332, 335-342, **336**, **343**, 343-344, **344**, 348, **349**, 350-356, **354**, 447, 450, 454
Breen, Philip M. 385
Briant, Shane 121, 126
Brimley, Wilfred 188
Bronson, Charles x, xviii, 97-98, 99, 100, 101-102, **103**, 105, **106**, 106, **107**, 108, **109**, 111, **111**, **112**, 113, **114**, 114, 115, 116, 117, **117**, 118-120, 179, 180-181, **180**, **181**, 182, **182**, **183**, 184, **185**, 187, 188, **189**, **191**, 192, 193, 194, **195**, 210, 211, 286, 303, 369-370, 505, 507
Brough, Candi and Randi 8
Bruner, James 469, 472-473, 484, 493-503
Buchholz, Horst 322

Buntzman, David 439
Buntzman, Mark 427, 429, 431, 435, 436, 437, 439, 439, 442

Caesar, Sid 303, 304, 308
Caffaro, Cheri 11-12
Cagney, James 457
Caligula 223, 238, 240
Cameron, James 427, 434, 445
Canalito, Lee 412
Cannon, Mary 23, 24, 28
Cardiff, Jack 288
Carew, Topper 346
Carlucci, Milly 229
Carney, Art 369, 373
Carradine, John 197, 199-200, **200**, 201, 202
Carrey, Jim 361
Carter, T.K. 25
Carver, Steve 119, 500
Cassavetes, John x, xviii, 351, 395-408, **396**, **397**, **402**, **406**, **407**, 505
Cassel, Seymour 397, 401
Cassinelli, Claudio 218, 229
Cassisi, John 148
Cenci, Renzo **185**
Chambers, Michael see Boogaloo Shrimp
Chan, Jackie 282, 283
Chiba, Sonny 459
Child is Waiting, A 398-399
Chung, David 448, **455**
Clair, Cyrielle 385, 389
Clay, Andrew Dice 357, 359, 361
Clay, Nicholas 121, **123**, 127
Clinton, George S. 46
Coates, Lewis see Cozzi, Luigi
Coelho, Susie 339
Colgin, Russell W. 207
Comin' At Ya! 163
Connery, Sean 385, 387-388, **387**, 389, 391, 393, 394
Conti, Bill 157
Coogan, Jackie 38
Coppola, Francis Ford xxii, 33
Corman, Roger xxi-xxii, xxiii, 32, 38, 135, 217, 380
Correll, Rich 348
Corsaro, Frank 240
Courtney, Alex 81
Cox, Tony 38
Cozzi, Luigi 213, 216, 218, 220, 222, 224, 225, 226, 227, 228, 233, 234-238, 240, 241, 245, 383

Cramer, Grant 61, 64-65
Craven, Wes 340
Cushing, Peter 197, 199, **200**, 201, 203, 385, 391
Cyborg xix

D'Abo, Olivia 417-418, 425
D'Amato, Joe 174, 220, 381
D'Angelo, Mirella 223, 238-245, **239**, **243**
Dancers 226
Dangerously Close 176
Danning, Sybil 213, 216, 217, **217**, 218, 219, 226, 228, 377, 379, **379**, 380, 382-383
David, Keith 486
Davidson, Boaz xxv, 23, 28-29, 67, 69, 72, 131, 132, 137, 140, 143-144, 148, 150
Davis, Gene 179, 185, **187**, **191**, **192**, 192-193, 194
De Laurentiis, Dino 97, 101
De Stefane, Ed **210**
Deacon, Richard 3, 8, 12
Death Hunt 194
Death Sentence 100
Death Wish xiv, 25, 97, 97-120, 207, 211, 286, 288, 369, 429, 494
Death Wish II xviii, 3, **96**, 100-107, **103**, **106**, 108, 179, 188, 209, 288, 429
Death Wish 3 3, **107**, 108-114, **109**, **111**, **112**, **114**, 114, 118, 120, 288, 292
Death Wish 4: The Crackdown 3, **114**, 114-118, **117**, 120, 179, 184, 439
Death Wish V: The Face of Death 118-119
DeBevoise, Allen 325
Déjà vu 226, 304
Del Ruth, Thomas 102
Delta Force 2: The Colombian Connection 115, 248, 370, 456, 485, 494
Delta Force 3: The Killing Game 29, 210
Delta Force, The xviii, 110, 166, 304, 308, 416, 472, 488, 493, 494
Dementia 13 xxii
Deoul, Stefani 353
Depp, Johnny 340
Derek, Bo 167, 301, 322, 386, 409-412, **410**, **413**, 414, **415**, 415, **417**, **418**, **420**, 420, 421-426, **421**
Derek, John 409, 411, 412, 414, 416, 421-426, **426**
Dern, Bruce 151, **152**, **153**, 154
Desert Warrior 9
Desmond, Dick 73
Dewey, Chris xxvi
Diamonds xxvi, 260
Dickerson, George 116
Dickey, Lucinda **267**, **271**, 272, **272**, 325, **326**, 328, 329, 342, 447, **453**, 454, 463
"Do the Bartman" 342, 345, 347
Doin' Time on Planet Earth 7, 370
Donaggio, Pino 225-226, 303
Dr. Heckyl and Mr. Hype 8, 31-39, **32**, **33**, **35**, **37**, 127, 176

Dubin, Gary **138**
Dudikoff, Michael xviii, 188, 266, 303, 455, 505
Duet for One 157, 287
Duffy, Thomas F. 103
Dunaway, Faye 110, 285, **286**, 286-287, **287**, 288, **291**, **292**, **294**, 295, 298, 318, 414
Dye, John 361

Ebert, Roger 153, 193, 218
Edmonds, Michael see Jakoby, Don
Efroni, Yehuda 5, 222-223, 303, 379, 487, **490**
Eilbacher, Lisa 179, 188, **191**
El Dorado xxii-xxxiii
Elliott, Denholm 285, 287, 288
Emmanuelle 123-124
Endless Love 311, 313, 314, 321
Engelbach, David 97, 101, 104, 108
English, Louise 204
Enter the Ninja xviii, 63, 73-87, **74**, **76**, **82**, **86**, 247, 252, 255, 263, 279, 459
Escape from Beyond 170
Evil That Men Do, The 108
Exorcist, The 43, 155, 156, 453
Expendables, The 29-30, 197
Exterminator 2 3, 310, 427-445, **428**, **429**, **431**, **437**, **438**, **443**
Exterminator, The 427, 428-429, 430, 431
Eye for an Eye, An 493, 498, 499, 500

Faison, Frankie 432
Falcon, Bruno "Pop N Taco" 328
Family Matters 342, 345, 347, 348
Fellini, Federico 238, 239, 242, 244, 404
Ferman, James 293
Ferrare, Ashley 250, 279
Ferrers, Lady Katherine 296
Ferrigno, Carla see Green, Carlotta
Ferrigno, Lou 213-216, **214**, **215**, **217**, 218, 220-221, 226-228, **227**, 230, **232**, 233, 234, 236, 237-238, 242-243, **243**, 377, 378, 379, **379**, 382-383, 414
Ferro, Dan 116
Firewalker 184, 248, 320, 391, 456
Firstenberg, Sam ix-xi, 247-248, 257, **257**, 258-277, **267**, **271**, **272**, 325, 328, 336, 447, 454, 455, 459, 461-462, 465, 466
Fishburne, Laurence 103
Foldes, Lawrence D. 207, 212
Forbes, Bryan 369, 371-372, 374
Forbidden Planet 229
Forrest, Steve 318
Fragasso, Claudio 377, 381-382
Franklin, Diane 131, 135-136, **136**, **141**, 141-147, **145**

Freedman, Winifred 134, 138-139
Freya, Jan 350-356
Friedkin, William 156-157, 166
Friedland, Dennis xxvi
Frye, Sean 252
Frye, Soleil Moon 252
Frye, Virgil 38, 252

Gale, Charles 357, 361-362
Gallardo, Silvana 103
Garcia, Sabrina 339, **344**
Gardenia, Vincent 105
Garfield, Brian 98, 100
Garfield, John 91
Garland, Judy 41, 338, 398
Gawain and the Green Knight 386
Gazzo, Mike 92
Geffner, Deborah 432
Geleng, Massimo Antonello 242
Gellar, Sarah Michelle 308
George, Christopher 73, 83, 85, 87
George, Lynda Day 209
George, Susan 73, 81
Ger, Aviva 299, 301
Ghosts Can't Do It 426
Gielgud, John 285, 287, 291
Gilmour, George 41, 46
Ginty, Robert 427, 430, 431, 434, 435-436, 442, 444
Glennon, Cordon 285
Glickenhaus, James 429
Globus, Yoram ix, xi, xiv, xvii-xviii, xix, **xx**, xx, xxi, xxiii-xxiv, xxv-xxvii, 3, 5, 7, 8, 12, 29, 42, 63, 69, 76, 81, 100, 118, 124, 131, 132, 143, 172, 179, 180, 196, 200, 218, 223, 247, 258, 259, 262, 276, 299, 306, 318, 326, 328, 346, 347, 351, 383, 385, 386, 398, 399, 435, 440, 473, 505
Godard, Jean-Luc xviii
Going Bananas 29, 226
Golan, Menahem ix-x, xi, xiv, xvii-xviii, xix, **xx**, xx-xxiii, xxiv-xxvi, xxvii, 3, 5, 7, 8, 12, 18, 29, 32-33, 34, 39, 41, 42, 43, 47, 54, 55, 56, 63, 69, 72, 73, 76, 77, 81, 100, 101, 108, 118, 119, 124, 128, 131, 132, 143, 157, 158, 172, 179, 180, 196, 200-201, 205, 217, 218, 223, 228, 247-248, 258, 259, 260, 262, 270, 272, 276, 277, 299, 303, 306, 308, 310, 311, 314, 315, 316, 318, 321, 322, 325, 326, 327, 328, 344, 346, 347, 351, 383, 385, 386, 398, 399, 408, 421, 423, 424, 435, 440, 454, 461, 465, 473, 501, 505
Goldenberg, Devin 3
Goldstein, Allan A. 119
Goodson, Bill 274-275
Gor 226

Gossett, Robert 308-309
Gould, Elliot 303, **307**, 307-308, 369, 372, 465
Grace Quigley 310, 430
Graduates of Malibu High, The see Young Warriors
Grandi, Serena 231
Great Escape, The 98, 102
Green, Carlotta 230, 237-238, 382
Greenberg, Adam 303, 306
Greene, Bob 20-21
Greene, Graham 244
Greene, John 66
Griffith, Charles B. xxii, 31, 32-33, 34, 38-39
Grizzly 220, 224
Gross, Arye 439
Gross, Jerry 23
Guillermin, John 315, 316
Gurfinkel, David 302
Gygax, Gary 495
H.O.T.S. 8, 10, 11, 12
Hadar, Ronnie 8
Hamill, Mark 188, 386
Hancock, Herbie 288, 434
Happy Hooker Goes Hollywood, The xxvii, **2**, 3-14, **6**, **10**, 33, 370
Happy Hooker Goes to Washington, The 6
Happy Hooker, The xxvii, 4, 6
Happy Hooker: My Own Story, The 6
Hare, Will 81
Harpaz, Shraga 299, 300
Harris, Brad 222, 377, 379, 382
Harryhausen, Ray 7, 225, 236, 327, 345
Haunted Summer 110
Hayes, Isaac 106
Heatherton, Joey 6
Hefner, Hugh 67, 156
Hellbound 300
Hemingway, Margaux 303, 305, **307**, 309
Hemsey, Yvonne 158
Hercules **163**, 174, 213-228, **214**, **215**, **217**, 233, 235, 236-237, 238-239, **239**, 240-245, **243**, 377-378, 379, 380, 383
Hercules II: The Adventures of Hercules **221**, 226, **227**, 228-234, **232**, 235, **235**, 237-238, **239**, 380, 447
Hero and the Terror 139, 210
Herzog, Werner 17-18
Hickman, Gail Morgan 97, 114-115, 116, 117
Hill, Marianna 15, 18
Hitman, The 119
Ho, Godfrey 74

Holden, William 157
Holland, Steve 146
Hollander, Xaviera 4, 5-6, 7
Hong, James 450
Hool, Lance 181-182, 469, 472, 473, 474, 500-501, 502
Hooper, Tobe 108, 176
Hospital Massacre 29, 62, 67-72, **68**, **71**, 125, 172
Hot Chili 65, 133, 135, 148, 150, 166, 308, 435, 440, 450
Hot Resort 29, 308, 360, 450
House of the Long Shadows 197-205, **198**, **200**, **203**, 391
House on Chelouche Street, The xxiv
Howard, Kevyn Major 103
Howard, Trevor 387
Howerton, Charles 38
Hudson, Rock 422
Hunter, Richard 204
Huntly, Leslie 14

"I Feel for You" 344
I Love You Rosa xxiv, 306
I'm Almost Not Crazy: John Cassavetes – The Man and His Work 351, **407**, 408
"I'm Coming" 51, 58
Ice-T 332, 341, 346
Idol, Gerri **133**, 134
"In Your Eyes (Freedom)" 492
Inga xxvi
Innocence of Muslims 9, 12
Invaders from Mars 38, 108, 176, 248, 456
Invasion U.S.A. xiii, xviii, 62, 113, 472, 478
Ireland, Jill 99, 101-102, 118
Ireland, Kathy 323

Jackson, Michael 42, 190, 198, 311, 327, 333, 342, 345, 346, 348
Jaeckin, Just 121, 124-125, 128
Jakoby, Don 97, 108, 114
Joe xxvi, 435, 440, 442
Johari, Azizi 26, 93
Johnson, E. Lamont 103
Johnson, Sunny 31, 35
Jump, Gordon 361

Kalani, Jr., Charles see Tanaka, Professor Toru
Kane, Carol 308
Karloff, Boris 201
Kazablan xxiv, 259
Keach, Stacy 151-152, **153**, 154
Kedrova, Lila 389-390

Keeler, Christine 177
Keith, Paul 8
Keith, Sheila 203
Kelly, Roz 61, 63
Kempinski, Tom 287
Kennedy, George 409, 416, 425
Kennedy, Grace 47
Kennedy, Jayne 89, 90, 91, 92, **93**, 94-95
Kennedy, Jr., John F. 318
Kennedy, Leon Isaac 89-91, 92, **93**, 94-95
Keough, Jeana 186, **187**
Keyes, Irwin 439
Khan, Chaka 327, 344, 346
Khashoggi, Adnan 318
Kickboxer 332
Kiger, Susan 8, 12
King Solomon's Mines 165, 184, 315, 320, 391, 505
King-Hall, Magdalen 285
King, Stephen 173, 371
Kinjite: Forbidden Subjects 116, 179, 184, 370
Kinski, Klaus xxiv, 19-16, **16**, 20
Kinski, Nastassja 17
Kline, Richard 102-103
Kohner, Pancho 179-180, 181, 182
Kosugi, Kane 247, 250, 253, 254, 256, **277**, 277-284, **280**
Kosugi, Shane 248
Kosugi, Sho xiv, 63, 73, **74**, 77-79, 80, 85, 247, 248, 250, **255**, 255, 257, **257**, **263**, 264, 269, 270, 273, 274, **277**, 277, 278, 279, 280, 281, 283, 447, 451, 452, 454-455, 456, 460-461, 462
Krieger, Stu 23, 28
Kristel, Sylvia 24, 121, 123, **123**, 124, 125, 126, 127, **128**, 128-129, 140
Kurosawa, Akira 116, 264, 377, 380

Lacey, Ronald 311, 320, 360, 391
Lady Chatterley's Lover 24, 72, 121-129, **122**, **123**, **125**, **128**, 172
Lambada 302, 328, 342
Lambert, Steven 248, 253, 256-257, 269, 274, 448, **455**, 456-463, **460**
LaMotta, John 454
Lanchester, Elsa 202
Landis, John 485
Lang, Perry 92, 320
Last American Virgin, The xviii, xxv, 8, 29, 38, **130**, 131-150, **132**, **133**, **135**, **136**, **138**, **139**, **141**, **145**, **147**, **149**, 176, 208, 302, 306
Lauter, Ed 109
Lawford, Peter 92
Lawrence, D.H. 123, 125, 127
Lawson, Leigh 389

Lazarus, Jerry 166, 303, 308
Leadbetter, Cindy 229
Lee-Thompson, Peter 118
Lee, Bruce 73, 77, 256, 283, 458, 470
Lee, Christopher 197, 199, **200**, 201, 204
Lee, Jonna 357, 359, **362**, 363-367
Lemmon, Chris 3, 4, 12, 13
Lemmon, Jack 4, 13, 99
Lemon Popsicle xxv, 29, 69, 81, 131, 132, 140, 143, 144, 150, 302
Lenz, Kay 115
Lenzi, Laura 230
Leonard, Elmore 260
Lepke xxvi, 247, 259, 260
Leprechaun 62, 435, 440, 441-442
Les Miserables 463, 466, 467
Levinson, Larry 469, 472
Lew, James 458
Lewis, Geoffrey 189
Lifeforce 108, 176, 200, 342, 447, 505
Little Shop of Horrors xxii, 32, 38, 105
Lloyd, Christopher 15, 20, 149
Lockhart, Anne 210
Lockwood, Margaret 285
Lokey, Ben 329, 333
London, Lisa 8, 10-14
Lone Wolf McQuade 26, 95, 470, 500
Lopez, Perry 116
Love Streams 351, 395-408, **396**, **397**, **402**, **406**, **407**, 505
Love, Allan 47
Lugosi, Bela 201
Lumet, Sidney 99
Lyons, Robert F. 188
MacLaine, "Captain" James 296
Madame Rosa xxiv
Magician of Lublin, The xxvi
Magnificent Seven, The 98, 182, 217, 322, 377, 378, 380, 382, 419
Making the Grade 165, 320, 357-367, **358**, **360**, **362**, 391
Man with the Rubber Head, The 225
Mangine, Joe 445
Margolyes, Miriam 49
Maria's Lovers 17, 159, 318
Marvin, Lee 108
Marx, Groucho 65
Mason, James 285
Mata Hari 124, 128
Mataix, Enrique **195**, **333**, **452**
Mattei, Bruno 216, 236, 237, 377, 381-382

Maximum Overdrive 173, 432
May, Brian 484
McCallum, David 102
McCallum, Jason 118
McCallum, Paul 188
McDonald, Christopher 330, 332
McDonald, Julie 347, 348
McGinley, Ted 318
McGinnis, Scott 359, **362**
McLaglen, Andrew V. 311, 316
McShane, Ian 127
Messenger of Death 179, 184, 192
Midnight Ride 159
Miller, Dick 38
Miller, Jason 151, 155, 156, 157-158, 159-160
Mills, John 322
Mingozzi, Gianfranco 244
Missing in Action xiv, xviii, 182, 210, 450, **468**, 469-503, **471**, **499**, 505, 508
Missing in Action 2: The Beginning 116, 254, 448, **473**, 474-484, **475**, **478**, **479**, **482**, 487
Mission MIA 472
Mitchum, Robert 151, 153, **153**, 154, 157, 158-159, **159**, 184, 422
Mizrahi, Moshe xxiv
Mommie Dearest 286, 318, 414
Monaghan, Jim 500
Monoson, Lawrence 131, **132**, 132, 133, **135**, 143, **145**
Moore, Roger **368**, 369, **370**, 370-372, **373**, 374-375,
Moore, Wildey 111
Moritz, Louisa 65, 134, 135, **135**, 135, 150
Moroff, Mike 116
Morricone, Ennio 169, 173, 225, 321
Mortimer, John 293
Murder By Mail see *Schizoid*
Murphy, Audie xxiii
Murphy's Law 114, 115, 166, 179, 184, 188, 308, 370
Myers, Kenny 348

Naked Cage, The 10, 11, 13, 14
Naked Face, The 303, 307, **368**, 369-375, **370**, **373**
Nakoula, Nakoula Basseley 9
Nana, the True Key of Pleasure 72, 169, 171-178, **172**, **173**, **175**, 221, 225, 379
Nannuzzi, Armando 173
Nebe, Chris 14
Neeson, Liam 100
Nelson, Judd 357, 359, 361, **362**, 363
Nero, Franco 73, **74**, **76**, 77, 79, 80, 82, **82**, 87, 247
Neubauer, Leonard 61

New Year's Evil xiii, 61-66, **66**, 67, 79, 135, 454
Newborn III, Phineas 330, 333
Newton, Margie 230
Nicholas, Paul 13, 14
Nightmare on Elm Street, A 340
Ninja III: The Domination 75, 79, 248, 258, **267**, 268, 269, 270, 272, 315, 328, 336, **446**, 447-467, **449**, **451**, **452**, **453**, **455**, **464**
Ninja: Shadow of a Tear 250, 278, 283
Niven, Kip 61, 64
Norris, Aaron 469, 484, 489, 498, 500, 501, 502
Norris, Chuck x, xviii, 3, 26, 29, 95, 113, 116, 119, 139, 210, 254, 283, 303, 370, 380, 441, 456, 457, 458, **468**, 469-471, **471**, 472-473, **473**, 474, **475**, 476, 477, **478**, 479, **479**, **480**, 481, 482, **482**, **483**, 484, 485, **486**, 487, **488**, 488, 489, **490**, 491, **491**, **492**, 493, 494, 498, **499**, 499-503, **503**, 505
Norris, Mike 210
Novak, Mel 498
Noy, Zachi 81
Number One With A Bullet 115

O'Connell, Taaffe 65
O'Herlihy, Gavan 110
O'Keeffe, Miles 385, 386-387, 412
O'Neill, Terry 286, 287
O'Toole, Peter 240
Obregon, Ana 161, 166-167, 409, 415
Occhipinti, Andrea 409, 417, **421**, 425
Olkewicz, Walter 360
Ollie & Jerry 335
Olsen, Dana 357, 361
Omaggio, Maria 230
One More Chance 248, 260, 262, 454
Operation Thunderbolt xxiv, 18, 217, 260
Otello x
Outlaw of Gor 226
Over the Brooklyn Bridge 166, 226, 303-310, **304**, **305**, **307**, **309**, 372
Over the Top 101, 505
Oy Vey, My Son Is Gay 38-39

P.O.W. The Escape 494
Page, Jimmy **106**, 106-107, 288
Palzis, Kelly 190
Parker, Charles 325
Parks, Michael 119
Paulsen, David 15, 18
Peasgood, Julie 202
Peck, Brian 139
Pen, Howard C. 385

Penitentiary 90, 91
Penitentiary III 90, 94, 95
Penitentiary II 90, 95
Picardo, Robert 467
Pinocchio 108
Pinups, The 11, 13
Platoon Leader 188
Podestà, Rossanna 218
Poggi, Ferdinando 230
Pollock, J.C. 472, 500
Potts, Cliff 320
Powell, Dave 450
Preppies see *Making the Grade*
Preston, Kelly see Palzis, Kelly
Price, Vincent 197-198, **200**, 201, 203, 204, 205

Qissi, Michael 332
Quigley, Linnea 208
Quinn, Anthony 426
Quiñones, Adolfo see Shabba-Doo
Quintano, Gene 161, 163, 165, 357, 361

Raab, Max 156
Rabal, Francisco "Paco" 161, 166
Rader, Jack 487
Raffin, Deborah 113
Rappaport, David 391
Rappin' 302, 328, 332, 342, 432
Ravel, Maurice 414
Ray, Ola 190
Reagan, Ronald 479
Recht, Coby and Iris 43
Redgrave, Lynn 6
Redondo, Emiliano 166
Reed, Oliver 31, 34, 36, 127
Reeve, Christopher 370
Reeves, Steve 213, 215, 382
Reichert, Julie 325, 335-336, 350-356
Reilly, Tom **210**, 210
Reiner, Carl 466-467
Reisz, Karel 293
Revenge of the Ninja xi, 38, 75, 79, 84, 208, **246**, 247-268, **249**, **251**, **255**, **257**, **263**, 270, 274, 277-279, **277**, **280**, 283, 315, 336, 433, 452, 453, 454, 456, 459, **460**, 461, 462, 484
Rhys-Davies, John 311, 320, 321, 385, 391
Rice-Davies, Mandy 177, 379
Richarde, Tessa 134

Richie, Lionel 327, 344, 346
River of Death 119
Road Warrior, The 432, 484
Robbins, Eva **221**, 222, 231
Roberts, Alan
Roberts, Arthur 3, 8-9, 12, 247, 249, 462
Roberts, William 179, 182
Robertson, Kimmy 138, **147**
Robinson, Stuart 103
Rochon, Lela 332
Rockula 38
Rodriguez, Vidal "Lil Coco" 328
Rogers, Jaime 330
Ross, Ricco 110
Rossington, Norman 202
Roundtree, Richard xxvi, 207, 209
Rowlands, Gena 395, **396**, 397-398, **397**, 400, **402**, 403, **406**
Royal Wedding, The 330, 339
Rubbo, Joe 131, **132**, 133, **135**, 135, 143, **147**, 148-150
Runaway Train x, 25, 115, 400, 485
Ryan, John P. 115, 266

Sachs, William 427, 435-436, 437, **438**, 439-445, **443**
Sahara 92, 169, 173, 225, 311-324, **312**, **314**, **317**, **319**, **323**, 360, 391, 425
Sallah xxiv
Salsa 29, 302
Samson and Delilah 414
Sanchez, Ana "Lollipop" 328
Sanderson, William 26
Sarandon, Susan 435, 440
Savage Weekend 18
Scaife, Gerald 325
Schiavelli, Vincent 26
Schizoid 15-21, **16**, **19**, 66, 67
Schlesigner, John 293
Schneider, Dan 360, **362**
Schroeder, Barbet xviii
Schwarzenegger, Arnold x, 213, 215, 216, 288
Sciotti, Enzo **185**
Scott, Carey 359
Scott, George C. 156, 157
Secret of Yolanda, The 299-302, **300**, 328
Seed of Innocence see *Teen Mothers*
Selzer, Julie 465
Servants of Twilight 441
Seven Keys to Baldpate 201
Seven Magnificent Gladiators 216, 217, 227, 228, 237-238, **276**, 377-383, **379**, **381**

Seven Samurai 217, 377, 382
Shabba-Doo **272**, 273, 274-275, 325, **326**, 327, 329, 332, 340, 342, 352
Shadows 397
Shanks, Don 256-257
Sheen, Martin 151, 152, **153**, 154, 158
Sheldon, Sidney 371
Sherwood, Robin 102
Sheybal, Vladek 41, 45, 59
Shields, Brooke 169, 311-318, **312**, **314**, **317**, **319**, 321, 322-324, **323**
Shields, Teri 313-318, 323-324
Silberg, Joel 272, 299, 302, 325, 326, 328, 342
Silke, James 247, 270, 311, 315, 447, 454
Silver, Arthur 469, 472
Silverman, Jeff 423
Silvers, Phil 7, 12
Simpsons Sing the Blues, The 348
Sirtis, Marina 110, 292-293, **292**
Siskel, Gene 322
Solomon, Timothy "Popin' Pete" 328
Somkin, Arnold 303, 306
Sorvino, Paul 151, 152, **153**, 154, 156
Spano, Vincent 318
Speck, Richard 182, 190
"Speed" 49, **55**, 58
St. John, Jill 68
Stamboul Train 244
Star Wars xxvi, 161, 188, 199, 216, 235, 236, 391
Starcrash 216, 234-235, 236, 237
Steiger, Rod 369, 372, 374
Stevens, Andrew 179, 186, 188, **193**, 194-196
Stevens, Elizabeth 494, 499
Stewart, Catherine Mary 41, 45, **49**, **55**, 55-60, **57**
Stoler, Shirley 26
Stone, Mike 73, 76, **76**, 78, 80
Strasberg, Susan 240
Street Smart 370
Struzan, Drew **312**
Stuart, Aimee 285
Surrender 166, 308
Sword of the Valiant 199, 320, 360, **384**, 385-394, **387**, **390**, **392**, 412
Symeoni, Sandro **111**, **112**, **331**, **453**, **471**

Talbot, Paul 192
Tanaka, Professor Toru 254, 484
Tarantino, Quentin 13, 32
Tarzan, The Ape Man 386, 412, 414, 426
Tavor, Eli 299, 302

Taylor, Chris "The Glove" 476
Taylor, Kirk 110
Teen Mothers **22**, 23-30, **27**, 69, 93
Teenage Mother 23
Tek-Oh, Soon 116, 469, 480, **482**
Terminator, The 38, 306, 427, 434, 445
Terry, Joe Michael 484
Testi, Fabio 421-422
Texas Chainsaw Massacre 2, The 176, 505
That Championship Season 151-160, **152**, **153**, **155**, **159**
Thatcher, Margaret 322
Thatcher, Mark 322
Thompson, J. Lee 97, 115, 117-118, 179, 184, 192, 194
Tobias, Oliver 290
Todd, Richard 201, 202
Tompkins, Angel 14
Topol, Chaim xxiii
Tourista, The 362, 366
Towne, Robert xxii, 33
Townes, Carol Lynn 341
Treasure of the Four Crowns 161-170, **162**, **163**, **165**, **168**, **169**, 173, 225, 308, 361, 415, 447
Trejo, Danny 116
Trump, Donald 426
Trunk to Cairo xxiii, 72
Turturro, John 439
Twilight Zone: The Movie, The 485
Tzarfati, Asher 299, 300

Uranium Conspiracy, The xxvi, 18

Vadis, Dan 378
Valcauda, Armando 222
Van Damme, Jean-Claude x, xviii, 30, 79, 108, 280-281, 283, 332, 455, 478
Van Dyke, Dick 8, 34
Van Patten, James 207, 209, **210**
Van Patten, Nels 209
Van Peebles, Mario 427, **431**, 431-432, 434, 442
Vendrell, Michael 458, 459
Ventura, Jan see Freya, Jan
Ventura, Michael 350, **407**, 408
Vidal, Gore 240
Vitali, Keith 247, 252
Viviani, Sonia 229, **232**
Voigt, Jon 400

Wagner, Chuck 202

Walker, Dorian 357, 362
Walker, Pete 197, 200, 201, 204
Walker, Texas Ranger 470
Wallace, Chris 65
Walsh, M. Emmett 469, 476, 477, 487
Walsh, Rob 208, 257
Ward, Lyman 8
Wasson, Craig 15, 20
Way of the Dragon 458, 470
Wead, Timothy 23, 24, 28
Weeks, Stephen 385, 386
Weldon, Fay 293
Welles, Mel 38
Wesley, John 484
West Side Story xxiv, 330, 340
West, Adam 3, 7, 9, 12, 370
Wicked Lady, The 110, 178, 284-298, **286**, **287**, **289**, **291**, **292**, **294**, **297**
Wicked Lady, *The* (1945) 285, 289, 296
Wicking, Christopher 121, 125
Wild Style 346
Wilkes, Donna 15, 20
Williams, Russell 365
Williams, Steven 484
Wilson, Lambert 311, 320, 321
Winner, Michael 97, 99, 100, 101, 102, 104, 106, 107, 108, 110, 114, 115, 118, 209, 285, 286, 288, 289, 292, 293-294, 494
Winter, Alex 110
Winters, Shelley xxvi, 303-304, 308
Wolman, Dan 171, 172, 178
Womark, David 261, 263, 459

X-Ray see *Hospital Massacre*
Young Racers, The xxi-xxii, 32
Young Warriors **206**, 207-212, **210**, **211**
Young, Burt 308

Zapped! 363
Zeffirelli, Franco xviii, 313
Zito, Joe 441, 469, 473-474, 484, 502
Zola, Émile 171, 177, 178

www.ingramcontent.com/pod-product-compliance
Lightning Source LLC
Chambersburg PA
CBHW051106230426
43667CB00014B/2459